Coalition Strategy and the End of the First World War

When the Germans requested an armistice in October 1918, it was a shock to the Allied political and military leadership. They had been expecting, and planning for, the war to continue into 1919, the year they hoped to achieve a complete military victory over the Central Powers. Meighen McCrae illuminates how, throughout this planning process, the Supreme War Council evolved to become the predominant mechanism for coalition war-making. She analyses the Council's role in the formulation of an Allied strategy for 1918–1919 across the various theatres of war and compares the perspectives of the British, French, Americans, and Italians. In doing so we learn how, in an early example of modern alliance warfare, the Supreme War Council had to coordinate national needs with coalition ones.

MEIGHEN MCCRAE is a Lecturer in the Strategic and Defence Studies Centre at The Australian National University.

Cambridge Military Histories

Edited by

HEW STRACHAN, Professor of International Relations, University of St Andrews and Emeritus Fellow of All Souls College, Oxford

GEOFFREY WAWRO, Professor of Military History and Director of the Military History Center, University of North Texas

The aim of this series is to publish outstanding works of research on warfare throughout the ages and throughout the world. Books in the series take a broad approach to military history, examining war in all its military, strategic, political and economic aspects. The series complements *Studies in the Social and Cultural History of Modern Warfare* by focusing on the 'hard' military history of armies, tactics, strategy, and warfare. Books in the series consist mainly of single author works – academically rigorous and groundbreaking – which are accessible to both academics and the interested general reader.

A full list of titles in the series can be found at:
www.cambridge.org/militaryhistories

Coalition Strategy and the End of the First World War

The Supreme War Council and War Planning, 1917–1918

Meighen McCrae

The Australian National University

CAMBRIDGE
UNIVERSITY PRESS

CAMBRIDGE
UNIVERSITY PRESS

University Printing House, Cambridge CB2 8BS, United Kingdom

One Liberty Plaza, 20th Floor, New York, NY 10006, USA

477 Williamstown Road, Port Melbourne, VIC 3207, Australia

314–321, 3rd Floor, Plot 3, Splendor Forum, Jasola District Centre, New Delhi – 110025, India

79 Anson Road, #06–04/06, Singapore 079906

Cambridge University Press is part of the University of Cambridge.

It furthers the University's mission by disseminating knowledge in the pursuit of education, learning, and research at the highest international levels of excellence.

www.cambridge.org
Information on this title: www.cambridge.org/9781108475303
DOI: 10.1017/9781108566711

© Meighen McCrae 2019

First published 2019

Printed and bound in Great Britain by Clays Ltd, Elcograf S.p.A.

A catalogue record for this publication is available from the British Library

Library of Congress Cataloging-in-Publication Data
Names: McCrae, Meighen, 1982- author.
Title: Coalition strategy and the end of the First World War : the Supreme
    War Council and war planning, 1917-1918 / Meighen McCrae, Australian
    National University, Canberra.
Other titles: Supreme War Council and war planning, 1917-1918
Description: First edition. | Cambridge ; New York, NY : Cambridge
    University Press, [2019] | Series: Cambridge military histories | Includes
    bibliographical references and index.
Identifiers: LCCN 2018047154 | ISBN 9781108475303 (hardback : alk. paper) |
    ISBN 9781108466684 (pbk. : alk. paper)
Subjects: LCSH: Allied and Associated Powers (1914-1920). Supreme War
    Council. | World War, 1914-1918. | Military planning–Europe–History–20th
    century. | World War, 1914-1918–Diplomatic history.
Classification: LCC D544 .M37 2019 | DDC 940.4/012–dc23
LC record available at https://lccn.loc.gov/2018047154

ISBN 978-1-108-47530-3 Hardback

Contents

Illustrations

Acknowledgements

This work would not have been possible without the guidance and encouragement of a number of individuals. I am particularly indebted to my former thesis supervisor, Hew Strachan, for his advice and support. Adrian Gregory, who acted as my interim supervisor, broadened my understanding of the First World War. Rob Johnson brainstormed with me on concepts of future war, without which I never would have concentrated on the years 1918 and 1919. While at Oxford, I was also fortunate to benefit from the learning environment created by the Changing Character of War programme.

The following scholars have offered valuable remarks on parts of this project at various stages of its conception: Martin Alexander, James Belich, John Darwin, Gabriela Frei, Robert Gildea, Elizabeth Greenhalgh, Holger Herwig, John Lunan, David Morgan-Owen, and Mark Mulholland. During my viva Margaret MacMillan and David French provided many thoughtful observations. I also owe a debt of thanks to the two anonymous readers, whose comments have strengthened every aspect of this book.

As I have developed this project, I have also benefitted from engagement with colleagues at a number of institutions. I am indebted to my former colleagues at the Joint Services Command and Staff College, King's College London, who, over tea breaks discussed aspects of this work. In the Department of International Politics at Aberystwyth University, my colleagues have created a stimulating scholarly environment. My *alma mater*, the University of Calgary, continues to foster my scholarship through its faculty. John Ferris provided crucial insights on the entirety of this manuscript. Without his encouragement at the MA level I would not have continued my academic journey. Pat Brennan always generously offered his time by both reading and discussing this work as it progressed. The International Society of the First World War members have generated a multi-faceted forum for scholars, with which I have been privileged to interact. Furthermore, I would like to thank the

Centre International de Recherche de l' Historial de la Grande Guerre for awarding me a Gerda Henkel Scholarship in 2011.

This study was made possible through a rich body of archival sources. As such, I would like to thank a number of archives and their staff: the Albert and Shirley Small Special Collections Library, the Bodleian Library, the Imperial War Museum, the Library of Congress, the National Archives (Washington, DC), the National Archives (Kew), the Seeley G. Mudd Manuscript Library and Service Historique de la Défense (Département de l'Armée de Terre, Château de Vincennes). By permission of the Warden and Fellows of New College, Oxford, by permission of the Master and Fellows of Churchill College, Cambridge, and by permission of the Parliamentary Archives, I have quoted from materials that they hold. I would also like to thank the editorial team at Cambridge University Press for helping me navigate my first book publication.

Finally, I am grateful to my family members for each supporting me in their own way. In particular, Rick and Bev McCrae brought clarity to aspects of this work by proofreading the entire manuscript and asking helpful questions. Wanda Molson and James Chamberlain did everything in their power to make my academic pursuits possible. While the First World War is my obsession, Garry has accepted it as a near third (demanding) member of our family without complaint and with tremendous support and patience.

Chronology

1917

November	7	First Session of the SWC.
		October Revolution in Russia. The Provisional Government was overthrown causing Russia's immediate withdrawal from the war (Julian calendar, 25 October).
		EEF seized Gaza and sent forces in two directions: along the coast to Jaffa and inland toward Jerusalem.
	9	Diaz replaced Cadorna as Chief-of-Staff of the Italian army.
11 Nov–24 Dec		The Italians stopped retreating after the Battle of Caporetto (launched 24 October), halted two additional Austro-Hungarian attacks, and began to stabilise the front.
	16	Clemenceau replaced Painlevé as the French Premier.
		EEF took Jaffa.
17 Nov–30 Dec		Allenby captured Jerusalem.
	18	Marshall replaced Maude as commander of Allied forces in Mesopotamia.
20 Nov–7 Dec		First Battle of Cambrai saw the first major employment of tanks in the war. Significant initial Allied gains were lost to the German counter-attack.
26 Nov–22 Dec		The Bolsheviks called for an armistice with the Central Powers. Once an agreement was reached peace negotiations began at Brest.
December	7	The United States declared war on Austria-Hungary.

	9	The Central Powers and Romanians signed the Focşani armistice.
	23	PMRs signed Joint Note 4: 'The Balkan Problem'.
1918		
January	8	Woodrow Wilson presented his Fourteen Points.
	28	Russia severed diplomatic ties with Romania.
February	9	Part of the Treaty of Brest-Litovsk negotiations resulted in the 'Ukrainian Brest'. The Ukrainian People's Republic agreed to exchange foodstuffs for German military protection.
	12–22	Smuts and Amery travelled to Egypt to investigate Joint Note 12.
12 Feb–25 Apr		Ottoman forces resumed their offensive in Armenia capturing Erzingan, Trebizond, and then Erzerum before moving on to Batum and Kars.
	18	The IEF began to advance along the Euphrates.
18 Feb–3 Mar		Operation Faustschlag occurred after the armistice between the Central Powers and the Soviets expired. When the Bolsheviks refused the Central Powers' demands for additional territory the Central Powers went back on the offensive capturing Reval (modern-day Tallinn) and Pskov (20 km east of the modern-day Russian/Estonian border), Minsk (in modern-day Belarus) and Kiev before the Bolsheviks signed the treaty.
	19–21	The EEF captured Jericho and began to occupy the Jordan Valley.
March	7	The newly declared independent state of Finland signed a peace treaty with Germany.
	9	IEF occupied Hit.
	13	The Germans entered Odessa.
	14	Trabzon peace conference began between the Ottoman Empire and a delegation of the Transcaucasian Diet and government.
1 Mar–5 Apr		The Michael Offensive, the first of a series of German offensives on the Western Front, forced the retreat of British Fifth Army, captured thousands of prisoners, and threatened the vital railway junction of Amiens. In the north, British Third Army held around Vimy Ridge.

	23	Lithuania declared independence.
	25	IEF occupied Khan Baghdadi.
	26	Doullens Conference. Foch was appointed Supreme Commander of the Allied Armies on the Western Front and given coordinating power.
April	3	Foch given 'the strategic direction of military operations'.
	4	Ottoman forces captured Van.
	5	Japanese troops landed at Vladivostock.
	8	The Germans occupied Kharkov (modern-day Ukraine).
	9–29	With Operation Georgette the Germans struck at the British in Flanders. While bloody, the British halted the offensive without the Germans gaining any critical territorial objectives.
	20	The Germans entered the Crimea.
May	1	The Germans seized Sevastopol.
	7	The Central Powers and Romania signed the Treaty of Bucharest.
11 May–4 June		The Conference of Batum was held between the Transcaucasian states (Armenia, Azerbaijan, and Georgia) and the Ottoman Empire; however, fighting continued between regional powers, the Ottomans, the Germans, and the British.
	26–28	The Ottomans defeated the Armenians at Karakalise.
	26	Georgia declared independence.
27 May–6 June		During Operation Blücher the Germans attacked the French on the Chemin des Dames. They advanced to within 35 miles of Paris.
	27	Allies landed troops at Archangel.
	28	Both Armenia and Azerbaijan declared independence.
	30	Battle of Skra-di-Legen. The Allies successfully attacked the Bulgarians in the Greek army's first major offensive of the war.
June	2	Foch raised the issue of expanding the American programme to 100 divisions by July 1919.

8	The Germans began an expedition into the Caucasus to secure resources.
9–15	During Operation Gneisenau the Germans attacked between Noyon and Montdidier. The French, with support from American troops, counter-attacked at Château-Thierry and Belleau Wood.
14	Ottoman forces captured Tabriz.
15–23	The Battle of the Piave was Austria-Hungary's last offensive of the war. Despite initial success, the Allies pushed the Austro-Hungarians back across the Asiago Plateau and beyond the Piave River.
23	Clemenceau, Foch, Mordacq, and Pershing discussed the shipment of American troops to meet the 100 division programme.

July

4 July–10 Sept	PMRs considered policy for the autumn of 1918 and spring of 1919.
11 July–3 Aug	Diplomatic and Military Commission established to consider whether or not an offensive should occur in Macedonia in 1918.
15	The final German spring offensive attempted to capture Reims with a pincer attack; however, the French successfully defended against it.
18–22	In the Battle of Soissons the French, with support from American forces, counter-attacked the recent German advances west of Reims. It was the first major German defeat.
18	D'Espèrey publicly declared that an offensive against the Bulgarians should occur no later than early October. The US War Department decided on the 80 division programme.
20	Foch asked Clemenceau to call up the conscript class of 1920 so they could be trained for use in 1919.
24	Commanders discussed future operations including action for 1919.
25	Henry Wilson presented 'British Policy 1918–1919' to the War Cabinet.

August	2	Ottoman forces captured Urmia.
	8–12	In the Battle of Amiens the Allies successful attacked and broke through the German lines, capturing thousands of prisoners. Ludendorff called 8 August 'the black day of the German army'.
	11	Allied forces landed at Vladivostok.
	20	French offensive between Aisne and Oise.
	26	PMRs and Foch discussed plans for autumn 1918 and the year 1919.
	26 Aug–2 Sept	A series of Allied attacks pushed the Germans back to their last redoubt (the Hindenburg Line).
September	12	In the St Mihiel Offensive the French and American forces undertook a successful two pronged assault on the St Mihiel salient in the first large-scale action by the AEF.
	14	Baku was captured by Ottoman forces after a six-week siege. Troops were then directed to capture Derbent.
	15–29	With the Vardar Offensive Franchet d'Espèry led an Allied offensive that compelled the Bulgarians to call for an armistice.
	19–21	In the Battle of Megiddo the EEF broke Turko-German defences, opening the roads to Damascus, Beirut, and Aleppo.
	26 Sept–1 Oct	The EEF entered Damascus.
	26 Sept–11 Nov	The American army launched its first major offensive on the Meuse-Argonne.
	27 Sept–9 Oct	Major offensives by the British First, Third, and Fourth Armies broke through the Hindenburg Line.
	26 Sept–11 Nov	British, French, and Belgian forces captured Passchendaele.
	30	Bulgarians signed an armistice.
October	4	First German note requesting an armistice was sent to Woodrow Wilson.
	5	Clemenceau, Foch, Orlando, Lloyd George, H. Wilson, Hope, and Hankey discussed operations in the Balkans.
	8	PMRs and the Committee of Prime Ministers discussed armistice terms.

Abbreviations

AEF	American Expeditionary Force
AFGG	Les Armées françaises dans la Grande Guerre (French official history)
AMEL	Leopold Amery Papers, Churchill College Archive Centre, Cambridge
AMTC	Allied Maritime Transport Council
AMTE	Allied Maritime Transport Executive
ANC	Allied Naval Council
Baker	Newton D. Baker Papers, LOC
Baruch	Bernard Baruch Papers, Seeley G. Mudd Manuscript Library, Princeton Library
BEF	British Expeditionary Force
Bliss	Tasker Bliss Papers, LOC
CAB	Cabinet Papers, TNA, Kew
CHAR	Winston Churchill Papers, Churchill College Archive Centre, Cambridge
CIAM	Conseil Interallié de l'Armement et des Munitions
CIGS	Chief of the Imperial General Staff
DWT	Dead Weight Tonnes
EEF	Egyptian Expeditionary Force
EFC	Emergency Fleet Corporation
EWB	Executive War Board
FO	Foreign Office Papers, TNA
FRUS	Foreign Relations of the United States
GHQ	General Headquarters
GQG	Grand Quartier-Général (French high command)
HHW	Henry Wilson Papers, Imperial War Museum, London
HNKY	Maurice Hankey Papers, Churchill College Archive Centre, Cambridge
IACWPF	Inter-Allied Council on War Purchases and Finance
IAMC	Inter-Allied Munitions Council
IATC	Inter-Allied Transport Council

IEF	Indian Expeditionary Force
IWM	Imperial War Museum
LG	David Lloyd George Papers, Parliamentary Archives, London
LOC	Manuscripts Division, Library of Congress
March	Peyton March Papers, LOC
MUN	Ministry of Munitions Papers, TNA
NARA	National Archives and Records Administration, College Park, MD
Pershing	John Pershing Papers, LOC
PMRs	Permanent Military Representatives
PWW	A. S. Link et al., eds., The Papers of Woodrow Wilson
RG	Record Group, National Archives, DC.
Rodd	Rennell of Rodd Papers, Bodleian Library, Oxford
SHD-	Service Historique de la Défense – Département de
DAT	l'Armée de Terre, Château de Vincennes
Stettinius	Edward R. Stettinius Papers, Albert and Shirley Small Special Collections Library, University of Virginia
SWC	Supreme War Council
TNA	The National Archives, Kew
USAWW	The United States Army in the World War (American official history)
USSB	United States Shipping Board
WIB	War Industries Board
Wilson	Woodrow Wilson Papers, LOC
WO	War Office Papers, TNA

0.1 The Balkan Campaign, 1917–1918

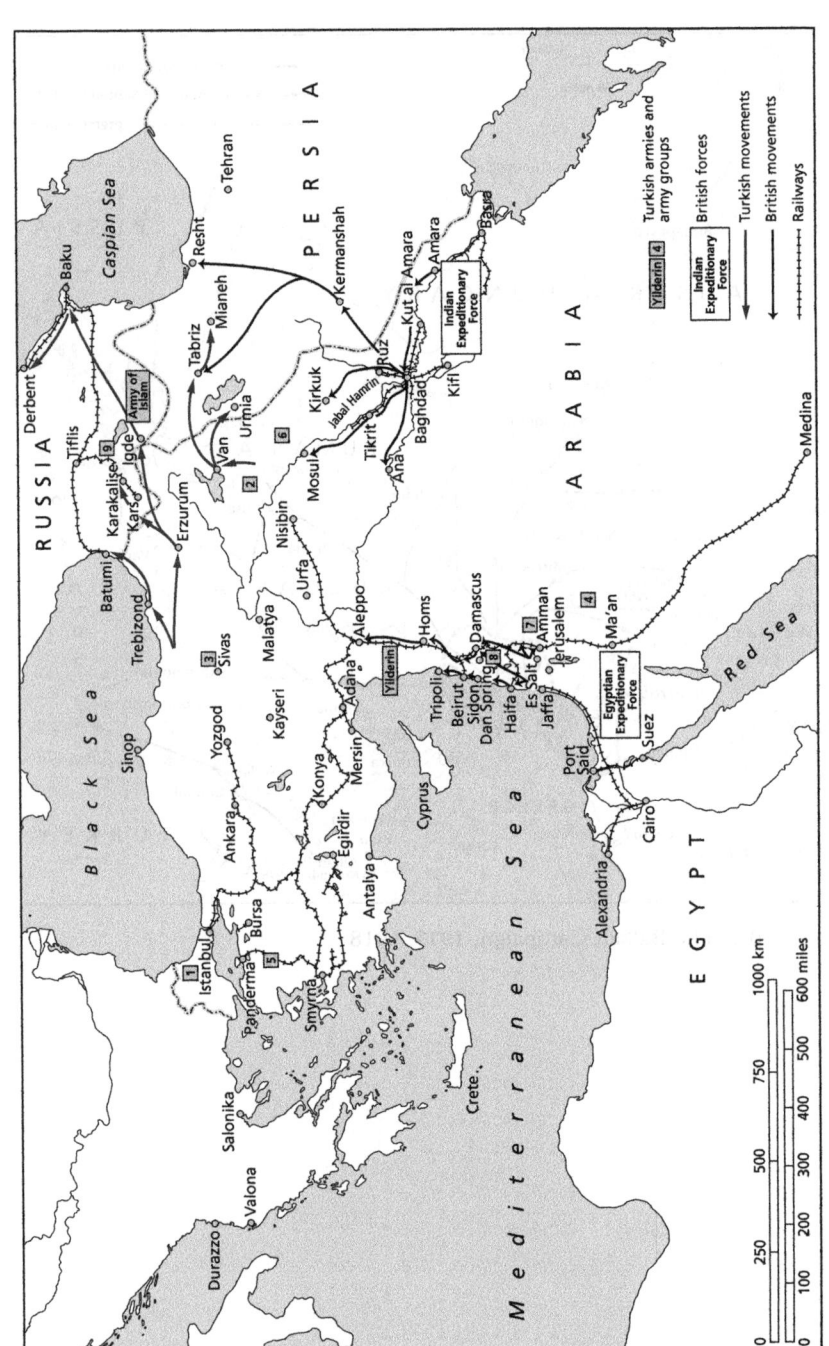

0.2 Palestine and Mesopotamia Campaigns, 1917–1918

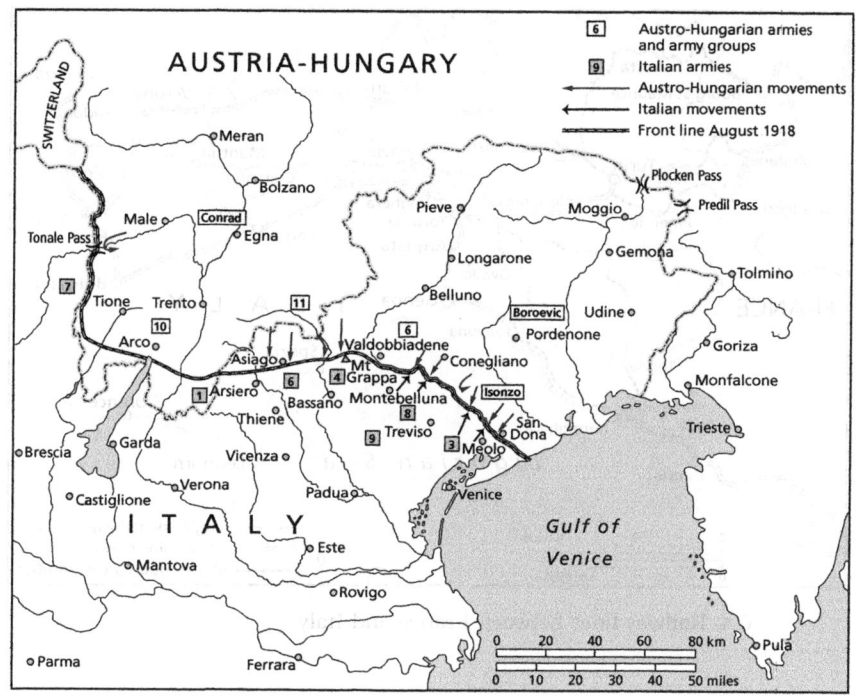

0.3 The Italian Front, 1918

0.4 Railway lines between France and Italy

Introduction

When the Germans approached the American President for an armistice in October 1918, it came as a great shock to the Allied political and military leaders.[1] They had been planning to continue the war into 1919, convinced that only then could a military victory be won. This book investigates the depth and extent of Allied planning for a campaign in 1919 through the mechanism of the Supreme War Council (SWC). It analyses the workings of the SWC as an inter-allied body and an early example of modern coalition warfare, comparing the perspectives of the British, French, American, and Italian representatives in their willingness and unwillingness to coordinate national needs with alliance imperatives. It finds that the key points driving Allied decision-making and strategy-making in 1918 were resolved through the SWC.

The first key commonality was a shared notion of victory. The very creation of the SWC saw its members focus on a decisive military defeat of the German army in 1919. The timeline to victory that they developed was affected by their perception of the enemy's strength, their assessment of the difficulties inherent in overcoming the military advantage offered by the Central Powers' interior lines of communication, their appraisal of the European allies' morale (both on the home-front and within their militaries) to continue the war, and their ability to gather the necessary superiority in material and manpower. Furthermore, the collapse of the Russian Front created uncertainty about German resources in the east and how they might be redeployed to tip the balance on other fronts. After the Allies' shock at the Battle of Caporetto and the subsequent German spring offensives, they were determined never to underestimate the enemy again. Erring thereafter on the side of prudence, the SWC

---

[1] While recognising that the Americans were technically an 'Associate' power in the coalition, as opposed to a formal 'ally', the term 'Allies' is used throughout this book to refer to British, French, Americans, and Italians as that is how the Supreme War Council used the term at the time.

consistently overestimated the remaining capabilities of the German war machine and thus the resources required to defeat it on the battlefield.

Second, manpower continued to be the main ingredient for winning the war in 1918 because of this notion of victory and perception of the German menace. Specifically, the deployment of American troops became *the* crucial resource and factor in strategic planning, with the French, British, and Italians facing serious resource shortages by the end of 1917. Connected directly to American manpower is the third key point: the US army and the American administrative boards that mobilised resources for it chose to deal with their European counter-parts essentially through the SWC. In turn, the European allies realised that the SWC was the essential forum for negotiating with the United States on the single most important issue, the deployment of American forces for 1919. This made the SWC the locus for what all decision-makers thought were the central decisions being made in 1918, those about fighting the war in 1919.

Fourth, Allied strategy focussed on the global context of the war and the interdependent nature of the different theatres of war. As the United States increased its material contribution to the war effort, the Americans insisted on being informed on what was happening globally so as to ensure that Allied manpower and other resources were not being frittered away in peripheral campaigns. This focus married with the SWC's mandate to view developments and efforts on the Western Front in relation to the other theatres. The collapse of the Russian and Romanian Fronts created the impression that the Germans would be able to draw down dramatically their manpower commitments in those areas. This Allied fear brought to the forefront the connection between the various fighting zones. Action in the Balkans, Italy, Palestine, and Mesopotamia was framed in relation to the effect it would have on the Franco-Belgian Front, whether that was drawing away troops or impacting the morale of enemy or Allied forces. In this way, this book builds upon David French's argument in *The Strategy of the Lloyd George Coalition* that disagreements between the British military and political leadership centred on when the war would be won, as opposed to whether the war would be won in the West or the East.[2] In fact, this argument was also central in Allied discussions. By considering Allied strategy in these various theatres, this book emphasises their interdependent nature and contextualises the Franco-Belgian Front in this wider framework of a global war.

[2] David French, *The Strategy of the Lloyd George Coalition, 1916–1918* (Oxford, 1995).

Despite these significant positive contributions, any evaluation of the SWC as a mechanism for coalition war-making also needs to consider the limitations of the institution. Here, the book stresses two major challenges to the SWC's planning efforts. The first was balancing national interests with international ones. The SWC member nations were willing to subordinate national sovereignty when a coalition effort was required to defeat the enemy; however, when it was perceived that they could act unilaterally, especially when they disagreed with their partners, they did so. In reality, the nation with the largest fielded military in a theatre determined the action there – so the French largely determined operations in the Balkans, while the British did the same in the Middle East. This study demonstrates and explores how the SWC acted in these theatres as a limited channel for communication and a symbol of Allied unity, but not as an authority for the direction of action.

While the Permanent Military Representatives of the SWC (PMRs) were able to reach a compromise on policy, their political counter-parts struggled to do so. It was more difficult for the political leadership to set aside postwar ambitions whereas the PMRs could focus on winning a military victory. However, both the political and military leadership recognised the importance of maintaining the coalition as an objective in itself – what William Philpott refers to as one of the key 'fronts' of the war effort.[3] They were not going to allow the coalition to fall apart, especially not as long as they could each pursue their own interests in the secondary theatres while also maintaining pressure on the Western Front. After all, the main role of the SWC was to oversee action on the Western Front in the context of the global war. It accomplished this task.

The second major challenge to the SWC coalition planning was the complicated relationship between an evolving and dynamic strategy and the reality of operations on the ground. What the component chapters of this book demonstrate is that a coalition strategy did not always meet the demands of the rapidly unfolding actions in all theatres. This caused tension between the PMRs, who were attempting to control policy and resources for the future with the idea that military action in 1918 would have a direct effect on how the war would be won in 1919, and those of the commanders-in-chief on the ground, who were responding to immediate events. Naturally, the Allies sacrificed plans for the future to respond to the surprising collapse of the Central Powers in late 1918. Plans for 1919 had to be brought forward or abandoned altogether out of recognition of the changing circumstances. In some cases, the SWC was

---

[3] William J. Philpott, *Attrition: Fighting the First World War* (London, 2014), 9.

bypassed in favour of quick decision-making that it was simply not capable of producing. The SWC and their policies for 1919 demonstrate the aspirations of coalition decision-making and its inherent complications. Despite its limitations, the SWC still acted as an enabler for the coalition war effort.

To downplay the contribution of the SWC is to misconstrue Allied decision-making in 1918, which is precisely what has happened in the existing literature. In making the overall argument that the SWC was *the* key mechanism for coalition war-making, this study contributes to the existing literature in two primary ways. First, it emphasises the centrality of the idea that the war would be carried into 1919 and details how this belief influenced Allied decision-making. Second, it readdresses how the coalition operated in the final year of the war.

A substantial body of First World War literature focusses on how and why the war was won by the Allies in 1918. A number of insightful case studies have been produced at the army, corps, and divisional levels that explore tactical and operational developments that contributed to victory in this year.[4] While these studies often recognise that the Allies were surprised by victory, the focus is on how means were applied to achieve victory in that year rather than on the longer term notions of victory. David Stevenson also addresses the question of how the war was won in *With Our Backs to the Wall*.[5] He considers the higher levels of national strategies and coalitions through a comparison of a series of factors – military action (and the means available), shipping, finance, and attitudes on the home-front – that led to victory for the Allies and defeat for the Central Powers in 1918. However, Stevenson's work does not evaluate the mechanism for coalition war-making which enabled the Allies.

Other works reflect on the challenges the Allies faced in late 1918 and the pessimistic mentality of British leadership. In *Winning and Losing on the Western Front*, Jonathan Boff analyses the slow advance of the Third Army in November and highlights the strength of German resistance up

[4] S. Bidwell and D. Graham, *Fire-Power: British Army Weapons and Theories of War 1904–1945* (London, 1982); J. P. Harris, *Amiens to the Armistice: The B. E. F. In the Hundred Days' Campaign, 8 August–11 November 1918* (London, 1998); Nick Lloyd, *Hundred Days: The End of the Great War* (London, 2014); Michael Neiberg, *The Second Battle of the Marne* (Bloomington, IN, 2008); Robin Prior and Trevor Wilson, *Command on the Western Front: The Military Career of Sir Henry Rawlinson 1914–1918* (Barnsley, 2004); Gary Sheffield, *Forgotten Victory: The First World War Myths and Realities* (London, 2002); Gary Sheffield and Peter Gray, eds., *The British Army, the Hundred Days Campaign and the Birth of the Royal Air Force, 1918* (London: Bloomsbury 2015); John Terraine, *White Heat: The New Warfare, 1914–1918* (London, 1992); John Terraine, *To Win a War: 1918, the Year of Victory* (London, 2000).

[5] David Stevenson, *With Our Backs to the Wall: Victory and Defeat in 1918* (London, 2012).

to its collapse.[6] Ian Brown, too, illustrates that the British had serious reservations about their ability to bring the war to a conclusion in 1918 through his description of the strains of pursuing the Germans and the disarray of American administration and supply.[7] In *Haig's Intelligence: GHQ and the German Army, 1916–1918,* James Beach illuminates how the British Expeditionary Force (BEF) commander overestimated the German army's capabilities in 1918.[8] Brock Millman examines the mentality of key British decision-makers, arguing that they doubted their ability to win the war militarily and feared a second war with Germany.[9] Millman does consider some of the thinking done by the PMRs for 1919; however, his focus (and sources) are based too heavily on Henry Wilson, and in this way Millman misses the broader trends in thinking about the future. In addition, by not considering the American perspective or resources that the Americans would bring to bear in 1919, he fails to consider the greatest asset that the British had for 1919. Although these various works demonstrate that the British were surprised by victory, they tell us little about the Allies' thinking and concrete planning to carry the war into the following year.

Studies of coalition war also focus on the theme of how the war was won in 1918. Frequently the SWC is ignored or relegated to a mere 'military debating society' because much of its labour was toward the 1919 campaign which never occurred.[10] While Philpott considers how the SWC acted as a forum for venting grievances, his analysis does not go beyond this body's contribution to unified command. Elizabeth Greenhalgh's *Victory through Coalition: Britain and France during the First World War,* analyses Anglo-French military and economic coordination over the entire course of the war, details the formation of some of the SWC sub-committees, and briefly considers their roles in achieving victory in 1918. By focusing on how the war was won, Greenhalgh does not consider the long-term arrangements nor the decision-making for achieving a victory that was focussed on 1919. While building on her groundwork, this book challenges her assessment of the SWC as merely a 'talking shop'.[11] It does so by emphasising the Americans as an integral

---

[6] Jonathan Boff, *Winning and Losing on the Western Front: The British Third Army and the Defeat of Germany in 1918* (Cambridge, 2012).

[7] Ian Malcolm Brown, *British Logistics on the Western Front 1914–1919* (Westport, CT, 1998).

[8] Jim Beach, *Haig's Intelligence* (Cambridge, 2013).

[9] Brock Millman, *Pessimism and British War Policy 1916–1918* (London, 2001).

[10] William J. Philpott, *Anglo-French Relations and Strategy on the Western Front, 1914–18* (London, 1996), 151.

[11] Elizabeth Greenhalgh, *Victory through Coalition: Britain and France during the First World War* (Cambridge, 2005), 179.

partner, specifically their use of the SWC as both a major avenue of communication and coordination with their fellow allies for the 1919 campaign.

What brought about victory in 1918 is an important question that these works address. While it is understandable that their focus would be on 1918 given that the war was won in that year, three questions remain: What was Allied strategy focussed on? How did the Allies come to a decision about strategy? How did they plan to execute this strategy? It is these questions that this work addresses and in doing so it demonstrates the centrality of the SWC to Allied decision-making.

Studies of the SWC have offered limited insight into these important questions. Thomas Daniel Shumate pioneered a study of the SWC in 1952, prior to the release of many official documents.[12] Historian David Trask later expanded on Shumate's study; however, his focus is much less international than that of his predecessor.[13] Although Trask does examine the Russian intervention and the Balkans, his work is tightly focussed on the American contribution to the SWC. In this way he fails to consider the wider strategic concerns of a coalition fighting a global war.

Early accounts of the SWC considered how it operated, how it contributed to unified command, or how certain individuals contributed to its running.[14] In Britain, discussions of the SWC were embroiled with debates on who was responsible for the war's numbing casualty rates. Civilian leaders, such as British Prime Minister David Lloyd George, presented the creation of the SWC as evidence of their efforts for an alternative (Allied) strategy from that of the battles of attrition conducted by the generals on the Western Front.[15] When historians began to

---

[12] Thomas Daniel Shumate, 'The Allied Supreme War Council, 1917–1918' (PhD diss., University of Virginia, 1952).

[13] David Trask, *The United States in the Supreme War Council: American War Aims and Inter-Allied Strategy* (Middletown, CT, 1961).

[14] R. H. Beadon, 'The Supreme War Council of the Allied and Associated Nations: Its Origin, Organization, and Work', *The Journal of the Royal United Services Institute*, 65/457 (1920); Daniel R. Beaver, *Newton D. Baker and the American War Effort, 1917–1919* (Lincoln, 1966); Tasker H. Bliss, 'The Evolution of the Unified Command', *Foreign Affairs*, 1/2 (1922); Frederick Palmer, *Newton D. Baker: America at War* (2 vols., New York, 1931); Frederick Palmer, *Bliss, Peacemaker: The Life and Letters of General Tasker Howard Bliss* (New York, 1934); Anonymous, *The Supreme War Council* (Boston, 1918).

[15] L. S. Amery, *My Political Life* (3 vols., London, 1953), ii; Beadon, 'The Supreme War Council of the Allied and Associated Nations'; David Lloyd George, *War Memoirs of David Lloyd George* (London, 1934), vi; General Sir William Robertson, *Soldiers and Statesmen* (London, 1926); Captain Peter E. Wright, *At the Supreme War Council* (London, 1921).

examine civil-military relations, the SWC was once again considered as part of this controversy and not in its own right.[16]

Other historians have approached the study of coalition war either by comparing the relations of two nations, or by detailing the experiences of one nation fighting as part of a coalition. The strength of both approaches is that they highlight the effects of civil-military relations and national interests on coalition warfare. These works range from military, diplomatic, and economic studies. Bruce Cohen analyses the close relationship between the French and Americans through France's training and arming of the American army. David Woodward examines Anglo-American relations, including the issue of amalgamation of American troops in British formation, to argue that the British, conscious of the relationship between the size of their army and the audibility of their voice at the peace table, wanted to use American soldiers to supplement deficiencies in British manpower. Kathleen Burk examines the economic relationship between America and Britain and how the war was financed.[17] Jeduha Wallach's *Uneasy Coalition* may consider the Allied partnership from a multi-national perspective but his study of coordination is shallow.[18] He does illustrate how the Allies' various visions for a postwar settlement put them at odds and how, because they were relatively equal partners, they had to negotiate in 1918. This study builds on these earlier contributions by examining the SWC as a point of interception through which both equal and junior partners hammered out broadly effective war-making relations.

Overall, the existing historiography is limited; first, in its engagement with the role of the SWC in coalition war-making and second, in its exploration of how far the Allied political and military leadership planned to continue the war into 1919. This book, in contrast, focusses on decision-making at the international level examining the coalition's creation of a strategy from the perspective of the four national contributors, as opposed to examining national or bi-lateral relationships and agreements. By 1918 there was no hegemon on the Western Front. Each partner had a significant bargaining chip in which to balance the

[16] David Woodward, *The Military Correspondence of Field-Marshal Sir William Robertson, Chief of the Imperial General Staff, December 1915-February 1918* (London, 1990), 183; D. R. Woodward, *Lloyd George and the Generals* (Newark, 1983).

[17] Robert B. Bruce, *A Fraternity of Arms: America and France in the Great War* (Lawrence, KS 2003); David Woodward, *Trial by Friendship: Anglo-American Relations, 1917–18* (Lexington, KY, 1993); Kathleen Burk, *Britain, America and the Sinews of War, 1914–1918* (Boston, 1985).

[18] Jehuda L. Wallach, *Uneasy Coalition: The Entente Experience in World War I* (Westport, CT, 1993).

coalition: the Americans were supplying a significant amount of man-power, the British were shipping many of these troops, the French (and British to a lesser extent) were supplying the Americans with equipment, and the Italians were protecting the backdoor to France. None of these nations had recent experience of conducting a multi-party coalition of relative equals. This book enhances the current literature by demonstrat-ing how the coordination of a coalition through the institution of the SWC was of landmark significance in the history of coalition war-marking. Furthermore, not only did the Allies coordinate a strategy but they also established a complex network of committees to organise Allied resources to deliver that strategy into 1919.

This book is a close study of the development of an Allied strategy through the discussions of the SWC, its military advisers (PMRs), and the committees that examined Allied shipping (Allied Maritime Transport Council), munitions (Inter-Allied Munitions Council), and transport (Inter-Allied Transport Council). It was these committees that were central to improving Allied coordination in 1918 for a campaign in 1919. This work prioritises these central committees ahead of those that discussed developing technologies.[19] Tanks were an innovative idea, but Allied strategy prioritised gaining numerical superiority over the enemy through manpower, so the key debates were about raising, transporting, and supplying this manpower. Therefore, J. F. C. Fuller's idea for 'Plan 1919', a large-scale tank offensive focussed on attacking the 'brain' (command centre) of the German army, is not discussed.[20] His innova-tive and fanciful ideas for the employment of tanks have since been dispelled through an examination of its capabilities and production.[21] Outside of the issue of shipping, the naval dimension is not a central focus of this study.[22] Although the PMRs had a liaison with the Allied

---

[19] On chemical warfare, see Albert Palazzo, 'Plan 1919 – The Other One', *The Journal of the Society for Army Historical Research*, 77/309 (1999); Roy Macleod and Jeffrey A. Johnson, eds., *Comparative Perspectives on the Chemical Industry at War, 1914–1924* (Dordrecht Springer, 2006).

[20] J. F. C. Fuller, *Tanks in the Great War, 1914–1918* (London, 1920).

[21] J. P. Harris details how the plans circulating within the British military on the use of tanks in 1919 were unrealistic. See J. P. Harris, *Men, Ideas and Tanks: British Military Thought and Armoured Forces, 1903–1939.* (Manchester, 1995). Greenhalgh has shown that, although mechanical means were becoming increasingly popular, in 1918 the technology was too underdeveloped to play a decisive role. See Elizabeth Greenhalgh, 'Technology Development in Coalition: The Case of the First World War Tank', *The International History Review*, 22/4 (2000). On French tanks, see Tim Gale, *French Tanks of the Great War: Development, Tactics and Operations* (Barnsley, 2016).

[22] The navy was in fact making its own plans for 1919 that included aviation plans to attack the German fleet. See Paul Halpern, *A Naval History of World War I* (London, 1994), 441–443.

Naval Council (ANC) they rarely met with it and the two groups operated separately.[23] The backgrounds of the PMRs lay in the army. Furthermore, this study considers the Russian Front through Allied discussions on the Germans gaining resources in this theatre rather than specifically examining the Russian intervention.[24]

The central sources of this study are the minutes of the SWC, including those from the meetings of its military advisers and the relevant sub-committees. The *procès-verbaux* have been treated as direct quotations, not indirect ones. In cases where there was no substantial difference between copies of the *procès-verbaux*, the British minutes are cited. While recognising that the Americans were technically an 'Associate' power in the coalition, as opposed to a formal 'ally', the term 'Allies' is used throughout this book to refer to British, French, Americans, and Italians as that is how the SWC used the term at the time.[25]

Outline of Chapters

The chapters of this study are generally organised by theatre of war and their relevance to a coalition strategy for 1918–1919. This chapter structure draws out the sub-themes of how the coalition perceived enemy and allied forces and their morale, the interdependent nature of the theatres, and the interaction between the SWC and the commanders in the field.

The first chapter outlines how the SWC was organised and how it functioned. Chapters 2–4 then explore the roles of the 'secondary' theatres, drawing upon the evolving PMR debates over an Allied policy for 1918–1919. Chapter 2 examines the campaign in the Balkans, while Chapter 3 considers those of Palestine and Mesopotamia. These two chapters are intimately linked as resources for peripheral theatres were

---

[23] For a detailed study of the ANC, see David Trask, *Captains and Cabinets: Anglo-American Naval Relations, 1917–1918* (Columbia, MO, 1972).

[24] The British SWC records comprised some of the earliest documents made available, and they have been utilised by scholars to discuss the Russian intervention. On SWC as a source, see B. Schwarz, 'Divided Attention: Britain's Perception of a German Threat to Her Eastern Position in 1918', *Journal of Contemporary History*, 28/1 (1993), 119–120n14. On the Russian intervention, see French, *Lloyd George Coalition*, 241–245; Elizabeth Greenhalgh, *Foch in Command: The Forging of a First World War General* (Cambridge, 2011), 274; Carol Melton, *Between War and Peace: Woodrow Wilson and the American Expeditionary Force in Siberia, 1918–19* (Macon, GA, 2001). Current research understands the Russian intervention to have commenced as an effort to prevent the Germans from moving troops from the Russian to the Western Front and not primarily as an attempt to stop the spread of Bolshevism.

[25] For example, when the British War Office calculated the rifle strength of the Allies they included the Americans. War Office to War Cabinet, 13 August 1918, The National Archives [hereon referred to as TNA], War Office Papers [hereon WO], WO 158/107.

limited. Imperial rivalry and each coalition partner's vision of the postwar settlement have frequently been credited with driving Allied strategy in these areas. At the international level, the PMRs' discussions centred on how these theatres could contribute to a victory against the Germans – specifically how action might draw enemy forces away from the efforts being made in the West. This argument was also being made by many of the commanders. When the PMRs discussed war aims, they did so as a means to conduct the war – as a way to gain allies – rather than as objectives in themselves. Chapter 4 examines the Italian theatre and the extent to which the coalition partners used the SWC to support the Italians. All three of these chapters demonstrate each theatre's relationship to the Franco-Belgian Front and how they were considered to be an integral part of a wider global strategy to defeat the Germans.

Chapter 5 examines the predominance of the Western Front and the operational notion of victory through discussions by the Allied political and military leadership on the creation of a larger US army. The American war effort was central to Allied strategy for 1919. With an overwhelming superiority in manpower the Allies would unquestionably have been able to deliver a mortal blow to the German army. These discussions alone show how the skewed perception of the German menace affected the ways in which the coalition partners believed this military victory could be achieved.

Chapter 6 underpins the previous chapter by exploring the extent to which the Allies coordinated resources to deliver the expanded American programme aimed entirely to reinforce the Western Front. It uses the sub-committees of the SWC to focus on two issues critical to this build-up – those of shipping and munitions.

The conclusion examines how the armistice terms perpetuated Allied military action by exploring the terms of the armistice drawn up by the PMRs and comparing them with the terms that were accepted by the SWC and then by the Germans. It argues that the PMRs wanted to achieve with the armistice what *they believed* they had been denied on the battlefield – a complete military victory. Additionally, the conclusion evaluates the challenges faced by the SWC and the extent to which it was able to overcome them. These challenges included inexperience at various levels in conducting a war of this scale, a lack of executive authority, and varying national interests. Despite the challenges it encountered, the SWC was successful in improving Allied communications, coordinating essential resources for the 1919 campaign, and in supporting a junior (but vital) partner. The limitations of this body included its inability to react in a timely manner to unfolding events, and in its failure to assess the enemy with sufficient accuracy. Finally, the conclusion briefly discusses the legacy of the SWC for the Allied coordination in the Second World War.

Together, these chapters detail how the SWC provided an arena for the creation of an Allied strategy based on the realistic idea and, for a long time, highly likely expectation that the war would continue into 1919. In doing so this work readdresses the role of the SWC in coalition war-making.

1   The Supreme War Council

Over there, over there,
Send the word, send the word over there
That the Yanks are coming, the Yanks are coming
The drums rum-tumming everywhere.
So prepare, say a prayer,
Send the word, send the word to beware –
We'll be over, we're coming over,
And we won't come back till it's over, over there.[1]

In November 1917, the 'Yanks' might have been arriving in Europe, but they were not doing so at a rate that impressed their European partners. After such a challenging year the Entente was desperate for their American partner to be fully mobilised and active on the battlefield. The Nivelle offensive that had promised a decisive battle in mid-April 1917 had failed to achieve this goal. Instead it had worn down the French army and sparked mutiny, which necessitated a recovery period for the French forces. The Battle of Passchendaele, underway from 31 July to 10 November, also failed to achieve the results that the Allied political leadership was expecting. Although attrition rates on both sides of the battlefield were high, the Allies had not broken through enemy lines at Ypres to capture German U-boat bases on the Belgian coast. In Italy, the situation was grave as the Central Powers delivered a crushing defeat at Caporetto in autumn.

The news from the Russian home front also raised concerns. With the forming of a provisional government in March 1917 and the abdication of Nicolas II, the Entente questioned the extent to which political events would weaken Russia's military ability. Initially Russia's Kerensky offensive in July drove back the Austro-Hungarian forces; however, once German reinforcements arrived a successful counter-offensive broke

[1] Geo M. Cohan (composer) and Billy Murray (performer), *Over There*, (1917), Library of Congress [hereon LOC], accessed 18 August 2018, at www.loc.gov/item/ihas.10001056.

Russian morale. By November a second revolution took Russia completely out of the war.

In the Balkans, on the Vardar sector, the Allies attempted an offensive in spring 1917; however, it was derailed when the Serbians refused to attack. And while Greece joined the war on the side of the Allies in late June their army had to be raised, trained, and equipped before it could make a major contribution. In Romania the French had assisted in the creation of fifteen new divisions which allowed the Romanians to launch an offensive in late July. Lacking Russian support, however, the Allies only narrowly managed to stabilise this front after the Central Powers counter-attacked. In September French forces made some positive gains by taking Pogradec in Albania, but these were hardly compensation for the setbacks elsewhere.

The major points of optimism in 1917 were the gains made in the campaigns of Sinai and Palestine and Mesopotamia. In spring 1917 Allenby had replaced Marshall with orders to take Jerusalem by Christmas. By 31 October the Egyptian Expeditionary Force (EEF) was assaulting the Gaza-Beersheba line. Moving to take Jaffa, Allenby continued his advance on Jerusalem. In Mesopotamia General Maude had taken Kut in February and moved into Baghdad by 11 March. That same month the Russians had pursued Turkish troops in Persia. Eventually planning to connect with the Russians, as well as take the oil fields at Mosul, Maude divided his forces into three groups. The Indian Expeditionary Force (IEF) began moving up the Tigris, Euphrates, and Diyala Rivers before logistical problems and the onset of the summer weather paused their advance. In autumn the IEF resumed its march up the Tigris.

It was within this uncertain climate that the Supreme War Council (SWC) was created. A joint venture undertaken by the British, French, American, and Italian governments, its purpose was to improve the coordination of the coalition war effort. The concept of implementing a body that would oversee strategy was suggested throughout the war. The pressing need for allied unity had resulted in closer discussions between the French and British political leadership, as well as the creation of a standard monthly meeting of the allies in 1917.[2] In mid-1917 the idea of creating an allied institution re-emerged as the Allies began to realise the Russians were likely out of the war, and that this would mean the Germans would be able to move substantial forces to the Western Front

[2] Greenhalgh, *Victory through Coalition*, 23, 137; William J. Philpott, 'Squaring the Circle: The Coordination of the Entente in the Winter of 1915–16', *English Historical Reivew* 114 (1999), 875–898.

for a major offensive. Greater coordination might provide an answer to this threat – but what would that coordination actually mean? It was not until November 1917 that a combination of military events and political and military support demanded the creation of a formal body that could channel the direction of the war beyond the immediate.

The British and French prime ministers met in late September to discuss the details of an allied war committee. The French Prime Minister, Paul Painlevé, was eager to force the British to take up more of the front line in France. Depending on how it was constructed, this body could provide him with leverage.[3] He envisaged Foch, who was Army Chief of the General Staff, as the head of an Allied general staff that controlled Franco-British reserves, with the idea that his position would eventually evolve to generalissimo.[4] Lloyd George did not want the SWC to simply evolve into unified command and was adamant that it should maintain both a political and a military side (even after Foch became generalissimo in spring 1918). By early October 1917, the British Prime Minister could see how such an institution would give him greater political control over military affairs. His own ideas for a policy in 1918 were in stark opposition to those of British Field Marshal Douglas Haig, the Commander-in-Chief in France, and General 'Wully' Roberston, Chief of the Imperial General Staff (CIGS). Haig persisted with the idea that the war could be won with the launch of a major offensive that would achieve a breakthrough on the Western Front in the spring of 1918. Robertson agreed that the war had to be won on the Western Front, but preferred a policy of attrition.[5] Lloyd George voiced his support for the French Commander-in-Chief (in the field) Pétain's policy of 'active defence' in France in 1918. It allowed for the arrival of American troops before a decisive victory was attempted in 1919. For Britain, this would ensure the British army played a determining role in winning the war, thus giving Britain a leading role in the peace settlements. Meanwhile, a victory against the Ottoman Empire would raise morale in Britain and aid in securing its Asiatic Empire, while the naval blockade continued to wear down the enemy.[6]

While the idea of an Allied institution was being developed, the crushing Italian defeat at Caporetto gave the British Prime Minister the impetus to push for its creation. However, the matter was complicated

---

[3] French, *Lloyd George Coalition*, 161.
[4] Greenhalgh, *Victory through Coalition*, 166. She also provides detail on a number of other individuals who supported this idea, including Foch and Wilson.
[5] David Woodward, *The Military Correspondence of Field-Marshal Sir William Robertson, Chief of the Imperial General Staff, December 1915–February 1918* (London, 1990), 133.
[6] French, *Lloyd George Coalition*, 192.

by British political-military relations, which ensured that this body would not supersede the general staffs. The Italians were in need of British and French aid for their own front. Conscious that one of the first issues to be discussed by the SWC was the defence of the Piave front, they, too, agreed. The Americans wanted a purely military organisation, with a president that could execute decisions.[7] These different expectations of the SWC's responsibilities and composition created tension between its members. The SWC as an institution was further complicated by its evolving structure that had to respond to changes in the war's conduct.

When a new French government was formed under Clemenceau on 19 November 1917, the idea of a French generalissimo gained increasing support. Clemenceau's main aim for the SWC was that it would bring about unified command. He had little interest in using it for other discussions and did not think that a committee could substitute for a single commander.[8] The result was that he attempted to by-pass the SWC whenever possible. However, as this work demonstrates, American support for this body forced discussions on key issues to take place through this forum. The SWC survived the appointment of an Allied Generalissimo. This was partly due to its central role in supporting the Americans expanded manpower programme. When it served national interests to use the SWC, Clemenceau did so. Foch also did so – he worked with the Americans through the SWC, and sent questions to the various Permanent Military Representatives (PMRs) on issues such as tanks, the American programme, and improvements to railway lines. The French fed information into the SWC, which was then digested by the various SWC committees. Tasker Bliss, the American PMR, himself stressed to the American secretary of war, Newton D. Baker that, 'Of course there is only one power that would think that it could gain any advantage by the dissolution of the Supreme War council. M. Clemenceau wants to put the whole direction of the war in all theatres in the hands of General Foch'.[9] However, the Americans and the British would not allow this to happen, forcing the French to work through the SWC, as this book demonstrates.

---

[7] Trask, *Supreme War Council*, 33.
[8] Robert K. Hanks, 'Culture versus Diplomacy: Georges Clemenceau and Anglo-American Relations during the First World War' (University of Toronto, PhD thesis, 2002), 201.
[9] Bliss to Baker, 26 June 1918, LOC, Bliss Papers [hereon Bliss] 250.

What Was the Supreme War Council?

Meeting monthly at Versailles the SWC consisted of two representatives each from Britain, France, and Italy. The head of government was the permanent member and while, in theory, the second representative could vary depending on the topic of discussion (although he had to be member of the government) so as to provide the most pertinent information, these were usually Alfred Milner of the British War Cabinet (and by April 1918 Secretary of War), French Foreign Minister Stephen Pichon, and Italian Foreign Minister Sydney Sonnino. The US position was slightly different. Fearful of losing diplomatic independence, President Wilson refused to sit on this political committee; however, he sent Arthur Hugh Frazier, the American ambassador to Paris, to act as 'an ear but not a mouth'.[10] This placed the Americans in a favourable situation where they could keep an eye on their partners, while still claiming to be politically detached. It also thwarted attempts to use the SWC for the creation of an Allied approach to major political questions, such as the pronouncement of Allied war aims. It also gave the American Military Representative a central position at the SWC as will be discussed.

Technically the SWC had no executive power; however, these key members were able to use their positions within their own governments to advocate the implementation of the agreements made by the SWC. In their desire to maintain the coalition and coordinate action, they frequently did so. It was not a perfect system of agreement, but this forum also allowed the Allies to hold their partners accountable and solicit information. For this reason, the SWC invited various individuals to present information, which meant that these meetings frequently became overwhelmed with opinions, as illustrated by its being nicknamed 'the circus'. The result was that often the agreements reached at the SWC were negotiated in small group sessions, with the resolutions being made at the official meetings. They also served to illustrate Allied unity to the world, which was believed to have a positive effect on Allied morale.

Permanent Military Representatives

The SWC was assisted in military matters by technical advisers known as the PMRs, who are at the centre of this study.[11] They concerned

---

[10] Hankey recorded that this was the nickname Clemenceau gave Frazier. Maurice Hankey, *Diplomacy by Conference: Studies in Public Affairs, 1920–1946* (London, 1946), 24.

[11] On 8 December 1917, the PMRs decided to call themselves the 'Military Representatives'. 'Minutes of the Permanent Military Representatives', 8 December

themselves with what they termed 'policy'. They purposefully avoided using the term 'plan' as they recognised that this term was commonly used to refer to what the commanders-in-chief created for operational purposes.[12] The main responsibility of the PMRs was to prepare and submit recommendations for the consideration of the SWC on questions that the SWC directed to them. Proposals put forth by the PMRs could either be discussed by the SWC and decided upon, or decided upon by each individual government outside the SWC. The policies created by the PMRs detailed the limits within which the commanders should function, rather than giving specific instructions to the field commanders.[13] They functioned at a level comparable to that of the general staffs and created a strategy that considered all of the theatres of war in relation to one another. They were concerned with how to conduct the war and only considered political issues to the degree that it affected the former. What they meant by the term 'policy' today would be called strategy. The general policies they created were compiled into guidelines (not detailed plans) that rarely considered specific operational details and never considering tactics. What they offered was an alternate opinion to the national ones put forward by the general staffs in each country. So while the general staffs had information about their coalition partners via liaisons, the PMRs were working together daily and aimed to reflect a coalition perspective. The result was that they were able to make recommendations on how best to coordinate the coalition war effort, which included identifying existing areas of poor coordination and advising on the creation of a number of sub-committees.

It was this group that created much of the controversy over the implementation of the SWC, as they challenged the roles of the general staffs.[14] They were instructed to analyse the military situation from the broad view of the Allies, and not just of their own country. Lloyd George hoped that they would act as much as advisors to the other governments as they would to their own.[15] One of their first tasks was to consider whether an offensive or defensive stance should be adopted in 1918 and

---

1917, TNA, Cabinet Papers [hereon CAB] CAB 25/120/SWC17. Shumate refers to them as 'military diplomats'. Shumate, *Allied Supreme War Council*.

[12] Tasker Bliss, 'Supreme War Council: American Report of the First Six Sessions', 28 November 1918, Bliss/252/p. 10.

[13] 'Report of T. H. Bliss on the Supreme War Council', February 1920, Bliss/253/p. 40.

[14] For more on this controversy, see David R. Woodward, *Field Marshal Sir William Robertson: Chief of the Imperial General Staff in the Great War* (London, 1998), 187–204.

[15] *Proces-Verbal* of a Conference of the British, French, and Italian Governments, Held at the "New Casino Hotel", Rapallo, on Wednesday, November 7, 1917, at 11 A.M.', TNA, CAB 28/3/I.C.30.

also whether, in the meantime, any of Germany's allies could be knocked out of the war. When Foch became Allied Generalissimo, their importance as a body that considered future policy was reinforced.[16] Foch would be responsible for immediate military action, while the PMRs were charged with future campaign planning for the upcoming autumn, as well as for 1919.[17]

One PMR was appointed for each country represented at the SWC. Initially the Allies disagreed over who should sit on the body. Both General Henry Wilson and Lloyd George were adamant that the PMR should be independent of the War Office. They claimed it would allow the PMRs to express an independent military opinion. The French and the Americans, who both hoped the SWC would result in a unified command, did not see why the roles should be divided.

The original British PMR was Henry Wilson, who had experience liaising with the French and who was close to Foch. From the onset the relationship between Wilson and the British Chief of Staff was a struggle for power. The British Army Council adamantly disagreed with the PMRs' ability to propose plans of operation differing from its own. It affirmed that the Army Council was the supreme authority on the military forces of the British Empire. Wilson, as an officer, should receive instructions from the Army Council when his work as PMR affected the military forces of Britain. The Army Council insisted that Wilson not give advice without the Army Council's permission.[18] In the end, the War Cabinet compromised, agreeing with the Army Council but giving Wilson 'unfettered discretion as to the advice he offered'.[19] As this work will show, these tensions permeated into Allied discussions, in particular during discussions over action in Palestine and Mesopotamia. When Wilson replaced Robertson as Chief of the Imperial General Staff (CIGS), Rawlinson briefly took up the role as PMR. A month later, Rawlinson was recalled to field command, at which point any tension between the British PMR and the Army Council had ebbed. Charles Sackville-West, the man Henry Wilson affectionately referred to as

---

[16] A notable achievement of the SWC was its formation of the Executive War Board (EWB). It was an evolutionary step toward Foch's promotion to generalissimo on the Western Front. Most studies on the SWC have been focussed on the EWB and Foch's evolution to generalissimo, therefore it is unnecessary to repeat that work here. See Greenhalgh, *Victory through Coalition*, 181–185; D. R. Woodward, *Lloyd George and the Generals* (Newark, 1983), ch. 11; Tasker H. Bliss, 'The Evolution of the Unified Command', *Foreign Affairs* 1/2 (1922), 10–25.

[17] Also see Greenhalgh, *Foch*, 381–387; Greenhalgh, *Victory*, 221–223.

[18] 'Relations between Army Council and British Representative', 12 November 1917, TNA, CAB 27/8/WP65A.

[19] Ibid.

'Tit Willow' and who was known as 'Wilson's own man', became PMR for the remainder of the war.[20]

In contrast to the British, the other countries PMRs were closely linked to the general staffs of their respective countries. Foch was initially appointed the French PMR, but after British objections that he could not hold both this position and Chief of the General Staff (CGS) he was replaced by General Maxime Weygand. Formerly Foch's Chief of Staff and still his alter ego, in April 1918 Weygand returned to this position in support of Foch when he was promoted to generalissimo. Weygand was replaced by Émile Belin, who had been Chief of Staff to Joffre in 1914. Belin had proved to be a capable staff officer. His skills of working with people and the fact that he was a trusted bureaucrat (who would not overstep his responsibilities) likely recommended him for the position of PMR.

Italy's first PMR was the ruthless and stubborn General Luigi Cadorna, who had lost his command of the Italian army after the infamous battle of Caporetto. He was the most senior ranking officer of the PMR, but he retired in February 1918 when the decision to investigate Caporetto was made. Cadorna was replaced by General Mario Nicolis di Robilant who, at this time, was best known for his own blunder at Caporetto. He had failed to immediately execute Cadorna's order to retreat the Fourth Italian Army, resulting in the capture of thousands of his men. However, his capabilities as a commander where recognised when Diaz brought him back to field command in early 1918.

The Americans took longer to establish their PMR and his staff as they had to be organised from the other side of the Atlantic. General Tasker Bliss, who had recently vacated the position of chief of staff, was appointed to this position. He had recently been the military representative to Colonel House's mission in November 1917, which was focussed on improving coordination with the European partners, thus he was an obvious choice. Bliss was known for his diplomatic and analytical skills, and he worked well with the Secretary of War, Newton D. Baker, who appointed him to this role.[21] As the Americans lacked a political voice on the SWC, Bliss's role as PMR was unique amongst the PMRs and he had a considerable amount of power. He became one of two main channels for coordination between the Americans and their European partners: Wilson – Baker – Bliss and Wilson – Baker – March – Pershing. The issue with the latter channel was that the personalities of Pershing, the

---

[20] Maurice Hankey, *The Supreme Command, 1914 to 1918* (2 vols., London, 1961), ii, 797.
[21] For more on Bliss, see Frederick Palmer, *Bliss, Peacemaker: The Life and Letters of General Tasker Howard Bliss* (New York, 1934).

commander of the American army in Europe, and that of Peyton March, who became the American army chief of staff in early 1918, severely clashed. While all three men were four star generals, Bliss was able to subordinate himself to Pershing when necessary whereas Pershing and March continued to be entangled in a power struggle throughout the war. As will be explored in this book, Bliss was an asset in two major ways. First, as he communicated well with March, he was able to smooth some of the difficulties that were raised because of the Pershing-March rivalry. This was essential if the Americans were to get the correct army configuration in Europe that could cooperate with their European partners. Second, Bliss's diplomatic abilities allowed him to present his government's position to the European partners while at the same time remaining politically detached. This was no small feat.

Organisation of PMR Staffs

The PMRs worked in the Hôtel de Trianon in Versailles and lived nearby in various villas. The hotel provided ample room for the staffs to work; the British and the French each had half of the first floor for their offices, while the American and Italians had divided the second. This meant that they could easily discuss and exchange information. They set up a hub for communications, as their staffs included telephone operators, cyclists/motorcyclists, and a number of drivers (ten automobile drivers for the British alone) which could take them to and fro as they gathered information from various channels.[22] They ensured they had translators, as well as multilingual officers where possible. With the assistance of the incredibly capable Maurice Hankey, who was the British War Cabinet Secretary and British SWC Secretary, Henry Wilson organised the British Section of the PMRs into three main branches and one smaller fourth branch.[23] Branch 'A' (Allies) dealt with the strategic and military situations of the Allied and neutral forces. It considered where the enemy might launch an offensive, and how that offensive could be thwarted. This section was further sub-divided by theatre. Branch 'E' (Enemies) adopted the viewpoint of the German High Command, and envisaged scenarios it might execute. There was a large mirror in the room where 'E' staff worked. It was Wilson's preference that these officers wear their

---

[22] 'Instructions relatives à l'installation à Versailles du Conseil Supérieur de Guerre', 21 November 1917, Service Historique de la Défense – Département de l'Armée de Terre, Château de Vincennes [hereon referred to as SHD-DAT], Fonds Clemenceau, 6N 61.

[23] Hankey, *The Supreme Command*, 719.

caps with the peak to the back, so that when they looked up from their work they would see themselves as Germans (Wilson himself enjoyed impersonating a German officer).[24] This method of roleplaying was not unlike that undertaken by officers at *Deuxième Bureau* (French Intelligence) who used it as a tool to get into the mind-set of German decision makers.[25] The third branch, 'M' (Material), considered manpower, munitions, and transport issues. Its main responsibility was to advise the SWC about manpower and material requirements for military plans. It worked closely with the Inter-Allied Transport Council to evaluate the capacity of various railways of both the Allies and their enemies. This work was an essential component in transforming the plans of the other two branches into reality. In addition, this branch also co-ordinated administration among the various Allied sections. The fourth and smallest branch was the political branch. From both the Allied and enemy perspectives, it analysed the extent to which political situations affected military action. Altogether, the British Section comprised 150 men.[26]

After speaking with Henry Wilson, Bliss chose to style the American Section on the British example, with the exclusion of the political branch, as the Americans believed it would hinder their diplomatic independence. This section comprised a staff of twelve officers and approximately forty enlisted men and army field clerks. Liaison officers were assigned to both Pershing's and Foch's headquarters in order to keep Bliss informed of happenings at the front. Frazier provided a link between Bliss and the State Department, as Frazier reported to the latter, and provided information to Bliss, although Bliss forwarded joint notes and minutes directly to the State Department. Again, this organisation was specifically designed to maintain American diplomatic independence. Bliss's relationship with the American General Staff and War Department was much closer, as General Peyton C. March (Army Chief of Staff), and Newton D. Baker (Secretary of War) were amongst his regular correspondents.[27]

The French also organised their section into three branches, but they were divided into Eastern Section (Section d'Orient), Western Section (Section d'Occident), and a joint Political and Economic Section (Section Économique et Politique). The French staff consisted of

---

[24] Charles Edward Callwell, *Field-Marshal Sir Henry Wilson: His Life and Diaries* (2 vols., London, 1927), ii, 41.

[25] Terrence Finnegan, 'Military Intelligence at the Front, 1914–18', *Studies in Intelligence* 53/4 (2009), 37.

[26] 'Historical Record of the Supreme War Council', n.d., TNA, CAB 25/127.

[27] 'Report of T. H. Bliss', Bliss/253/p. 45.

approximately twelve officers and sixty personnel. In contrast, the Italians did not divide their group into branches. The Italian PMR was supported by a mere eight officers, two drivers, and twenty soldiers, thus ensuring their status as a junior partner.[28] The enormous size of the British staff meant that they had the potential to dominate the other PMRs. They conducted more studies than their colleagues and put forward many of the draft joint notes that were turned into PMR recommendations. At the end of the war, however, the French made the alterative claim that it was the French Section that had undertaken the majority of the work.[29] In reality, the procedures followed by the PMRs prevented any one nation from dominating. Controversial issues were debated at their meetings and had to be agreed upon if the PMRs wanted them to take the form of a joint note. Also, by rotating the chairman of the meeting (who set the agenda), each nation was able to put forward issues that concerned them.

Each PMR was provided with military information (including all documents and proposals relating to the conduct of the war) from his individual country. Intelligence was also provided by their respective army chiefs of staff and foreign offices. The PMRs had the freedom to solicit material from other government bodies (shipping, finance, food, munitions, aviation, transport, and manpower).[30] Intelligence (both diplomatic and military) came in the form of military attaché reports, intelligence summaries, charts, and maps. It included information relating to the organisation, strength, disposition, and tactics of the German army. Each week the British Section was sent a copy of the comparative figures of the British and enemy troops which were communicated to the War Office from the General Staff (M.O.3).[31] After Foch's appointment as generalissimo he established a liaison between his headquarters (Grand Quartier-Général) and each PMR section. The PMRs also saw reports passed between the War Office and the British liaison at Foch's Grand Quartier-Général (GQG), as well as the reports created by each liaison officer. In addition, Bliss received intelligence from Pershing's headquarters (G-2) while Belin was privy to intelligence from *Deuxième Bureau* and from Pétain. Under the SWC, no formal body for sharing intelligence between the Allies was established (the Inter-Allied Commission

[28] 'Note relative à l'installation à Versailles de l'État -Major Italien', 23 November 1917, SHD-DAT, Fonds Clemenceau, 6N 61.

[29] 'Historique du Conseil Supérieur de Guerre', 9 October 1919, SHD-DAT, Fonds Clemenceau, 6N 61.

[30] 'Procès-verbal of the Second Session of the Supreme War Council', 1 December 1917, TNA, CAB 25/121/SWC165, pp. 7–8.

[31] See TNA, WO 106/324.

was established in August 1918, but it functioned outside of the SWC). The PMRs did exchange intelligence with one another, which they then used to estimate German capabilities and project these onto the comparable strength of the Allies and the Central Powers. The Americans relied on British and French statistical summaries; Bliss determined that his own staff was too small for it to repeat this work. The British made a detailed map of enemy and allied positions that was available to all sections.[32] These assessments and projections of relative strengths were central to the PMRs evolving strategy.

The PMRs made policy recommendations to the political side of the SWC that were communicated in the form of joint notes. The PMRs had to unanimously agree upon each note, otherwise the information could be put into a 'special report' instead. These notes were then discussed at the monthly SWC meetings were they could be altered before being accepted or rejected. The majority of notes were approved; however, there were challenges in implementing them. Like the political side of the SWC, the PMRs did not have executive authority. After approval, any notes related to military policy were sent from the PMRs to the General Staff of their countries. It was then the responsibility of the General Staff to advise the government on the note and execute any plans. In reality, this sequence of implementation meant that the general staffs could delay any suggestions with which they did not agree. The political members of the SWC followed the notes' progress, and they could enquire as to why no action was being undertaken either with their own general staff, or return the issue to the SWC. Alternatively, the PMRs could petition the SWC which could then result in the political side of the SWC becoming involved once again. Given that the meetings were monthly, this was a slow process. It was also a useful stalling tactic if one wanted to maintain the visage of Allied unity but not undertake action. In this way the recommendations met with varying degrees of success. The PMRs' recommendations were more successful when they supported the work of the Generalissimo with a view to future action. Communications between the other SWC committees and councils were less complicated than those sent to the general staffs due to the fact that the SWC and PMRs were often soliciting information. These councils comprised the leading national decision makers; therefore those implementing the decisions were usually the same people who had made the recommendation.

---

[32] 'Report of T. H. Bliss', Bliss/253/p. 46.

During the PMR meetings one of its members would act as the chairman in order to direct the proceedings. With each meeting the chairman rotated based on the date of each country's entry into the war, as did the secretary, whose nationality matched that of the chairman. The secretaries remained fairly independent of one another, as neither a common registry nor record office was ever established despite the idea having been discussed.[33] It was the secretary of the day who assembled the agendas for the PMR meetings, as well as the joint notes, in consultation with the other three secretaries. This secretary also created a draft of the summary of decisions and minutes for the meetings, which were then circulated to the other branches. If they could not agree on the recording of an issue then it was excluded and discussed at the next meeting. Those who had participated in the meeting could make amendments to the draft. The PMR secretaries then worked together to make a common record (written in the official language of the PMR keeping the record) which had to be approved by all sections. The secretary assured the members 'that the Minutes correctly present the views expressed by them at the Council'.[34] The result was that the formatting of these joint documents was different but the content was usually the same. This procedure was followed for all joint reporting, including Joint Notes. These documents were passed on by each joint secretary to their respective governments. Copies of information received from their respective governments were not given to each section. Instead, it was the responsibility of each section to inform the others of the attitudes and interests of its own government.[35] Naturally, the PMRs used the information they received from their own governments to strengthen their position against the other PMRs when necessary.

The Advisory Committees

The SWC and PMRs were assisted by a number of bodies. While not all of these organisations will be discussed in this work, the ones central to the creation of an Allied policy – the Allied Maritime Transport Council, the Inter-Allied Munitions Council, and the Inter-Allied Transportation Council (IATC) – will be evaluated in the appropriate chapters. Members of the PMR staff attended the meetings of the inter-allied councils and committees. Technically, as of 28 May 1918, these groups

---

[33] 'Historical Record of the Supreme War Council', n.d., TNA, CAB 25/127/p. 19.

[34] Colonel Storr (British Section) 'Notes on the Genesis and Functions of the Joint Secretariat of the Supreme War Council', 22 May 1918, Bliss/323/SWC217.

[35] 'Report of T. H. Bliss', Bliss/253/p. 46.

were to report to the PMRs on the 1st and 15th of each month regarding the developments related to the decisions made by the SWC that affected their body.[36] Hankey described that, 'the inter-Allied organisations were functioning as advisers to the Supreme War Council (political side) exactly as British Government Departments functioned vis-à-vis the War Cabinet'.[37] However, this is to underestimate the reality of the growing authority and responsibilities of these bodies throughout 1918. Initially Allied shipping needs were discussed as part of the House Mission to Europe in November 1917, but with the creation of the SWC, the AMTC came under the umbrella of the SWC. So while these organisations could work independently of the SWC, they complemented the work being done at the SWC by enabling the SWC members to refer questions to them, and thus enabled the Allies to align their strategy with their means. In particular, the AMTC and IAMC became central to Allied coordination as the Americans insisted on using these forums to discuss their needs and contributions (a central focus of Chapter 6).

Prior to the creation of the SWC, the mechanisms for communication between the allied political and military leadership included military and civilian missions and allied liaisons that communicated between soldiers, diplomats, and war offices. Individual personalities were particularly central to how these channels functioned, as personal relationships frequently dictated what information was passed to liaison officers. This meant that these channels could be problematic and unreliable, as is exemplified by Clemenceau's reference to his own diplomatic corps as lamentable.[38] Personality clashes also caused difficulties at the SWC, but despite them, it became increasingly employed for the discussion and coordination of the Allied war effort. Naturally bi-lateral discussions still occurred, but it was through the channels of the SWC that Allied decisions were finalised, and expected to be done so by the coalition partners who wanted to know how the component parts of the coalition were working toward a shared vision. The SWC provided an opportunity to formalise the international conferences that were already part of the Allied communication system and to create a reliable system for the discussion of coalition issues (see Figure 1.1).

---

[36] 'Summary of Conclusions [attached to Proceedings of 32nd Meeting of Military Representatives]', 28 May 1918, TNA, CAB 25/121/SWC224.
[37] Hankey, *The Supreme Command*, 783.   [38] Hanks, 'Culture versus Diplomacy', 187.

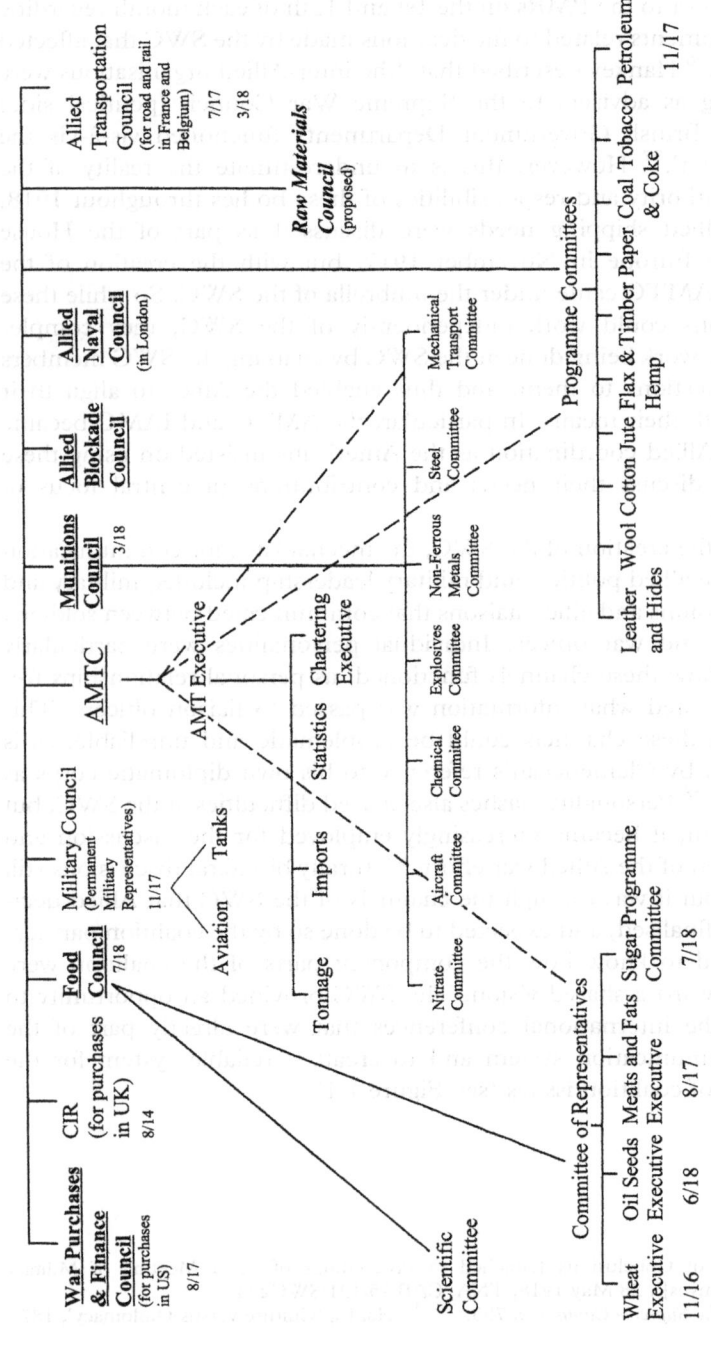

Figure 1.1 Diagram of the Supreme War Council Organisation, November 1917
Reproduced from Elizabeth Greenhalgh, *Victory through Coalition: Britain and France during the First World War* (Cambridge: Cambridge University Press, 2005), 278.

2   Offensive Action in the Balkans?

> The present position in the Balkans is deplorable – French and Italians
> working against each other, Serbs and Greeks working together in
> secret, a general mistrust of the French, and isolated attempts by one
> Secret Service or another to bring off a deal with the Bulgarian enemy at
> the expense of their Allies. Nobody trusts anyone else, and the whole
> peninsula is a nest of intrigue.[1]

This quotation indicates the complicated nature of coalition war in the
Balkans. More than in any other theatre the coalition partners had
varying perspectives on what could be achieved against the Central
Powers. It was after defeat at Gallipoli that British and French troops
were diverted to Salonika in a failing attempt to assist the Serbians. In
1915 it offered an alternative strategy to the stalemate on the Western
Front.[2] The French led the expedition in Macedonia, where they had
imperial and economic interests. Despite losing Serbia, the French and
British agreed to maintain a force of approximately 150,000 men to hold
Salonika in an effort to encourage the Balkan states, especially the
Greeks, to join them.[3] Both the British and the French wanted to block
German aspirations in the Near East. Success in this region would allow
Germany to economically dominate from the North Sea to the Indian
Ocean and from Hamburg to the Persian Gulf via Constantinople. With
the Serbian army driven out of its homeland, the Germans had a continu-
ous line of communication to the Ottomans via the Berlin-Baghdad
Railway, which increased British anxiety that the Central Powers would

---

[1] Bliss quoting 'a British Officer', Bliss to Baker, 3 July, 1918, Bliss/318.
[2] David Dutton, *The Politics of Diplomacy: Britain and France in the Balkans in the First
World War* (London and New York, 1998), 29. Dutton illustrates Lloyd George's
leading role in proposing an expedition to Salonika as early as 1915. On the
relationship between alternative strategies and political-military relations, see Philpott,
Anglo-French Relations, 71.
[3] Leonard V. Smith, Stéphane Audoin-Rouzeau, and Annette Becker, *France and the Great
War 1914–1918* (Cambridge, 2003), 79.

attack Egypt or India.[4] Furthermore, without an Allied presence in Salonika, ports in Greece might provide the Central Powers with submarine bases.

Using the PMRs discussions as its central focus, this chapter examines how the varying positions of the coalition members made it difficult for them to create an Allied strategy in the Balkans, despite the fact that they had a forum to do so. At the Allied level of the SWC, the French, British, Americans, and Italians all recognised that to win the war they would have to throw their weight against the Germans on the Western Front; however, how the Balkan theatre would contribute to this victory was fiercely debated. Initially the French wanted to launch an offensive in the Balkans, as they believed it would improve Allied morale in this theatre. After the German spring offensive, they argued that offensive action in the Balkans would support their efforts on the Western Front by pinning down enemy resources. In stark contrast, the British wanted Allied efforts to focus on the defence. This would ensure that the Germans did not obtain submarine bases along the Greek coast and would also allow the British to safely shift troops further east to Palestine and to the Western Front. Given the primacy of the Franco-Belgian theatre, the Allies had limited resources to shift between the secondary theatres. This reality placed the British and French at odds over where their resources could best be positioned.

In addition to maintaining the defensive, the British advocated for diplomatic action. In turn, by attempting to involve their partners in political discussions, the British isolated the Americans. Distrustful of the Entente's political intentions and aware that their partners were trying to involve them in a theatre where they had not declared war against the main adversary – the Bulgarians – the Americans tried to remain militarily and politically detached. The extent of their interest was to monitor their allies so that they did not divert any more forces from the Western Front, where the Americans intended to make their decisive assault in 1919. Under pressure from the French to support the campaign in the Balkans, the Italians had deployed the *Corpo special italiano d'Albania* and formed a base at Valona.[5] This presence allowed them to pursue one of their own foreign policy objectives, that being to dominate the Adriatic. Additionally they sent an expeditionary force to Salonika,

[4] Dutton, *The Politics of Diplomacy*, 92, 99, 150–153; Schwarz, 'Divided Attention', 104.
[5] On the various opinions and debates on sending forces to the Balkans, see John Gooch, *The Italian Army and the First World War* (New York, 2014), 71–80; 118–122.

which, by January 1918, comprised 41,000 combatants.[6] Like the British, the Italians supported the defensive position. Regrouping after Caporetto and then preparing for another Austrian attack on the Piave in June (see Chapter 4) meant they could not afford to send additional forces to the Balkans, as they could not be replaced. Furthermore, the Italians were concerned that if the Greeks had a major role in a successful offensive they might threaten Italy's territorial ambitions in Northern Epirus.[7] Therefore it was not until they were convinced the Greeks were a strong fighting force that they shifted to accepting an offensive policy in this theatre. Finally, as this chapter will illustrate, the Italians used the SWC to challenge some decisions made by the French Commander.

With the Allies being divided between two opposing camps supporting either offensive action or defensive action, it was difficult for the SWC to reach an agreement. Added to these opposing views was the reality was that the French largely controlled this theatre. The French were the hegemonic power, with overall command in this theatre appointed to the commander of the armée d'Orient. His instructions came from Clemenceau, not the PMRs. For the French it was clear who should create the strategy in the Balkans – the French. However, the SWC provided a forum for the other coalition partners to attempt to affect this strategy. Furthermore, as the PMRs were instructed to investigate the situation in the Balkans, they had little choice but to continue to press the French for information and attempt to reach an agreement. Ultimately, no party wanted to be responsible for the demise of the coalition. The result was that the PMRs created an ambiguous agreement that maintained the substance of the coalition, but did not reflect the reality of the unfolding military situation. Without executive power, and in competition with other planning groups, this coalition institution was limited. Discussions over military action in Macedonia illustrate the complicated nature of policy making between the coalition members.

Polarisation in 1917

One of the first issues discussed by the PMRs on their formation was to decide Allied policy in the Balkans. The French and British political and military leadership had frequently met earlier in 1917 to discuss this issue and had established a pattern of disagreement with which the PMRs had to contend. After the February Revolution in Russia, the

---

[6] 'État comparatif des forces alliées et ennemies sur le front de Macédoine', 7 January 1918, SHD-DAT, Conseil Supérieur de la Guerre, 4N 53.
[7] Angeliki Sfika-Theodosiou, 'The Italian Presence on the Balkan Front', *Balkan Studies*, 36/1 (1995), 78.

Allies attempted to assess how far political unrest would constrain Russia's military action and what the knock-on effect would be for the other Allies. Both assumed that the Germans would strike a major blow on one of the fronts in autumn 1917 – as they had done to Serbia in 1915 and Romania in 1916 – but they could not agree on where this attack would occur. The British contended that Mesopotamia was under threat whereas the French argued that an attack in the Balkans was more likely.

The situation was made worse when the British announced that they would withdraw troops from Salonika to move to Palestine. Ferocious debates ensued between the British and French about the feasibility of this manpower distribution. The British situation in the Middle East had devolved with the loss of Russian support in Asia Minor, leaving Mesopotamia vulnerable to an attack. They assessed that the most efficient way to minimise this danger would be by placing pressure on the Turkish army in Palestine. When the Greeks joined the war on the side of the Allies in June, this gave the British further justification to withdraw divisions as, they argued, they could be replaced by Greek ones.[8] In contrast, the French Minister of War, Paul Painlevé, insisted that a British withdrawal of troops would result in a 'bad moral effect' in the Balkans, and that militarily it would indicate to the enemy that the Allies had no intention of attacking in this theatre. More worryingly, it would indicate that the Allies themselves were ripe for an attack. The Italians and the Serbians supported this view while the Russian representative went further, arguing that 'in the Balkans it [the British division] could serve the interests of the Allies as a whole far more effectively than it could in Palestine or Mesopotamia, where a reverse, though unfortunate, would not affect the whole of the Allies ...' As the British recorded, 'the implication of this argument was that the Palestine and Mesopotamia campaigns were a selfish British interest'.[9]

In contrast, the British representatives defended their position by reminding their allies that the enemy could not make realistic gains in the Balkans because the balance of troops was in favour of the Allies. Furthermore, intelligence indicated that the Turkish army was going to attack in Mesopotamia. Finally, they argued that the Allies were unable to conduct an offensive in the Balkans, as the Russians were unable to provide essential support in the north. The conclusion reached by the British was that this division, which was not required to maintain the defence, was an 'inexcusable' waste given 'the really important work to

---

[8] 'The Allied Conference held in Paris on July 25 to 26, 1917', TNA, CAB 28/2/I. C. 24.
[9] Ibid.

be done elsewhere'.[10] These discussions served to further illustrate the diverging positions of the British and French in these theatres.

As the British confirmed they would move divisions from Salonika, the French became increasingly desperate and alarmed at the effect this would have on morale in this theatre. They went as far as to suggest that the British withdraw a division from France (where the French were also insisting that the British take up more of the line).[11] The French Premier, Alexandre Ribot alternatively offered to temporarily send a French division from Salonica to Egypt until it could be replaced by a British division from France. When this tactic did not work, he then threatened to inform the French Parliament that the British were ignoring French needs. The British explained that it was merely a case of the French making a moral argument while the British were making a military one. The French representative reminded the British that, militarily, the French could send a division to Palestine too, 'because they had a political and moral right, in the interests of France, to strengthen their military representation in Palestine'.[12] The Italians followed suit by saying that this applied to their armies as well. Both Arthur Balfour, the British Secretary of State for Foreign Affairs, and the resolutions of this meeting clarified the various spheres of influence of the powers. In the case of France and Italy: 'both nations were already represented in Palestine by, it was true, a nominal force, but the only object of that force was to preserve French and Italian claims by showing the French and Italian flags. To mix diplomatic questions with purely military considerations did not help on the war'.[13] Symbolically neither the French nor Italian representatives denied this point. The final resolution recognised 'the special responsibilities of the British government in Mesopotamia and Palestine ...' and agreed to the withdrawal of one British division.[14]

A discussion between the British and the French on what victory in the Balkans would mean further served to polarise British and French approaches to the Balkans. While at a previous meeting Lloyd George had advocated that Turkey and Austria could be detached through a combination of military and diplomatic action if the Russians could not be revived, he also asked the commanders to consider how the war would be won without the Russians.[15] Lloyd George was irritated that Foch,

[10] Ibid.   [11] Ibid.
[12] 'Notes of an Inter-Ally Conference held at 10, Downing Street, S.W., on Tuesday and Wednesday, August 7 and 8, 1917', TNA, CAB 28/2/I.C.25.
[13] Ibid.   [14] Ibid.
[15] 'Notes of an Allied Conference, Held in the President of the Council's Room at the Foreign Office, Paris, on Thursday, July 26, 1917, at 3:15', TNA, CAB 28/2/I.C.24(a).

who was Chief of the General Staff of the French Army, offered a pessimistic vision. In regards to the Balkans, Foch's description of defeating the Bulgarian army highlighted the challenging terrain in this theatre. The two routes to Sofia were from the Vardar and Struma Valleys, both of which would require crossing the difficult Rhodope Mountains with its deep river gorges and complex peak system. Communications were poor with only one railway, while the geography leant itself to a strong defensive position. For these reasons any offensive would have to progress slowly and carefully. Despite these difficulties Foch recommended offensive action emphasising it was important 'more especially because Greece had not yet reached her maximum military effort'.[16] Foch knew that a successful limited offensive would improve morale at a key moment when the Greek army was being raised. This idea was one that the French would continue to promote throughout late 1917 and into 1918 in regards to offensive action in the Balkans. These meetings throughout 1917 established a pattern of the British advocating for diplomatic action in the Balkans while they turned their sights to the Middle East. In contrast the French, who were leading the Allied armies in this theatre, sought to maintain morale, and thus advocated for offensive action. It was within this polarised environment that the PMRs had to operate.

Challenging Roles

Foch

When Clemenceau became Premier and War Minister in November 1917 he refocussed efforts in the Balkans on military action by replacing Sarrail, the commander of the Armée d'Orient, with Guillaumat. Sarrail had been criticised for his economic meddling in the Balkans with many suspecting that he was more concerned with preparing for the postwar world as opposed to conducting military operations that would win the war.[17] The British Commander in Salonika, George Milne, looked favourably upon the new commander. He appreciated that Guillaumat listened to the opinions of others while still maintaining clear ideas of his own.[18] This change in command presented an opportunity for better

---

[16] 'Procès-verbal of a Meeting between Representatives of the British, French, and Italian Governments', 8 August 1917, TNA, CAB 28/2/I.C.25(E).

[17] See David Dutton, 'The Balkan Campaign and French War Aims in the Great War', *The English Historical Review*, 94/370, 91–113.

[18] Dutton, *The Politics of Diplomacy*, 131.

relations between the Allies, and it also meant that new instructions were to be given to the commander of the Armeé d'Orient.

Foch, who as Chief of the French General Staff was the technical adviser to the French government in all theatres, had been digesting the situation reports coming from the Balkans.[19] With a report entitled 'Points to be addressed by the Commander-in-Chief of the Allied Armed Forces' he, too, reinforced that action in the Balkans would now be considered by the military results they could achieve.[20] Foch emphasised that the mission of the Allied Armies should be to prevent the enemy from conquering Greece. Precautionary measures were to be taken, alongside the Greeks, to ensure the protection of the naval base of Corfu, as it guaranteed Allied communications throughout the Adriatic. Foch also directed Guillaumat to create additional bases from that of Salonika. It was also essential that Guillaumat prepare the Greek army, first to take a defensive position and then an offensive one.[21] While the majority of his points focussed on the defensive, in a final section on 'preparing for the future resumption of offensive operations', Foch discussed the importance of moving onto the offensive when possible. From Foch's perspective, defensive organisation was already in the process of being carried out, and so Guillaumat should spend some of his time studying the *possibility* of an offensive 'to take action in the best interests of the Coalition against enemy armies, according to the circumstances of the moment'.[22] Signed by Clemenceau, these instructions did not indicate a major shift in policy but rather a sensible approach to military planning given the concern about morale, the wording of the instructions, and the fact that defensive arrangements were already underway (giving Guillaumat time to consider offensive action). Furthermore, Guillaumat confirmed Foch's suspicions about the morale of the Allied armies in the Balkans, going as far as to suggest the possibility of a mutiny. It is not surprising that offensive action would be suggested, as limited offensives were seen to shore up morale.

While Foch drew up these instructions for Guillaumat, the PMRs were also discussing action in the Balkans. On 23 December 1917, they signed Joint Note 4 entitled 'The Balkan Problem', in which the PMRs agreed the Allies should remain on the defensive in Macedonia for the year 1918.[23] Like Foch, the PMRs highlighted the importance of mainland

---

[19] 'Compte – Rendu des Operations des Armées Alliées d'Orient. 1er-15 Novembre 1917', 7 December 1917, SHD-DAT, Conseil Supérieur de la Guerre, 4N 52.

[20] Foch, 'Points sur lesquels doit se porter l'attention du Général Commandant en chef les Armées Alliées d'Orient', 9 December 1917, Conseil Supérieur de la Guerre, 4N 52.

[21] Ibid.   [22] Ibid.   [23] Joint Note 4, CAB 25/120/SWC27.

Greece; however, they were more concerned about the abilities of the enemy than was Foch. As reinforcements for this front were not available, the PMRs feared that the Allies would be forced to retreat to Salonika, where their stores were located, in the case of the enemy converging their forces for a powerful offensive. They predicted that such a retreat would result in a serious disaster if the Allies were to lose mainland Greece with its various harbours suited to conversion into submarine bases by the enemy. The Allies had already lost substantial amounts of merchant shipping in the Mediterranean in 1917 with the German Mediterranean flotilla group having sunk approximately 1,514,050 gross tonnes.[24] The PMRs implied that losing mainland Greece would have severe consequences for the naval war in the Mediterranean, which Foch had also acknowledged. Although both the French General Staff and the PMRs recognised the vulnerability of the Allies in the Balkans, the PMRs did not recommended offensive action. Their recommendations were sent to the SWC and reserved for further consideration. They also approved the plans put forward by Foch, despite the fact that the British PMR was irritated that they had been cut out of the official instructions.[25]

Guillaumat

It was not until April 1918 that the PMRs were able to consider Guillaumat's own plans for the Balkans. By this point the situation had dramatically changed for the Allies, who were scrambling to meet the German spring offensive in the west. In February, the PMRs had received a summary of Guillaumat's idea, but his full plan had been sent with one of his staff officers who physically had to make the slow journey from Salonika to France.[26] After this long wait, the British, Americans, and Italians were not pleased with the content, which ignored earlier instructions to build-up defences and instead wrote of offensive action. During a meeting on 8 April, the PMRs discussed Guillaumat's neglect of Greece's defences. They were still concerned that mainland Greece might be invaded if an attack were to occur in the immediate future. As it was their responsibility to report to the SWC on these plans, the PMRs worried that they would be held accountable. They insisted that

---

[24] John Ellis and Mike Cox, *The World War I Databook: The Essential Facts and Figures for All the Combatants* (London, 2001), 280.

[25] Callwell, *Field-Marshal*, 46.

[26] 'Minutes of the Meeting of the Military Representatives', 28 February 1918, CAB 25/120/SWC/(MR)18.

Guillaumat supply them with information on the bases in Old Greece and Valona and that he establish new bases immediately. Coming to the French commander's rescue, Belin, the French PMR, explained that Guillaumat was still working on more detailed plans which would incorporate the PMRs' demand for the formation of other bases. Frustrated with his French colleagues, the Italian PMR retorted that it had been four months since Guillaumat received his instructions. Remaining composed at this meeting, Sackville-West later confided to the former PMR and his close friend, Henry Wilson, that he was exasperated that the French commander was not taking seriously the fact that Allied forces were likely to prove inadequate against an enemy attack. Sackville-West also had doubts over the value of the Greek and Serbian armies, thinking it unwise of Guillaumat to assume they could have a large role in any offensive action. He feared that the Serbian army was tired and, therefore, the Serbs should prepare defensive positions. With no way to enforce action, Sackville-West pressed Belin to discover when the more detailed studies by Guillaumat would be ready and when the formation of the bases would begin.[27] Despite his frustration with Guillaumat, Sackville-West said that he found the French PMR 'very pleasant' and 'ready to help'.[28]

As the seriousness of the German spring offensives was realised, the British PMR was increasingly sceptical about offensive action in Macedonia, suggesting that the British withdraw from Salonika and instead focus these resources on the Western Front: 'We ought to get out of Salonika let Guillaumat hold Greece – in fact if we can reduce our shipping in the Mediterranean to zero and if we can supply Egypt-Palestine and Mesopotamia from India we should be able to contemplate a more serious situation should it arise in France with less anxiety'.[29] Sackville-West was in communication with Captain Stead, the British War Office representative at Salonika, who had observed the poor military situation in Macedonia and emphasised to the British PMR the lack of Allied unity and poor relations between the various commanders in this theatre. Stead believed the probability of an attack by the Central Powers was quite high as the German navy now had access to the Russian fleet, which could assist them in dominating the southern Mediterranean. He predicted 'that an attack on Salonika, as an essential naval base,

<hr />

[27] 8 April 1918, PMR Meeting, CAB 25/121/SWC(MR)25.
[28] Sackville-West to Henry Wilson, 8 April 1918, Imperial War Museum, Henry Wilson Papers [hereon HHW], HHW/2/128/14/ff.43.
[29] Sackville-West to Henry Wilson, n.d., HHW/2/12C/1/ff.75.

may well become the selected alternative plan following a check in France'.[30] This negative report was reinforced when French intelligence reported that the Germans intended to employ the Russian Black Sea Fleet (in reality the Germans did seek control of this fleet, but never planned a major sortie).[31] In addition, Stead told Sackville-West that the Greek army was 'rather a weakness than a strength'.[32] Already sceptical of Allied strength in this theatre, the British PMR was resolved to prevent offensive action. Sackville-West's opinion was aligned with his government.

Guillaumat and Foch, however, were focussed on how best to combat the German onslaught on the Western Front. In contrast to the PMRs' agreement that the protection of mainland Greece was an immediate need, Foch's focus had shifted. Recently given command on the Western Front, Foch feared that the Germans might withdraw troops from Bulgaria to bolster their strength in France. On 4 April he wrote to Guillaumat asking him to prepare for an offensive in case it became necessary to hold the Germans in the East.[33] Although Foch had no command over Guillaumat, these instructions fitted with his own operational desires. In March, Clemenceau had directed Guillaumat to prioritise defensive preparations over offensive ones, initially favouring the transfer of four divisions from Salonika to assist the Allies in the Franco-Belgian theatre. However, Foch preferred these troops be used to hold enemy forces away from the Western Front. Foch pressed Clemenceau to accept these offensive operations, with the knowledge that the military agreement between Bulgaria and Germany expired on 23 September, and that Bulgarian morale was low.[34] It was hoped that the Bulgarians could be pressured to withdraw from the war through a combination of political pressure and military force. In a separate action, Foch went as far as to offer Guillaumat everything that could be spared.[35] Convinced, Clemenceau instructed Guillaumat to be ready to go on the offensive if circumstances deemed it necessary.[36]

---

[30] Captain Stead to Sackville-West, 12 April 1918, HHW/2/12C/2/ff.84–5.
[31] Trask, *Captains and Cabinets*, 254. By July, the Germans obtained nine battleships, six cruisers, ten destroyers, and ten U-boats. For a more detailed explanation of the actual situation in the Black Sea, see Trask, 271–272.
[32] Captain Stead to Sackville-West, 12 April 1918.
[33] Foch to Guillaumat, 4 April 1918, AFGG 6/1, annex 472.
[34] Doughty, *Pyrrhic Victory: French Strategy and Operations in the Great War*, 485; Greenhalgh, *Foch*, 447.
[35] Foch, 19 April 1918, AFGG 8/3, annex 16.
[36] Clemenceau summarises previous instructions in Clemenceau to Guillaumat, 12 May 1918, SHD-DAT, Conseil Supérieur de la Guerre, 4N 53.

In contrast to Foch's idea that action in the Balkans could support the Western Front through an offensive, the British high command believed support would come through withdrawing manpower from their divisions for use in the Franco-Belgian theatre. As part of their policy to reduce divisions from twelve to nine battalions, the British made plans to withdraw twelve battalions from Salonika without consulting their French partners. These forces would then be replaced with manpower from India. When the French learned of British intentions they were both surprised and infuriated. Guillaumat, who was considering offensive action, wondered why the British had not informed him of their intentions and why the matter had not been discussed at the SWC given the obvious effects on Allied capabilities. He encouraged his government to force the British to suspend or withdraw this order.[37] The matter was also referred to the SWC in early May after insistence from the French General Staff.[38] Both the British and French representatives held their positions until they finally resolved to send a French-led mission to investigate whether these troops could be safely moved.[39] In less than a week Clemenceau communicated to the French commander that in addition to the British withdrawal of forces, the French were going to progressively withdraw forces from one division, excluding artillerymen, for use in France. He instructed that given that the British would replace their forces with ones from India, French manpower could be replaced with Greek infantrymen. This would allow the commander to pursue an offensive.[40] Within a few weeks and in the context of the Greek army performing well during limited attacks, Guillaumat reported that the transfer of these battalions should proceed.[41]

Meanwhile the British War Cabinet was becoming concerned with events in the Balkans. Guillaumat had been slow in considering the SWC instructions and then the French suddenly replaced him with Franchet d'Espèrey without consulting the other coalition members.[42] On 12 June 1918, Lloyd George told Sackville-West to raise the question of the Balkans with the other PMRS, as 'the War Cabinet feel some anxiety'.[43] At the February Supreme War Council meeting it had been

---

[37] Guillaumat to the War Minister, 23 April 1918, *AFGG* 8/3, annex 83.

[38] État-Major Général de l'Armée, 'Note sur la situation générale', 10 April 1918, *AFGG* 8/3, annex 32.

[39] Clemenceau, 'Order de mission', 7 May 1918, SHD-DAT, Conseil Supérieur de la Guerre, 4N 53.

[40] Clemenceau to Guillaumat, 12 May 1918, Conseil Supérieur de la Guerre, 4N 53.

[41] Guillaumat to Clemenceau, 1 June 1918, AFGG 8/3, annex 216.

[42] Guillaumat was called back to France in case they needed him to replace Foch, not because the French government was unhappy with his performance.

[43] Arthur Balfour to Britoil, 12 June 1918, Bliss/318.

decided that the policy for 1918 would remain defensive on all fronts. No decision could be made in the Balkans in 1918. This agreement was reinforced when, at the SWC in early June, after having been delayed since the beginning of the year, Joint Note 4 was quickly accepted.[44] The British, however, still had reservations about whether the French would abide by the resolution. On 6 June, after a meeting with the War Cabinet, Henry Wilson wrote to Sackville-West: 'We are sending you instructions about Note 4 so now you can push along and *do* push. Don't be put off by the withdrawal of Guillaumat and substitution of Franchet. Of course the French will try and put us off on these grounds. *Don't* let them; especially as we are now greatly reducing the strength of forces there'.[45] The British and French were increasingly at odds over strategy in the Balkans with the British insisting the French hold to the defensive ideas outlined in Joint Note 4 while the French advocated for offensive action.

The situation worsened in late June when Guillaumat, now the military governor of Paris, reacted negatively to a memo written by Sackville-West. He explained, 'The documents sent by Sackville-West demonstrate a complete ignorance of the question. He pushed it [offensive action] back by six months and then completely contradicted the directives I received …'[46] Sackville-West did not seem to have considered the reality of the situation in Macedonia. D'Espèrey had illustrated that the Armée d'Orient could successfully undertake a series of local offensives. Part of the Greek army had even succeeded in taking a Bulgarian stronghold at Skra-di-Legen. From the French perspective, it was time to undertake a large scale offensive.

In an attempt to rectify the discrepancy between the PMRs over Allied strategy, Guillaumat wrote to Belin to inform him of a 'new situation' in the Balkans which led him to propose moving from the defensive to the offensive in order to knock the Bulgarians out of the war. This letter described the favourable conditions of the Allies in Macedonia and how it presented an opportunity to strike the Central Powers where they were weak. He described how the Greek army was performing well and how competition between Serbia and Greece meant that they were both willing to fight. Earlier concerns about the possibility of an offensive by the Russian Black Sea fleet under command of the Germans had been handled by the Allied navies. He recommended progressively increasing

---

[44] 'Procès-verbaux of the Three Meetings of the Sixth Session of the Supreme War Council', 3 June 1918, TNA, CAB 25/122/SWC307.

[45] Henry Wilson to Sackville-West, 6 June 1918, HHW/2/12C/17/ff.102.

[46] Guillaumat to Alby (le général chef d'état-major general de l'armée), 20 June 1918, *AFGG* 8/3, annex 278.

offensive action, and rather than attacking on the sides of the Vardar shores, as had been suggested in March, he now wanted to employ the Greek and Serbian Armies by having them attack in their sectors. '[I]n order to obtain maximum gains . . .' the position of these attacks would be purposefully related to national aspirations, explained Guillaumat. The Serbians would fight hard because they were gaining back their own territory. Guillaumat envisaged the Greek army attacking by the valley of the Struma towards the Sérés or Cavalla. They would begin with small offensives and progressively work towards larger ones that would crush the morale of the Bulgarians and potentially the Austro-Hungarians and Ottomans.[47]

Oddly, Belin did not pass this information to the other PMRs until 27 June, and this was only after the issue of policy in the Balkans had finally boiled over. Sackville-West attended this meeting in a frustrated state, as despite asking for information about the situation in the Balkans on a daily basis he had yet to receive an update. He began the 35th meeting of the PMRs by insisting that Belin inform his colleagues of French military policy in Macedonia. Strangely unprepared, given that Guillaumat had sent him an appraisal of the situation, Belin asked that the meeting be postponed while he gathered further information.[48] When discussions were resumed five days later, Belin presented his colleagues with a draft joint note on policy in the Balkans, along with a series of French papers on policy in Macedonia covering the past few months.[49] This information reaffirmed what the other PMRs suspected; the French had not been keeping them informed. It was also obvious that the French had ignored earlier instructions to build defensive bases in favour of working on plans for offensive action.[50]

Despite French omissions about their plans in Macedonia, both the American and Italian representatives, after questioning the French PMR, were willing to agree to offensive action in the Balkans. Bliss made it clear (asking that it be added to the procès-verbal) that the American government was indifferent as to whether Allied policy in the Balkans was offensive or defensive. The two key points were, first, that no assistance should be requested from the Americans, and second, that whatever

---

[47] Guillaumat to Belin, 22 June 1918, SHD-DAT, Conseil Supérieur de la Guerre, 4N 53.

[48] 'Procès-Verbal de la 35e séance des représentants militaires', 24 June 1918, Bliss/324; 'Summary of Conclusions', 24 June 1918, CAB/25/122/SWC252.

[49] 'Projet de note collective – Situation dans les Balkans', 27 June 1918, SHD-DAT, Conseil Supérieur de la Guerre, 4N 53.

[50] 'Minutes of the 36th Meeting of the Military Representatives', 29 June 1918, CAB 25/122/SWC254/1.

policy was decided upon be adhered to.[51] Di Robilant, the Italian PMR, had concerns about the abilities of the Allied armies in Macedonia, as the British were in the process of replacing European troops with ones from India and, even more damning, the Greek army had recently experienced a series of mutinies. He was willing to trust Guillaumat's positive assessment of the Allied armies, but he wanted defences to be built and an actual date set for offensive action. As Belin had covered these points in his draft note, di Robilant was satisfied, and immediately called for the PMRs at least to agree that offensive action should occur. Sackville-West, however, was not as easily swayed, interjecting that 'apparently orders for an offensive had already been issued. M. Clemenceau had already given the necessary instruction on this point'.[52] Flabbergasted, Belin explained that, that was not true: 'Guillaumat had merely been called upon to submit proposals regarding an offensive . . .' In fact Clemenceau wanted the commander to be prepared to take offensive action if the opportunity was presented to do so. Guillaumat, no longer French Commander-in-Chief in the theatre, was offering an alternate opinion on military policy in the Balkans. And while it was natural for the French government to seek his views given his experience, his advice competed with that of the PMRs.

Sackville-West finally conceded to a change in policy – that offensive action should be considered in the Balkans – once Belin agreed to invite Guillaumat to the next meeting. The British PMR, however, had not agreed to a date for an offensive which left the matter open for further discussion. The next day Belin sent a note to the other PMRs informing them that he had communicated their various perspectives to Clemenceau. The French Prime Minister's response was to hold his opinion, reiterating that he had given d'Espèrey definite instructions to take the offensive for reasons equivalent to those which Belin had explained in the PMR meeting the previous day.[53] In fact Clemenceau had instructed Franchet d'Espèrey to plan an offensive in Macedonia for autumn 1918. Together d'Espèrey and Guillaumat led the planning and attack on Bulgaria in 1918.[54] This was on the same day that Clemenceau told d'Espèrey that to relieve pressure on the Western Front it was time go on the offensive in the Balkans. To the great displeasure of the British, despite having agreed on Joint Note 4,

---

[51] 'Corrected Text for Minutes of 36th Meeting of the Military Representatives', 8 July 1918, Bliss/324.

[52] 'Minutes of the 36th Meeting', 29 June 1918.

[53] Belin to PMRs, 30 June 1918, SHD-DAT, Conseil Supérieur de la Guerre, 4N 53.

[54] David Stevenson, *With Our Backs to the Wall: Victory and Defeat in 1918* (London, 2012), 143.

Clemenceau altered the instructions given to Guillaumat by refocussing attention on the protection of Salonika. This gave secondary import- ance to the forming of other bases that would serve to protect Old Greece. The British were particularly appalled to learn that Foch had created and signed d'Espèrey's instructions which were then endorsed by Clemenceau. This was an obvious breach of Foch's power as Allied Generalissimo of the *Western* Front.[55]

Following closely after the PMR meeting, the 7th SWC Meeting, in early July highlighted tensions between the British and the French at the political level, as it gave Lloyd George the opportunity to vent his frustrations with French action in the Balkans and made it glaringly apparent that he and Clemenceau had opposing views on policy in the theatre. To address and mend these differences, the PMRs were asked to study the possibility of an offensive in Macedonia.[56] They would do so alongside special diplomatic representatives. This meeting also resulted in the PMRs' investigation into what would become Joint Note 37, 'General Military Policy of the Allies for the Autumn of 1918 and for the Year 1919', of which policy in Macedonia was part. The result was two, almost identical, forums for the PMRs to consider policy for this theatre. The first forum drew its final decisions on 3 August 1918, whereas policy for Joint Note 37 was not agreed upon until 10 September.

Diplomatic and Military Commission

The title of this commission, 'the Diplomatic and Military Commission' represents the different approaches the British and French took; the former attempted to focus on the diplomatic aspect of offensive action against Bulgaria while the latter focussed on the military issues. Prior to the start of the meeting on 11 July, Sackville-West met with Lord Robert Cecil, the British diplomatic representative, and Lord Derby, the British ambassador to Paris, to discuss the British position on Macedonia.[57] Recognising that the Bulgarians and the Austro-Hungarians were the weakest of the Central Powers, they thought the Bulgarians, if they could be detached from the Central Powers, could still prove to be a useful ally against the Turks as an 'expedition might be undertaken in Bulgaria

---

[55] Dutton, *The Politics of Diplomacy*, 176.

[56] 'Procès-verbal de la troisième séance de la septième session du conseil supérieur de Guerre', 4 July 1918, *AFGG* 8/3, annex 368.

[57] David Dutton, ed., *Paris: 1918: The War Diary of the British Ambassador, the 17th Earl of Derby* (Liverpool, 2001), 95.

against Constantinople if we are prepared to give that place to Bulgaria'.[58] To gain the Bulgarians as partner, they would first have to isolate the Bulgarians from the Central Powers, which they argued could be achieved through internal revolution in Bulgaria or by convincing the Bulgarians to withdraw from their alliance with the Central Powers. The issue they had with the French argument for knocking the Bulgarians out of the war through military action was that the Allies would have to divert more resources to Macedonia to achieve this aim. A limited offensive, or one that failed to defeat Bulgaria, would only serve to further tighten the link between Germany and Bulgaria. The solution the British proposed was that an offensive in the Balkans should not be attempted in 1918.[59]

Having spent the morning preparing, Sackville-West and Cecil were in a strong position to advocate these ideas. What they found, however, was that the French and Italians were enthusiastic about an offensive. When Cecil remained 'non-committal' and emphasised that the British wanted to continue to keep negotiations open with the Bulgarians, the French Foreign Minister, Stephen Pichon, gave what Sackville-West described as 'an impassioned oration to the effect that never, never would they give Bulgaria anything, never would they betray their friends Greece and Serbia'.[60] Pichon refused to use Constantinople or Adrianople as bargaining pieces with Bulgaria, both of which Greece coveted. Surprised by the French Minister's strong stance, Sackville-West advised Henry Wilson to inform the British Foreign Office that there had been a change in French policy. Whereas the French had, in the past, advocated for both military and diplomatic approaches, at this meeting they were highlighting the need for military action and feared demoralising their Greek and Serbian allies by negotiating with the Bulgarians.

The French, too, were well-prepared for this meeting, especially as they had the knowledgeable Guillaumat on their side. His location in Paris (he had taken over as military governor of Paris on his return from Salonika) made it convenient for him to attend the meetings while his experience in the Balkans made him an expert representative. With this position, Guillaumat was able to act as an authoritative supporter of both d'Espèrey and offensive action in the Balkans. It was at this diplomatic meeting that Guillaumat's campaign began to have significant influence on key individuals. He began his speech by expressing an alternative view of the situation in Salonika from that of Cecil and Sackville-West. He

[58] Sackville-West to Wilson, 11 July 1918, HHW/2/12C/23.
[59] 'Procès-Verbal de la Séance de la Commission Diplomatique et Militaire', 11 July 1918, SHD-DAT, Conseil Supérieur de la Guerre, 4N 53.
[60] Ibid.

said that the whole question was a purely military one. He then described how, to his delight, the Greek army had been performing well and, given the low morale of the Bulgarians, an Allied offensive had the potential to liberate Serbia (although he doubted it would break into Bulgarian territory).[61] Furthermore, he questioned what would happen if offensive action were not undertaken and reminded the commission members that the morale of the Greek army was still fragile. Once again the French made the argument that a successful offensive was key to maintaining and raising morale.[62] Guillaumat recommended an offensive before October, and following on from this Pichon suggested that the PMRs investigate the question. Emphasis was placed on the idea that an offensive could not be a half success and would need to eliminate the Bulgarians from the war. On the ground in Macedonia, the French continued to pursue an offensive strategy with Clemenceau ordering d'Espèrey to continue to direct the activities of his armies with a view to the preparation and further development of a possible large scale offensive. A small but important clause was added to satisfy the PMRs, that this action would be undertaken 'should it be deemed appropriate by the Allied Governments'.[63]

American Position

The Americans did not offer diplomatic advice to this conference. As at the SWC meetings, Arthur Frazier observed the meeting without contribution; however, Bliss attended as the American PMR. In his correspondence with the American Secretary of War, Newton D. Baker, Bliss described the interdependent nature of the various fronts and growing concern over the morale of Allied troops in this theatre. He explained:

One serious thing was admitted by all, – that the Greek Army would melt away before the coming winter, just as the Serbian Army had to a considerable extent done, if no hope were given to them of an offensive movement by which they might win back certain lost territory.

The Allied Forces in Macedonia cannot afford to lose the Greek contingent because, on the strength of it they have withdrawn a very considerable British and French force for use on the Western Front.[64]

---

[61] Ibid. Also see French Section, 'Notes sur le moral bulgare', 13 July 1918, *AFGG* 8/3, annex 415.
[62] 'Procès-Verbal de la Séance de la Commission'.
[63] Belin to PMRs, 21 July 1918, SHD-DAT, Conseil Supérieur de la Guerre, 4N 53.
[64] Bliss to Baker, 31 July 1918, Bliss/250.

Bliss's letter to Baker illustrates how Guillaumat's positive assessment of the Greek army was used to advocate offensive action. The Greek army could undertake offensive action and, in fact, it needed to do so in order to maintain its morale. This argument also played on British fears, as they needed the strength of the Serbian and Greek armies to be maintained if they were to continue to withdraw troops from Salonika for a campaign in Palestine.

Policy in the Balkans presented additional difficulties for the American PMR that did not exist for his colleagues. As the Allies discussed moving from a defensive to an offensive strategy in Macedonia, the British and the French increasingly pressured Bliss to become politically involved, despite his government's policy to remain detached. As the British Section explained:

The Americans are conspicuous in the Balkan Peninsula by their absence, but they can play a very important part in Allied policy by reason of their obvious disinterestedness, which will make them trusted by all, including Bulgaria; and from the fact that a large number of Bulgarians are in the United States and that the American Minister is still at Sofia.

The question of a declaration of war by America against Bulgaria is therefore one of the very gravest importance – a weapon in the hands of the Allies that if used in the right way and at the right time may have great results. The French Chief of Staff at Salonika expressed the opinion that it is through the United States that the Allies should attempt to win over Bulgaria from Germany.[65]

The British and French had difficulty in understanding the American position, especially when the Americans could provide a unique approach and added weight to the campaign against the Bulgarians. Furthermore, the Americans had recently raised political questions themselves when they solicited their colleagues for advice on whether the American government should declare war on Bulgaria and the Ottoman Empire (see Chapter 3 on this issue). Soon after deciding not to declare war on Bulgaria, despite the advice of the SWC members (including Bliss), the American PMR quickly resumed his aloof political stance.

From the middle of 1918 to the end of the war, Bliss frequently complained to Baker and the US Chief of Staff, General Peyton C. March, that the Allies were harassing him to make political decisions. Convinced that formal instructions from his government to remain detached from action in Macedonia would dissuade his partners, Bliss sought assistance from Baker. The US Secretary of War instructed that,

---

[65] to the American Section, 'Notes on the Political Situation in the Balkans', 3 July 1918, Bliss/318.

as the Americans did not have forces in Macedonia, they were leaving it to the other Allies to adopt a military plan. Once again, the Americans explained they were willing to accept an Allied plan as long as they were not asked to send any resources.[66] With this cablegram in hand, Bliss explained to his British and French colleagues that his government had formally declared that they had no interest in getting involved in the Balkans. He was flabbergasted when they 'were inclined to shrug their shoulders . . .'.[67] This response heightened his frustration and suspicion of the Allies for the remainder of the year. In contrast, Sackville-West became increasingly convinced that an Allied policy was required in the Balkans.[68] Tension between the PMRs was created as the British favoured a military-diplomatic solution, the French favoured a military one, and the Americans attempted to remain politically detached.

These varying approaches continued to remain at the centre of PMR discussions. The issue once again was raised as part of drafting Joint Note 37. The Americans could not avoid mentioning this theatre, as the note was to incorporate all theatres. They kept their response focussed on military action. Bliss argued that the Central Powers had a distinct advantage in the Balkans because they were using troops that were not suitable for use on the Western Front, whereas the Allies not only had a greater number of forces in Macedonia, but ones that could be used elsewhere. The Germans thought so too, referring to Salonika as the Allies' 'largest internment camp'.[69] In fact, the Allies had approximately 650,000 troops to the Central Powers 450,000. The Allied forces were comprised of 28 divisions: 9 Greek, 8 French, 6 Serbian, 4 British, and 1 Italian.[70] If the Allies had been willing to abandon this front, the French and British divisions could have been moved elsewhere. A more moderate and realistic plan, however, was for the British to release British troops from this theatre by replacing them with Indian ones, for which plans had begun as early as April 1918.[71]

---

[66] Bliss to Baker, 3 October 1918, Bliss/250; Baker to the American Section, 1 July 1918, Bliss/329, cablegram #66. Bliss wrote that the US had no interest in Macedonia, 9 July 1918, Bliss/246.

[67] Bliss to Baker, 24 August 1918, Bliss/250.

[68] Sackville-West to Wilson – especially after July he continually mentions the desire to come to a political agreement with the other allies.

[69] Captain B. H Liddell Hart, *History of the First World War* (London, 2014), 110.

[70] Jean Delmas, 'Les Opérations Militaires Sur Le Front De Macédoine Octobre 1915 – Septembre 1918', *La France Et La Grece Dans La Grande Guerre* (Thessalonique, 1992), 6.

[71] Before this could be done they required thirty-six infantry and four pioneer battalions from India. James Kitchen, *The British Imperial Army in the Middle East: Morale and Military Identity in the Sinai and Palestine Campaigns, 1916–18* (London, 2014), 196.

Bliss's own section concluded that the Western Front was the main theatre of war, and, as nothing of great value would be gained by an offensive in Macedonia, the policy should remain defensive. The American Section explained, 'All Allied troops that can be spared from anywhere are now needed on the Western Front which is a decisive theatre of war. The people of the United States are making strenuous efforts to increase the strength of the Allies forces there. Manifestly it is important not to diminish these forces unnecessarily'.[72] Furthermore, Bliss was concerned that a large scale offensive in Macedonia would require additional manpower and tie up valuable shipping needed to supplying the force. As the Allies were desperate for shipping (see Chapter 6 on resources) Bliss did not want to gamble on an offensive in the Near East. Bliss's own attitude towards a defensive policy was illustrated by his support of British proposals to improve railway lines between Piraeus and Salonika in case Allied troops needed to be evacuated from the area.[73] The Americans' first draft note, submitted to the other PMRs on 15 July, discouraged action in the Balkans.[74] For the Americans, a campaign in Macedonia ran in direct opposition to their aim of focussing resources on the Western Front.

At the same time as he expressed his support for a defensive stance, Bliss, in accordance with the instructions from the joint diplomatic and military meeting, sent a series of questions to Guillaumat in order to assess the specific operational details and objectives that a campaign in Macedonia would require.[75] Bliss's questions illustrated his concern with resources being diverted from the Western Front. He focussed his attention on the material and manpower requirements for an offensive, as well as from where Guillaumat would resupply if losses were high. On 19 July Guillaumat sent a response that illustrated his confidence in the ability of the Allied troops in Macedonia.[76] He reassured the Americans of the value of his objectives and his ability to make effective use of the resources already allotted to this theatre, thus addressing their concern that he not request any additional resources. Guillaumat promoted the idea of an offensive against Bulgaria, writing, 'It is consequently neither possible nor convenient to fix in advance limits to an operation which

---

[72] Memorandum to Bliss from American Section, 9 July 1918, Bliss/318.
[73] Bliss to Mr Cravath, 1 July 1918, Bliss/318.
[74] 'The American Military Representative to the British Military Representative', 17 July 1918, CAB/25/84.
[75] 'Le représentant militaire américain au représentant militaire français', 15 July 1918, *AFGG* 8/3, annex 428.
[76] 'Sur le Projet d'Offensive des Armées Alliées en Orient', 19 July 1918, Bliss/318; SHD-DAT, Conseil Supérieur de la Guerre, 4N 53.

could lead us to liberate the main part of Serbia and to penetrate Bulgarian territories'.[77] For the French commander, manpower and materials were not an issue – the morale of victorious Greek and Serbian forces would trump any losses they would incur. In addition, he was certain that the Central Powers could not reinforce the Bulgarians. He summarised, 'the issue is much simpler. We have an Army in the East of 600,000 men in excellent physical and mental state, which has before it an army of 400,000 men whose moral condition is poor, at war for six years. Not to attack would be an unforgivable mistake, especially when one is sure that if even the impossible, a failure was to occur, it could not in any way jeopardize the current situation'.[78] He reinforced the necessity of an offensive by highlighting that it was the only way to achieve success. Despite American insistence that they would not declare war against the Bulgarians, Guillaumat reinforced that if they did do so, it would greatly affect the morale of the Bulgarian army.

British Position

Upon receiving the American proposal, Sackville-West found that his staff largely agreed with the American Section. Specifically 'M' (Material) Branch of the British PMR section, expressed their great concern over the material expense of a campaign in Macedonia explaining, 'we should probably find ourselves more and more involved and having to divert more and more shipping to support a distant expedition'. If this were to occur the result would be 'a "running sore" which would sap all the energy and vitality from the rest of the body'. Even worse, 'It is simply playing into the enemy's hands to attack him where he has the most opportunity of doing us the most serious damage ...'[79] Wastage was higher for campaigns in the East because the Mediterranean was still not secured from frequent submarine attacks (see p. 12 for losses to shipping between 1917 and 1918).[80] Sackville-West's report did not support the French timeline, explaining that autumn was a poor choice for an offensive in this theatre because the health of troops was affected during that season and because reinforcements could not be supplied.[81]

Sackville-West was beginning to find himself outnumbered. The commanders in the field, Franchet d'Espèrey and Sir George Milne (the local

---

[77] Ibid.   [78] Ibid.

[79] Beadon to Sackville-West, 25 July 1918, CAB 25/122, Minute Sheet.

[80] Also see Paul Halpern, *The Naval War in the Mediterranean, 1914–1918* (London and Annapolis, 1987).

[81] Sackville-West to British War Cabinet, 5 August 1918, CAB 25/26/SWC298.

British commander) also supported an offensive. By 18 July, d'Espèrey had publicly declared that an offensive should occur no later than early October. Milne recognised that the opportunity was ripe for attacking the Bulgarians, since they were exhausted and the Central Powers were too busy in Italy and France to reinforce them.[82] The British PMR was becoming increasingly discouraged. Guillaumat's response to Sackville-West's questions about the possibility of an offensive in Macedonia was of varied quality. When asked his reasons for believing the Bulgarian army would suffer a major defeat, Guillaumat provided a shallow response. He told Sackville-West that this point had already been covered in the diplomatic meeting and that 'Every army is destined to undergo a great defeat when it is decided to inflict it'.[83] Given that the PMRs' role was to create a report about how an offensive could bring about defeat, this answer was unhelpful. After months of attempting to influence policy in Macedonia, Sackville-West vented his frustrations to Henry Wilson:

now you say it is time we thought of ourselves – a thing *I* do ... *because* I am disillusioned, *because* I am a pessimist that I fancy altruism is right – high ideals are right – therefore if we can help to win by altruism – it will pay in the end – Persia, India, etc will be all right but not if we try the French, Greek, Roumanian, Italian method of doing business – It is *because* we have no interest in the Balkans that we are the people to boss that show ... We must have an allied policy in the Balkans and the British must be responsible. Kick out these little Frenchmen – they have become 'she bash wallahs' – the Americans are doing all the fighting in France and they are strutting about saying they direct.[84]

It is interesting that Sackville-West envisioned that coming to a decision on an Allied policy in the Balkans would involve the British dominating their colleagues. He was becoming disheartened with the role the PMRs were playing in creating a strategy in the Balkans. While it had seemed that by inviting Guillaumat to answer questions about strategy in this theatre it would empower him with knowledge, it had in fact only served to overshadow Sackville-West's ideas. Instead the French were largely dictating action in this theatre, as with the largest proportion of troops and overall command they could do so.

The British position was made worse when Guillaumat manged to convert Bliss to his cause. For Bliss it was a meeting with Guillaumat that changed his opinion that the Allies should maintain a defensive stance in

[82] Dutton, *The Politics of Diplomacy*, 177.
[83] Guillaumat to Sackville-West, 'Note sur le Project d'Offensive des Armée Alliés en Orient', 19 July 1918, SHD-DAT, Conseil Supérieur de la Guerre, 4N 53.
[84] Sackville-West to Wilson, 19 July 1918, HHW/2/12C/27/ff.128.

the Balkans. At first suspicious that a meeting with Guillaumat had been called under the instruction of 'higher authority', Bliss quickly warmed to Guillaumat referring to him as 'one of the most level headed Frenchmen I had met'. The fact that Bliss believed that Guillaumat 'stands high in the estimation of General Foch' certainly helped to gain Bliss's respect.[85] When it came to strategy for Macedonia specifically, Bliss told Guillaumat that he would not make any decisions and that he did not want to act as an intermediary between France and Britain. He did, however, offer to read over Guillaumat's plan for an offensive with him, indicating a level of acceptance of the French plan.

Bliss had this meeting 'fresh in mind' when the PMRs met on 29 July 1918 to discuss the policy they would recommend to their governments. Despite earlier insistence by the British and Americans that the policy should be defensive, it was decided that a military offensive was justified and should occur by October 1918, and that planning, which was already underway, should be continued. Although it appeared that the French had won a victory against the British in terms of policy, Sackville-West withheld full commitment to this theatre by refusing to set a specific date for the campaign, saying that one would be agreed upon closer to October, when preparations would almost be complete. Bliss recorded that 'The French still wanted a positive declaration *now* that an offensive would be undertaken in October'.[86] He surmised that, although they were unhappy with this clause, 'the French yielded'.[87]

The outcome of this meeting was that the French Section was instructed by its colleagues to prepare a memo on the Balkans, which was submitted and approved by the PMRs on 3 August. The report highlighted that Bulgaria was weak and that the morale of the Serbian and Greek armies was low. It gave the date of 1 October 1918 for the offensive to start, but it also included a clause that, 'it is expedient, in principle to leave the General Commanding-in-Chief the Allied Armies of the East free to launch this offensive at the moment he considers most favourable, unless new and unforeseen circumstances arise which compel the SWC to fix the time itself or abandon the enterprise altogether'.[88] The Allies had reached a compromise – albeit a vague one riddled with animosity. Their memo was received by each Allied government by mid-August and it formed the basis of discussion between the Allied governments as events unfolded. In practical terms this clause meant that technically, according to the protocols of this

---

[85] Bliss to Baker, 31 July 1918, Bliss/250.   [86] Ibid.   [87] Ibid.

[88] 'Rapport sur la Situation dans le Balkans', 3 August 1918, Bliss/318; *AFGG* 8/3, annex 583.

Inter-Allied institution, the Allies should still reassess the political and military conditions before a major offensive. It also meant that the British could continue to negotiate military policy for this theatre, which they did. For the French, it gave them Allied permission to proceed with preparing for offensive action.[89]

When the British PMR reported to the War Cabinet on 5 August he illustrated his concerns about Greek morale and said that, although Guillaumat was pressuring for offensive action in October, he was unsure about the material results it would achieve. Sackville-West had legitimate concerns about the lack of shipping for this theatre and the dangers to ships in the Mediterranean.[90] D'Espèrey's unwillingness to build-up additional bases heightened the British PMR's fears that the Allies could face serious losses – to their resources and strategic position in Macedonia – if an offensive were unsuccessful. However, the British PMR found himself further isolated. Despite earlier reservations, Cecil switched positions after Guillaumat assured him that his military plan allotted time for the British to evaluate any political concerns they might have. With the British PMR still holding his position, discussions on Macedonia were far from being concluded.

The Final Drawing of Joint Note 37: The Balkan Dimension

The creation of an Allied strategy for autumn 1918 and the 1919 year continued to provide an avenue for discussion. The PMRs had been dealing with the present situation, but now they had to do so with a view to winning the war in 1919. Although the American PMR file records that by 8 August the three PMR sections 'concurred' over policy in the Balkans, an examination of the detailed notes illustrates that they still held varying opinions. While the Americans were willing to accept the offensive plans of the French, they continued to strongly advocate that no additional ocean tonnage, material, or troops should be diverted to Macedonia. Their arguments remained the same up to the signing of final Joint Note 37 on 10 September.[91]

---

[89] D'Espèrey to Clemenceau, 3 August 1918, SHD-DAT, Conseil Supérieur de la Guerre, 4N 53.

[90] Sackville-West to Wilson, 28 July 1918, HHW/2/12C/28/ff.130.

[91] French notes are CAB 25/84 and Bliss/324; American ones in Bliss/324; British notes in CAB 25/84. The final 'Joint Note No.37', 13 September 1918, CAB/25/122/SWC320; Bliss 324/SWC316/1; 'Note Collective N. 37 Politique Militaire Générale des Allies pour l'Automne 1918 et l'Année 1919', SHD-DAT, Conseil Supérieur de la Guerre, 4N 6.

In contrast, the British continued to analyse the Balkan situation as it related to instructions to the PMRs to plan for the future, and used it as an attempt to renegotiate the date for an offensive. Even before the Allies had agreed on the 3 August proposal, the British had submitted an extensive draft Joint Note 37 to their colleagues. As Sackville-West wrote to Bliss, 'the note embodies I think the views we agreed on in principle the other day'.[92] The note highlighted the inter-dependence of the various theatres of war by reiterating that no additional forces could be supplied to this theatre and that the date of the offensive must depend on the situation in *all* other theatres. The British resumed their argument that an offensive in autumn 1918 was undesirable and that, instead, the spring 1919 would offer better results, as the Germans would have difficulty in reinforcing the Bulgarians as they, themselves, would need all of their troops to fight on the Western Front.

On 12 August the British sent a note to the other PMRs about the Balkan situation that related to the study of 1919, 'one of a series now being prepared in connection with proposals as to Allied policy in the Autumn of 1918 and Year 1919'.[93] What is revealing about this report is that it was actually created by the 'E' (Enemy) Branch of the British PMR section on 24 July and was still being referred to by the British Section, with slight amendments to Allied and Enemy forces, as late as 24 September, a day before the armistice with Bulgaria was signed. They were adamant to hold their position. This plan was written from the perspective of the enemy. It examined the main issues that the PMRs explored when considering a policy in the Balkans. In many ways their assessment of the Central Powers was accurate.

'E' Branch began its study with an assessment of the low morale of the Bulgarian army, arguing that it was a result of few German troops still reinforcing the Bulgarian army, war weariness, and poor relations with the other members of the Central Powers.[94] As early as January 1917, the Germans themselves feared that Bulgarian morale was so low that they might sue for peace. Like the earlier assessment of the Bulgarians by Guillaumat, the British Section also accurately argued that Bulgaria would not launch an offensive due to tensions over the sovereignty of territory between the Central Powers. In reality, serious disputes existed not only between Germany and Bulgaria over Dobrudzha, but also

---

[92] 'British PMR to French, Italian and American Sections', 31 July 1918, CAB 25/84/116.
[93] 'British PMR to American, French and Italian PMRs', 12 August 1918, Bliss/318; CAB 25/122.
[94] Richard Hall, *Balkan Breakthrough: The Battle of Dobro Pole 1918* (Bloomington, 2010), 93.

between the Ottomans and the Bulgarians, also over Dobrudzha, as well as the lower Marista Valley, and the area from Western Thrace to the Mesta River (which Bulgaria had won in the First Balkan War). With the Treaty of Bucharest, signed in May, the Bulgarians only received 15 percent of the territory gained by the Central Powers, despite their desperate need for resources.[95] The result was that the defeat of Romania acted to highlight tension between the Central Powers rather than raise morale, as the Bulgarians questioned whether their allies would fulfil their promises (in terms of Bulgaria's war aims).[96] Overall, the British Section did not think the Bulgarians would participate in offensive operations because these would weaken the Bulgarian amy and only lead to gains for both the Ottomans and the Germans.[97] In fact, the Bulgarians did not launch any offensive against the Allies in 1918.

One area in which the British Section's assessment was not pessimistic enough was towards the food situation. Believing food conditions had improved in 1918, they wrote that the Bulgarians had access to rice, with which to feed the population, which had previously been exported. And although they recognised that rations for soldiers were poor, the British still considered that the overall health of Bulgarian soldiers was good. In reality, by December 1917 officers and soldiers at the Bulgarian Front received a mere 800 grams of bread a day, rear-echelon soldiers 600 grams, and civilians 400 grams of bread or grain or 300 grams of flour. By July 1918 the food situation had worsened with rations down to 600 grams a day for men on the front, with few vegetables and no meat to supplement them.[98] Poor food, clothing, and military equipment and declining manpower led to resentment towards the Germans, who treated Macedonia as a 'conquered land' from which food could be extracted at will. Bulgarian soldiers were also aware of the poor conditions on the home-front, which added to their deteriorating morale.[99] However, despite the challenges facing the Bulgarians and the difficulty they would encounter if they mounted an offensive, the British did not conclude that they would be easily beaten on the battlefield. If attacked the Bulgarians would defend, making it difficult for the Allies to negotiate a political settlement. The good news presented by 'E' Branch was that they did not think the Bulgarians had any stomach for offensive action, arguing that their soldiers generally believed that their national

---

[95] Ibid., 107.

[96] Ibid., 112. For more on the details of this territorial disputes, see pp. 91–112.

[97] 'Macedonian Front From the Point of View of the Central Powers', 24 July 1918, CAB 25/122/SWC288.

[98] Hall, *Balkan Breakthrough*, 104.   [99] Ibid., 112.

goals had already been obtained. Without German reinforcements, the British concluded, the Bulgarians would remain on the defensive.

The British assessment of the Allies, however, was far from positive. The situation was complicated by their having to negotiate between five different nationalities in the Balkans. The British Section calculated that this weakness off-set the low morale in the Bulgarian army. Furthermore, they did not rule out the possibility, even if unlikely, that the Germans could reinforce the Bulgarians with troops from the Western Front. This scenario was more likely to occur if the Germans failed to make large gains elsewhere, as they needed a victory in 1918 to raise the morale of the Central Powers. Arguing that the Bulgarians were in a reasonable position to attack the Allies, with German reinforcements, the Central Powers had the ability to make serious gains in Macedonia.[100] In reality the Germans had withdrawn their forces from Macedonia for use on the Western Front for the March offensive. By the summer of 1918 only 3 battalions and 32 batteries remained (the British Section estimated that the Germans had two battalions in Bulgaria as of 20 July).[101]

In all, the British Section wrote that an offensive by the Bulgarians was unlikely. If it did occur the attack would come down the Vardar Valley in September or October, and if successful Salonika might be isolated. This last clause hinted towards earlier policy that other bases should be established. It was with this joint note that the British indicated that the Bulgarians could be knocked out of the war. They used this idea to shift the focus from military discussions to political ones.

On 17 August, Bliss informed Sackville-West that he agreed with this memo; however, as discussions for a campaign in Macedonia continued, Bliss's reservations about the Allies grew.[102] Specifically a British memorandum suggesting the Allies discuss political questions relating to peace in the Balkans concerned him. He felt the Allies were constantly trying to involve the Americans in political questions, 'for the purpose of enabling them better to shape their military campaigns'.[103] It was his belief that political questions should only be settled once the Central Powers had been defeated, and any discussions before that distracted them from obtaining this victory. On 9 August Bliss had explained to Baker:

---

[100] 'Macedonian Front from the Point of View of the Central Powers', 24 July 1918, CAB 25/122/SWC288.

[101] For Bulgarian figures, see Hall, *Breakthrough*, 104. For British figures, see 'Assessment of the Enemy', 20 July 1918, Bliss/320.

[102] Bliss to Sackville-West, 17 August 1918, Bliss/318.

[103] Bliss to Baker, 22 August 1918, Bliss/250.

I believe that the United States should aim at a successful termination of the war in 1919, and should make that the paramount question and in all of its dealings with its Allies should keep that question to the front. You may think that this is purely an academic question; that our Allies will say that they are as much interested in ending the war in 1919 as we can be. That of course is what they would say; but in practice they may not be ready to do the things and to make the sacrifices which will be necessary to end the war in that time. They all agree that it can be ended only by American troops, supplies, and money. But I can see it in every discussion at which I am present, and in nearly every paper that is submitted to me, that when the end comes they want certain favourable military situations to have been created in different parts of the world that will warrant demands to be made of the United States which they think will be, perhaps, the principal arbiter of peace terms. If these sufficiently favourable military situations are not created on certain secondary theatres by the beginning of autumn of next year our Allies may be willing to continue through 1920, at the cost of United States troops and money, a war which may possibly if not probably be ended with complete success, as far as we are concerned, by operations on the western front in 1919 . . .[104]

This was an unfair assessment of his partners, who, with troops fighting in multiple theatres, had to seriously consider their contribution to the war effort and the strategy for a global war. The British hoped the Americans would act as a mediator between the Allies, to assist in smoothing relations that could negatively affect military operations. They even went as far as to suggest a new political-diplomatic representative to sit on the SWC arguing that 'unity of policy' had not been obtained in the secondary theatres. Once again the Americans refused.[105] Pressure from the British to come to an agreement served to further isolate the Americans, while the British became frustrated with their aloof American colleagues.

As the Americans became more comfortable about the idea of an Allied offensive in the Balkans, they became more uncomfortable with the British placing them under pressure to make political decisions for the area. For Bliss, the decisive theatre was the Western Front. His interest in Macedonia went no further then to prevent it from sapping any resources that could go to the Western Front. These concerns were transmitted to Baker and on to President Woodrow Wilson. On 17 August Baker confided to President Wilson, 'The tremendous effort which America is making, and the vast force which we will have in 1919 will win the war, if our allies want it won, and are willing to make any correspondingly devoted effort'.[106] The Americans continually

---

[104] Bliss to Baker, 9 August 1918, Bliss/250.   [105] Ibid.
[106] Baker to President Wilson, 17 August 1918, LOC, Newton D. Baker Papers [hereon Baker] Baker/8/6.

reaffirmed that their concern for the Balkans went as far as its relationship to the Western Front. As the Allies struggled to come to an agreement in this theatre, the Americans kept their focus on winning the war in France.

In contrast to the PMRs growing confidence for an offensive in the Balkans, the British War Office were increasingly negative towards such action. Meeting with Captain Stead on 24 August, Bliss was informed that the Greek army was weak and morale low. The Greek government had amassed men, 'who otherwise would make trouble at home ...' under the pretext of being a service-of-the-rear force, so that the Allies would feed them.[107] The War Office had serious reservations about the military abilities of their Italian partners, fearing that in the event of a German offensive in Salonika, the Italians would withdraw to Valona (which fulfilled Italian foreign policy in giving them a foothold on the Adriatic coast, with the aim of gaining Dalmatia), as opposed to protecting mainland Greece. Stead put forward the popular argument that an offensive would occur if the Germans had spare troops, as they would need a victory to increase morale since they had had little success all year. Stead was still focussed on the recommendations made in Joint Note 4 ('The Balkan Problem – written in December 1917). He warned that if the Allies were forced to retreat, they would have to do so to Salonika, as the other bases still had not been established. He did not recommend an offensive until this situation was improved. The following day, on 25 August, Bliss learned that the British Section of the PMRs disagreed with Stead about the possibility of a German offensive in Macedonia or Italy. Instead they thought that the Germans were now on the defensive 'against increasing odds, with famine at home and Allies ready to desert them at the first safe opportunity'.[108] Adopting a stance in line with the British Commander-in-Chief in Macedonia and the French PMR, the British Section no longer recommended spring 1919 as the optimal time for an offensive. Instead they refrained from proposing a date and reminded their partners of Joint Note 4; that Franchet d'Espèrey should create other bases in order to protect Old Greece in case of an Allied retreat in the area. What may seem like a minor detail was actually a significant shift in position that brought the British closer to a compromise with their colleagues. They did however, continue to frustrate the Americans by once again suggesting that political discussions should commence. With the Central Powers beginning to unravel and the possibility of some of its members suing for peace in the next few weeks,

---

[107] Bliss to Baker, 24 August 1918, Bliss/250.
[108] Bliss to Baker, 26 August 1918, Bliss/250.

the British argued that it was essential for the Allies to discuss the postwar settlement. The British were correct to be concerned that, unless political matters were settled, the Allies would find themselves in a precarious situation when the war ended, a detail that Bliss was unable to appreciate.

The frustration felt by the British War Office with the French Commander-in-Chief, because he was ignoring earlier instructions to defend Old Greece, was also felt by the American representative. While Bliss had been encouraged to support the French in offensive action, the PMRs still wanted these defences to be built. As Bliss explained to Baker after the PMRs met with Stead:

We have repeatedly called attention to the small progress that has been made in this work but as all of the orders that go to the Italian contingent on the Macedonian Front are sent from Rome and those to the remainder of the Allied force there are sent by the French Government from Paris, it is difficult to enforce the decisions of the Supreme War Council in these remote theatres. I have sometimes thought that the only way to secure prompt and unified action in such cases would be to give Marshal Foch a strong Staff and give him *general* control on all other theatres as he now has detailed control on the Western Front.[109]

Recommendations made by the PMRs did not go directly to the commanders in the field. Once approved by the SWC, these instructions were sent to Rome, London, Paris, or Washington for approval before being sent out as formal instructions to the commanders (in the case of these governments approving the recommendations). Depending on how these memos were sent between parties (messenger as opposed to telegraph) it could take weeks. It would also depend on how quickly these bodies passed on the instructions. The main way of transmitting large amounts of information securely and quickly was the telegraph, making use of undersea cable networks. Across land (outside of Western Europe) this system was poorly developed, vulnerable to breakdowns, and less secure. As everything had to go in code, there were delays in de-coding. Breakdowns in the land network also occurred. Couriers could only go as fast as the transport that was carrying them. Radio was still in its infancy and vulnerable to 'atmospherics' (interruption by natural causes) and very erratic over long distances. In addition, everyone could intercept radio, so that even if it was in code at least they possessed the message and could try to decipher it. Communications themselves could be fast (if not always reliable) as long as there were working land telegraph connections to connect with any undersea telegraph cable, human factors

[109] Ibid.

could interfere to slow them down. And while it would not have taken from December to August for a SWC recommendation to reach the commanders in Macedonia, slow communications (especially those sent by courier) could be used as a stalling tactic, particularly when the French Prime Minister's opinion did not align with those of his coalition partners. Long lines of communication and a lack of executive power were partly to blame for the problems Bliss and Sackville-West were experiencing, but more significantly, the French were in control in Salonika.

Eleven days later, on 13 September, the PMRs reached an agreement on Joint Note 37. At first all members put their proposals forward as the basis of discussion; however, both Bliss and di Robilant, the Italian PMR, quickly withdrew their own plans, citing that the British and French notes incorporated the main points to be discussed. Bliss even explained, as recorded in the American version of the meeting's minutes, that '[b]oth these notes contained the substance of what he was prepared to accept'.[110] This left either the British or the French note to be discussed. Bliss suggested that given the straight-forward layout of the French note, it should be chosen. Although an agreement was reached, this scenario illustrates that to the end the French and the British were at odds for control over the smallest of details.[111]

With the writing of Joint Note 37 the idea of interdependent theatres came to the forefront. The section on 'General Considerations' for the secondary theatres recommended that the Allies hold the Central Powers in the various areas and, if possible, draw additional forces to alleviate pressure from the Western Front. The way to achieve this goal was clearly by attacking, although the Allies phrased it as 'a vigorous attitude'.[112] On the predominance of the Franco-Belgian Front, the Allies could agree. Working outwards, they gave ambiguous information to reinforce the idea of Allied unity. The joint note reiterated the decisions made on 3 August and still did not state a date for an offensive; however, it did allude to one occurring in 1918. Furthermore, they still instructed d'Espèrey to establish new bases for the protection of Old Greece. This wording illustrates a compromise between the PMRs. And while an offensive in 1918 now seemed likely, they also believed the war would continue into 1919. They refrained from making specific plans for 1919 because they wanted to see what happened in the Balkans in 1918.

[110] 'Minutes of the 45th Meeting of the Military Representatives', CAB 25/122/SWC316; Bliss/257, 324.
[111] Joint Note No. 37', 13 September 1918, CAB 25/122/SWC320.   [112] Ibid.

Before Joint Note 37 could be implemented, d'Espèrey had grown impatient with progress as the campaigning season would soon draw to a close. And while he wanted to react immediately to events on the ground, having learned his lesson in July, the French sought endorsement from the SWC for offensive action.[113] Travelling to London Guillaumat informed the British War Cabinet that an offensive was being launched.[114] After this meeting the French took a unilateral policy in the Balkans. Even Henry Wilson, the British Chief of the Imperial General Staff, recorded: 'I have been given no information concerning the further intentions with regard to operations in the Balkans ...'[115] By the time he wrote this note to Sackville-West, d'Espèrey's successful offensive had led to an armistice with the Bulgarians. The French commander's offensive action had effectively accelerated an armistice with the Bulgarians. He had advanced 130 km into Bulgarian territory, taking 90,000 prisoners.[116]

The Issue of Valona

At the end of August, the PMRs attention was brought to the issue of Valona when the Austrians launched an offensive in Albania. Concerns were further heightened when intelligence indicated that the Austrians were sending additional forces to bolster their troops in order to continue and intensify their offensive. The PMRs were asked to study the military situation in Valona, where the majority of forces were Italian. There was tremendous tension in this area between the Allies, as the Italians held Valona partially in an effort to block their rivals, Greece and Serbia, from moving north into Albania. On the ground, the forces in Albania formed d'Espèrey's left wing. For the Allied effort, the Italians aided their partners by reinforcing the Allied supply bases in the Adriatic.[117] Maintaining Valona was essential to the naval effort in the Mediterranean.

Prior to the PMR meetings on this issue, the Allied Naval Council (ANC) reinforced the importance of maintaining this port, as they did not want the enemy to be able to use it as a submarine base. They reiterated,

---

[113] Clemenceau to Franchet d'Espèrey, 6 September 1918, AFGG 8/3, annex 878.
[114] Dutton, *The Politics of Diplomacy*, 178.
[115] Wilson to Sackville-West, 26 September 1918, CAB 25/26.
[116] Delmas, 'Les Opérations Militaires', 10.
[117] Sfika-Theodosiou, 'The Italian Presence on the Balkan Front', 70.

The security of Valona is of vital importance to the operations of the Allied Navies in the Adriatic, and for this reason it appears probable that the enemy may attempt to dominate or secure that Base. If the Allies lose effective possession of Valona, the whole of the Naval operations in the Lower Adriatic against enemy Submarines will be seriously prejudiced ...[118]

The ANC also expressed their concern about the Austrian forces facing the Italians. The War Cabinet went further, instructing Sackville-West, 'to represent the extreme importance attached to the Italian positions covering VALONA by the Admiralty, loss of which would affect naval situation in the Mediterranean most gravely'.[119] The Allies had gone to great effort to build (and continue to improve upon) a 'barrage' in the Strait of Otranto in an attempt to prevent enemy submarines from exiting the Adriatic. The First Lord of the Admiralty believed that the anti-submarine barrage vitally reduced the number of ships sunk by submarines.[120] Furthermore, Valona was seen as playing an essential role in future naval operations in the Adriatic. The Admiralty wanted the Malakastra Heights to be held. From here Valona Harbour, and thus naval operations being undertaken, could be viewed. The Admiralty wanted to maintain secrecy for preparation and concentration, especially if they decided to advance on Durazzo in spring 1919.[121] The British determined that it was essential for the Italians to hold these areas.

The situation in Valona became further complicated by French-Italian relations, specifically the issue of command in the Balkans. As part of shoring up Italian forces in Valona, the Italian Commander-in-Chief, Diaz, had sent forces from the Western Front in Italy to Valona. However, he could not move any additional forces as Foch opposed this action. Another way to bolster these forces was to move some of the forces the Italians had stationed in Macedonia. Earlier in the year the PMRs had discussed moving the Italians 35th division and had gone as far as to recommend that it be transferred in the direction of Valona but only once d'Espèrey said he could spare it.[122]

[118] 'Report of the Fifth Meeting of the Allied Naval Council', 13 and 14 September 1918, TNA, Admiralty papers [hereon referred to as ADM] ADM 137/836/No. 213.

[119] War Office to Britcil, 3 September 1918, CAB 25/45/44.

[120] 'Extract from War Cabinet 468, dated September 3, Minute No. 6', CAB 25/45. For more on the barrage see Halpern, *A Naval History of World War I*, 159–166. Halpern argues that the barrage was largely unsuccessful in imprisoning submarines. Paul Halpern, 'The War at Sea', in *A Companion to World War I*, ed. John Horne (Chichester, 2010), 152. Also see Halpern, *The Naval War in the Mediterranean, 1914–1918*.

[121] War Office to Britcil, 7 September 1918, CAB 25/45/22.

[122] 'Procès-verbal of the 45th Meeting of Military Representatives', CAB 25/122/SWC.316/1.

In an attempt to bypass d'Espèrey, and knowing that the British would be sympathetic to the Italian cause, Diaz contacted di Robilant seeking support from the PMRs for the transfer to Valona of one brigade of the 35th division. Meanwhile, Weygand had sent this question to Foch, who had responded that while this theatre was outside his jurisdiction, and that the question should be sent to Versailles, he would also bring the matter to Clemenceau's attention. At Versailles, the other PMRs found that Belin had been instructed by his government not to comment on the transfer of these forces. As the Italian PMR admitted, '35th Italian Division was altogether under the orders of the Commander-in-Chief of the Allied Armies of the East, the latter was entitled on principle to place it wherever he might think best'.[123] However, this conflict made the Italians rethink command in this theatre. The Italian Commander in Albania was not subordinate to the Commander-in-Chief of the Allied Armies of the East. As di Robilant explained, this meant that the latter could only intervene if the Italian Commander-in-Chief *or* the Supreme War Council requested him to do so. This point explains why the Italians also sought to use the SWC to intervene on this matter.

The British PMR was willing to recommend the transfer of this brigade, especially as the Italians limited their demand to it being moved closer to Valona. In this case the brigade could be transferred either to Valona or back to Salonika as danger arose.[124] Bliss saw a wider implication in the entire scenario over the issue of command in the theatre. He suspected that, given d'Espèrey's concern that the Austrians were going to attack Valona, the only reason the French commander was not supporting the transfer of this brigade was because he had been given 'superior orders' not to do so. Here the American PMR indicated Clemenceau was working outside the SWC. Bliss concluded that it was definitely a question for the PMRs and the SWC. The problem was that the French government had vetoed a PMR resolution on the matter. As all joint notes had to have unanimity, the three PMRs could create a special report that was sent to the various government for their consideration. Meanwhile, the Italians secured this port. In October, after the Bulgarians had signed an armistice, the Italians took the issue further by creating what they referred to as 'a superior command of the Italian forces in the Balkans' that was based in Valona. This position, appointed to General Comm. Settimio Piacentini, placed the discipline of the 35th Division under the Italians. This meant that Piacentini would have to be kept well-informed of its actions and was one way the Italians could begin

---

[123] Ibid.   [124] Ibid.

to resume control over their division. The Italians reasserted their independence by also giving this command control over 'all matters relating to the Government of the territories occupied'.[125] Clearly the Italians did not want the French interfering in their areas of influence along the Adriatic coast. More significantly to the evaluation of the SWC, the PMRs' study of the situation in Valona illustrates how, in the case of the Balkans, Clemenceau attempted to limit the ability of the SWC to even make recommendations. Without the willing efforts of all four members, it was difficult for this institution to function.

Armistice

Strategically the armistice with Bulgaria, signed on 30 September, allowed the coalition to rethink how they might defeat the Austro-Hungarian forces and Ottoman forces. It also brought the British and French leaders to clash, once again, on strategy for this theatre. The terms of the armistice, set by Franchet d'Espèrey, aimed to bring Romania back into the conflict.[126] Lloyd George wanted to position Milne's army under Allenby (in Palestine) before having them proceed towards Constantinople. While the British Prime Minster cabled Clemenceau to express these views, the French Prime Minster responded with a different idea. Having communicated with Berthelot (former chief of the French military mission to Romania), Guillaumat, and Foch, Clemenceau informed Lloyd George that the preferred action of Berthelot and Guillaumat was to advance up the Danube and link with the Romanians before proceeding towards Austria. In contrast, Foch recommended taking limited objectives, commencing with the occupation of strategic points in Bulgaria and the cutting of the Constantinople railway at Nish and on the Maritza.[127] In fact, if given the choice, Foch preferred to focus on defeating the Germans on the French Front as opposed to using forces for an advance in the eastern theatres.[128] Clemenceau concluded that once these limited objectives were achieved, the coalition forces could then link with Romania.

[125] Italian PMR to French, British and American Military Representatives, 28 October 1918, CAB 25/45.

[126] J.-C. Allain, 'Le France Et Les Armistices De 1918 En Orient', *La France Et La Grece Dans La Grande Guerre* (Thessalonique, 2012), 30. For more about the terms of the armistice, see Bruno Hamard, 'Quand la victoire s'est gagnée dans les Balkans: l'assuat de l'armée d'Orient de septembre à novembre 1918', Guerres Mondiales Et Conflits Contemporains', *Guerres mondiales et conflits contemporains*, 46/184 (1996).

[127] Hankey, *The Supreme Command*, 841.

[128] General Staff to DMO, 2 October 1918, WO 158/84/173.

In the afternoon of 5 October, a meeting was held at the Villa Romaine between Clemenceau, Foch, Orlando, Lloyd George, H. Wilson, Hope, and Hankey. Despite having learned that the Germans had approached President Wilson for an armistice, Lloyd George and Clemenceau continued to argue over a plan by d'Espèrey, which recommended that the British army in Macedonia (Struma region) proceed into Bulgaria. Meanwhile one French, one British and three Greek divisions would march on Constantinople.[129] Lloyd George, fearing that the French would steal a British victory over the Ottomans, threatened to remove Milne from d'Espèrey's command and instead to have the former march independently on Constantinople. The issue was taken up later in the day at a meeting at the Quai d'Orsay, where both Lloyd George and Clemenceau compromised. The British Prime Minister kept Milne's army under d'Espèrey in exchange for Milne being put in command of the section to move on Constantinople.[130] With this precarious military compromise, Lloyd George concluded 'It is a political and not a military plan'.[131] Clemenceau's subsequent instructions to d'Espèrey and Guillaumat envisaged sending one force east through Bulgaria towards Constantinople in an attempt to isolate the Ottomans and force them to sign an armistice, a second force north to join with Romania and then move towards southern Russia, a third force to liberate Serbia before moving north towards Hungary, and a fourth force to move up the Adriatic coast (for distance these forces reached between September and November, see Map 0.1).[132]

The final compromise embodies the nature of alliance warfare in the Balkans. The SWC was supposed to coordinate Allied efforts and yet the reality was that with a hegemonic power in this theatre, there was little the other Allies could do to force the French to coordinate with them. None of the other powers would threaten the French with repercussions in France. The French argument was difficult to counter given that they promised positive consequences for the Western Front while not diverting additional resources. The French, who led the expedition to Salonika, were able to determine military action in this theatre.

---

[129] Hankey diary, 7 October 1918, Churchill College Archive, Cambridge, Maurice Hankey Papers [hereon HNKY] HNKY/1/6; Franchet to armée serbe, britannique, hellénqiue, A.F.O., 1er groupement de D.I., 'Instruction pour les armées', 5 October 1918, *AFGG* 8/3, annex 1347.

[130] Franchet to Clemenceau, 6 October 1918, *AFGG* 8/3, annex 1347.

[131] Lloyd George quoted in Hankey diary, 7 October 1918, HNKY/1/6.

[132] Clemenceau to d'Espèrey and Guillaumat, 'Plan d'action Militaire en Orient', 7 October 1918, *AFGG* 8/3, annex 1378.

The French, British, and Americans all had varying viewpoints on what should occur in the Balkans – the French wanted offensive action to relieve forces from the Western Front, the British wanted defensive action so as to scale down their efforts in the theatre to move resources elsewhere, and the Americans wanted to keep the focus on the Western Front and prevent additional manpower and materials from being devoted to this theatre. Throughout 1918 the French maintained that Bulgarian weakness and growing Allied strength (and the improvement of the Greek army) offered an opportunity to remove one of the Central Powers from the conflict. And while the British slowly came to recognise these weaknesses, they also continued to doubt the abilities of the Greek army, as well as those of the Allies, to coordinate in this theatre.

What the PMRs agreed to and even discussed had little bearing on the actual events in the Balkans – in the end the British and French commanders in the field determined when the time was ripe for an offensive. However, through these discussions the Allies had a better understanding of what was taking place, and could factor these events into the creation of a global Allied strategy for 1919. The SWC and PMR discussions provided them with a forum to question one another – the French may have been able to act on the ground, but their partners 'took them to task' through the SWC. For the Americans, in particular, it allowed them to monitor what their Allies were doing and ensure that manpower and materials were not being diverted from the Western Front. Although the three nations often seemed to be working at cross purposes with one another, ultimately they had to agree if they wanted to preserve the idea of the coalition. Compromises, albeit ambiguous ones, occurred because they believed in the substance of the alliance. In the end, what was common about all three approaches was that developments in the Balkans were interdependent with, and subordinate to, those on the Western Front.

3   Eliminate the Ottoman Empire?

Policy discussions for 1918 and 1919 by the PMRs expanded beyond the Western Front to include both Palestine and Mesopotamia. The British, who had reached an agreement with Russia in 1907 on their frontiers in the Middle East and Central Asia, now found themselves facing a Turco-German threat. British troops were initially sent to these regions to protect Britain's Asiatic empire.[1] In comparison to their partners, the British had by far the greatest military presence in Palestine, while they had the only Allied military presence in Mesopotamia. These forces comprised close to one million men. To maintain its influence in this region the French deployed the Détachement Français de Palestine (DFP), which by September 1917 comprised 2,732 men. Despite rival interests in Palestine, the British and French recognised the importance of keeping the Central Powers out of southern Russia, where they believed the Germans would be able to obtain resources that would aid their military effort.[2] In the long term, neither government wanted to see the Germans expand their influence from Constantinople to China.[3] Hoping to gain Libya, the Italians sent an even smaller force; a mere 593 men. By the time the SWC was formed, the Italians attention was firmly on events unfolding on the Italian Front, thus they contributed little to these discussions.[4] The Americans did not take military action in these theatres, although they did contemplate declaring war on the Ottoman Empire. Despite that the majority of the forces in the Middle East were British, these theatres were discussed as part of the PMRs'

---

[1] For more on the origins of the intervention and the threat the Germans posed to the British Empire, see Hew Strachan, *The First World War: To Arms* (Oxford, 2001), 696–814.

[2] For the German side of this issue, see Stevenson, *With Our Backs*, 91–98.

[3] Schwarz, 'Divided Attention', 4.

[4] M. Larcher, *La Guerre Turque Dans La Guerre Mondiale* (Paris, 1926), 633. In the pre-war period they had taken the Dodecanese islands from the Ottomans. Anthony Bruce, *The Last Crusade: The Palestine Campaign in the First World War* (London, 2003), 6.

global perspective. For the PMRs policy in the Middle East was related to how to win the war against the Central Powers.

By early 1918 the PMRs agreed that strategy on the Western Front should remain defensive while the coalition built up forces for a decisive assault in 1919. Eliminating the Ottoman Empire from the war formed part of the PMR policy. If the Allies were successful, this action would force the Germans to send men and material away from the Western Front to the East. After the signing of the Treaty of Brest-Litovsk and German spring offensives, the PMRs no longer argued that the Ottoman Empire could be knocked out of the war; however, they still believed they could hold enemy forces in this theatre and prevent Germany from obtaining material resources in southern Russia. Through the PMRs' discussions, the interdependent nature of the various theatres of war came to the forefront, while their decisions reasserted that the Western Front was the main theatre of war.

Although the PMRs were able to reach a broad agreement on policy in Palestine and Mesopotamia, their discussions were complicated by their lack of executive authority. It was unclear as to who was responsible for creating an Allied policy in these theatres. Should it be determined by the nation with the largest army in the field, or, given the implications for other theatres of war, should it be a coalition decision? The result was a 'tug of war' between the British, who wanted a free hand in the Middle East, and the French and Americans who wanted all efforts to contribute to the Franco-Belgian Front. The British tested how much decision-making and information they had to share with their partners. They were determined to limit the extent to which they made national needs sub-servient to international ones in a theatre outside the Western Front and one where they had an overwhelming superiority of forces within the coalition. Meanwhile, their partners were determined to use the SWC to gain information about the allocation of resources.

In the case of the British, coalition strategy making was further compli-cated by internal debates between the British political and military elites in ways that did not did not occur between the French and American Sections. The desire of both Clemenceau and President Wilson to keep efforts focussed on the Western Front was clear to their PMRs. However, as the British political and military leadership did not have a unified strategy, the position of the British PMR was unclear. British strategy was divided between those who thought all efforts should be focussed on the Western Front in 1918 and those who believed gains could be made elsewhere while resources were built up in France for the decisive cam-paign in 1919. While both groups recognised that the war had to be won on the Western Front, the main difference in their approach was whether fighting in one of the 'sideshow' theatres would delay or hasten victory on the Western Front. In early 1918 Henry Wilson (at that time British PMR) and Lloyd George agreed on an Eastern strategy; however, by the end of July, Wilson, as CIGS, advocated focussing resources on the Western Front with limited action in the Middle East. As a result, the new PMR, Sackville-West, was caught between the opinions of Wilson, who was his friend and adviser, and the Prime Minister, who was also the political representative on the SWC. The debates at the international level placed the British national ones clearly in the context of how action against the Ottomans would benefit a decisive result on the Franco-Belgian Front. Although Lloyd George had intended that the SWC would extend his control over the British generals and their 'Western' ideas, the SWC proved a more difficult forum and the PMRs more independent from their political leadership than he had anticipated.

In December 1917 the Allies faced a changing strategic climate as an armistice between Russia and Germany was signed and treaty negotiations began. In Mesopotamia, the Indian Expeditionary Force (IEF), having taken Baghdad in the spring, now had to rethink its offensive plans. With Russia out of the war, it was no longer possible to execute the combined operation the Allies had been planning, which would have seen the Russians advance on Mosul while the IEF moved north, up the Tigris river. While in late 1917 the IEF occupied Jabal (north of Baghdad on the Tigris and south-east of Tuz), the new commander of Allied forces in Mesopotamia, General Marshall, having replaced General Maude who died of cholera in mid-November, began thinking of possible operations for 1918. Meanwhile, in Palestine, Allenby triumphantly marched into Jerusalem on 11 December 1917, giving the coalition a victory to celebrate after a very bleak year. The Allies anxiously contemplated what the loss of Russia would mean to their global strategy.

PMR Planning

By mid-January both Maxime Weygand and Henry Wilson had begun to digest the strategic changes in the Middle East, each producing draft notes on this subject which were circulated to the other PMR sections prior to their meeting in person. The Italians did not produce their own draft, and as the Americans were not yet established at Versailles, neither did they. Weygand's note illustrated French support for a campaign against the Ottoman forces, emphasising that, of the members of the Central Powers outside the main theatre of war, the Ottoman Empire was the one which could be most easily be attacked. The French Section considered that the Turkish army was worn out and crippled by low morale, in part, because they recognised (and resented) the imbalance in their relationship with Germany.[5] If British forces were to take advantage of the enemy's weakness, the French Section argued, the defeat of the Ottomans would give access to the Straits (Bosporus); re-establish direct lines of communication with the Caucasus, Armenia, southern Russia, and Romania; improve the effectiveness of the blockade by keeping German merchant ships out of the Black Sea; and economise on shipping tonnage by making it possible to import food from southern Russia as opposed to the United States. In addition, the French highlighted that defeating the Ottomans would adversely affect German submarine operations in the Mediterranean and stop German ambitions in the Orient, so contributing to Germany's long-term defeat. They also hoped that it might have a negative impact on Bulgarian morale. Finally, the defeat of the Ottomans would mean the release of British troops which could then be used on the Franco-Belgian Front where manpower was badly needed.[6]

Rather than attack in Palestine or Mesopotamia, Weygand recommended that the Entente focus its military efforts on an offensive aimed at the Dardanelles or Alexandretta, which he considered to be the vital regions. This idea was not a new one as it had been suggested in 1914–1915, and then revisited in September 1917 when Lloyd George asked the French to consider sending an expedition to coordinate with Allenby's advance.[7] The advantage of capturing Alexandretta was that it was close to the main rail-line used by the Ottomans to supply the Middle East from Istanbul. Success there would allow the Entente to isolate Turkish forces in Palestine and Mesopotamia by cutting their supply lines. As historian Matthew Hughes writes, 'All things considered, an amphibious landing stood more chance of seriously destabilising the Ottoman empire than the gradual advance on which Allenby was embarking'.[8]

This action was only part of what the French Section envisaged, as they also wanted to coordinate it with three other actions: an offensive into Mesopotamia that should aim to open the route along the Tigris, into Mosul and up towards Van; an assault in Palestine towards Aleppo; and

[5] Following the style of the PMRs, the terms 'Ottoman' and 'Turkish' forces are used interchangeably; 'L'offensive contre la Turquie', 30 November 1917, SHD-DAT, Conseil Supérieur de la Guerre, 4N 8.
[6] 'Nécessite et possibilités d'une action de l'entente contre Turquie en 1918', 4 January 1918, SHD-DAT, Conseil Supérieur de la Guerre, 4N 8.
[7] Hankey, Supreme Command, 699, 767.
[8] Matthew Hughes, Allenby and British Strategy in the Middle East 1917–1919 (London, 1999), 23.

an attack in Macedonia to tie up the enemy in the north. The French Section was not alone in considering an attack against a port. While conducting their own studies, 'A' Branch of the British Section advised that an operation against Port Ayas or Mersina would have an effect on morale equal to one against Alexandretta or Aleppo while requiring fewer resources.[9] Where the French were unique, however, was in suggesting that the Japanese be approached to undertake this amphibious landing, given that in their assessment such an operation required more men, material, and maritime resources than the British, French, Americans, or Italians could supply.[10] Although this was true, the French were also concerned about the British intervening in France's traditional sphere of influence along the Lebanese coast or in southern Cilicia.[11]

The French Section was adamant that Japanese support should be pursued.[12] The Japanese government had recently informed the French Ambassador to Tokyo that they had no interest in intervening in the Mediterranean (beyond the 12 destroyers they already currently had in use).[13] However, the French believed the Japanese misunderstood the situation and feared weakening their military while the United States was re-arming. They wanted the Japanese to be presented with a fresh study emphasising the many reasons why the latter should become involved in the Middle East. These covered the gamut: the Japanese should guarantee the security of India as part of their treaty alliance with Britain; the growing strength of Germany would challenge Japan and China; Japan should try and preserve the high military reputation it had gained after the Russo-Japanese War; Japan needed the support of its allies to resolve the issues of China, Manchuria, and Mongolia; and although the Japanese were not technically at war with the Ottoman Empire, the Turkish army could only be seen as the mercenary army of Germany.[14] Simply put, the French hoped to utilise the unrealised potential of the Japanese army as they were alarmed by the Allies' manpower figures.

The French note, however, was not discussed on 21 January when the PMRs met. Instead the unique aspect of Weygand's proposal, a landing on the Syrian coast, was sent directly by the French to London. Henry

---

[9] 'A' Branch, 'The Military and Strategical Position in the Turkish Theatre and South Russia as a Whole', 6 January 1918, CAB 25/68/p. 6.

[10] 'Nécessite et possibilities', 4 January 1918, 4N 8.

[11] Hughes, *Allenby and British Strategy*, 24.

[12] Weygand to Vice-Amiral, Chef d'État Major Général de la Marine, 19 January 1918, SHD-DAT, Conseil Supérieur de la Guerre, 4N 1. Weygand's note from 4 January was given slight amendments before it was approved by the naval section (sub-section of the French Section) and then the French Section.

[13] For these figures, see Halpern, *A Naval History of World War I*, 26.

[14] 'Nécessite et possibilities', 4 January 1918, 4N 8.

Wilson said he would follow up on the reply from London; however, his efforts came to naught when he found that he could not gain the information about the Japanese navy that he required to complete the study.[15] This left the British PMR's note for discussion, to which only one small amendment was made before being agreed upon and officially made Joint Note 12, 'The Campaign in 1918'.[16] In drawing up his draft joint note, General Wilson was assisted by Leo Amery, a political officer at the SWC and also an ardent advocate of action in the East. Amery was in close contact with Lloyd George and frequently circulated papers to the War Cabinet.[17] It was Amery's opinion that the PMRs would support Lloyd George in his quest for an Eastern strategy, explaining to the Prime Minister, 'With Wilson at Versailles and the East delegated to Smuts, I don't think the old gang can give you too much trouble – if they do you can deal with them'.[18]

Lloyd George hoped to use the SWC to advocate his own strategic ideas and saw that Henry Wilson was given plenty of ammunition to follow his 'Eastern' ideas. Despite the British Section having completed their studies on Palestine, Lloyd George first wanted Henry Wilson to speak to Jan Smuts, the multifaceted South African representative on the Imperial War Cabinet (later he joined the British War Cabinet), before it submitted anything to the other PMRs. The British PMR responded by holding a meeting where he asked his staff,

to change their minds as to the best way to approach the problem, and to first find out whether we were safe in England, France and Italy, and then, if the answer was in the affirmative, examine the Palestine and Mesopotamian problem and see what could be done. Not to approach the problem in the way that the War Office had done, by starting at the wrong end and ruling out Palestine and Mesopotamia to start with.[19]

While working at Versailles, General Wilson read Robertson's memorandums on strategy for 1918. He disagreed with the CIGS's proposal to do nothing in Palestine and to withdraw all forces besides those required for a defensive stance in order to gain extra forces for use on the Western

---

[15] 'Draft Minutes of the Meeting of the Military Representatives', 21 January 1918, CAB 25/120/SWC50.
[16] 'Minutes of the Meeting of the Military Representatives', 21 January 1918, CAB 25/120/SWC56; 'Procès-verbal de la séance des representants militaires au consel supérieur de guerre', 21 January 1918, SHD-DAT, Conseil Supérieur de la Guerre, 4N 4. Little discussion of this joint note was recorded in the minutes of the meeting.
[17] Shumate, *Allied Supreme War Council*, 252. Shumate interviewed Amery.
[18] Amery to Lloyd George, 12 January 1918, Parliamentary Archives, London, David Lloyd George Papers [hereon LG] LG/F/2/2/1/11.
[19] Henry Wilson, 15 January, 1918, quoted in Callwell, *Field-Marshal*, 51–52.

Front. Robertson feared the Germans would make large gains in France once they transferred their forces from the Eastern Front, whereas the British Section argued that attacking the Ottomans would draw German forces away from the Western Front.[20]

Joint Note 12 did not set out operational objectives. Its purpose was to establish a general policy for the coalition. The French and the British Sections agreed that, with the change in the strategic situation caused by the second Russian revolution, which they feared had allowed the Germans to release as many as 60 divisions from the Russo-Romanian Fronts, the Allies were not strong enough to attack on the Western Front. As such, they would have to remain on the defensive while building up American manpower.[21] The PMRs determined that the main theatres of war, the Franco-Belgian and Italian ones, would be safe. However they did not think the coalition could afford to remain on the defensive in all theatres: 'To allow this year to pass without an attempt to secure a decision in any theatre of war, and to leave the initiative entirely to the enemy would, in the opinion of the Military Representatives, be a grave error in strategy apart from the moral effect such a policy would produce upon the Allied Nations'.[22] Furthermore the coalition had a responsibility 'to consider how that strategy must be modified in order to take the fullest advantage out of such opportunities as remain open to them during the phase of deadlock on the Western fronts ...' The PMRs were also concerned about how morale would be maintained on the home-fronts if the Allies achieved nothing in 1918.

While the responsibility of the PMRs did not extend to giving instructions to the Commanders-in-Chief, they did suggest what Allied objectives in the Middle East should be, recommending in late January:

There are certain more immediate objectives, indeed, such as Haifa, the friendly grain producing region of the Haran, Damascus and Beirut, which seem clearly indicated not only by their military, economic and political importance, but also by the prospect of striking effective blows at the Turkish forces which are not likely to abandon them without a contest.[23]

The PMRs imagined that by attacking these regions they would force the Germans to go to the assistance of the Ottoman forces. In general, going on the offensive in Palestine and Mesopotamia might assist anti-German

---

[20] Leo Amery, 'The Turkish and South Russian Problem', 4 January 1918; 'A' Branch, 'Military Action for 1918', 6 January, 1918, CAB 25/68.

[21] 'E' Branch, 'The General Situation with Notes on "A German Offensive in France"', 1 January 1918, CAB 25/68; French PMR to Clemenceau 'Projet de Plan d'Action', 22 January 1918, SHD-DAT, Conseil Supérieur de la Guerre, 4N 1.

[22] 'Joint Note 12', 21 January 1918, CAB 25/120/SWC57.   [23] Ibid.

forces in both southern Russia and Romania, which in turn would force the Germans to divert resources to these areas.[24]

The PMRs were careful not to demand manpower from the Western Front for a campaign in the East as they knew there was a shortage of shipping tonnage and that manpower was needed in France. They argued that they could use the Allied forces and resources that were already in Palestine and Mesopotamia as well as possibly gain 'minor reinforcements' from a number of regions which could be formed into new units: East Africa, when that campaign ended; Salonika when two divisions could be spared; India, by raising new units; and finally the Western Front, in the form of extra mounted troops (which were of little use there). Regardless, manpower was only a secondary issue compared to that of poor communications in Palestine and Mesopotamia. They argued that the difficulty was not dislodging the Ottoman forces from various positions, but rather pursuing and defeating them. Doing so required not only that the Allied forces themselves be mobile and able to operate at large distances from their base, but also that they be able to repair and construct railway lines of various gauges and provide them with rolling stock. In addition they would need to open up new bases at the ports.

In reality these operations was not nearly as minor as the PMRs tried to indicate. Fielding and moving an army in the Middle East required extensive logistical preparations, including building roads, railways, and water pipelines.[25] As limited shipping was available for this theatre, moving materials, when they were available, proved challenging (see Chapter 6 on resources). The large scale of what they were suggesting is further demonstrated by the PMRs' desire to increase aerial attacks against the Ottoman forces. They suggested the creation of an independent strategic aviation base in Cyprus and in the Aegean as well as the organisation of a naval air service in the Eastern Mediterranean, arguing that the use of airpower for 'concentrated strategic offensives' was 'essential to any scheme of serious operations against Turkey'.[26] But the Allies already lacked sufficient airpower on the Western Front, leaving little for operations in the Middle East.

In their assessment of potential action against Turkey, the PMRs began their discussion modestly; however, once they had reached the conclusion of the joint note their recommendations had become extravagant:

---

[24] Ibid.
[25] See Kristian Ulrichsen, *The Logistics and Politics of the British Campaigns in the Middle East, 1914–22* (Basingstoke, 2011), 63–78.
[26] 'Joint Note 12'.

the need for the most energetic co-operation and the closest co-ordination not only of the Allied Military forces in Palestine, Mesopotamia and Armenia, but also of the Allied Naval and Air forces along the whole coast of Asiatic Turkey, of the local governments in Egypt, India, Cyprus, or from whatever country materials, supplies or labour can be furnished, and not least, of the Allied Foreign Offices. It is essential to the success of the offensive against Turkey that it should be envisaged not as a series of disconnected operations, but as a single co-ordinated scheme whose object is to eliminate one of the Enemy Powers from the War.[27]

For reasons previously described (see Chapter 2 on Macedonia), they excluded any action in the Balkans. To coordinate the coalition's operations in Macedonia, Palestine, and Mesopotamia would have been ideal; however, the reality was that it would require too many military resources at a time when the Allied coalition was concerned about manpower and only beginning to organise their resources as a coalition. To ask for this level of coordination in 1918 was unrealistic. This sort of thinking did, however, encourage the SWC to begin to establish bodies for greater unity. Overall, the PMRs recommended an offensive against Turkey because they thought they could make strategic gains that would justify the resources action would require. Knocking the Ottoman Empire out of the war would not defeat the Germans, but it would place pressure on them, presumably remove forces from the Western Front, and gain the Allies territory with which to negotiate once the war had ended.

Prior to the SWC meeting at the end of January, when Joint Note 12 was discussed and agreed upon, the British General Staff examined and commented on its content.[28] 'There is no question as to the great advantage which we should obtain from the collapse of Turkey', they acknowledged, for 'Turkey has been a millstone round our neck throughout the war and her collapse should bring us very important and immediate relief'.[29] The concern was whether or not they had the resources to do so. They disagreed with the PMRs' assessment that the Ottoman army's morale was low and concluded it had adequate supplies, transport, and ammunition. They also disagreed with the strength of the forces opposing Allenby in Palestine, arguing for 425,000 men rather than the PMR's estimate of 250,000. In reality, when Allenby finally renewed his offensive in August he found there were only 100,000 Turkish forces south of Damascus and that only 32,000 of the infantry

---

[27] Ibid.
[28] 'Comments by the General State Upon Joint Note 12', 28 January 1918, CAB 25/68.
[29] Ibid.

could be considered front line troops. In fact the PMRs were correct about Turkish morale being low. The Ottoman forces had begun to desert in large numbers, with those remaining facing food and clothing shortages due to the breakdown in communications.[30] The General Staff also criticised the PMRs' suggestion as to where to obtain manpower. It was also not possible to draw upon troops from East Africa as they required rest after enduring tropical conditions and malaria before they could be sent to the Western Front. Transferring mounted troops from the Western Front was the only viable option in bolstering the under-strength forces in Palestine.

In Mesopotamia, the General Staff thought a major offensive could not occur until rail-lines had been constructed between Basra and Baghdad, delaying such a thrust until at least September 1918 (see Map 0.2).[31] Instead they wanted to focus on securing the Persian Front, but this would necessitate a delay of nine months while they assisted in reorganising Russian and Armenian troops. Given Allenby had to operate on his own, the most they thought could be achieved from the PMRs' plan was the capture of Haifa. But as the General Staff considered the town to be of little value to the Turks, they determined it was not worth the effort. The General Staff thus recommended that Allenby only advance to the Hejaz railway. Communications were a serious issue. The Ottoman rail-lines were 3' 6" gauge which meant that the British had to get locomotives and wagons that would fit this line from Australia and South Africa or they had to build standard gauge rail-lines.[32] A campaign in Palestine in early 1918 would have sapped British resources and was very unlikely to have knocked the Ottoman Empire out of the war.[33]

Despite the objections raised by the British General Staff, the content of Joint Note 12, of which Palestine and Mesopotamia were only a part, remained unchanged. This note provided Lloyd George with the impetus to push an Eastern strategy onto the coalition. Furthermore, he used the SWC to assert authority over the commanders by suggesting they be excluded from Allied discussions until the political leaders requested their input.[34] This approach worked for part of the SWC's third session; however, Lloyd George was confronted by Clemenceau, whose natural instinct was to advocate that all efforts be focussed on the Western Front. He expressed concern that Paris was under threat, an opinion he

[30] Bruce, *The Last Crusade*, 208.   [31] 'Comments by the General Staff', CAB 25/68.
[32] 'Note by D.G.M.R.', 26 January 1918, CAB 25/68.
[33] Hughes, *Allenby and British Strategy*, 61.
[34] Lloyd George to Clemenceau, 31 January 1918, SHD-DAT, Fonds Clemenceau, 6N 61.

vigorously maintained throughout the war.[35] In particular Clemenceau was concerned that the shortage of manpower on the Western Front meant that none could be spared elsewhere.[36] The French closely scrutinised the availability and employment of British manpower. It was Joint Note 12's reference to an offensive against Turkey that caused the most friction between the coalition partners. As Hankey described, it was only 'agreed to after a terrific struggle, as the soldiers had got at Clemenceau to oppose it and concentrate everything in the west'.[37]

When he first came to power, Clemenceau had gone so far as to tell Lloyd George that he was willing to make peace with Turkey on any terms, including the sacrifice of French interests in Syria.[38] At this meeting, clemenceau insisted that Joint Note 12 be altered by removing the section on attacking the Ottoman Empire and that instead the British could themselves conduct a campaign in the East. Lloyd George retorted by asking Clemenceau if the Allies should withdraw from Salonika, Baghdad, and Jerusalem, insinuating that if British interests were to be sacrificed, so too should French ones in Macedonia. Lloyd George explained that at most two divisions would be gained by assuming a defensive position in the Middle East and that 'that was all even Sir Douglas Haig hoped for'.[39] This was a tremendous slight coming from Lloyd George – but his point was that a gain of two divisions was not worth sacrificing the option of offensive action against the Ottomans. In early 1918 the British had 'Indianised' their armies in the Middle East by taking one complete company from each Indian battalion in Egypt and Mesopotamia and amalgamating them to form new units. Drafts came from India to make up shortages. By creating these new units they could withdraw British ones for use elsewhere at a time when the British were desperate for manpower.[40] In fact, by the end of August Allenby had sent 60,000 men to the Western Front.[41]

---

[35] 'Procés-Verbal of the Second Meeting of the Third Session of the SWC', 31 January 1918, CAB 25/120/SWC71.

[36] See E. Greenhalgh, 'Errors and Omissions in Franco-British Co-Operation over Munitions Production, 1914–1918', *War in History*, 14/2 (2007).

[37] Hankey diary, 1 February 1918, HNKY/1/4.

[38] Christopher M. Andrew and A. S. Kanya-Forstner, *France Overseas: The Great War and the Climax of French Imperial Expansion* (London, 1981), 152.

[39] 'Procés-Verbal of the Second Meeting', CAB 25/120/SWC71.

[40] Kitchen, *The British Imperial Army*, 195. Also see Keith Grieves, *The Politics of Manpower, 1914–1918* (Manchester, 1988).

[41] David R. Woodward, *Hell in the Holy Land: World War I in the Middle East* (Lexington, KY, 2006), 170. Concerned about his own manpower shortages, Allenby recommended that his government obtain three to four divisions of highly trained Japanese soldiers for use in Palestine. Kitchen, *The British Imperial Army*, 196.

It may have seemed that the remaining forces, especially the 54th Division, which was all British, could have been withdrawn, but for a variety of reasons, the British would not do so. An examination of the order of battle for the British forces illustrates that many of the 'white' troops that remained in the Middle East were mounted or cavalry divisions, both of which would have required significant retraining to fight on the Western Front.[42] Having already experimented with the Indian army on the Western Front in 1915, these forces had been withdrawn, due to difficulty in replacing losses of officers and concerns about the low morale of the Indian troops.[43] As Martin Gregory has argued, however, the British never realised the full potential of the Indian army due to long-held prejudice. While these troops might have been capable of fighting in France, the maintenance of the 'martial doctrine' limited recruiting and the reserve structure, which in turn made it difficult for the Indian army to maintain its unit strength.[44] It also meant that the British were unable to withdraw all of their 'white' troops from the Indian army. A reluctance to recruit Indian officers meant that not only was there a shortage of technically trained Indian officers, but due to the language skills required to command an Indian unit, there was also a shortage of British ones. Given the high wastage on the Western Front in 1918 it would have been difficult to maintain the Indian troops if they had been moved to the Western Front. In addition, the British required the Indian army for the defence of India itself. While in January, the French had suggested that the defeat of the Turks would mean the British could move 250,000 troops to the Western Front, the British had responded that some, but not all troops could be transported.[45] An additional reality of moving troops from the Middle East to the Western Front was that it would require troop transport ships that were desperately needed to move American troops across the Atlantic.

While Lloyd George's argument for an Eastern strategy was supported by the Italians, Clemenceau would not yield.[46] Unable to reach an agreement in the main meeting of the SWC, Clemenceau, Pichon, Lloyd George, Milner, Orlando, and Sonnino met in private session where a

---

[42] Ellis and Cox, *The World War I Databook*, 208–209.
[43] Jeffrey Greenhut, 'The Imperial Reserve: The Indian Corps on the Western Front, 1914–15', *The Journal of Imperial and Commonwealth History*, 12/1 (1983), 68–69.
[44] Gregory Martin, 'The Influence of Racial Attitudes on British Policy towards India during the First World War', *The Journal of Imperial and Commonwealth History*, 14/2 (1986), 100.
[45] 'Nécessite et possibilities d'une action de l'entente contre turquie en 1918', 4 January 1918, CAB/25/43.
[46] Nothing else was said other than the Italians agreed.

compromise was reached.[47] Reassembling at the main SWC meeting, Lloyd George announced that he had agreed to amend Joint Note 12 with a paragraph that stated:

The Supreme War Council accepts Note 12 of the Military Representatives on the Plan of Campaign for 1918, the British Government having made it clear that, in utilising in the most effective fashion the forces already at its disposal in the Eastern theatre, it has no intention of diverting forces from the Western Front or in any way relaxing its efforts to maintain the safety of that front which it regards as a vital interest of the whole Alliance.[48]

With this compromise Lloyd George received agreement from his coalition partners that the British could pursue action in the Middle East, while Clemenceau received reassurance that the Western Front remained the main theatre of war.

For the time being the French General Staff (L'État -Major de l'Armée) abandoned the idea of a landing on the coast of Syria, as it was determined that the naval resources were not available. Given that the British were going to resume action in the Middle East, the French did not want to be completely inactive in this region.[49] While Clemenceau did not have war aims outside of Europe, others in his government did.[50] The idea that the French army should increase its presence in the Palestine campaign was circulating in Paris. Foreign Minister and French representative at the SWC Stephen Pichon advocated to Clemenceau directly on this issue; however, he found Clemenceau reluctant to bolster the DFP.[51] Nevertheless, a palatable scheme was devised to increase French presence in the Palestine campaign without detracting from efforts in France. Colonel Brémond, head of the French mission in Egypt, recommended to Clemenceau that the size of the DFP be increased. The 'Orient' Section under Weygand at the SWC reinforced these ideas.[52] It did so by highlighting that it was 'of vital interest to

---

[47] No minutes were kept, Hankey, *The Supreme Command*, 765.

[48] 'Procés-Verbal of the Third Meeting of the Third Session of the SWC', 1 February 1918, CAB/25/120/SWC72. The Bliss papers did not have anything about this meeting; however, he did tell a colleague that on Joint Note 12 the British had pushed for a campaign in Asia Minor, which the Italians supported and the French opposed. Bliss to Henry Pickney McCain, 4 February 1918 in Arthur Link, et al., eds., *The Papers of Woodrow Wilson* [hereon *PWW*] (Princeton, NJ: Princeton University Press, 1984) 46: 240.

[49] 'Note sur les possibilités de renforcement du détachement français de Palestine', 5 February 1918, SHD-DAT, Conseil Supérieur de la Guerre, 4N 8.

[50] The various groups working for a French Empire are described in Andrew and Kanya-Forstner, *France Overseas*, 143.

[51] Le ministre des Affaires étrangères à Monsieur le président du Conseil, 31 January 1918, AFGG 9/1, annex 538.

[52] AFGG, 9/1, p. 92.

France' to increase French forces as it would enable the DFP to undertake more significant military action and reassert French interests in this region. The 'Orient' Section suggested to send the Légion d'Orient to join the DFP. Based in Cyprus, this force was comprised of Armenian and Syrian volunteers who were determined to fight the Ottomans. Given these circumstances it would take a minor amount of tonnage to transport them and would not drain manpower from France. In mid-February the decision was made to deploy the Légion d'Orient.[53] Between May and September 1918 the DFP (now the DFPS as it included Syria) grew from 3,925 to 7,378 effectives.[54] The French recognised that this was a fraction of the size of Allenby's forces, which they estimated at 150,000 in March 1918.

The British political and military leadership continued to quarrel over what to do with these forces. Although Joint Note 12 had outlined a coalition policy and direction, when the SWC instructed the Commanders-in-Chief and British General Staff to draw up and submit their plans to the SWC, Robertson passionately raised his concerns about Joint Note 12 and 'entered a solemn protest against the Turkish campaign'.[55] He argued that a campaign against the Ottomans was impractical due to the limited resources available in Palestine. In an attempt to dissuade his government from sending resources to the Middle East, Robertson used British intelligence, which overestimated the strength of enemy forces facing Allenby, to discourage the War Cabinet from recommending offensive action.[56] He wanted to restrict action outside the Western Front as the General Staff was aware that the Germans were moving forces from the East to France.[57] Allenby himself had informed the War Cabinet on the 14 December that he did not foresee a successful advance prior to the summer of 1918. Due to the upcoming rainy season, he recommended a gradual advance in order to double track his rail-line up the coast. He also intended to attack the Hejaz railway which supplied the Ottoman forces at Medina.[58] When Allenby was further pressed by the War Cabinet to consider the occupation of Palestine up to the Dan spring (by Mount Hermon) or to advance to Aleppo (which would cut the Turkish supply route to Mesopotamia), he responded that he would require more than double his current number of infantry divisions,

---

[53] Ibid., 9/1, p. 87.   [54] Ibid., 9/1, p. 229.
[55] Hankey diary, 2 February 1918, HNKY/1/4.
[56] Yigal Sheffy, *British Military Intelligence in the Palestine Campaign, 1914–1918* (London, 1998), 289, 330.
[57] Hughes, *Allenby and British Strategy*, 55.   [58] Ibid., 52.

expanding his force from 7 to 16 or even 18 divisions.[59] In addition Aleppo was approximately 360 miles from British lines.[60]

Instead, Allenby's plan detailed a limited advance to the Beirut-Damascus line, as opposed to the substantial plan set out in Joint Note 12. His plans were based on an overestimation of Ottoman forces. A report prepared within the EEF estimated that Allenby would face a minimum of 60,000 enemy combat troops if he moved up to the Sidon-Qunaytra line, when in reality, the Turks could field no more than 20,000 infantry in this area.[61] As Yigal Sheffy has explained, despite that the EEF had several techniques to calculate the strength of Ottoman units, it did not provide them with the whole picture, and as the strength of divisions was difficult to calculate, they frequently overestimated the enemy.[62]

Meanwhile, as the British War Office made its concerns heard, Lloyd George sent Smuts, along with Amery, to Egypt from the 12 to 22 February to investigate whether the PMRs' plan could be executed, instructing these two men 'that the efforts [in the Middle East] should no longer be haphazard as they had hitherto been, but should now be coordinated with the view of seeing how far it was possible to force this ally of the Central Powers out of the war'.[63] The Prime Minister was attempting to use Smuts, along with the SWC, as an alternative opinion to that of the War Office and commanders-in-chief. Unfortunately for Lloyd George, the recommendations which came from this mission were overshadowed when the Germans launched their powerful offensive on 21 March on the Western Front. Coupled with the signing of the Treaty of Brest-Litovsk early that month, the strategic situation had dramatically changed and Entente fears about German and Ottoman ambitions in the East were confirmed. As a result, Allenby's plan to push along the Mediterranean coast was postponed, and in late March he was instructed to prepare troops for movement to the Western Front and to remain on active defence in Palestine. This stance was reinforced by his sending approximately 60,000 of his men to France between May and August.[64]

These events also had a profound impact on the PMRs' creation of a global Allied strategy.[65] Responding quickly to the change in the strategic situation, the PMRs produced Joint Note 20 'The Situation in the

[59] Sheffy, British Military Intelligence, 288.   [60] Kitchen, British Imperial Army, 193.
[61] Sheffy, British Military Intelligence, 287–288.   [62] Ibid., 292.
[63] Smuts to Mrs Smuts, 11 March 1918 in William Keith Hancock (ed.), The Smuts Papers (London, 1956), 612.
[64] Woodward, Hell in the Holy Land, 170.
[65] 'Les Conséquences de la Catastrophe Russe en Asie', 10 March 1918, SHD-DAT, Conseil Supérieur de la Guerre, 4N 8.

Eastern Theatre' at the end of March, which recommended that the British consider taking action to prevent the Germans from gaining access to food, manpower, and raw materials in the East. They were especially concerned about the three-fold advantage this treaty gave the Germans in increasing their manpower, arguing that not only could the Germans now move a large portion of their 47 divisions in Russia (the estimate of the number of divisions fluctuated) to the Western Front (in reality, between 1 November 1917 and 21 March 1918 the Germans transferred 48 divisions to the Western Front), but they could also add to their numerical supremacy by obtaining as many as 500,000 Russian subjects to add to the German army, and use a limitless number of slaves in German industry and farming.[66] Fixated on the objectives of the Central Powers, the PMRs estimated that the former would:

utilise relatively small German military forces, in conjunction with Turkish troops, and with the native Moslem populations, in order to secure control of the whole of Transcaucasia, and of Northern and Central Persia, with the object both of threatening the flanks of the British forces in Mesopotamia, and of inciting the Afghans to attack India.[67]

The PMRs contended that the Germans now had the upper hand in this region and could use it to compel the British to divert large numbers of forces to the Middle East or, even worse, 'frighten it [the British government] into concluding peace'.[68] British military intelligence was itself concerned that Ottoman forces would be successful in occupying part of the Caucasus and in exterminating the Armenians. The PMRs also argued that the Germans and Turks had the ability to send agents into Turkestan to stir-up Pan-Turanian propaganda, and from there 'work up an anti-British agitation in Afghanistan'.[69]

The desire to prevent German gains in Mesopotamia had to be balanced with efforts on the Western Front. With the altering of the strategic context, the PMRs were also wary lest Persia and Trans-Caucasus become a drain on limited British capabilities. The coalition was making plans to rush American troops to France and utilise all available resources to stop the German spring offensives. The solution they proposed was for British forces to quickly take the initiative in Mesopotamia, arguing that by doing so fewer forces would be needed to prevent a pro-German coup in Teheran and to prevent German and Ottoman forces

---

[66] On actual German forces, see, Giordan Fong, 'The Movement of German Divisions to the Western Front, Winter 1917–1918', *War in History*, 7/2 (2000), 229; 'Joint Note 20', CAB 25/121/SWC 151. This note was written on the 29 March; however, it was not signed by the PMRs until 8 April 1918.
[67] 'Joint Note 20', CAB 25/121/SWC 151.   [68] Ibid.   [69] Ibid.

from entering Afghanistan.[70] The French Section supported British action in Mesopotamia and had gone as far as to suggest a British occupation of the road from Tabriz to Teheran.[71] An examination of the background to this joint notes illustrates that military action was advised by the PMRs to prevent the Germans from making gains which would assist them in sustaining their military forces and home-front morale (by gaining access to food and other resources) and to prevent German economic ambitions after the war. These two objectives were intertwined as German gains during the war would establish their position for the postwar world. The French Section agreed that the Germans posed a serious threat to British interests in Persia, India, and Afghanistan.[72] Meanwhile, Marshall, the British commander in Mesopotamia, attempted to reduce hysteria about the loss of their Russian ally by arguing that neither the Germans nor Turks were capable of significant military movement across Persia.[73]

Clemenceau's response to the German spring offensive was, unsurprisingly, for pressure to be relieved from the French Front. Knowing that Lloyd George was a strong proponent of action in the East, he was suspicious that the British were unnecessarily conserving resources in this theatre. The War Office had informed the French that due to the reorganisation of British forces, offensive action could not be undertaken in Palestine for several months. However, the French General Staff was keeping a close eye on British action and assessed the campaign in Palestine in the context of efforts on the Franco-Belgian Front. They surveyed the comparable strength of British and Ottoman forces and found the British had a two-to-one advantage. Given these figures, the French General Staff advocated British forces in Palestine contribute to resisting the German offensives on the Western Front in one of two ways: by launching a major offensive in Palestine, or by transferring a greater number of divisions back to France.[74] By giving two options, the French allowed Lloyd George to pursue his earlier policy in the East or to follow Clemenceau's earlier request to bolster their forces in France – either way Clemenceau wanted the effect to be felt in France.

---

[70] Ibid.
[71] 'Sur Les Menaces Allemandes contre la sécurité des indes', 16 March 1918, SHD-DAT, Conseil Supérieur de la Guerre, 4N 8.
[72] Ibid.
[73] Charles Townshend, *When God Made Hell: The British Invasion of Mesopotamia and the Creation of Iraq, 1914–1921* (London, 2010), 418.
[74] 'Note sur la situation militaire en Palestine', 19 May 1918, AFGG 9/1, annex 624.

He pushed the matter by soliciting an assessment of the War Offices figures from the PMRs.[75]

Belin, who had replaced Weygand as the French PMR, used information from the French General Staff to create a draft joint note entitled, 'The Situation of the British Army in Palestine', which he circulated prior to the PMRs 33rd meeting.[76] At the meeting, Belin found Sackville-West to be abrasive about considering French views. The British PMR reminded his colleagues that 'practically all the troops in Palestine were British ...' therefore Allenby was receiving policy information, 'more or less approved by the Supreme War Council ...' directly from the British government.[77] Sackville-West reassured the other PMRs that they were following an Allied policy as much as possible and that the reorganisation of forces in Palestine would lead to the bolstering of forces in France. However, he also indicated that the British were the overwhelming dominant power in the Middle East. He reinforced this point when Belin suggested the French send a mission to Persia to combat the expansion of German interests. It was in Bliss that Belin found support. The American representative also wanted detailed information on the British army in Palestine and wanted the PMRs to closely watch this theatre. What the PMRs found was that the British Section was willing to communicate information about activities in the Middle East in order to reassure them that they were focussed on action in France, but they were not willing to accept direction or interference. In this regard the British were behaving in a similar manner to the French in the Balkans.

Enter the Americans with Political Considerations

While Bliss had attended the third meeting of the SWC (held from 29 January to 2 February), where Joint Note 12 was discussed, his contribution had been limited to ensuring that forces were not diverted from the Western Front. He was unable to submit his own study of Joint Note 12, as he was still in the midst of establishing the American Section, whose members had to make the journey across the Atlantic. In May, deviating from the American stance of remaining politically detached from their European partners, Bliss involved his colleagues in discussions about whether or not the Americans should declare war on Turkey or Bulgaria. This question stemmed from the heavy support in

[75] Clemenceau to Belin, 20 May 1918, AFGG 9/1, annex 625.
[76] 'Projet de Note Collective: La Situation Militaire de l'Armée Britannique de Palestine', 26 May 1918, Bliss 323.
[77] 'Minutes of the 33rd Meeting of the Military Representatives', CAB 25/121/SWC235.

Congress for a declaration of war against both countries. In fact, Congress had asked the Senate Committee on Foreign Relations to investigate this question. It, in turn, asked both the Entente governments and the SWC if they believed a declaration of war on both Turkey and Bulgaria, or either of them, would contribute significantly to the defeat of the Central Powers.[78]

Although this question was of a political nature, the PMRs nonetheless investigated the impact declarations of war would have on military victory.[79] Bliss's initial opinion was that a declaration of war, 'might have a good moral effect for the Allies on the peoples of the Near East', concluding, 'there might perhaps be an advantage in such a declaration and he could see no possible disadvantage'.[80] Bliss told his colleagues that the United States had hoped the Turks would appeal to them for a separate peace, 'but that this hope of a diplomatic settlement had now grown very feeble'.[81] General di Robilant, the Italian PMR, expressed his concern that the collapse of Russia would enable Germany to penetrate Persia and establish supremacy in the East. A declaration of war by the United States against Turkey, he argued, would make it easier for the Americans to assist the Entente in the Near East; indeed, 'this intervention of the United States might be a most important element in terminating the war'.[82] The French representative was more hesitant then his colleagues, pointing out that the Americans did not have the troops to intervene and it could lead to an embarrassing situation if they declared war and could not contribute militarily. Di Robilant disagreed and suggested that the best form of assistance that the Americans could provide would be to aid the British in improving their lines of communication in Palestine, Persia, and Mesopotamia. Sackville-West recommended the Americans declare war on both Turkey and Bulgaria 'because of the great moral effect it would have on the people of those countries to know that the Allies are really together in everything ...'[83]

The joint recommendation that originated from this meeting largely amalgamated the opinions of all four PMRs and proposed that the Americans should declare war on the Ottoman Empire. They also suggested an American declaration of war on Bulgaria, with the stipulation

[78] Robert Lansing to Woodrow Wilson, 2 May 1918, FRUS, II: 121.
[79] Bliss to the Military Representatives, SWC, 5 May 1918, Bliss/323. For British PMR's notes on the issue, see the entire folder of CAB 25/40 entitled 'Relations between America and Turkey and Bulgaria'.
[80] 'Draft Minutes of the 29th Meeting of the Military Representatives', 6 May 1918, CAB 25/121/SWC205. For a copy of the American, French, and Italian minutes, see Bliss/323/SWC205.
[81] Ibid.   [82] Ibid.   [83] Ibid.

that the Americans should give Bulgaria a time limit so as to foster negotiations – a suggestion made by the British Section. The PMRs highlighted that these actions would not oblige the Americans to commit troops to these theatres, but would be a purely political stance.[84] With Russia out of the war, the coalition partners could offer Constantinople to Bulgaria with the understanding that the Straits would be internationalised. While the United States would first declare war on the Ottomans, Washington could then be used as the channel through which to bring Bulgaria over to the side of the Entente.[85] The PMR recommendations gained additional support from their naval counterpart, the Allied Naval Council.[86]

Lansing informed President Wilson that the British, French, and Italian governments advised the US government to declare war on both Turkey and Bulgaria. He understood the signing of the joint recommendation by the PMRs to be the view of each government.[87] In addition, the British Foreign Office attempted to encourage an American declaration of war by reminding them that it would give 'a significant role for the United States at the peace table in regard to the settlements to be reached concerning the Near East and Middle East'.[88] Lansing encouraged the President to respond promptly.[89] Balfour, the British Foreign Minister and frequent British representative on the SWC, told Edward House, President Wilson's confidant and unofficial foreign policy advisor, that an American declaration of war on Bulgaria would negatively affect Bulgarian morale. Wilson responded that the United States and Bulgaria had a friendship and that a declaration of war would not be effective propaganda.

While the PMRs considered the impact that these declarations of war would have on the military situation, President Wilson was concerned about the humanitarian ones. As Sir William Wiseman, the head of the British intelligence division in the United States and friend of Colonel House, explained to Sir Eric Drummond, the private secretary to Balfour:

---

[84] 'Joint Recommendation', 7 May 1918, CAB 25/40/SWC205, annex 'A'.

[85] Note by H. W. Studd, 5 May 1918, CAB 25/40. It was not the first time 'A' Branch had suggested using territory to bribe one of the Central Powers to drop out of the war. On 6 January 1918, H. W. Studd suggested bribing the Ottomans, CAB 25/68.

[86] 'Relations of United States with Ottoman Empire and Bulgaria', 15 May 1918, CAB 25/40/GT4554; ADM 137/836.

[87] Lansing to Woodrow Wilson, 8 May 1918, in Link, *PWW*, 47: 568.

[88] Lansing paraphrased a note from the Foreign Office, W. H. Page to Robert Lansing, 17 May 1918 in Link, et al., *PWW*, 48: 80n1.

[89] Robert Lansing to Woodrow Wilson, 20 May 1918, in Link, et al., *PWW*, 48: 80.

I have discussed relations of U. S. with Turkey and Bulgaria with both Col. House and the President. The President's views are broadly as follows: He has no sympathy for Bulgaria, nor does he believe in the so-called 'traditional friendship' with the States. He does not regard the Bulgarians as dupes of the Germans with whom he classes them. Whilst he admits that a declaration of war against Bulgaria might achieve a certain political advance he is reluctant to declare a war which would be unaccompanied by any definite military action on the part of the U.S., considering such a situation empty and undignified. Nevertheless, I think he could be persuaded to take the step, but I gather from your No. 710 of July 27th that this would be undesirable unless a declaration of war on Turkey had been previously made. His views regarding Turkey are somewhat different. He has no sympathy or liking for the Turks, but he believes that the presence of American missionaries and others has up to now prevented massacres and atrocities which would otherwise have occurred. Advisers whom he trusts (mostly connected with various education and religious organizations in Turkey) have convinced him that a terrible outburst of savagery would follow on a declaration of war. This reason, a curious one I admit, added to the fact that he cannot see any direct military advantage to be gained and only an indirect political one, make him definitely opposed to the idea of a declaration of war on Turkey by the U.S.[90]

Colonel House's diary entries also confirm that Wilson's main qualm against declaring war on the Ottoman Empire was his belief the Turks would massacre the entire Christian population. House, instead, focussed on the military situation, writing, 'I considered the best reason for not declaring war on Bulgaria was that there were no Bulgarian soldiers on the Western Front, and as long as they refused to help the Germans there, we might well refuse to declare war on them'.[91] Despite the advice of the PMRs and the Entente governments, President Wilson would not alter his opinion. This discussion, which began in spring 1918, encouraged the Entente powers to promote the idea of an American declaration of war on Turkey and Bulgaria throughout 1918. However, it also contributed to tension within the coalition, as it frustrated America's partners that the President would open and close the door on political discussions when it suited him.

Joint Note 37: The Middle Eastern Dimension

By July, Lloyd George was once again pushing for an offensive against the Ottoman Empire now that the Germans had been held off on the

---

[90] Wiseman to House, 27 August 1918, in Link, et al., *PWW*, 49: 365. As Wiseman told Arthur Cecil Murray, President Wilson 'has no sympathy whatever for Bulgaria or Turkey', 30 August 1918, in Link, et al., *PWW*, 48: 398–399.

[91] House Diary, 19 May 1918, in Link, et al., *PWW*, 48: 70.

Western Front and Foch had begun to successfully counter-attack. Maurice Hankey, the very capable War Cabinet Secretary, as well as the SWC secretary, was concerned that this issue was going to upset Anglo-French relations. For an offensive to be launched in Palestine by the autumn British troops would have to be withdrawn from France, something both Clemenceau and Foch adamantly opposed. The testy atmosphere created by these discussions was recorded by Hankey:

We are really on the verge of a serious conflict of British and French policy, which must come to a head by the autumn ... The question is whether to take your fight with Clemenceau & Foch now or later. Wilson thinks it fairer to take it now. The P. M. & Milner are inclined to get everything ready in Palestine, and then in the autumn to insist on withdrawing them. It is a matter of tactics.[92]

In contrast, when the issue of an offensive against the Ottoman Empire was once again discussed by the PMRs, as part of policy discussions for the autumn of 1918 and spring of 1919 (Joint Note 37), the PMRs had little difficulty in coming to an agreement. By July they had completely reversed the advice they had given in Joint Note 12 about what was possible. In contrast to their earlier suggestion of offensive action, they now agreed that 'the Allies, must ... concentrate their resources both in man power and material on the Western Front for the decisive struggle'.[93]

The initial drafts for Joint Note 37 drawn by all sections reflected this new opinion. On 17 July the Americans submitted their first draft to the other PMRs. It highlighted their concern that military conditions in Palestine, Mesopotamia, and Macedonia were favourable to the enemy. Earlier hopes that Turkey might be detached from Germany were thought to be dashed now that Russia and Romania had been defeated. An important consideration by the PMRs was that the forces used by the Central Powers in these theatres were ones that they could not use in the main theatre of war. Meanwhile these troops held down Allied troops, 'considerable parts which are suitable for use on the Western Front, at least for replacement purposes ...'[94] While in Palestine the PMRs estimated that Allied and enemy forces were relatively equal, in Mesopotamia they estimated the Allies were using 119,000 more combatants than the Turks.[95]

---

[92] Hankey diary, 3 July 1918, HNKY/1/4.
[93] 'Joint Note No. 37', 13 September 1918, CAB 25/122/SWC320.
[94] 'Allied Operations in the Autumn and Winter of 1918 and Summer of 1919', 17 July 1918, CAB 25/84.
[95] 'A' Branch, 'How Are We to Win the War in 1919?' 21 July 1918, CAB 25/84/SWC280

For Bliss, the other major concern was the amount of sea-going tonnage used to maintain the Allied troops in the Middle East theatre. British 'M' Branch expressed the same opinion, commenting, 'This appears to be indisputable. Even a comparatively small operation in the East might have a very considerable effect on the rate of arrival of Americans in France'.[96] Furthermore, 'M' Branch emphasised, 'We simply cannot afford at this stage, if we wish to win the war, to take any unnecessary risk with large quantities of shipping, much less go gambling with it in Oriental adventures'.[97] In terms of objectives to be achieved in Palestine, Bliss also had doubts. He did not think that an Allied advance was likely to capture Damascus prior to the spring of 1919. Even if it did, 'the capture of that city would appear to be an accomplishment of comparatively no military value ...'[98] The Americans were not willing to support a venture in this theatre, especially after they balanced the resources required – more ocean tonnage, rolling stock, personnel, plus 150 miles of railway construction – against potential strategic gains that were limited, especially as these resources were needed in France (see Chapter 6 on resources).

'E' Branch's examination of the situation in Palestine, written from the perspective of the enemy, asserted that, while it was still crucial for the Germans to keep the Ottoman Empire in the war, due to limited resources, the former could only give minimal support to the latter. The British Section determined that the Central Powers did not have enough forces in Palestine to launch an offensive, nor would an offensive form part of their essential policy. For the latter reason, the Germans would only reinforce the Turks enough to keep them fighting and opposing the British forces. Like the Americans, 'E' Branch questioned the strategic goals in Palestine, reporting that although the loss of Aleppo or Damascus would have a moral effect on the Turks, neither was of great strategic value to the Central Powers.[99]

As Sackville-West composed a draft for Joint Note 37, he received a number of papers from his section and was also in close communication with Henry Wilson. The CIGS, too was in the process of writing his own paper for the War Cabinet which he completed on 25 July 1918. While

---

[96] Macready, 'M' Branch, 'Comments on Enclosure 10.B', 23 July 1918, CAB 25/84, minute sheet, 2.

[97] Beadon, 'M' Branch, 25 July 1918, CAB 25/84, minute sheet 3.

[98] 'Allied Operations in the Autumn and Winter of 1918 and Summer of 1919', CAB 25/84.

[99] 'E' Branch, 'Situation in Palestine, Mesopotamia and the East', 24 July 1918, CAB 25/122/SWC287; 'E' Branch, 'Probably Enemy Action in the Balkans and Turkey in the Autumn of 1918', 22 July 1918, CAB 25/78.

the PMRs considered the needs of the coalition as a whole, Wilson's paper assessed British military policy for 1918–1919, 'so that the policy of our war aims and the strategy of our war effort may harmonise in securing for the British Empire the best possible position at the dawn of the peace'.[100] He no longer advocated action in the East. Instead, Wilson reasserted that it was imperative to secure the Western Front (see Chapter 5 on the France-Belgian theatre). It was within this framework that he considered what could be done in the secondary theatres while the Allies built up forces on the Western Front for a decisive attack by 1 July 1919. He based his assessment on intelligence indicating that the Germans and Ottomans were no longer quarrelling over Baku. Previously the Germans had been trying to keep the Turkish forces away from Baku by sending them towards Palestine. Wilson believed that the Germans had secured southern Russia along with control of the Black Sea, and thus their path to the East lay through Mesopotamia, Persia, and the Trans-Caspian, as opposed to via Egypt and Syria. In this scenario Palestine lost much of its importance although it still had a central role in protecting Egypt (and the essential shipping route through the Suez Canal). In fact the Germans had made significant gains with Russia's demise. They had occupied parts of modern-day Ukraine, entered the Crimea, and offered military support to a number of nations declaring independence from the Bolsheviks. Coupled with Ottoman advances in Armenia, the situation in this region was bound to cause the Allies to reassess.

Sackville-West's strategic assessment was in line with both the American Section and Henry Wilson's memo. The defeat of Romania and Russia had given the Ottoman Empire new lines of communications from the Black Sea to Caucasia, which meant that Aleppo was no longer an objective for the Allied forces in Egypt and Mesopotamia. In terms of capturing cities for propaganda and morale value, the British had already taken Jerusalem. As the British Section wrote:

The centre of gravity of the Middle East is now between BAGHDAD and the CASPIAN SEA and the importance of operations in PALESTINE has decreased. Any considerable advance by the British Army in PALESTINE would be impossible without increases of troops and material, neither of which are available. Our activities in this theatre should be confined to such local enterprises as are necessary to ensure our present position and as can be undertaken without addition to the resources already at General Allenby's disposal.[101]

---

[100] Henry Wilson, 'British Policy 1918–1919', 25 July 1918, CAB 27/8/257.
[101] 'Proposed Joint Note', 31 July 1918, CAB 25/84; Bliss/324.

Its description was a condensed version of Wilson's paper. As Sackville-West explained to Wilson, 'I purposefully omit details nor do I lay too much stress on Eastern policy because that is a British affair and is being dealt with by you. The only thing we want is a free hand for the future'.[102] Wilson did not think that the Germans would send a large number of troops to the Middle East; rather he believed they would continue their policy of using a small number of Germans 'to stiffen Turkish units and stimulate their offensive activities'.[103] The War Office had inquired as to what Allenby proposed to do in this theatre if given or loaned an additional three or four divisions in the autumn (to be returned to the Western Front in the spring). Allenby had replied that in stages he could work his way as far as the Tiberias-Acre line. Wilson did not think that this area offered a strategic advantage to the British, and would be costly in material. He was also concerned that in the spring of 1919 the Germans could attack the EEF on this line with the effect that three or four divisions could not be withdrawn for use on the Western Front for the decisive attack planned there. Like the British PMR, he recommended a policy of active defence. However he also suggested a limited campaign to secure the Hejaz railway in the area of Amman, an objective that would improve communications with the Arab forces.

While remaining on active defence in Palestine, the main effort in the Middle East should focus on Mesopotamia and Persia. The CIGS detailed that if the Germans had superior communications in Northern Persia and if they controlled the Caspian Sea, then they might succeed in controlling the Trans-Caspian railway to the border of Afghanistan, thus threatening India. The British Section wrote that British forces should aim to control the Caspian Sea and prevent the Germans from acting in that area. It wanted to cut German supplies from Turkestan and to support anti-German forces in southern Russia. The objective was to hinder German ambitions in the East. These efforts would complement those being made by the Allies in Siberia and the Arctic ports. The goal was to 'constitute a serious threat to German ambitions in the East and by aiding such healthy elements as still exist in Russia to crystallise into efficient fighting bodies we shall absorb large German forces and relieve the pressure on the Western Front'.[104] This objective was in line with a suggestion made by the American Section in mid-July that the coalition investigate how to use the forces in Mesopotamia to supplement those in Siberia and Archangel. Henry Wilson also suggested that a division from

---

[102] Sackville-West to Henry Wilson, 31 July 1918, HHW/2/12D/2/7.
[103] Henry Wilson, 'British Policy 1918–1919', 25 July 1918, CAB 27/8/273; CAB 25/85.
[104] 'Proposed Joint Note', 31 July 1918, CAB 25/84; Bliss/324.

Mesopotamia could be used in Siberia if it encouraged a larger intervention in Russia by the Americans and the Japanese.

While the British Section's staff included ardent advocates of action in the East like Leo Amery, the policy it recommended corresponded with the opinions of the CIGS rather than with Milner, Smuts, and Lloyd George. And while Lloyd George may have wanted to leave his partners to do the majority of the fighting in France while the British army made efforts elsewhere, the reality remained that the British would have to fight with the coalition on the Western Front if they wanted to be given a serious role during the peace talks.[105] Whereas in early 1918 Lloyd George had been able to utilise the advice of the SWC, whose British member at that time was Henry Wilson, against the CIGS (who, at that time, was Robertson), he now found that Henry Wilson's military opinions were 'simply "Wully *redivivus*"'.[106] As Hankey colourfully recorded, 'It is Irish instead of Scotch, but it is still whisky'.[107] Amery attempted to raise awareness of the Eastern strategy by writing a response to Wilson's paper.[108] He argued that efforts could still be made in the East and suggested linking the armies in Palestine and Mesopotamia at the Mosul-Aleppo line. However, it was Wilson's line of reasoning, as well as that of the other PMRs, that the British Section followed. As Henry Wilson told Sackville-West, 'Yes I quite agree to the sketch note on "the Allied policy ..." It travels in the same order of ideas as our Note here, a copy of which you have had'.[109] Sackville-West did not alter the content of his joint notes despite the fact that it was not in line with the Prime Minister, who was also the British political representative on the SWC. As the war ended before Joint Note 37 could be discussed, one can only speculate how Lloyd George could have advanced an Eastern strategy against such rival opinions.

After receiving the British draft, the Americans reinforced and enhanced their earlier position on action in the Middle East. However, they were also willing to agree to British action in Mesopotamia if it did not require shipping resources. In a letter to Sackville-West, Bliss agreed to follow the British Section's policy in Palestine and Mesopotamia, 'with the understanding that the proposed extension of operations in the Mesopotamian theatre to include the Caspian Sea and the Caucasus, shall not involve the allotment to that theatre of any ocean tonnage

---

[105] French, *Lloyd George Coalition*, 257.   [106] Hankey, *The Supreme Command*, 830.
[107] Ibid.
[108] Amery to Hankey, 1 August 1918, Churchill College Archive Centre, Cambridge, Leopold Amery Papers [hereon AMEL] AMEL/2/1/1. For a copy of Wilson's paper with Amery's notes in the margins, see AMEL/1/3/54.
[109] Henry Wilson to Sackville-West, 5 August 1918, HW/2/12D/4/ 16.

necessary to produce the maximum effort on the Western Front, as to which the Military Representatives have substantially agreed'.[110] Behind the scenes, Bliss had written to March to explain how his approach to strategy was different from his colleagues as 'naturally enough, the Representatives of our Allies cast more side glances at the situation in the Balkans, in Palestine, Mesopotamia, and elsewhere than I do'.[111] With this compromise the Americans reasserted that the Western Front was the main theatre and should continue to be the focus of resources.

The French Section asserted a similar opinion to their British and American colleagues calling for an active attitude in the 'théâtres extérieurs'. Their assessment had changed little from March: they still expressed deep concern about German ambitions in the East, they believed the Ottoman armies were weak and poorly supplied in comparison to the British troops, and they blamed poor communications for the weakness of the British position to go on the offensive. They also still correctly assessed that Ottoman morale was low, their supplies were limited, and the Allies maintained a two-to-one advantage over the Turkish forces.[112] However now, the French, like their colleagues, also highlighted that strategic points, including Aleppo, had lost much of their importance since the Ottomans now had access to the Black Sea and no longer had to rely on the Baghdad railway. Instead of setting distant objectives, the French Section recommended that limited operations be undertaken which would attract enemy forces. In the autumn, British forces could progress toward Tul Kéram (where the Turkish 8th Army was located), the Naplouse line (modern day Nablus, 49 kilometres north of Jerusalem), as well as attack Es Salt (in the Jordan Valley) and Amman. For the winter of 1918, they believed troops should be withdrawn from this theatre and sent elsewhere, with the EEF progressing to the Haifa-Tiberias-Dera line in the spring of 1919.[113] While the French may have wanted more manpower in other theatres (especially France) it was costly to move them there.

After the PMRs met with Foch on 26 August, the content of the British, French, and American notes did not change (the Italians had yet to submit anything). Although the PMR records do not recount

[110] American Section, 'Allied Plans of Campaign for the Autumn 1918 and for the Year 1919', 1 August 1918, CAB 25/84; Bliss to Sackville-West, 17 August 1918, CAB 25/78; Bliss/324.

[111] Bliss to Baker, 9 August 1918, LOC, Woodrow Wilson Papers [hereon Wilson] Wilson/98.

[112] Bruce, The Last Crusade, 208.

[113] French Section, 'Projet de Plan d'Operations pour les Armées Alliés pendant l'automne 1918 et l'Ete 1919', 6 August 1918, CAB 25/84.

Foch's comments on the Middle East, they do illustrate those of the American commander. In early September Pershing considered what could be done in Mesopotamia as part of a wider strategy. As Lansing told President Wilson:

He [Pershing] believes that the successful advance of the Allies on the western front will continue and while he does not consider that the Germans are yet beaten, he is satisfied that the morale of their troops is bad. Under these circumstances, he thinks that united action should be taken to bring about the end of the (*) if possible before next year. He believes that if the President were now to urge the Allies to attack simultaneously on the Italian front at Saloniki [sic] and in Mesopotamia if possible, if he were to address words of encouragement to that section of the Russian public which is pro-Ally; if an intimation from the same source were conveyed to Austria-Hungary, Bulgaria and Turkey that the time has come for them to yield and if pressure were brought to bear upon the neutrals, especially Spain, to join the Allies, the defeat of Germany which he now considers certain would be hastened. General Pershing informs me that according to his Intelligence Service, the Germans are already moving supplies to the right bank of the Rhine and that an attack by the American army is now imminent.[114]

On the same day Pershing expressed these opinions he had a meeting with Foch who informed him that the Germans were in complete disorder and must be attacked to take advantage of the situation.[115] President Wilson was surprised that Pershing would offer political advice of this kind. And yet despite the urging of his commander-in-chief, Wilson still would not take political action against Bulgaria or the Ottoman Empire, explaining to the American Chief-of-Staff, 'I am clear that it would be out of the question for me to urge, without the (at least intimated) concurrence of the Supreme Military Council, such action in all military theatres of the war; and it is equally clear to me that events, not any suggestions from us, will determine the action of Bulgaria and Turkey'. He continued by noting, 'You know the advances that have been made to us from Bulgaria and Turkey and how imprudent and unwise it would be for us to use the only channels that are open'.[116] Wilson preferred to leave the issue unresolved, hoping that the American Secretary of War would reinforce the President's stance when he met with the European partners in person.

As the meeting to discuss Joint Note 37 drew nearer, the Italians finally submitted their draft to the other PMRs on 3 September. They added

---

[114] Lansing to Wilson, 30 August 1918, in Link, et al., *PWW*, 49: 404.
[115] 'Conversation between Foch and Pershing', 30 August 1918, National Archives, DC., Record Group [hereon RG], RG/120/268/3143/986-A.
[116] Wilson to March, 2 September 1918, in Link, et al., *PWW*, 49: 416.

nothing new to the discussion on the Middle East, writing that, in the theatres outside France operations should be defensive or, at most, local so that all efforts could focus on the main theatres, by which they meant the Franco-Belgian and Italian ones. They argued that to take offensive action in the Middle East would result in the use of additional resources that could be better utilised in the main theatres of war. The next day the Americans went further in focussing on the Western Front:

That operations in all other theatres of war should be regarded as subordinate to those of the Front in France; should be confined to only such as will harmonize with, and contribute to the accomplishment of, the plans for that Front; and that there must be no diversions to those theatres of men, materials, and ocean tonnage that will weaken the effort on the Front in France except as may be approved by the Allied Commander-in-Chief on that Front.[117]

Otherwise the Americans held to their earlier opinions.

At the PMRs' 45th meeting, where they discussed Joint Note 37, it was clear the focus of Allied efforts would be the Western Front.[118] The substance of the various PMRs' drafts on the Middle East was very similar. Although the PMRs considered that the British were superior to Ottoman forces in Palestine and in a position to launch an offensive, communication difficulties that would arise from any significant advance, as well as the low strategic value of objectives in the area, meant that the PMRs did not recommend a large scale offensive. Instead they argued for a limited one that would both hold and attract Ottoman forces. Over the winter troops could also be withdrawn from this theatre 'in order to reinforce the Armies on other fronts'.[119] Henry Wilson too had suggested withdrawing troops from Palestine over the winter months. In Mesopotamia, given that British forces were limited, they would focus on securing a foothold on the Caspian Sea and securing the Baghdad-Hamadan-Enzeli road. The objective was to draw German forces away from the Western Front. The final note did, however, have one major difference – it included a clause that said the Commander-in-Chief was free to advance to Mosul if he could do so and if it did not detract from the efforts on the Caspian Sea.

Armistice

The tension between the British and French PMRs that had been lying under the surface while they constructed a policy in the Middle East

[117] Bliss to the Military Representatives, 4 September 1918, Bliss/324.
[118] 'Minutes of the 45th Meeting of the Military Representatives', CAB 25/122/SWC316.
[119] 'Joint Note No. 37', 13 September 1918, CAB 25/122/SWC320; Bliss/324/SWC316/1.

during 1918 and 1919 finally boiled over when the Central Powers began
to collapse. The signing of the armistice with Bulgaria on 30 September,
in which the French took a leading role, had left the British bitter at being
excluded from these discussions. They refused to allow the French to
take the lead in defeating the Ottomans. They also attempted to leave the
Americans and the Italians on the periphery of decision-making.
Although the Italians attended meetings with the French and British,
there was tension within the Entente: 'Orlando, who had seemed serene
and smiling at the meeting with Clemenceau was really seething with
indignation against the old bag and poured it out in this conversation at
the Embassy in a veritable torrent. Ll.G's observation was that these
Latins are very odd people'.[120] Meanwhile Frazier expressed to Hankey
his concern that the Americans were being excluded from discussions.
Later that evening Hankey explained the situation in his diary:

We could hardly tell him point blank that we were holding Conferences, instead
of the S.W.C., because President Wilson would not declare war on Turkey &
Bulgaria, in spite of our advice, and that we do not feel obliged to consult him
either as to our military operations or peace discussions in regard to these regions.
But we had to give Frazier a hint of it. However, we did not comment to him on
the unreasonableness of President Wilson's attitude in refusing on the one hand
to call himself an 'ally' or to speak of us any more than 'associated nations' in
sending no accredited representative to speak with any authority on his behalf and
yet on the other hand expecting to be told everything, and consulted on
everything.[121]

Given the content of this entry, it is not surprising that it was excluded
from Hankey's published memoir. The British had continued to encourage the US government to declare war on the Ottoman Empire throughout 1918.[122] As late as 18 September Balfour asked the American
government to reconsider declaring war on Bulgaria prior to an Allied
offensive, as he thought it would weaken the morale of the Bulgarians.
However before the question was discussed by the Americans the offensive occurred and the Bulgarians requested an armistice.[123] This situation ensured that the Entente would exclude the Americans from
discussions where possible. The European partners were now able to
give vent to the frustration they felt with President Wilson's habit of
stopping and starting political discussions at his own discretion.

---

[120] Hankey diary, 5 October 1918, HNKY/1/6.   [121] Ibid.
[122] Drum to Wise, 27 July 1918 and 24 August 1918, in Link, et al., *PWW*, 49: 365n1.
[123] House diary, 18 September 1918, in Seymour, *The Intimate Papers of Colonel House*,
     4: 57.

After the signing of the Bulgarian armistice, the British and French had quarrelled over the form military action should take against the Turkish forces. Tensions resumed when the Ottomans called for armistice negotiations, this time over who would command the fleet sent up the Dardanelles. Even once a British admiral was chosen, the British continued to exclude the French admiral from being involved, causing a 'fearful row'.[124] When the French objected, Lloyd George reminded Clemenceau that Franchet d'Espèrey had not consulted the British when he concluded negotiations with the Bulgarians, and in this way Hankey explained that Lloyd George 'gave more than he got'.[125] The reality was that the British had the majority of forces in the Middle East, and once Allied unity was no longer considered necessary to defeat the Central Powers, they could undertake unilateral action without concerning themselves with repercussions from their partners. From their perspective these theatres were a British affair, and they would only coordinate as far as they were forced to by their partners. Furthermore, it was easier for the British, French, American and Italian governments to come to an understanding when peace was in the distant future and beating the enemy was by far the foremost issue. With the looming prospect of the end of hostilities, national needs began to be reasserted.

Discussions for a policy in the Middle East for 1918 and 1919 illustrate that it was possible for the coalition to create a unified policy when their interests coincided. Furthermore, the SWC had created an expectation that, despite national dominance in a particular theatre, each theatre would be considered in relation to its contribution to a victory against the Germany army. It was no longer acceptable for the British to work in isolation on policy in Palestine and Mesopotamia. Try as they might, the British could never fully rid themselves of this expectation – even if they only went as far as to communicate their intentions to their partners. In order to place the greatest military pressure on the Germans in 1919, all theatres had to be coordinated.

The PMRs' responsibility was to consider strategy from the Allied perspective. And while Lloyd George attempted to push his Eastern agenda onto the SWC, by September the PMRs agreed that to win the war in 1919, the greatest contribution the IEF and EEF could make was to draw and hold forces in these areas. With this decision they reasserted that the secondary theatres were subordinate to the Western Front. Lloyd George lost his ability to use the PMRs as an alternate military

---

[124] 29 October 1918, HNKY/1/6. Not quoted in published diary.   [125] Ibid.

opinion to those of the commanders-in-chief and chiefs-of-staff. By working with Foch, Pershing, and Henry Wilson, the PMRs aligned themselves with the most influential military opinions in their home nations. This allowed them to create a policy for 1919 that evolved, albeit slowly, in relation to the immediate military situation.

4 Maintaining the Italians
The Role of the Italian Theatre in Creating an Allied Strategy

In autumn 1917, the Germans, concerned that Austria-Hungary might be knocked out of the war, reinforced the Austro-Hungarian army with their own elite units and launched an offensive against the Italian army near Caporetto, driving it back all the way to the Piave river, within 20 miles of Venice. Earlier in the year, the Allies, in particular Lloyd George, had considered reinforcing the Italian army with heavy artillery, but they had instead decided to focus their efforts on the Franco-Belgian theatre. With general plans already in place to move troops from France to Italy, the Allies were able to rush four British and six French divisions to help stabilise the Italian Front when the Central Powers began their attack in October. Slowly, the Italians managed to regroup what remained of their forces and munition, having lost more than 305,000 men through injury, death, capture, and desertion, as well as approximately 3,000 machine guns, 3,152 artillery pieces, and 1,732 trench mortars.[1] Severely crippled, the Italian government and army underwent a reformation, starting with the newly appointed Prime Minister Vittorio Orlando who, in turn, under the pressure of the Allied leaders, sent General Cadorna, the former army commander, to Versailles and replaced him with General Armando Diaz. The Battle of Caporetto, as it came to be known, had a devastating psychological effect on the Italians. For the remainder of the war they were convinced that the Germans, with their superior railway lines, would quickly reinforce the Austro-Hungarian army and launch an offensive that would knock them out of the war. If the Allies lost Italy, not only would it mean that the 44 Austro-Hungarian divisions the Italians pinned down would be free to move to other theatres, but it also meant that the backdoor to France would be open.[2] The need to keep Italy an active

---

[1] John Gooch, *The Italian Army in the First World War* (Cambridge, 2014) 245–246.
[2] Mark Thompson, *The White War: Life and Death on the Italian Front, 1915–1919* (London), 338. That is what the Allies thought they held down. Thompson (ed. Horne) said that they actually held down between 50–60 Austrian divisions that otherwise would have been sent to the Western Front.

belligerent was never questioned in London, Paris, or Washington – bluntly put, with Russia out of the war the Entente could not afford to lose another ally, especially one so close to France.

This chapter assesses the role of the Italian theatre in the wider Allied strategy that the Supreme War Council developed throughout 1918 for autumn 1918 and 1919. The PMRs' discussions about strategy revolved around three main issues. The first was the ability to improve railways between France and Italy, as the Allies came to recognise the importance of being able to rush troops between these theatres during an emergency. At the centre of these discussions was a sub-committee of the PMRs, the Inter-Allied Transport Council, one of whose responsibilities was to assess and make recommendations for the improvement of railway lines between France and Italy. The IATC's studies highlighted the Allied perception of the German menace, which had the advantage of interior lines of communication. Already concerned that the Central Powers could transport troops from the east to any other theatre, giving them the numerical advantage they required for a successful offensive, the Central Powers' superior lines of communication meant that the Italians were not simply facing the Austro-Hungarians. Indeed, as the Germans could move forces at any time to the Italian theatre, the formidable foe the Allies faced included elite German units, like the ones that had successfully crashed through their lines at Caporetto.

The second issue, raised by discussions of strategy, was whether the Italians required material assistance from their partners. Holding the view that the Central Powers had superior forces in Italy, the Italians argued that the Allies should send resources to the Italian theatre if they wanted to keep Italy in the war. Defeat at Caporetto acted as a catalyst for the formation of an Allied body that could act as a forum for Allied coordination for all theatres. When the idea of the SWC was raised by Lloyd George at Rapallo, where the Allies had gathered to discuss how best to deal with the Caporetto disaster, the Italians, desperate for military assistance, were agreeable to such an idea.[3] For the remainder of the war the Italians used this body to advocate greater military assistance on their front, and while the British, French, and American representatives were not willing to sacrifice gains in France for ones in Italy, they listened to the grievances and concerns of their junior partner, while conducting studies of their own. In the end, the Italians did not gain all the resources they wanted from their partners, but, through the

[3] Hankey diary, 7 November 1917, HNKY/1/4.

SWC, they were successful in obtaining what they needed to win a military victory over the Austro-Hungarians.

The third issue which affected discussions for an Allied strategy was what role Foch had in determining action in this theatre. These discussions were rendered more difficult when Rome refused to give Foch authority over the Italian theatre in the spring of 1918, complicating the responsibilities of the PMRs in relation to Italy and serving to undermine the American-Italian relationship, as the Italians ceaselessly pressed the Americans for manpower. Supporting the Allied Generalissimo, the Americans refused to encroach on Foch's responsibilities, which in turn reinforced the predominance of the Franco-Belgian Front as the main theatre of war. However, these discussions also elevated the importance of the Italian theatre, as the Allies developed a notion of the 'Western Front' that incorporated both the Franco-Belgian and Italian theatres.

When, in December 1917, the Allies met to discuss how to coordinate their efforts in the future the French and Italian representatives presented opposing ideas as to what should occur in the Italian theatre. The British and French divisions had arrived in Italy and had already begun to improve the defensive positions of the Italian army and reinforced the need for Diaz to do the same.[4] While Clemenceau recommended a joint Allied offensive on the Italian Front, neither the Italian political nor military leadership were enthused about this prospect. In contrast, they were fixated on the manifest weaknesses of the Italian army and requested greater assistance from their Allies. Specifically, the Italians wanted the British to send an additional division (the 6th) to Italy to reinforce the Italian Front; however, Lloyd George was concerned about any undermining of the Allies' numerical supremacy on the Franco-Belgian Front in the face of a possible German offensive in the spring of 1918. Given the varying opinions on the Italian theatre, the SWC instructed the PMRs to study the possibility of both defensive and offensive action in Italy. The British War Cabinet had also asked Henry Wilson, then the British PMR, to confer with his colleagues and report on whether the Italians required more artillery or more men.[5]

Meanwhile, the Austro-Hungarians continued to attack on the Monte Grappa and Asiago sectors (see Map 0.3). While the British and French commanders in Italy, Plumer and Fayolle, remained confident that they

---

[4] For more on the specific improvements undertaken, see George Cassar, *The Forgotten Front: The British Campaign in Italy, 1917–18* (London and Rio Grande, 1998), 112–116.

[5] 'Minutes of the Meeting of the Permanent Military Representatives', 19 December 1917, CAB 25/120/SWC22.

could hold the line, Diaz was not.[6] Cadorna, now acting as the Italian PMR, asked that the British send the 6th Division immediately; however, Wilson and Weygand said that nothing had changed materially for the British to need to do so. Cadorna shifted approaches and instead asked for artillery. But given the precarious situation on the Franco-Belgian Front, due to the Russian revolution and the likelihood of German forces being transferred to France in the spring, the French and British PMRs were not willing to send such resources to Italy. Pointing out that the Italians had already received substantial artillery reinforcement, they would only go as far as to refer the Italian PMR's request to their respective general staffs.[7] On Christmas day, a summary of this discussion was written as Joint Note 6 and referred to the SWC. The following day the PMRs met once again to discuss 'The Italian Problem' as they entitled it. This time the French and British PMRs argued that the situation in Italy was less worrying, as the Italians had been successful in holding along the Piave-Grappa-Altiplani line and the PMRs believed they could continue to do so. While they would not send further reinforcements, the PMRs did recommend that the Italians build-up their lines of defence, as well expedite the retraining and reorganisation of their army. The commanders in Italy also made similar recommendations to the British War Office.[8] Furthermore, the PMRs suggested that, once this work was completed, the Anglo-French troops should be returned to the Franco-Belgian theatre in order to meet the German offensive, which the Allies predicted was coming in spring 1918.[9]

Although the PMRs determined that further resources should not be sent to Italy, they did continue to consider other ways to improve the situation there. From their studies in December 1917, the British Section deemed that Italy was safe if the earlier recommendations of reorganisation and training were followed. In addition they pressed for the improvement of rail transport both between France and Italy and within Italy itself, 'in order to secure strategic unity of action over the two theatres'.[10] They had additional concerns about how to combat war weariness in Italy, as they feared a complete collapse of Italian forces or another disaster like Caporetto unless morale was improved. To prevent

[6] Cassar, *Forgotten Front*, 122–123.
[7] 'Minutes of the Meeting of the PMRs', 19 December 1917.
[8] Cassar, *Forgotten Front*, 117. While notes by neither of the commanders were found in the papers of the PMRs, they likely received this information through unofficial channels. For example, Henry Wilson was in close contact with Lord Cavan (who commanded the 14th Corps in Italy and who succeeded Plumer in March 1918).
[9] 'Joint Note 6: The Italian Problem', 25 December 1917, CAB 25/120.
[10] 'Joint Note 12', 21 January 1918, CAB 25/120/SWC57.

such an occurrence, they suggested that Italy's partners stabilise the country economically by assisting with coal, wheat, and other resources which would 'prevent the creation of economic conditions which would favour the operations of pacifist agitators . . .'[11] They even went as far as to consider lending funds to the Italians so that they could increase pay for the troops and the allowances for their dependents.[12] While the latter ideas were cut from the draft joint note they sent to the other PMRs, they do illustrate the extent to which the British Section was concerned about Italian morale.

Predicting an Attack by the Central Powers –
In France or Italy?

Coinciding with the PMRs' studies on Italy were others considering the security of the Franco-Belgian Front. In February, the British and French representatives argued that, given an impending German attack in France and a lack of Allied manpower, the British and French should withdraw any troops they could from Italy to France (ideally three British and three French divisions from the five and six respective divisions they had in Italy).[13] The complicating factor was that Italian and British intelligence did not concur, as the Italian Minister of Foreign Affairs, Sidney Sonnino, said that the Germans were concentrating forces on the Italian Front whereas British intelligence said they were concentrating on the Franco-Belgian one.[14] The Italians were concerned, that with Romania's recent defeat, the Austro-Hungarians would have an additional 250 battalions to employ in the Italian theatre. They argued that, if the Anglo-French troops were withdrawn, Italy would surely be knocked out of the war.[15]

At the third SWC meeting, held during late January and early February, Henry Wilson presented a solution to the Allied difficulty in predicting the movement of German forces. It was an idea which both he and Foch had been developing and which the SWC accepted at the end of January. As part of discussions of strategy for 1918, he recommended the creation of the General Reserve, as it was called, which could be manoeuvred between the Franco-Belgian and Italian Fronts. It would be controlled by a parent body known as the Executive War Board (EWB),

[11] 'Memo by General Wilson: 1918 Campaign', 19 January 1918, CAB 25/120SWC52.
[12] Ibid.
[13] 'A' Branch, 'The Security of the Allied Line in France', 20 January 1918, CAB 25/120.
[14] 'Procès-Verbal of the Third Meeting of the Third Session of the SWC', 1 February 1918, CAB 25/121/IC-41.
[15] Cassar, *Forgotten Front*, 126–127.

whose members would comprise the PMRs with Foch acting as its president. In theory it offered the advantage of flexibility in the defence as it could be used to fill gaps in the line when and where needed.[16] The creation of the General Reserve resulted in the Allies redefining what they meant by 'Western Front'.[17] As the forces were ideally to be made up of 14 French, 10 British, and 7 Italian divisions, it would not be confined to the Franco-Belgian theatre.[18] The relative proximity of the Italian and Franco-Belgian theatres meant that troops could be transferred quickly between the two by all belligerents. As a consequence, the SWC now defined the 'Western Front' as the area from the North Sea to the Adriatic.[19]

At the March SWC meeting, Lloyd George also raised the issue of the Germans attacking Italy. The SWC members had expected that by the time they met for this meeting, the EWB would have completed a study on the possible employment of Italian troops on the Western Front. The British Prime Minister asked the commanders-in-chief in France what arrangements had been made in the case of such a decision. He also wanted both Versailles and the commanders to conduct further studies on how best to support Italy.[20] Specifically the PMRs were asked to examine, with the assistance of the IATC, the problem of rushing troops across the Alps in case of an Austro-Hungarian offensive. The complicating factor was that the role of the PMRs in relation to Italy was confused, first by the existence of the EWB and then by the appointment of Foch as generalissimo at the end of March. The dual role of the PMRs as both military advisers to the SWC and members of the EWB made it difficult for them to determine which forum was appropriate for certain issues. In particular, on the matter of moving forces between Italy and France, the PMRs preferred the EWB forum, as otherwise they would be excluding Foch from the discussions.

As the Allies nervously awaited an imminent German attack in the spring of 1918, the PMR sections continued to assess the Italian theatre's overall role in both enemy and Allied strategy. In March, 'E' Branch of

---

[16] Greenhalgh, *Foch*, 281.

[17] For more on the General Reserve, EWB, and Foch's evolution to generalissimo, see ibid., 281–300. Trask, *Supreme War Council*, 59–69.

[18] Trask, *Supreme War Council*, 59.

[19] Filippo Cappellano, 'Les Relations Entre Les Armées Italienne Et Française Pendant La Grande Guerre', *Revue historique des armées*, 250 (2008). Filippo Cappellano argues that the close relationship established between French and Italian high command illustrates the extent to which the French and Italian theatres were no longer considered independent from one another.

[20] 'Procès-verbal of the Third Meeting of the Fourth Session of the SWC', 15 March 1918, CAB 25/121/IC-50.

the British Section predicted that the Austro-Hungarians would launch an attack to apply pressure on the Italian Front, thus preventing the Allies from sending any divisions to France. If the Austro-Hungarians continued to hold down these forces in Italy, the Germans would have greater numerical superiority in France when they subsequently attacked. 'E' Branch estimated that the Allies had 60 (including 9 British and French) divisions in Italy facing 48 ½ (including 3 German) divisions of the Central Powers. Weather permitting, they predicted an attack would occur around 15 April.[21] Another of the British branches, 'A' Branch, used the same numerical estimates for the Allies and Central Powers. Broken down they represented a comparative strength for the latter of 458,380 rifles, 3,158 field guns, and 1,603 heavy guns to the former's 652,000 rifles, 3,658 field guns, and 2,420 heavy guns. While these figures illustrated that the Allies were numerically superior to the Central Powers in Italy, 'A' Branch was concerned that by mid-April the Austro-Hungarians would have an additional ten fresh divisions from Russia and Romania, as well as more artillery.[22] The French Section's estimate of the Central Powers was higher at 54 ½ divisions.[23] On 20 March, one day before the German spring offensives commenced, 'A' Branch expanded its study, arguing that the Central Powers were likely to attack Italy because of the potential for larger gains. Indeed, 'If it succeeded it would probably knock Italy out of the war and would in the opinion of the Germans probably incline the hearts of the Allies to peace'.[24] However, if the Allies continued to fight, 'a conquered Italy would provide a new avenue of attack against France without entering Switzerland and would deprive us of the use of the land route to Taranto [an important naval base for Mediterranean operations]'.[25] While the PMRs were aware German forces were likely to attack in France, they underestimated the scale of the attack while at the same time misreading the situation in Italy.

Notions of 'race' also affected 'A' Branch's assessment of action in Italy. They feared the collapse of Italian morale, as they believed the

[21] 'E' Branch, 'An Austro-German Offensive in Italy', 2 March 1918, CAB 25/120/SWC100.

[22] 'A' Branch, 'Proposed Plan to Meet Certain Possible Offensive Operations by the Central Powers against Italy', 3 March 1918, CAB 25/120/SWC116. The enemy figures came from the War Office, wrote 'E' Branch, 23 March 1918, CAB 25/120/SWC144.

[23] Analyses télégrammes 3ieme Bureau A to French Section, 11 March 1918, SHD-DAT, Conseil Supérieur de la Guerre, 4N 27.

[24] 'A' Branch, 'Proposed Plan to Meet Certain Possible Offensive Operations by the Central Powers against Italy'.

[25] Ibid.

'Italian race' was highly susceptible to propaganda and thus thought that, while the Central Powers might fail to achieve a decision through an attack, they might do so through the deft use of propaganda. However, they also assessed the Austro-Hungarians troops as second class. The solution, as they proposed it, was for the Allies to give the Italian army 'morale reinforcement rather than any further supply of material force', that being, to 'stamp out' enemy propaganda and to maintain four French and four British divisions in Italy to help maintain Italian morale.[26] In exchange for each British and French division in Italy 'A' Branch recommended that two Italian divisions be sent to France, in order to prevent Allied strength from being reduced. They also argued that, while crucial rail-lines were being improved, all forces in Italy should remain on the defensive.

At their meeting on 18 May 1918, it was clear the PMRs were uncertain as to whether or not it was their responsibility to consider the transfer of Italian troops to France. Although the French PMR prepared a draft joint note that supported the idea of keeping in Italy all remaining French troops, the PMRs agreed that this question should be decided between Foch and the Italian Commander-in-Chief.[27] When Foch became Allied Generalissimo in March, the EWB was abolished and he absorbed its responsibilities. Despite these changes, some individuals, such as the CIGS, argued that the PMRs duties should include troop movement between France and Italy.[28] One of the first and only acts of the EWB was to recommend the transfer of two Italian, two French, and one British divisions from Italy to France to meet the onslaught of the German spring offensives. Their withdrawal, which began immediately and was completed in mid-April, left three British and three French divisions in Italy.[29]

Foch's appointment also created tension between the Italians and their partners. General Bliss explained to his government:

Doullens, of March 26 last ... purported to confer on General Foch the powers of an Allied Commander-in-Chief over all the troops operating in France. As a matter of fact, it gave him only power to consult with the different national Commanders-in-Chief and the so-called 'power of coordination'. He found, in practice, that he could do nothing except to confer with the different Commanders-in-Chief and try to persuade them to adopt a common plan. He could give no orders that would transfer a British Division beyond the immediate

---

[26] Ibid.
[27] 'Procès-verbal de la 30éme séance des Représentatives Militaires', 18 March 1918, 4N 4.
[28] Wilson to Amery, 30 March 1918, AMEL/2/1/1.   [29] Cassar, *Forgotten Front*, 132.

command of Marshal Haig, nor a French Division beyond the immediate command of General Pétain.

This led to the Convention in Beauvais on April 3 ... It was then unanimously agreed, with the consent of all Commanders-in-Chief who were there present, to give him the complete powers of a Commander-in-Chief, including that of giving and enforcing any order for the strategic movement of troops in France.[30]

The Italian members of the SWC initially agreed to place their army under Foch. Surprised to learn that this meant Foch could shift Italian troops to France, they clawed back his responsibilities. They maintained that they could not give Foch the power to command in the Italian theatre until the Allied armies functioned in Italy in the same way as they did France. As Bliss noted to Baker, 'As a matter of fact the British and French Divisions now in Italy do not form British and French Armies but are amalgamated in the Italian Army'.[31] The Italian leadership was indicating that, if the Allies had greater manpower resources in Italy, then they would have reason to give Foch greater responsibility in this theatre – an argument they recycled throughout 1918 in an attempt to gain additional resources.

The Creation of the Inter-Allied Transport Council

To assist the PMRs in their studies of communications on the Western Front, the SWC finally approved the creation of the IATC at their meeting in mid-March. As early as December, the SWC, in light of the dangerously slow movement of resources between France and Italy during the attack at Caporetto, had agreed that an expert should examine and report on the transport situation from the Adriatic to the North Sea. In January 1918 Major-General Nash (British) was assigned to recommend a system for Allied coordination. His subsequent report, submitted to the SWC in March, highlighted Allied competition for railway facilities and material. He recommended the creation of the IATC.[32]

Correspondingly, the PMRs had produced Joint Note 8, 'Transportation' in January, which also recommended the creation of an expert transport committee. This body would be responsible for improving

[30] Bliss to Baker, 24 August 1918, Bliss/250/No. 15.   [31] Ibid.

[32] Greenhalgh, *Victory through Coalition*, 243; Colonel A. M. Henniker, *Transportation of the Western Front 1914–1918* (London, 1937), 198–199. Joint Note 28, 'Inter-Allied Transportation Council: Procedure and Appointment of a Chairman', 18 May 1918, Churchill College Archive Centre, Cambridge, Winston Churchill Papers [hereon CHAR] CHAR/27/53; CAB 25/121/SWC212 annex H; Bliss/323; Weygand to Clemenceau, 9 March 1918, SHD-DAT, Conseil Supérieur de la Guerre, 4N 9.

rail-lines between the British, French, and Italian Fronts, making it possible for men and material to be rushed between the French and Italian Fronts when necessary.[33] Improving railway lines would also allow the Allies to economise sea transport.[34] Formed of four members from each of the SWC nations, the French appointed to this role an ex-offico president, the French Minister of Public Works (an official intimately concerned with military transport problems) to ensure that the IATC worked in close cooperation with his office.[35] Nash, the British member of the IATC, was also the BEF's Inspector-General of Transportation for the Western Front.[36] The joint-role of these members gave the IATC's recommendations additional clout. Subordinate to the PMRs, one of the first tasks assigned to the IATC was to make recommendations on how to improve the military use of railways between France and Italy. That the Allies subscribed to this body illustrates the importance they placed on improving communications between the two countries. However, as Clemenceau reminded Weygand, this body did not have executive authority, therefore direct orders for any changes would still have to come from the governments.[37]

Planning during the German Spring Offensives

At the same time as Foch's powers were being redefined in March, the PMRs met to discuss support required for the Italian army in case the Austro-Hungarian and German forces attacked. Ever cautious, Diaz had requested eight divisions from his partners, arguing that the Central Powers might attack in the region of Mantua. However, it was the question of how to improve railway transportation that the other PMRs wanted to discuss. They divided the problem of transportation into two areas: the first referred to the rail-lines between France and Italy, which needed to be improved to increase their carrying capacity; and the second area was within Italy itself, where rail-lines became utterly congested whenever they had to move large numbers of troops and stores during a crisis. It was recommended that the Italians build-up

---

[33] Joint Note 8 'Transportation', 9 January 1918, CAB/25/120/SWC(MR)10; 'Organisation du Comité Inter-alliés des Transports', n.d., SHD-DAT, Conseil Supérieur de la Guerre, 4N 9.
[34] Hankey to Nicholson, 13 April 1918, CAB 25/110.
[35] 'Draft Minutes of the 30th Meeting', 18 March 1918.
[36] Henniker, *Transportation*, 199.
[37] Le Président du Conseil, Clemenceau to Weygand, 19 March 1918, SHD-DAT, Conseil Supérieur de la Guerre, 4N 9.

reserve stocks (especially of coal) to free up lines from civilian use when necessary.[38]

The PMRs immediately sent a questionnaire to the IATC, inviting it to investigate how transport between Italy and France could be improved.[39] Two railway lines linked France and Italy – an inland route via Modane and a coastal route via Ventimiglia (see Map 0.4). They stretched as far as Amiens (via Paris) in northern France and the region of Padua (via Turin) in north-eastern Italy. The former line could carry 20 trains per day. Its capacity was limited by a section that was electrified. The latter route had a maximum capacity of 21 trains per day due to a portion of single-tracked line. The maximum number of wagons in each train was 32, resulting in an average net load of 260 tonnes. Outside the daily traffic of passengers and mail, which could be suppressed for a few days during an emergency, essential resources were moved along these two lines, including coal for industrial and civilian use in Italy and supplies to the British and French forces in Italy.[40] In addition, the French and British moved supplies for their campaign in Macedonia via rail to the Italian port of Taranto, in southern Italy, before shipping them onwards.[41]

During the crisis in October, troops had been sent from France to Italy at a rate of 42 trains a day. However, when the British divisions had been recalled from Italy to France they had only been transported at a rate of 16 trains per day – a rate considered insufficient by the PMRs. They instructed the IATC to report on how transport could be improved on both the Modane and Ventimiglia lines, specifically requesting that the IATC consider a number of solution: how, during critical periods, the Allies could reduce the transportation of supplies to military bases and the transportation of coal for non-essential uses; how to suppress trains for Taranto; and how to make better use of highways (through Aosta, Pienorol, San Damazzo, and Savone), which could help reduce the burden of traffic on railway lines.[42]

The IATC began their investigation by reporting on the current railway situation (see Table 4.1). In April they highlighted that, of the maximum number of trains running between France and Italy, 21 were used on the Modane route. Eight of these were used to carry coal. In the case of the Ventimiglia route, 12 of the 24 trains carried coal. On each line one train per day was used for passenger service.

[38] Bliss, 'Memorandum: Operations of Supreme War Council', n.d., Bliss/252/v. 7.
[39] 'Draft Minutes of 30th Meeting', 18 March 1918.   [40] Henniker, *Transportation*, 298.
[41] Sfika-Theodosiou, 'The Italian Presence on the Balkan Front', 76.
[42] 'Joint Questionnaire No.1', 27 March 1918, CAB 25/110/SWC154; Bliss/318/SWC154.

Table 4.1 *Rail capacity on the Modane and Ventimiglia Lines*

Route	Total trains per day	Coal[43]	Passenger service	Replacement of troops and materials for Allied divisions in Italy	Remaining
Modane	21	8	1	0	12
Ventimiglia	24	12	1	1	10

Source: Drawn from information in 'Transfer of Troops between France and Italy'.[44]

The figures presented were the full capacity of the lines that ran between France (Amiens) and Northern Italy. If the Allies used the railway's maximum capacity for troop transport, *all* other material, both military and civilian, between France and Italy, would be suppressed. Meanwhile other routes within Italy could continue to supply military material to the Italian Front.[45] If these trains were not suppressed, this left 22 trains (of 40 wagons each) for transferring troops.[46]

The IATC offered three solutions to improve the rate of transfer between these theatres. One was based on rail and road communications, the second utilized rail and sea, and the third was an all-rail solution. The first recommendation was to utilise additional train lines that did not span the Alps and have the troops march over the mountains for 40 miles before re-boarding the railway in Italy. By using these other lines, they estimated that they could mount an additional 12 to 16 troop trains per day. The second recommendation was to send 12 troop trains to Marseilles and then move the troops by sea to Genoa and Spezia. The third recommendation was that reserves of coal, supplies, and raw materials be built-up so as to free railway lines during a critical period. The first suggestion was not considered viable due to the organisation that would be required to disembark, march, and then re-embark troops through the Alps. The second suggestion was not considered desirable by the American Section because it believed that any available shipping should be used to bring American troops to Europe. The third recommendation was the most practical. If all supply trains could be temporarily discontinued (by husbanding resources beforehand) and diverted to troop transport, then the net capacity for troop movement from France to Italy

---

[43] Note: 9,000 tonnes of coal per day was sent from France to Italy per day by train. British Section to the American Section, 11 April 1918, Bliss/318.

[44] P. D. Lockridge to Bliss, 'Transfer of Troops between France and Italy', 17 April 1918, Bliss/318.

[45] Ibid.   [46] Ibid.

would be increased to 45 trains per day, with 40 wagons each. The IATC estimated 61 ½ trains were required to move a British division with its complement of corps and army troops and 52 ½ trains to move a French one. Given the maximum capacity that could be reached between France and Italy, 73 percent of a British or 85 percent of a French division could be moved in a single day.[47]

On 18 April the PMRs recast the IATC's ideas into Joint Note 22, entitled 'Transport between France and Italy'. This note indicated that the PMRs thought the Austro-German forces would attack at some point in Italy and thus, 'the transport of troops from France to Italy will eventually have to be carried out with the greatest possible rapidity'.[48] They concluded that the two railway lines via Modane and Ventimiglia would have to be used to their full capacity. They made a series of recommendations: that a reserve stock of coal of approximately 150,000 tonnes be created; that a stockpile of raw materials for Italian war industries be created; that supplies be built up for the Franco-British armies in both Italy and the Allied armies in Macedonia; that inquiries be made as to the possibility of moving coal from Italy to France via Switzerland (which could make use of alternative rail connections); and that the possibility of obtaining transport from the naval authorities be investigated. This note was sent to the SWC members, and approved by the French, American, and Italian governments. But leery of the proposed use of scarce British shipping to build-up resources in Italy, the British government did not.[49] Instead, the British shipping authorities agreed to investigate the question themselves.

Meanwhile the PMRs' responsibilities were once again questioned as the issue of whether the Allies should move two British divisions from Italy back to France was raised at Versailles. The French PMR thought the decision should be left to Foch whereas his British counterpart considered it was a matter for the PMRs.[50] At an earlier meeting the

---

[47] American Section, 'Notes on Reports of Inter-Allied Transportation Council of April 10th and 11, 1918', 15 April 1918, Bliss/318. Note: these estimates were updated around 17 April by General Nash. The original estimate was that a maximum of 50 trains per day could run between France and Italy; however, General Nash believed that no more than 45 could reasonably be used given the time required to unload other trains along the rail-line that would continue to run within Italy. Lockridge to Bliss, 'Transfer of Troops between France and Italy'.

[48] 'Joint Note 22: Transport between France and Italy', 18 April 1918, CAB 25/121/ SWC168.

[49] 'Procès-Verbal of the Third Meeting of the Sixth Session of the Supreme War Council', 3 June 1918, CAB/25/122/IC66SWC; 'American Report of the First Six Sessions', Bliss/ 252.

[50] 'American Report of the First Six Sessions', from the meeting on 27 April 1918, Bliss/ 252/v. 6.

British PMR, Sackville-West, had explained that both the French and British governments interpreted Foch's role as Generalissimo to apply only to France; however, a telegram from the French ambassador in Rome, which explained that Baron Sonnino agreed to Foch's power being extended to Italy in certain scenarios, confused this interpretation.[51] The PMRs themselves were unsure as to how to proceed and thus the issue was placed on hold until two days later when General di Robiliant presented General Diaz's opinions on the situation in Italy.

The Italian government needed to make a clear statement on Foch's relationship to the Italian theatre. The issue was complicated by the fact that Foch was pressing the Italians to attack the Austro-Hungarian army, arguing that this would pin down the Central Powers in Italy, while simultaneously preventing the Germans from moving more troops to the French Front. In contrast, as di Robilant explained to his colleagues, Diaz did not think an offensive in Italy was possible, nor did he think further British or French troops could safely be moved from the Italian Front if offensive action was going to be considered. As the Comando Supremo disagreed with Foch, Versailles offered the Italians an alternative forum to gain Allied support for a defensive stance in their theatre. As a result, the Italians continued to insist that the PMRs lead the discussions on troop movement.[52] To prevent the British and French from further withdrawing divisions from the Italian to the French theatre, di Robilant detailed the dire situation on the Italian Front, emphasising that reserves were dangerously low, partially as a result of the Italians sending two of their divisions to France and partially because Diaz was still in the process of forming a new corps. The PMRs resolved to delay further discussion until it was determined who was responsible for deciding this issue.

The Italian Commander-in-Chief was not the only one who thought the Germans likely to attack in Italy. A report by 'E' Branch on 'German Projects on Termination of the Offensive in France' supported Diaz's conclusions. Written from the perspective of the Germans, it argued that the Italian theatre was the only distraction from France that the Germans would consider: 'The attack on Italy may be considered as practically a part of the German campaign in the West'.[53] For this reason it considered that, if the offensive in France allowed, the Germans would send between six and eight divisions to Italy in order to launch an attack there in the latter half of June. 'E' Branch argued that the advantages of such an

---

[51] Ibid., v. 7.   [52] Ibid.
[53] 'E' Branch, 'German Projects on Termination of the Offensive in France', 30 April 1918, CAB 25/121/SWC201.

operation were that it would stave off political dissension in Austria-Hungary and raise morale in the army, with the main object of knocking the Italians out of the war. The Central Powers could then invade the south of France.

A further report explained how poor intelligence was making it difficult to assess both the strength of Austro-Hungarian forces on the Italian Front and the build-up of forces behind their lines (which would indicate an attack was coming). After consulting 'various Italian and British Intelligence Staffs', including a report by the War Office on the transfer of Austro-Hungarian troops to the Western Front, Hereward Wake, a British officer for 'E' Branch, eloquently explained the problem with trying to determine the size of Austro-Hungarian forces on the Italian Front:

Lack of identification on many parts of the front, the length of time during which many divisions have been lost sight of, and the absence of precise information as to whereabouts of divisions which are believed to have arrived from the Russo-Roumanian front make it difficult to express a confident opinion as to the strength and location of the enemy's concentrations. These difficulties are considerably increased by the reorganization and regrouping of units, the formation of new units and the arrival of detached units from the Eastern front which are taking place at the present time, and by the Austrian practice of transferring battalions and regiments from one division to another.[54]

The danger was that, while the Allies might be able to estimate forces currently facing them, the enemy could transfer troops from the East at any time, giving them the numerical advantage. And while, in February, the Allies had received some information as to the Austro-Hungarian order of battle in the East from the Romanian German Staff, this information was outdated. Furthermore, the intelligence Wake did have was of questionable value. Much of this information came second-hand from the War Office, which had obtained it from an informer who worked on the railway near Trento and from an agent in Stockholm (a Magyar journalist), both of whom reported on the movement of enemy divisions. Wake found the agent's information on Austro-Hungarian units to be 'unusually reliable' whereas the same agent's information on the German army had 'been proved to have been extremely poor'.[55]

Furthermore, the PMRs had difficulty assessing if the Austro-Hungarians were going to attack. As Wake complained, aerial photography of the rear-area of the Austro-Hungarian army was lacking due to

---

[54] 'E' Branch 'Austro-German Situation and Intentions on the Italian Front', 3 May 1918, CAB 25/121/W/37.
[55] 'E' Branch 'Appendix D: War Office Paper', 3 May 1918, CAB 25/121/W/37/D.

poor weather conditions throughout the latter half of March and all through April. He was also unimpressed with the inadequate use of sound ranging and flash spotting to locate enemy artillery. Photo evidence was too fragmentary to be of any assistance. Instead, intelligence was heavily based on information from prisoners and ground observations. And while 'E' Branch estimated that the Austro-Hungarians had an equal number of divisions to the Italians and Allies in Italy (53 divisions), the nature of intelligence led Wake to conclude that there was 'a considerable possibility of error in any forecast as to the enemy's intensions'.[56] He admitted that his estimates were 'liberal' in comparison to those of the War Office, which assessed that the Austro-Hungarians had 49 infantry divisions and 1 dismounted cavalry division.[57]

'E' Branch was more confident in using the information from informers and prisoners to predict the state of morale in the Austro-Hungarian army. Wake estimated that it was declining due to the recent 'Italo-Slav rapprochement', writing that, 'Several at least of the divisions from the Russo-Roumanian front are of poor quality, while the state of affairs in the UKRAINE, and the usually low morale of many of the divisions left in the Eastern theatre, make it unlikely that any large number of efficient troops can still be sent from there to the Italian front'.[58] Meanwhile, morale in the Italian army was 'satisfactory' now that that it had been reorganised and 'and [an] extensive system of defence lines has been constructed'.[59] Still, the British Section believed that the Germans were likely going to pressure the Austro-Hungarians to attack in order pin down Allied forces in Italy. Due to low Austrian morale 'the attack will be rather half hearted, in no great strength, and with no hope of obtaining the only result which is of vital importance to Austria at the moment, namely peace'.[60] So although they predicted an attack would occur, their assessment was less pessimistic than that of the Italian commander.

At the May SWC meeting, the dispute over who was to determine troop movement between Italy and France culminated. This time it was raised alongside discussions of an Italian offensive on the Austro-Hungarians. When General Wilson expressed his frustration that the PMRs had not determined if two more Italian divisions could safely be moved from Italy to France, di Robilant interjected that Diaz said that he could not spare these divisions. The Italian government itself was not prepared to transfer additional Italian troops without Diaz's approval.

---

[56] 'E' Branch 'Appendix A: Number and Disposition of Austro-Hungarian Forces in Italy', 3 May 1918, CAB 25/121/W/37/A.
[57] Ibid.   [58] 'E' Branch 'Austro-German Situation and Intentions'.   [59] Ibid.
[60] Ibid.

General Graziani, the (French) commander of the French troops in Italy, was urging an offensive on the Italian Front with the object of reducing pressure in the Franco-Belgian theatre. Still cautious after the disaster at Caporetto, the Italians explained that the weather was not suitable for such an attack, but that Diaz planned to attack once it improved. Orlando added that the situation in Italy was precarious, citing intelligence from deserters that said the Austro-Hungarian army was planning an attack. Aware that his colleagues were growing impatient with the Italians, Orlando astutely paid lip-service to the idea of moving Italian troops by agreeing that, 'his Government would release any divisions which could be spared', stating 'they welcome[d] anything which will establish more firmly the solidarity of the Allies'.[61]

When the SWC meeting resumed the following day, Orlando made it clear that the transfer of troops from Italy to France should be decided between Foch and Diaz. At his meeting, however, the British representatives complicated the matter by insisting that the PMRs should investigate troop movement between the various theatres. Careful not to relinquish all control of Allied organisations to the French, Lloyd George and Henry Wilson attempted to use the PMRs to rein in Foch's power. Meanwhile, Foch urged the Italians to adopt the same system of coordination as the one in France, highlighting if Diaz had this connection to the commanders in France he would have access to Foch's plans and vice versa. In this way they could coordinate action across the Western Front. Lloyd George recommended that the Italians accept the earlier Doullens agreement, which would allow Foch to coordinate the Italian army with the other Allied armies.[62] Foch, Clemenceau, Pershing, and Lloyd George reassured Orlando that, under the Beauvais agreement, Diaz would still have complete control of his troops and that, if he disagreed with the Generalissimo's ideas, he could appeal directly to his own government.

These arrangements, however, went too far for the Italian Prime Minister who instead accepted the principle of coordination embodied in the Doullens agreement. Meanwhile, the other SWC members pressed for a further extension of Foch's powers by agreeing among themselves on 'The Extension of General Foch's Powers to the Italian Front'. It recommended that Foch be made Commander-in-Chief of the

---

[61] 'Procès-verbal of First Meeting of the Fifth Session of the Supreme War Council', 1 May 1918, CAB 25/121/SWC188; Bliss/252.

[62] 'Procès-Verbal of Second Meeting of the Fifth Session of the Supreme War Council', 2 May 1918, CAB 25/121/SWC189.

Italian troops on the French Front (under the Beauvais agreement).[63] An additional note said that, if the three armies in Italy ever had to meet a large enemy offensive there, then the Italians would extend Foch's power. The Italians were ready to trade an extension of Foch's power in exchange for further manpower resources from their partners.[64] Finally, the Italians gave Foch the authority to consult with Diaz and coordinate action in Italy, but the execution of any action required Diaz's approval and would be led by the Italian commander.[65]

Shortly after this meeting Foch once again pressed Diaz to attack the Austro-Hungarians, specifically recommending they assault their communications in Val Sugana, a significant route through the Alps.[66] The Allies were aware that an attack was likely to occur against Italy in June; however, they were confident that the Italian army could hold. While the British had discussed withdrawing the remainder of their troops in Italy to France, they decided against doing so as it 'would have created a good deal of discussion and depression [among their Italian allies]'.[67] Instead they would send no more drafts to maintain the strength of these divisions and reduce their establishments from 12 down to 9 battalions (which the British had already done with their forces in France), freeing an additional 5,000 men to send elsewhere. This decision was questioned by both Lord Milner and General Wilson who were concerned that the Italian Front could collapse, which in turn would allow the Austro-Hungarians to send their divisions to France. When they argued that they 'did not want Italy to fall down', Clemenceau acerbically replied 'that he did not want Paris to fall down either'.[68] The British government moved forward with this decision.

The Battle of the Piave and the Analysis of Its Results for Future Strategy

On 15 June the Austro-Hungarian army launched their anticipated offensive against the Italians in order to support the German offensive

---

[63] Resolution 5, 'Procès-Verbal of Third Meeting of the Fifth Session of the SWC, 2 May 1918', CAB 25/122/SWC190; CAB/25/121/SWC190.

[64] Bliss, 'Memorandum: Operations of Supreme War Council: Vth Session', 1 and 2 May 1918, Bliss/252/v. 8.

[65] Bliss to March, 29 July 1918, The United States Army in the World War (hereon referred to as USAWW), 2: 557.

[66] Greenhalgh, Foch, 347.

[67] 'Secretary's Notes of a Conference held at the Trianon Palace Hotel', 1 June 1918, the uncatalogued papers of James Rennell Rodd, first Baron Rennell, Bodleian Library, University of Oxford (hereon Rodd), 19.

[68] Ibid.

on the Franco-Belgian Front.[69]Attacking the Italian Sixth, Seventh, and Third Armies, they made only small gains across the Piave. The Italian army's success in stopping the Austro-Hungarians troops on 23 June proved its reorganisation had been successful and equally illustrated the military weakness of the Austro-Hungarian army.[70] Foch, exuding optimism about the Italian Front, encouraged Diaz to move onto the offensive against the Austro-Hungarians hoping that the Italian army would advance to the Feltre road and provide the Italians with a base for future operations towards Trente. From this position the Italians would be able to participate in the coordinated attack by the Allies that Foch envisaged occurring in 1919.[71] From the Italian perspective there were still concrete reasons to delay offensive action. Although they had successfully stopped the enemy, they had done so at a cost of at least 85,000 casualties.[72] The result was that Diaz's reserves were almost entirely comprised of men born in 1900 who could not be used in combat until 1919.[73] Understandably, the Italian commander remained cautious.

Like Foch, Bliss was also optimistic as a result of the Italians holding on the Piave. As he explained to Baker, 'the splendid success of the Italian Army on the Piave has doubtless upset German calculations. It may cause a decided change in their plan'.[74] While Bliss had estimated that the Germans would maintain a substantial presence on the Italian Front to reinforcethe Austro-Hungarian forces, their defeat by the Italians pleasantly surprised him. He believed the Germans would now be compelled to send more troops to Italy to bolster the morale of their partners while success had increased the morale of the Italians. Bliss's assessment illustrated the importance of the failure of the Central Powers and highlighted the significant role of the Italian theatre in a global strategy. It was in Italy, Bliss reasoned, where 'the Germans had made the mistake which will lose them the war sooner than it otherwise would'.[75] He calculated that the German's erred by not sending sufficient reinforcements to the Austro-Hungarians for their offensive resulting in its failure. In order to improve the morale of the Austro-Hungarians and keep their ally in the

---

[69] Thompson, *White War*, 338.
[70] Pershing diary, 17 June 1918, LOC, Pershing Papers [hereon Pershing] Pershing/2; Marshal Ferdinand Foch, *The Memoirs of Marshal Foch*, trans. T. B. Mott (London, 1931), 403.
[71] Foch, *Memoirs*, 403.
[72] Analyses télégrammes 3ieme Bureau A to French Section, 4 July 1918, SHD-DAT, Conseil Supérieur de la Guerre, 4N 27.
[73] Giorgio Rochat, 'The Italian Front, 1915–18', in John Horne, ed., *A Companion to World War I*, 91. Rochat estimates casualties at 87,000.
[74] Bliss to Baker, 26 June 1918, Bliss/250/no. 10.   [75] Ibid.

war, the Germans would have to divert forces to Italy, disrupting the plans they had for 1918.

Despite the optimism expressed by the Allied Generalissimo and the American PMR, the information presented by the IATC and digested by the British Section, at the end of June, was still pessimistic. In response to a series of questions on transportation issues sent to them from the PMRs, the IATC reported that the Germans, using all available railway routes, were capable of assembling at least 2 ½ times more divisions in the Italian theatre than the Allies could deliver – some 24 to 32 divisions compared to the 10 to 12 divisions that the Allies could shift during the same time period. As 'A' Branch noted, while railway improvements would take only two months to complete once started, they would never give the Allies equal ability to move forces to that of the Central Powers due to a railway bottleneck along the Milan-Pavia-Parma line.[76] The IATC argued that the assembly of these additional divisions would give the Central Powers a numerical superiority of at least 42 percent.[77] Extrapolating from the IATC's study, 'E' Branch estimated that the Germans had 205 divisions on the Western Front, but given it was unlikely the Allies could launch an offensive that year, the Germans could safely reduce this force to 166. This action left 41 divisions which could be sent to Italy if the Germans did not want to attack elsewhere. Currently they believed that the strength of the opposing forces on the Italian Front had been increased from estimates in May to 64 Austro-Hungarian divisions facing 56 Allied divisions (including the remaining 3 British and 3 French). This figure was slightly higher than intelligence received by the French Section which estimated the Austro-Hungarians forces at 62 ½ divisions.[78] In fact, at the height of their attack in June, the Austro-Hungarians only had 58 divisions.[79] The IATC believed the Austro-Hungarian offensive would prevent further movement of Allied divisions to the French Front during the summer, which was true.[80] Furthermore, it expressed concern that, in the event of the Germans transferring troops to the Italian Front, poor intelligence in the theatre would make it difficult for the Allies to identify how many divisions had been sent until an attack began.

'E' Branch reasoned that the Germans would take advantage of their superior power of concentration to launch an offensive in the Italian

---

[76] 'A' Branch, 'How Are We to Win the War?' 31 May 1918, CAB/25/84/SWC280.
[77] 'E' Branch, 'An Austro-German Offensive in Italy', 27 June 1918, CAB/25/122.
[78] 'Analyse du rapport de quinzaine du Général Graziani en date du 2 Juillet', 9 July 1918, SHD-DAT, Conseil Supérieur de la Guerre, 4N 27.
[79] Rochat, *Italian Front*, 90.   [80] 'E' Branch, 'Austro-German Offensive in Italy'.

theatre in the autumn of 1918. It was because of, rather than despite, the failure of the Austro-Hungarian offensive in June that the Germans would consider an attack, as without success in 1918 unrest on the Austro-Hungarian home-front might cause their war-weary ally to withdraw from the conflict:

The integrity of Austria-Hungary and the continued repression of her subject races is a vital necessity for Germany. The creation of an independent Czech and Jugo-Slav States would cause a serious gap in the Central European bloc, and, although it is not expected that any effective move towards independence can be made by these peoples in the immediate future, there is undoubtedly a serious risk that a German failure to obtain a decision in the West, re-acting on the civil and military morale of Austria-Hungary, already depressed by bad food conditions and the failure of the offensive in Italy, might produce a situation of the utmost gravity.[81]

They argued that unless Austria-Hungary had peace in 1918 it would break-up; 'E' Branch also foresaw that, for the Central Powers, peace meant a military victory. For this to occur, the Germans would have to intervene on the Italian Front to keep their ally in the war. Furthermore, the IATC reasoned that, if the German offensive in France failed, then a military success by the Central Powers would be necessary to allay the resulting discontent on the German home-front as well.

On 5 July the PMRs once again convened to discuss the situation in Italy; however, their role had been redefined at the recent SWC session in order to avoid any overlap in Foch's duties. Now the main responsibility of the PMRs was to consider policy for the autumn of 1918 and the ensuing year. This affected their consideration of the Italian theatre as they were now less interested in commenting on the movement of troops and material between the Italian and French theatres in the immediate future (which was clearly Foch's domain). Instead they were concerned with making preparations for the future and improving railway communications between France and Italy. On the latter issue, they had received instructions from Foch, who urged them to undertake studies immediately.[82] For the remainder of the war Belin informed Foch on rail-improvements and agreements by the IATC. Foch wanted to know what transport he could rely upon.[83] Furthermore, it aided Foch's case for an offensive in Italy if he could reassure the Italians that support from France could be transferred to Italy in a timely manner.

---

[81] Ibid.
[82] Foch to Belin, 5 July 1918, SHD-DAT, Conseil Supérieur de la Guerre, 4N 9.
[83] Foch to Belin, 11 July 1918, SHD-DAT, Conseil Supérieur de la Guerre, 4N 9.

Since the PMRs last discussion on transportation, the IATC had already made large improvements to transportation between Italy and France. Instigating discussions between the Italian government and British Ministry of Shipping, it had been agreed that, while the British were unable to provide troop transport during an emergency, they could spare cargo tonnage. This tonnage could be used to move coal and other supplies, thus freeing up some space on the railway lines.[84] The IATC had also arranged, between the British and Italian governments, for a strategic reserve of 150,000 tonnes of coal to be created in Italy.[85] Together these two agreements increased the trains available to move troops during an emergency by 20 trains.[86] The Italians had also received 10,000 railway wagons from the French, while the British furnished the French with additional wagons to make up their shortages.[87] Given this contribution, the British made it known that they any further requests for wagons would come at the detriment of other war production.[88] Italy's partners were increasingly expecting the Italians to provide material support for these enhancements.

With these developments underway, the IATC had conducted a new study, which motivated the PMRs to recommend to the political side of the SWC improvements in the Modane railway line. Joint Note 33, entitled 'Measures Imperative to Take in Order to Increase the Capacity of the Modane Line with a View to Possible Strategic Demands', was based on the premise (put forward by 'E' Branch) that the Central Powers were likely to attack on the Italian Front given that they had failed to obtain a decision in France and because they would need a victory in 1918 in order to raise their own morale.[89] Incorporating the IATC's study, this note recommended necessary improvements to the rail-lines, which included double tracking parts of the line and enlarging certain railway stations.[90] Bliss warned that, unless Pershing was convinced that personnel for improving rail-lines between France and Italy would not come from those destined to improve rail-lines in France for

---

[84] British PMR to American PMR, 20 July 1918, Bliss/318; Joint Memorandum by the Ministry of Shipping and the Director of Movements (War Office), 'Transport of Troops between France and Italy', 26 June 1918, Bliss/318/GT4973.

[85] British (Milner) and Italian (Levi) governments, 'Agreement with Regard to Providing a Strategic Reserve of 150,000 Tons of Coal in Italy', 21 June 1918, Bliss/318.

[86] British Section, 'Annexure X to Joint Note 33', CAB/25/123.

[87] Rodd to Lloyd George, 12 July 1918, Rodd 19.

[88] Sackville-West to Belin, 7 August 1918, SHD-DAT, Conseil Supérieur de la Guerre, 4N 9.

[89] 'Joint Note 33','CAB 25/123/SWC265; Bliss/318.

[90] PMRs, 'Draft Joint Note: Increase of Transportation Facilities between France and Italy by the Modane Route' July 1918, Bliss/318.

the transportation of the American army there, the note would not be approved by the American government. To avoid such a rejection Bliss suggested that the PMRs submit a detailed plan of the work to be done, including information on who would supply the labour and material. Despite Bliss's suggestion, Joint Note 33 was sent to the coalition governments and, although it was approved by the American government by 16 July, they made it clear that, while the Americans agreed the Modane line should be upgraded, they would provide neither materials nor labour.[91] This note was also accepted by both the French and British governments and communicated to Foch, who wanted to know what improvements were being made to the railway lines between France and Italy.[92] Having recently received the figures on rail transport between France and Northern Italy, Foch emphasised the importance of improving railways. He wanted the IATC studies to be expanded beyond the Modane line to include those of Ventimiglia.[93] He pressed the IATC to undertake their studies as quickly as possible, giving urgency to the issue of transport between France and Italy.[94] While on the ground in France Foch had control of the railways, the PMRs provided him with an avenue for gauging what the railway situation in Italy was like.[95]

While the IATC undertook its more intensive study on who should provide the materials and labour, the Allies went ahead and agreed that the Italians would provide the latter, thus allowing improvements to begin as early as 28 July 1918.[96] In theory the expansion of the Modane line was to be a joint effort, as reflected by the plan put forward by the IATC in mid-August. It stated that the Americans were to provide the copper, bronze, and some of the steel and rails, the British steel and permanent way material, and the French porcelain, cement, and wood.[97] This study was disconnected from the action being taken by the Allied governments as the Americans had already refused to assist with materials.

[91] Bliss to the British, French, and Italian MRs, 16 July 1918, Bliss/246.
[92] American IATC representative to Bliss, 'Improvement Transportation Facilities between France and Italy', 8 August 1918, Bliss/318; Belin to Bliss, 7 July 1918, Bliss/318.
[93] Belin to Foch, 17 July 1918, SHD-DAT, Conseil Supérieur de la Guerre, 4N 1; Italian PMR to the American PMR, 21 July 1918, Bliss/324.
[94] Belin to Henaff (French IATC Representative), 7 July 1918, SHD-DAT, Conseil Supérieur de la Guerre, 4N 1.
[95] For more on Foch's involvement with railways in France, see Greenhalgh, *Victory*, 241.
[96] Nash to Sackville-West, 28 July 1918, Bliss/318.
[97] Director General of Transportation 'Improvement of Transportation Facilities between France and Italy', 16 August 1918, Bliss/318.

Despite the progress being made with communications, Italian pessimism dampened the increasingly optimistic outlook of their partners. Diaz pressed the British ambassador in Italy, Rennell Rodd, to encourage his government to send motorised vehicles for the Italian Front, arguing that an offensive by the enemy was imminent.[98] On 12 July, Rodd wrote to the Lloyd George to support Diaz's case. He argued that, with additional resources, Diaz's triumph against the Austro-Hungarian offensive could have been turned into a 'great success'. He relayed the opinion of Francesco Nitti, who was not only the Italian Minister of Finance but the second most influential member of Orlando's Cabinet, as he attempted to prophesy what German strategy would be:

the Germans will probably divert sufficient divisions here to make the enemy superiority in numbers if not overwhelming at any rate very menacing Nitti believes because, as he says, it is so obviously the best card for them to play. If they could get through to Milan and eventually even to Genoa it not only puts Italy out of action, but also menaces France in the South, and offers the best opportunity of terminating the war.[99]

Rodd continued that, in order to meet such a scenario, Diaz required material assistance, but that the French would never provide it unless forced to do so by their Allies as 'France never looks outside France and cannot see the urgent requirements of others ...'[100] He also took the opportunity to stress that Foch's powers as Generalissimo could not extend to Italy because he was too far away and thus did not comprehend the immediate situation in Italy. Finally Rodd turned to the recent attack by the Austro-Hungarians to explain why the Italians needed Allied resources. The Italians 'were practically annihilated' by the Austro-Hungarian machine guns.[101] The problem, he argued, was that the Italians did not have tanks, which would have given them the armour required to close with the Austrians. Although the Italians were constructing tanks, they were lagging behind due to the need to replace material losses at Caporetto and as they lacked coal and other raw materials. With 100 Allied tanks the Italians would be able to undertake counter-attacks without squandering lives. Rodd even went as far as to say that by the following spring the Italians would have upwards of 2,000 tanks of their own. His demands also included heavy gas shells from French stockpiles and one or two American divisions, which would 'have a good morale effect'.[102] The Italians were looking to the British to be

---

[98] Di Robilant 'Need of Motor Trucks in View of a Forthcoming Resumption of the Offensive by the Enemy on Our Front', 17 July 1918, Bliss/324.
[99] Rodd to Lloyd George, 12 July 1918, Rodd 19.   [100] Ibid.   [101] Ibid.   [102] Ibid.

sympathetic and to provide, or get the French to provide, these resources without having to extend the Beauvais agreement to Italy.

Meanwhile, as Rodd pressed the British government, the Italian PMR worked on gaining the support of his colleagues at Versailles. Di Robilant emphasised, although Italy had stopped the most recent Austro-German offensive, the Central Powers were gathering more manpower from the Eastern Front and the interior of the Dual Monarchy in order to launch another.[103] He provided his colleagues with four and a half pages of intelligence reports that had been gathered throughout June and July from enemy deserters, intercepted enemy correspondence, prisoners, informants, and circulated rumours. Using these reports that were 'substantially harmonious and ... largely drawn from different sources proved to be trustworthy' the Italians argued that between 10 and 30 German divisions would be sent to the Italian theatre in the near future.[104] In reality, these reports were highly subjective. In di Robilant's estimate, railway lines played a key part in the Central Powers' ability to trump the Italians, just as the IATC studies had shown. The Italian PMR urged the other PMRs to ensure that Joint Note 33 ('Measures Imperative to Take In Order to Increase the Capacity of the Modane Line with View to Possible Strategic Demands') was executed. Furthermore, di Robilant asked that units be pre-assigned for use in Italy in case of an emergency and that training camps be established in Italy for American divisions.

Even before the PMRs met to discuss this memo in late July, the United States government had sent a telegram to the other governments in response to demands being placed on the Americans to send troops to theatres outside of France.[105] Knowing it was highly unlikely Foch would send American divisions to Italy, Washington (to the delight and relief of Bliss) informed its partners that it would not send troops to Italy unless sanctioned by the Generalissimo. In a move that also reinforced its support of Foch, Washington stated that it would defer the question to him, 'as it would wish to defer all others'.[106] It considered the French Front to be so intimately linked to Italy that, if any American troops were sent to the Italian theatre, then Foch should coordinate them, writing that they were practically 'separate parts of a single line ...'[107]

---

[103] Italian PMR to the French, British, and American Military Representatives, 21 July 1918, Bliss/324/No. 3074.

[104] Italian Section, 'Probable Transfer of German Forces to the Italian Front', 22 July 1918, Bliss/318/no. 3074.

[105] Macchi di Cellere (Italian ambassador to Washington) to Robert Lansing, 28 August 1918, Wilson/99.

[106] 'Translation of Code Cablegram Received', 23 July 1918, Bliss/329.   [107] Ibid.

Furthermore, any American troops sent to Italy would come from those in France, and not comprise a separate force sent specifically to Italy from the United States. The Americans had already despatched the 332nd Infantry Regiment to Italy 'to show America's interest in the Italian situation and to strengthen Italian Morale'.[108] They were not likely to consider sending any more resources to Italy, despite Italian pressure to do so. Bliss hoped this telegram would settle the matter.

As the 40th PMR meeting was to prove, the Italians would not be easily dissuaded. Raising the issue as a draft joint note entitled, 'The Assignment of War Material to the Italian Army', once again Diaz, through di Robilant, attempted to gain substantial military supplies for the Italian Front. This time the Italian PMR explained that material resources were required if the Italians were to follow through on the offensive action recommended by Foch. Di Robilant told his colleagues that while Diaz and Foch had agreed on the action that the former would take, Diaz needed the resources to do so. Thus Diaz shrouded his request under the guise of executing Foch's wishes. Instead of receiving support from the other PMRs, however, di Robilant was confronted over the issue of Foch's lack of authority in Italy.

Di Robilant continued to press his colleagues, specifically requesting the PMRs to support the Italians in gaining motor transport from their partners. He argued that an Austro-Hungarian attack (supported by the Germans) on the Italian Front was still possible. 'Lorries' would improve the mobility of the Italian forces and compensate for a 'lack of [troop] numbers'.[109] The other PMRs immediately became suspicious as to why Diaz could not settle the matter with Foch himself. Di Robilant explained that Diaz merely wanted the PMRs to express an opinion on the matter. Bliss was convinced that the Italian theatre had to be considered alongside the other studies then underway. The PMRs were examining the future interaction of the various theatres of war (Joint Note 37), in order not to lose the pre-eminence of the French Front. Once again, the other PMRs refused to give advice on the movement of materials to Italy unless instructed to do so by Foch or the SWC.

Bliss took this opportunity to ask the Italians why they had not extended Foch's powers to that of the Beauvais agreement. If they were to do so, then Foch could order troops and materials (including the lorries) to the Italian theatre. Bliss also noted, that if di Robilant did indeed consider the Italian Front an integral part of the Western Front,

[108] 'Final Report of General John H. Pershing', 1 September 1919, *USAWW*, 12: 47.
[109] 'Minutes of the 40th Meeting of the Military Representative', 27 July 1918, CAB 25/122/SWC289.

then Foch's powers should be extended to Italy. Di Robilant retorted that what he had meant was that a break in the Italian line would have serious consequences for the French Front and that 'the discussion had strayed beyond the question he had submitted to the Meeting'.[110] This resolution, which had been constructed by Diaz and presented by di Robilant, was promptly withdrawn by the Italian PMR.

Two days later the question of the transfer of reserves from the French to the Italian Front was raised once more. Both the IATC and the Italian Section had conducted and completed independent studies on this question. From the Italian study a draft note had been put forward to its colleagues. Di Robilant said that the military situation in Italy was still not favourable for the Allies, despite the efforts being made to improve communications in Italy.[111] Specifically, he argued that the Germans could still transfer twice as many troops to the Italian theatre as the Allies in the same amount of time. Little work had been undertaken on the railway infrastructure. For example, work was supposedly ready to begin on the Chambéry-Turin line, but while labour agreements had been made, it was still unclear who was going to supply the raw materials and manufactured products.[112] Di Robilant contended that the only solution to the lagging rail-line improvements was to transfer reserve divisions to the Italian theatre. He divided these divisions into two groups: the first were American divisions that could continue their training in Italy. The second group included Allied divisions that would be specifically designated and prepared to move to Italy 'at a moment's notice' if required (this group would need to use trains, which further heightened the need for upgrading the railways between the two fronts). The Italian PMR emphasised that these two groups should together amount to at least 20 divisions.

Bliss was adamantly opposed to these suggestions. In particular, he insisted that any reference to the use of American troops on the Italian Front be omitted, reminding di Robilant that: 'All American troops in France, on the way to France, or about to start, were regarded as part of the forces under General Foch'.[113] Neither Bliss nor Washington wanted to undermine Foch's role as generalissimo. As Bliss continued, 'the United States had accepted in its entirety the principle of the Single

[110] Ibid.

[111] 'Draft Minutes of the 41st Meeting of the Military Representatives of the Supreme War Council', 29 July 1918, CAB 25/122/SWC296; 'Minutes of the 41st Meeting of the Military Representatives of the Supreme War Council', 29 July 1918, Bliss/324.

[112] Colonel Le Hénaff to General Belin, 27 July 1918, Bliss/324.

[113] 'Meeting of the Military Representatives of the Supreme War Council', 29 July 1918, CAB 25/122/SWC296.

Command on the Western Front, together with certain co-ordinating powers as regards Italy, and in every case the United States government would ask him whether he had consulted General Foch, whether General Foch had approved the plan, whether he asked for assistance to enable him to carry it out'.[114] Bliss later told Baker that the Italians were attempting to outmanoeuvre Foch and that he found the entire issue deplorable.[115] His approach was to reaffirm to his colleagues that a joint note sent to the American president would not be accepted and that the Americans recognised it as Foch's duty to move troops. Bliss insisted that the Italians contact Foch directly, rather than attempt to gain the support of the PMRs for an issue that was rightfully the responsibility of the Generalissimo.[116]

Before the debate became too heated, Sackville-West intervened by reminding his Italian colleague that Joint Note 33 ('Measures Imperative to Take In Order to Increase the Capacity of the Modane Line with View to Possible Strategic Demands') had been prepared to combat the possibility of the Germans moving troops to Italy once action on the Western Front had slowed down. The PMRs felt that many of the points raised by di Robilant had already been discussed. Frustrated, di Robilant countered that the situation in France had improved, implying that the French could afford to send these divisions to Italy whether or not Foch desired to do so. Met with contempt, he withdrew his note and agreed instead to compose a report which the French PMR would submit to Foch. If approved by Foch. If approved by Foch only then would the PMRs send it to the SWC. Tellingly, this note was never completed.

Still angry with the Italians, Bliss told March that the Italians needed to be pressured to accept Foch as Allied Generalissimo and that their continued suggestion of establishing training areas in Italy for American troops was unacceptable. He warned the Chief of Staff, 'I heard it quite openly said that one reason for the Italian demand for a large force of Americans is their belief that France is making a lot of money out of our troops, and they want a share!'[117] Bliss was relieved when March made an official announcement that the Western Front in France was the main area of military effort for American troops.[118]

The Italians were using the SWC in an attempt to gain additional resources, but what they found was that their partners were increasingly expecting the Italians to solve their own problems. The French Minister of Munitions, Louis Loucheur, had informed Belin that it was going to

---

[114] 'Draft Minutes of the 41st Meeting'; 'Minutes of the 41st Meeting', 29 July 1918.
[115] Bliss to Baker, 31 July 1918, Bliss/250.   [116] Ibid.
[117] Bliss to March, August 5 1918, Bliss/250.   [118] Ibid.

be impossible for the French to build-up additional stocks in Italy, in addition to the resources they were already providing. He warned Belin that the PMRs should avoid making resolutions to the SWC unless his ministry had been consulted.[119] The Italians would have to stockpile material as advised by both the SWC and Foch.[120] Belin also informed di Robilant of this opinion held by Foch and the French Minister of Munitions.[121] However, this note did not dissuade the Italians from seeking assistance from the SWC.

The Drafting of Joint Note 37 – The Italian Dimension

During the month of July, the PMRs had also begun drafting notes for what was to become Joint Note 37 'General Military Policy of Allies for the Autumn of 1918 and for the Year 1919'. The first draft put forward by the Americans supported the idea that, in Italy action should remain limited to counter-attacking and holding the line. Aware of the consequences of losing the Italians as an ally, the Americans explained that, '[the Italian] front may be considered as an integral part of the Western Front in the sense that the decisive defeat of either belligerent would probably release the troops of the other for service upon the Western Front'.[122] Like their American colleagues, the British highlighted the relationship between the French and Italian theatres, writing, 'In France and Italy alone can the immense Armies at the disposal of the Allies and Central Powers be deployed for battle', continuing that this was due to the fact that, 'the bulk of the forces available on both sides will be in France and Italy'.[123] Also like the Americans, and in contrast to Foch, they had serious reservations about the Italians launching a major offensive. However, unlike the Americans, the British Section hypothesised that in the autumn, once events had slowed on the French Front, the Germans would have the men to reinforce the Austro-Hungarian army and would then launch an offensive on the Italian Front. Given these conditions, the British Section recommended that the Allies prepare to meet such an offensive by creating a reserve in Italy, which the Italians also desired.

The British PMR was not the only individual with concerns. The CIGS, Henry Wilson, was also convinced that if the Germans failed in

[119] Loucheur to Belin, 8 August 1918, SHD-DAT, Conseil Supérieur de la Guerre, 4N 9.
[120] Belin to Loucheur, 14 August 1918, SHD-DAT, Conseil Supérieur de la Guerre, 4N 9.
[121] Belin to di Robilant, 14 August 1918.
[122] American Section, 'Allied Plan of Campaign for Autumn and Winter of 1918 and Summer of 1919', 15 July 1918, CAB 25/84.
[123] 'Proposed Joint Note', 31 July 1918, CAB 25/84; Bliss/324.

France then they would turn towards Italy in the autumn in order to achieve a success in 1918. The War Office had even gone so far as to suggest that the Austro-German forces could field up to 93 divisions in Italy. It imagined that once Italy was defeated the Central Powers could then turn back to the Franco-Belgian theatre to launch a massive offensive in 1919.[124]

By 1 August the Americans had produced a second draft which unintentionally made it sound as though they supported the Italians in their bid for resources, as it emphasised the central role Italy played in achieving victory: 'That this decision can be obtained only in the theatre lying between the North Sea and the Adriatic'.[125] The Americans were trying to explain the significance of the Italian theatre in relation to the French one – that the Italian theatre should support the French one. Further stipulations added depth to this point. They did not advise that troops be moved from France to Italy unless either the Germans moved divisions to the Italian Front or unless the security of the French Front could be ensured. In the latter scenario, troops could then be moved to Italy for an offensive, as success in Italy in 1918 would increase the likelihood for a war-winning offensive in France in 1919. While Bliss himself did not think the war could be won in the Italian theatre, the American phrasing was ambiguous and certainly encouraged the Italians. The British went as far as to warn the Americans of this fact by writing so directly on their draft copy of Bliss's proposal.[126]

The French produced their first draft note in August and, like their British and American partners, they discussed the Italian theatre as an integral part of the Western Front in general, illustrating how it supported the Franco-Belgian Front and held down forces that otherwise would have been sent to France. In order to assess whether troops should be moved between France and Italy, the French Section attempted to estimate the forces in Italy, concluding there were 56 Allied divisions (consisting of 715 battalions) facing 63 ½ Austro-Hungarian divisions (832 battalions strong) as of 1 August 1918.[127] Given these numbers they did not believe that Austria-Hungary would move forces to the Franco-Belgian Front; however, they also did not think the situation in Italy was positive enough to move divisions from Italy to France to assist with offensive action there. In autumn, however, if the Italians had ensured

---

[124] Henry Wilson, 'British Policy 1918–1919', 25 July 1918, CAB 25/85/Pt.I/9.
[125] American Section, 'Allied Plans of Campaign for the Autumn 1918 and for the Year 1919', 1 August 1918, CAB 25/84.
[126] Ibid.
[127] French Section, 'Projet de Plan d'Operations pour les Armées Alliés pendant l'automne 1918 et l'Ete 1919', 6 August 1918, CAB 25/84.

their defences were strong, they recommended that the other Allies should be prepared to take vigorous military action against the Austro-Hungarians in order to hold down as many of the Central Powers' forces as possible while the Allies attacked in France. In this scenario the Allies might send to Italy 10 divisions of French, British, or American troops. The decision for action in Italy rested on the situation in France: 'Only the results of operations in France during the end of the summer will allow us to judge if such withdrawals could be made'.[128] In 1919 as well, the French envisaged the Italians playing a supporting role to the Franco-Belgian Front, recommending that, once the offensive in France began, the Italian forces should attack the Austro-Hungarians. This action in Italy would prevent the Germans from having access to manpower resources in Italy and allow the Italians to take advantage of the weakness of the Austro-Hungarian forces while the Germans were busy elsewhere.

When the PMRs met Foch on 26 August, di Robilant was more optimistic about Italian abilities. He went as far as to suggest that the Allies focus on knocking the Austro-Hungarians out of the war, thus isolating Germany. The British draft Joint Note 37, which followed from these meetings, also reflected a positive outlook. It explained that, 'The Austrian Army might be crushed on the Italian Front and a portion of the German Army with it ...'; however, they made it clear that 'the final defeat of Germany, the real foundation of the hostile coalition can only be brought about where the main German Armies are to be found, that is to say between Switzerland and the North Sea'.[129] It was at the end of August that the British Section began to realise that, given the failure of the Austro-Hungarian offensive in June, in combination with the pressure being placed on the Germans in France (which had prevented the Germans from supporting the Austro-Hungarians), an attack by the Central Powers in Italy was unlikely to occur.[130] And yet they still wanted to be certain they would not be surprised again, as had happened at Caporetto. Thus the British Section promoted the recommendations of the PMRs and IATC that transport communications between Italy and France had to be improved.[131]

It was not until 4 September, only a few days before the PMRs were to meet to decide the final shape draft Joint Note 37 would take, that the Italians put forward their own ideas for the remainder of 1918 and 1919.

---

[128] Ibid.
[129] British Section, 'Proposed Joint Note: Allied Plans of Campaign for the Autumn 1918 and for the Year 1919', 30 August 1918, Bliss/324/SWC295/1.
[130] Chief of Staff, British Section, 28 August 1918, CAB 25/84, minute sheet, comment 22, p. 5.
[131] Ibid.

The Italians used this draft note as an opportunity to build on their earlier arguments for gaining resources from the Allies, by illustrating that, with these additional resources, they could knock Austria-Hungary out of the war. Doing so would then allow the Allies to focus on defeating Germany in 1919. Without these resources, they argued, Italy itself might be defeated. Political advantages of the former scenario were that the loss of Austria-Hungary could lead to Bulgaria detaching itself from the Central Powers, as its enthusiasm for the war was already waning, which in turn would lead to the isolation of Turkey and the severing of communications between the Germans and the East.

The Italians predicted that the Germans would settle in for the winter along a shortened line, giving their army time to recuperate, and put up heavy resistance in the spring. Knocking Austria-Hungary out of the war would limit German resistance on the Franco-Belgian Front by exposing Germany's left flank, as the Allies would have access to Bohemia via Austrian territory. Doing so would limit Germany's capacity to hold out on the Western Front, the length of which, the Italian's argued, should not be underestimated. Without the Austro-Hungarians as a member of the Central Powers, the strategic situation for both sides would be significantly altered. Furthermore, militarily defeating the Austro-Hungarians would also increase Allied numerical supremacy on the French Front for the decisive offensive in 1919 as 'a large number of Italian divisions' (the number was not specified) could be moved there.

In their draft note the Italians also indicated that they were prepared to launch an offensive in Trentino and on the Piave, 'provided that it is carried on in a strength and with the means necessary to successfully carry it through'.[132] To obtain this strength they requested greater support from the Allies – no less than 20–25 divisions which should include artillery and 'war material' – arguing that, given the arrival of American troops, the Allies could still succeed in the Franco-British sector without these resources. If the Austro-Hungarians were defeated first, victory over the Central Powers could be achieved by the summer of 1919. The operational plan being prepared by the Italian Supreme Command called first for an attack on the Trentino sector, with the object of preparing for a final attack in 1919.

The tone of the opening of this draft was one of enthusiasm, but it changed to caution and indecisiveness when it described operational plans. The Italians used their assessment of the Austro-Hungarian's numerical superiority, indeed markedly so by 1919, to underpin their

---

[132] Italian Section, 'Allied Plans of Campaign for the Autumn 1918 and for the Year 1919', 3 September 1918, Bliss/324.

Table 4.2 *Comparative strength of the Italian and Austro-Hungarian forces*

	In Line (,000)	Replacements (,000)	Totals (,000)	Numerical supremacy (,000)
1 Aug. 1918				
Italy	365	305	670	–
Austro-Hungarians	460	350	810	140
1 Jan. 1919				
Italy	365	215	580	–
Austro-Hungarians	460	725	1,185	605
1 Apr. 1919				
Italy	365	161	526	–
Austro-Hungarians	460	450	910	384

Source: 'Memorandum on the probable Relations as to Strength (in Rifles), From 1 August, 1918 to 1 April, 1919 between the Italian and Austro-Hungarian Armies'.[133]

demands for greater Allied resources. According to the Italians, their assessment of the force comparisons between the Austro-Hungarians and themselves was bleak (see Table 4.2). The Austro-Hungarian army not only had more men than the Italians but also had full strength and rested units as well as 'a really remarkable strength in artillery'.[134]

The Italians justified their assessment of the enemy by explaining that it was based on abundant intelligence gained from interviewing prisoners and from documents which they had captured during the battle of the Piave in June. These documents indicated that artillery from the Eastern Front was continually being added to the enemy divisions and that the Austrians were emulating the devastatingly effective German training systems.[135] Furthermore, in July the Italians had heard rumours (from sources which included prisoners, enemy deserters, and their own men who had escaped from Austrian captivity) that indicated that Austria-Hungary was able to replenish its units with men drawn from the interior of the Dual Monarchy. They also believed that the Germans had sent units to the Italian Front to boost morale. In general they assessed that enemy war material was sufficient, ammunition abundant, and personal

---

[133] Italian Section, 'Memorandum on the Condition of the Austro-Hungarian Army', 4 September 1918, Bliss/324. Note these figures do not include machine gunners, men of the baggage train, bomb throwers, flame throwers, etc., but rather line infantry, sharpshooters, cycle corps, and storm troops. They also exclude Allied forces in Italy; however, they do include the two Italian divisions in France, as well as the Italian forces in Albania (approximately 23,000 rifles). They evaluated units in battalions and companies, which they estimated at full strength, at 500 and 100–130 respectively.

[134] Ibid.   [135] Ibid.

equipment and trench arms renewed. The one item which the Austro-Hungarians lacked was uniforms (though their boots were still in good condition). To top these extraordinary assessments, Italian intelligence explained that '[i]t is positively known that the rations given the soldiers are equal to those given out in the other European armies'.[136]

Throughout 1918 the Italians grossly overestimated the abilities of the Austro-Hungarian and German armies. The reality of their situation, as described by historian Holger Herwig, was that, 'the once venerable k.u. k. [kaiserlich und königlich] Army was no longer a fighting force. Of the Isonzo Army's 15 divisions, seven were at one-third, three at one-half, and only five even at two-thirds of full strength. Dysentery, malaria, and malnutrition had reduced the army's rank and file to a pathetic shadow of its former self'.[137] One of the results of the battle of the Piave in June had been that the k.u.k. army had been demolished, with desertion rates steadily increasing until the signing of the armistice. By the end of June the Austro-Hungarian army stood at a total combat strength of 37 full divisions (although on paper the Austrian War Ministry still recorded it as 57).[138] The manpower that Austria-Hungary did have was surviving in tattered clothing and on a meagre 500g of meat a week, and around 450g of potatoes and vegetables served at most twice a week.[139]

The Italian draft note only adopted a sanguine tone when describing what an attack in Italy would look like if the Italians gained the necessary additional support from their partners. In this scenario, they argued they could defeat the Austro-Hungarians by May 1919. In contrast, without Allied assistance, 'the action of the Italian army should be limited to engaging the enemy forces opposed to it in actions of limited radius'.[140] The Italians also warned yet again of a possible combined Austro-Hungarian and German attack in the Italian theatre. To prepare, the Italians recommended that the Allies make provisions to reinforce the Italian Front quickly. For its part, the Italian army had to be prepared to move to the attack 'whenever the situation warrants it because of the shifting of Austrian forces from the Italian to the France-British theatre or because of occurrences in the latter theatre so favourable as to justify, on Italy's part, the employment of all their offensive strength to aid in a

---

[136] Ibid.
[137] Holger Herwig, *The First World War: Germany and Austria-Hungary, 1914–1918* (London, 1997), 434.
[138] Ibid., 373.
[139] Ibid., 435. Also see Thompson, *White War*, 342–245, 352–355. Mark Cornwall, *The Undermining of Austria-Hungary: The Battle for Hearts and Minds* (Basingstoke, 2000), 406–407.
[140] Italian Section, 'Allied Plans of Campaign'.

decision already assured'.[141] In fact the latter scenario is precisely what did occur on the Italian Front in October 1918. The Italians played on the well-known fears of their partners by hinting that, if the Italian army were not strong enough, it would not be able to hold forces in their theatre. The result would be that the enemy could move substantial forces to the Western Front, hindering Allied victory there in 1919.

At the same time as the Italians communicated their note to their colleagues, Bliss, reacting to pressure from the Italians, wrote a heated letter to March. Bliss complained that the Italians were pestering him for American manpower, which, the American PMR assessed, was because they overly feared the Germans, they lusted for money that could be made from American troops based in Italy, and they desired the political clout that would be obtained if Italy were to author the major blow against Germany. Unsurprisingly, Bliss supported Foch, who wanted the Italians to launch an offensive before the end of the year. However, the Italians quickly turned this request into an opportunity to ask for more resources. Compounding Bliss's frustration was a recommendation made by the American ambassador to Great Britain, Walter Hines Page, that the Americans send 500,000 of their men to Italy. The American PMR observed that Page had, 'like everyone else that goes to Italy . . . become saturated with the Italian idea'.[142] When Bliss suggested that Page consult Foch on the issue, Page replied that 'the Italians disliked the French very much and that the French reciprocated the feeling'.[143] Writing to March, Bliss relayed that 'He [Page] did not believe that he would get much encouragement at the Marshal's Headquarters. I told him frankly that I did not think he would get much encouragement at General Pershing's Headquarters'.[144] The American PMR was aware that Pershing had received positive news from an intelligence source (which was forwarded to Bliss) that conditions in Austria and Galicia were bad and thus it was unlikely that troops would be withdrawn from these areas and sent to support the Austro-Hungarian troops in Italy.[145] In fact Pershing had told Diaz that he too thought the Italians should attack, but Diaz, as usual, had been hesitant. Pershing inferred that Diaz wanted to conserve his troops for the spring of 1919.[146]

The final draft Joint Note 37 submitted by the Americans, on 4 September, reinforced the idea that American troops would not be sent to Italy unless Foch deemed it necessary. Not unsympathetic to the

---

[141] Ibid.   [142] Bliss to March, 3 September 1918, Bliss/250.   [143] Ibid.   [144] Ibid.
[145] From the American Military Attache (Petrodgrad) to GHQ, AEF, 10 July 1918 (but not processed by GHQ until 3 September), Bliss/321.
[146] Pershing diary, 3 September 1918, Pershing/2.

Italians, it also recognised the vulnerability of the Italian Front, writing that the war could be won in 1919 on the French Front 'after providing such forces for the Italian Front as may be necessary to insure its safety, and as, in the opinion of the Commander-in-Chief of the Allied Forces in France, can be employed to advantage in offensive operations on the Italian Front in supplementing Allied operations in France'.[147] However the Americans did not foresee upsetting Allied plans for an offensive in France in 1919 and thus 'no transfer of troops from France to Italy should be contemplated this year unless it be necessary to meet an enemy offensive ...'[148] The final joint note accepted by the PMRs, on 13 September, too, included a clause that both acknowledged the concerns expressed by the Italians but clarified that the Franco-Belgian Front was the main theatre of war: 'even though it might appear possible to crush the Austrian Army on the Italian Front, and a portion of the German Army with it, the final defeat of Germany, the real foundation of the hostile coalition, can only be brought about in the theatre where the main German Armies are to be found ...'[149] The PMRs, once again, recommended the improvement of rail-lines between France and Italy to allow for the concentration of troops in Italy – both to protect it against a potential attack from the Austro-Hungarians (reinforced by the Germans) and in case Marshal Foch determined that the Italians should launch their own offensive against the Central Powers (which he already had). The PMRs envisaged 'that a considerable offensive operation by the Italian Armies, if carried out in conjunction with the general offensive in France, might contribute largely to the final decision by the defeat of the Austrian Army, which could not at such a time count on any help from Germany'.[150] By September the PMRs were more positive about their ability to win the war, contemplating, 'that the opportunity may arise for the Allied Armies to undertake in Italy in the Autumn and Winter of 1918 the offensive intended for the Autumn and Winter of 1919'.[151]

Despite the increased optimism of the PMRs, the Italian political leadership was still hesitant. At the end of September, Nitti once again communicated his frustration with Italy's allies to Rodd. He explained that Italy joined the war to act as a 'complementary character, that is to say she had only to contain a portion of the Austrian army' and that

---

[147] American Section, 'Proposed Joint Note: Allied Plans of Campaign for the Autumn 1918 and for the Year 1919', Bliss/324.
[148] Ibid.
[149] 'Joint Note 37: General Military Policy of the Allies for the Autumn of 1918 and the Year 1919', 13 September 1918, CAB 25/84/SWC320.
[150] Ibid.   [151] Ibid.

instead Italy found itself 'alone against Austria-Hungary and in continual and sensible danger'.[152] He argued that the Allied forces in Italy were of comparable strength to the divisions and labourers that the Italians had sent to assist France in the spring of 1918 and complained that, '[i]t is hardly in the spirit of the compact of alliance that the Italian troops should be left face to face with an enemy largely superior in numbers'.[153] The French responded to Nitti's concerns by stating that the Austro-Hungarians forces were in a weakened state; however, this did not compel the Italian leadership to agree. Nitti's assessment was that 'Austria has as a matter of fact a great military capacity of resistance, a magnificent artillery organisation and a splendid tradition of discipline. All internal disorders therefore do not modify or modify little the efficiency of her military force which continues to be formidable'.[154] Nitti was passionate about this issue and met with Rodd to explain the Italian position in greater detail. While admitting that there were a variety of opinions on the magnitude (and quality) of the forces the Austro-Hungarians still had, he said that, even if the minimum calculation were taken, Austria-Hungary still had 12 more divisions than the Italians. Given these circumstances, the Italians did not want to attack. Nitti also warned that failure in Italy would affect the Allied position as a whole. However, he did say that, if an Allied reserve (of Americans) was created, then Italy would be in a position to attack even if these troops were not used in the front line.

Nitti then turned his attention to Italy's partner, France, accusing Clemenceau of cancelling the September meeting of the SWC in order to avoid discussing the return of Italian divisions and labourers from France. He complained that, 'France wished to concentrate not only the whole military but also the whole political direction of affairs in her own hands and had succeeded in drawing the American authorities into the orbit of her influence exclusively'.[155] Reverting to pre-war rivalries, Nitti said the French were paranoid about Italian population growth due to their own population's decline: 'Italy was also a future rival in economic development and it was the aim of French policy to retard and not to advance her national evolution'.[156]

The French were not the only ally the Italians were alienating. Their pestering of the Americans for resources was having a negative effect on the Italian-American relationship as well. When the American

---

[152] 'Notes on the Military Situation given by Signor Nitti to His Majesty's Ambassador', n. d., Rodd/19.
[153] Ibid.   [154] Ibid.   [155] Rodd to Lloyd George, 27 September 1918, Rodd/19.
[156] Ibid.

ambassador to Italy, Nelson Page, was approached about this issue by the Italian Minister of Foreign Affairs, he recommended that Diaz place his troops under the command of Foch in the same way that Pershing had done. Sonnino informed Page that the Italians were ready to do so. Page told President Wilson that both Diaz and the Italian king were also prepared to agree 'with the understanding that Italy would not be ordered to make an offensive against Austria until they had been given a sufficient number of Americans, as had been given by France at need'.[157] Once again the Italians tried to solicit manpower from their partners by offering to mount an offensive. Page later explained to Bliss that the 'future commercial relations of Italy and the United States would be benefited and international understanding promoted by further troops being sent there'.[158] While Page wished the Italians would make Foch Generalissimo in Italy, as this would settle the questions of American troop movement to Italy, he preferred the Italians would do so without being motivated by the idea that they would in fact be given American manpower.

The US Secretary of War, Newton D. Baker, was also bombarded with Italian pleas for manpower when he visited Europe in the autumn. Baker was aware that Pershing had been unreceptive to a request made by Diaz for Pershing to send him 25 divisions, and by the British to send forces to Italy (which might be placed under British command, although they did not say as much). He did not want to undermine Pershing and Foch by personally discussing these issues with the Italians.[159] Pershing had told the Italians, 'that we had one Western Front and that the question of sending troops to Italy should be regulated in the same manner that the question of sending them to Champagne, Picardy or any other sector was done'.[160] Not completely unsympathetic to the Italians, Baker asked that Bliss provide him with his opinion of the Italian theatre as well as suggesting that the Allies might consider the transfer of American troops over the winter when the fighting had ceased in France.[161]

Despite the American efforts to encourage the Italians to extend Foch's power to Italy, the Generalissimo was more concerned that the Comando Supremo partake in offensive action against the Central Powers than he was about having his responsibilities extended to Italy.[162] On 30 September Bulgaria had signed an armistice and, in an effort to

---

[157] Baker to Wilson, 26 September 1918, Wilson/100.
[158] Baker to Bliss, 14 October 1918, Bliss/250/no. 6.
[159] For the point on the British wanting the Americans to send forces to Italy, see Bruce, *Fraternity*, 256–257.
[160] Pershing diary, 24 July 1918, LOC, Pershing/2.
[161] Baker to Bliss, 14 October 1918, Bliss/250/no. 6.   [162] Greenhalgh, *Foch*, 449.

exploit this situation, the British and French encouraged an Italian offensive against the Austro-Hungarians to keep them from moving troops to the Balkans, where the Allied forces were planning to attack Austria-Hungary from the south and Constantinople from the east (as described in previous chapters).[163] In France, it was obvious to Foch that the Germans lacked the reserves to counter-attack. The Generalissimo urged the Italians to attack, as he wanted to bring pressure to bear on the Central Powers at as many points as possible, believing that the Germans would be unable to withstand this multi-pronged approach. Foch was not interested in exchanging resources required in France for extended power in Italy. He challenged the Italians to undertake an offensive role alongside their partners, writing, 'the allied armies, Belgian, British, French, American, Greek, Serb, are attacking without pause; from the Jordan to the North Sea all the front is shaken. There is no war without risks; the question is now to know whether those risks, with the shaken morale and the disorganisation of the Austrian army, the Italian Command is disposed to encounter them'.[164]

By early October Italian intelligence was more positive, accurately reporting the dire situation in Austria-Hungary. As one intelligence officer eloquently described, 'The Austrian army in line is still strong but it cannot be supported from the rear which is infected. It is like a pudding which has a crust of roasted almonds and is filled with cream. The crust which is the army in the front line is hard to break'.[165] Nonetheless, Italian high command still did not assume that Austria-Hungary would be easily defeated in the field.

Heavy rain forced Diaz to delay his offensive. Meanwhile Orlando learned that the Austro-Hungarians were preparing a peace proposal that would see them withdraw from Italian territory. Anxious for the Italian army to achieve a military victory which would ensure he had a voice at the peace table, Orlando spurred the Commando Supremo into action. Finally, on 24 October, the anniversary of Caporetto, Diaz moved forward with an attack. After six days of hard fighting, the Austro-Hungarians sued for an armistice. It came into effect on 4 November 1918.[166] If Diaz could have been encouraged to attack in September, the Allies would have achieved the sort of multi-theatre offensive action they had hoped to realise in 1919, as in the Balkans Franchet d'Espèrey

---

[163] Hankey diary, 1 October 1918, HNKY/1/5.
[164] Foch to Orlando, 28 September 1918.
[165] Cornwall, *The Undermining of Austria-Hungary*, 421.
[166] Ellis and Cox, *The World War I Databook*, 273.

attacked on 15 September and in Palestine Allenby attacked on 18 September.[167]

The Armistice of Villa Giusti, signed between Italy and Austria-Hungary, clearly illustrated that the Italians had achieved a military victory over their adversary. The Austro-Hungarian forces were to cease fighting immediately, surrender half of their artillery, reduce their peacetime forces to 20 divisions, and evacuate all territory which fell under the Treaty of London.[168] In addition, the Italians wrote in a 24-hour delay to the ceasefire terms, which allowed them to capture as much of the northern Adriatic and the Alto Adige regions as possible. This action enhanced the scale of their victory and highlighted their imperial ambitions. A final condition, allowing the Allies to pass through Austria in order to attack Bavaria, indicated the Allies' resolve to militarily defeat the Germans.

With this aim in mind, finally on 4 November Foch's role was expanded to include 'strategic direction' of all operations against Germany, including the Italian theatre.[169] This same day, the SWC approved a plan to attack Germany through Austria (via Bohemia and Galicia) as recommended by Foch, Bliss, H. Wilson, and di Robilant. Correspondingly the PMRs were directed to examine the details of such an offensive. Its aim was to prevent a German invasion of Austro-Hungarian territory, block Germany from obtaining strategic raw materials (such as coal and oil), and facilitate the creation of aerodromes from which to bomb Germany.[170] While at the SWC Foch gave support to this idea; his biographer, Elizabeth Greenhalgh, has written that 'given the weather at that time of year and the multinational nature of the force, it seems unlikely that Foch had much faith in the scheme worked out'.[171]

Serious shortages of railway equipment in autumn 1918 had caused the Allies' advance on the German army in France to slow. As the Germans retreated, they damaged roads, railways, and waterways which hindered the Allies' progress.[172] As Foch later recalled in his memoir, 'the restoration of these lines of communication was one of the most important problems which I and my staff had to solve during the autumn

---

[167] Hankey, *The Supreme Command*, 837.   [168] Thompson, *White War*, 362.
[169] Greenhalgh, *Foch*, 491.
[170] 'Eight Session Supreme War Council – Versailles, France', 4 November 1918, Bliss/ 252, p. 46; Hankey diary, 4 November 1918, HNKY/1/6. For more on the operational plan drawn up by Cavan, who shortly afterwards, changed his mind as he thought the Italian troops were not up for fighting the Germans, see Cassar, *Forgotten Front*, 217.
[171] Foch, *Memoir*, 491.
[172] Ibid., 494; Henniker, *Transportation*, xix; for transport problems faced by the BEF in autumn 1918 that would have continued into 1919, see Ian Brown, *British Logistics on the Western Front 1914–1919* (Westport, CT, 1998), 202.

of 1918'.[173] They needed men and material for this restoration work, and while the Americans alone shipped 70,000 tonnes of rails per month (amounting to 120 miles of line), the Allies also faced serious shortages of steel that affected railway transport (see Chapter 6).[174] The French had torn-up rail-lines elsewhere in France to use the materials to construct necessary military routes. Transportation materials needed for the campaign through Austria would compete with those required in France.

In September, the French and Italians had asked the Americans to provide them with rails, cars, and locomotives. Bernard Baruch, the president of the American War Industries Board, explained that 'it would be impossible to meet the present railroad programme of Secretary McAddo and of General Pershing, and these additional demands of France and Italy were simply making the situation hopeless'.[175] American railroad materials were over-committed, thus Baruch insisted that the Allies first standardise their railway resources and then present their needs to Versailles. The war ended before the coalition's railway transportation reached this level of coordination, however, the motivation to do so existed.

The situation facing motor transport was no better. In addition, the influenza epidemic also affected transportation. Not only did it cause the trains to stop running at times (due to a lack of able-bodied personnel), but as March explained to Pershing in mid-October:

The transportation end of the problem has given us some concern. We have commandeered the entire truck output of the United States and no trucks are allowed to go to any civilian at all, but just at this time when I hoped to get to you 10,000 trucks this month, the overwhelming epidemic of influenza has cut down the production of the plants to one-third, so that now the War Industries Board only promises us between 6 and 7,000 trucks instead of the 10,000 I hoped to get, but I will make it up later on.[176]

Under these conditions, it is hard to imagine that sufficient transportation resources would have been diverted to Italy for an attack on Germany through Austria when Foch desired to press the Germans in France. The PMRs, in any event, took the idea seriously. On 5 November Sackville-West recommended that the IATC travel to Italy to study the railway lines between Italy and Germany's southern frontier. Bliss was particularly

---

[173] Foch, *Memoir*, 494.   [174] Ibid., 495.

[175] William Gibbs McAdoo was the American Treasury Secretary. Colonel Summers to Bernard Baruch, 1 September 1918, Seeley G. Mudd Manuscript Library, Princeton University, Bernard Baruch Papers [hereon Baruch] Baruch/496/235.

[176] March to Pershing, 18 October 1918, LOC, Peyton March Papers [hereon March] March/22.

enthusiastic about this scheme, approving the British memo and recommending that the IATC begin its study immediately. The armistice with Germany was signed before these studies could be completed.[177]

While the final vision the PMRs had for a strategy in Italy never came to fruition, their discussions throughout 1918 on the role of Italy in a global strategy had served to highlight the essential, but secondary, role of Italy to that of France. Jointly they became known as the 'Western Front'. The forum of the SWC served the needs of the Italians and, although Italy was a junior partner, the British, French, and American representatives did not dominate the conversations about the strategic role of Italy in the wider coalition. Cautious not to press too hard an ally whose morale was shattered after Caporetto, the British, French, and American PMRs listened to and attempted to alleviate the grievances of their Italian partners. And while a number of voices, including the IATC, were pessimistic about what could be achieved on the Italian Front without substantial additional resources, the reality was that the coalition was not willing to sacrifice gains in France for ones in Italy. Studies conducted by the IATC highlighted the need to improve railway links between France and Italy, if the Allies wanted to neutralise the threat that superior interior lines of communication provided the Central Powers. These discussions illustrated the extent to which the idea of a German menace came to dominate the decision-making of various individuals. Throughout 1918 the PMRs considered the potential of an attack by the Austro-Hungarians; however, the defining factor in the level of danger that these attacks posed was whether or not they would be reinforced by German units. Thus throughout 1918, the PMRs, unlike the Allied Generalissimo, did not recommend offensive action in Italy, nor did they recommend the movement of further resources to Italy to bolster the Italian theatre as the Comando Supremo desired.

Determining an Allied strategy in Italy was also complicated by the establishment of various groups and individuals whose responsibilities overlapped – the PMRs, the EWB, and finally Foch. The Italians' reluctance to extend Foch's power as Allied Generalissimo to the Italian theatre resulted in the PMRs advocating the extension of Foch's powers, as opposed to their working in competition with him. Furthermore, American reluctance to send more than a token number of troops directly to Italy and insistence that the decision to send additional forces was Foch's, reinforced the idea that the Franco-Belgian Front was the main theatre of war.

---

[177] Bliss wrote these comments directly on 'Proposed Draft Note' by the British Section, 5 November 1918, Bliss/322.

Yet, despite these complications, for the Italians, the SWC provided an alternative venue for Allied cooperation to that provided by Foch. The SWC offered the Italian political and military leadership, who feared not being heard at all, the opportunity to make clear their needs and wants. And while Italy's partners did not meet all of their material and man-power demands they were able to provide the Italians with what they needed to stay in the war. Throughout 1918, when manpower was desperately required on the Franco-Belgian Front, three French and three British divisions, plus an American infantry regiment, were kept in Italy. These troops not only provided the Italians with a much needed morale boost, but they were also critical for the defence of Italy. They gave Diaz time to rebuild his army by providing the Italians with a counter to the possibility of German troops reinforcing the Austro-Hungarian army. With their endless demands for additional American manpower, the Italians came close to alienating their American partner, and relations with the British and French were also often strained when Italy's appetite for military resources appeared to exceed their appetite for fighting. Nevertheless, by acquiring what they needed, as distinct from everything they might have wished, to maintain their front, the Italians illustrated that the SWC could be successfully used – even by a junior partner – to influence their coalition partners.

5   The Role of the Franco-Belgian Front in Determining an Allied Policy for 1919

In late 1917 when the military and political leadership began to discuss a strategy for 1918, they recognised that they would have to hold on the Western Front in 1918 while they built up resources for a campaign in 1919. While in early February this strategy was agreed upon by the Supreme War Council, the German spring offensives heightened the need for manpower resources and traumatised the Allies into overestimating German capabilities. The result was that, for the remainder of the war, Allied thinking about a future campaign in 1919 was based on their having a numerical superiority over the Central Powers, with the main source of manpower provided by the Americans. As the British and French governments pressed the Americans to adjust the shipment of manpower to meet the immediate needs of the coalition, the issue of manpower for a campaign in 1919 was brought to the forefront of discussions. Initiated by Foch, the creation of an expanded American military programme was considered by the Commanders-in-Chief, the American War Department, and the British War Office. Meanwhile, at the international level, Allied policy for the autumn of 1918 and the year 1919 (what became Joint Note 37) was drawn up by the PMRs between July and September 1918. While the PMRs focussed on creating a policy for the global war, they adopted the advice of Foch on the Franco-Belgian Front while supporting his role as generalissimo. As part of the wider strategy for winning the war, the thinking and planning done by these various groups illustrates the predominance of the Franco-Belgian Front as the main theatre of war and the German army as the main enemy of the coalition. The final decisive campaign would be fought in 1919 because the Allied political and military leadership determined that, as well as being the earliest time that American manpower would give the Allies sufficient numerical superiority over the Central Powers, it was also the extent of time Allied morale could be maintained. In this way the Allies could overwhelm the German army and dictate the peace terms.

In December 1917, the PMRs promoted a policy of defence for 1918. After much discussion at the SWC's third meeting, held in late January and early February 1918, Joint Note 12, 'The Campaign in 1918', was accepted. As described in Chapter 3, with this note the SWC agreed to hold on the Western Front, giving them time to build-up resources for a campaign in 1919. The perspectives and discrepancies between Foch, Haig, and Pétain over the form that operations should take in 1918 have been examined in depth by historians, most recently by Elizabeth Green-halgh in *Foch in Command*, which this study will not repeat.[1] Relevant to this chapter is that the military leadership agreed that the only way the war would be won was with an offensive.[2] In the words of Henry Wilson, the former British PMR and newly appointed CIGS:

We can only obtain a favourable military decision by a decisive defeat of the German Armies, and this can only be obtained on the Western Front. It is agreed that we cannot hope for such a decision this year, and, therefore, we have to consider now what preparations we can make to obtain such a decision in 1919. We cannot decisively defeat the German Armies without breaking through their defensive system on a broad front, therefore our chances of obtaining this decision will turn mainly upon the question of whether a 'break-through' is militarily possible.[3]

To achieve a military victory, the Allies argued that they required greater numerical strength than the Germans. It was through the American army that the Entente hoped to gain this advantage. Yet, since late 1917, the British and French had deep concerns over the slow progress the Ameri-cans had been making in bringing their army to Europe. As a solution, they proposed the idea of 'amalgamation', which, by early 1918, was a request by the Entente for American units to act as reinforcements for British and French divisions. This system offered a number of advan-tages for the coalition as whole. First, it would expedite the American's entry into the front line because they could rely on the logistical support,

---

[1] Greenhalgh, *Foch*, 274. Doughty in *Pyrrhic Victory* describes how Pétain and Haig had different visions for 1918. Haig wanted large, but destructive offensives in 1918. He did not want the Allies to wait until August 1918 for a decision. Pétain first wanted the Germans to wear themselves out with attacks or by the Allies launching limited offensives before a large Allied offensive was launched; Doughty, *Pyrrhic Victory*, 393. By 23 October 1917, Pétain told Haig he did not support an offensive now that the Russians were out of the war and Pershing thought they should try to end the war in 1918 rather than 1919. Trask, *The A.E.F.*, 36. Woodward says that Pershing's policy was to slowly build-up American manpower in 1918 for the campaign of 1919 and that Bliss and Colonel House were horrified that the Allies might not hold out that long. Woodward, *Trial*, 121–122. André Kaspi discusses how Franco-American coordination for American transport and supply was originally based on the Americans limiting their fighting in 1918. They would make their major contribution in 1919. Kaspi, *Le Temps Des Américains* (Paris, 1976).

[2] Greenhalgh, *Foch*, 285. As early as September, Foch believed the war would continue into 1919 due to the Russian Revolution.

[3] Henry Wilson to the War Cabinet, 'Memorandum', 19 March 1918, CAB 25/73.

service-of-supply and experienced high-level commanders and staff officers of the army they were amalgamated into. Second, American divisions, training in quiet sectors, would release French and British divisions for use in combat. Third, American troops would improve the morale of the French soldiers they fought alongside.[4]

Pershing, however, was extremely resistant to the idea of amalgamation for both practical and personal reasons. He doubted the ability of the French and British armies to win the war, believing that victory could only be achieved by a large American army. Pershing also argued that the method of training and instruction in the Entente armies was very different from the American approach.[5] He did not want to be a general without an army and wanted an independent army complete with command, staff, and supporting services.[6] The American government, who preferred to give the AEF Commander freedom to make decisions, was also concerned about having American soldiers serve under a foreign flag and the effect this would have on the morale of both its soldiers and its home-front. Furthermore, political considerations underpinned the argument for an independent Army, as the Americans were determined to become an equal partner in the coalition, and, like their partners, were aware that the size of their army was likely to determine their position at the peace table.[7] Despite these reservations, these men recognised that the requirements of their partners might mean they would have, at least temporarily, to adopt amalgamation.[8] As discussions on amalgamation developed, the American War Department, as well as President Wilson's close friend and personal adviser, 'Colonel' Edward M. House, became sympathetic to the European's requests for temporary amalgamation at the same time as they questioned Pershing's burgeoning responsibilities.

In early January, Pershing, too, agreed with Pétain that, upon arriving in France, American regiments would serve for at least a month in French divisions. He also loaned African American regiments to the French.[9] An agreement was also made with the British in February, when Pershing finally agreed to allow the temporary amalgamation of six American divisions if the British shipped these troops. While these men would train in British lines, Pershing still had complete control over them and could withdraw them at any point (which he did). Pershing went as far as to

---

[4] On the issue of French morale, see Trask, *The A.E.F.*, 37.
[5] Trask, *The A.E.F*, 37, 39. In December, Robertson had suggested that the Americans insert their troops into British lines by companies or battalions. After their training was complete they could be combined into divisions as part of an American army.
[6] Bruce, *Fraternity*, 146.   [7] Ibid.   [8] Trask, *Supreme War Council*, 73.
[9] Doughty, *Pyrrhic Victory*, 421.

agree to temporary amalgamation during the German spring offensives.[10] Desperate for manpower throughout 1918, and aware that without a change in policy the number of their divisions would diminish in 1919, the Entente continued to argue for some form of amalgamation of American manpower into their armies, which in turn would increase the overall numerical superiority of the Allies.[11] This issue caused friction among all three partners, as the British and French competed for American manpower and the Americans resisted. Once the American Army was formed in August 1918 and proceeded to take up a French portion of the line, the British switched tactics, arguing for the American Army to take up a portion of their line, or for at least the French to do so. It was a contentious issue for the Entente, as in early 1918 they had quarrelled over how much of the line each army should be responsible for, with the result that the British had taken up an additional 27 km.[12]

The troops that had arrived in Europe during 1917 had been equipped by and trained with the French army; however, the British, recognising that the Americans were desperate for shipping, saw an opportunity to forge closer relations with the Americans by assisting them with troop transport in exchange for American manpower that would train with the British.[13] Furthermore, they questioned why, when they were providing substantial shipping assistance to the Americans, the Americans did not offer greater assistance to their British partners. As both David French and David Woodward have argued, the British were aware that the size of their army was likely to determine the say they would have in the postwar settlement.[14] Obtaining American troops would address the dwindling manpower resources of Britain. As this chapter (and the next) will illustrate, this exchange was driven by more immediate and practical needs. Concern over the postwar settlement was a secondary issue to winning the war, or in the case of spring 1918 – not losing it – for the coalition members.

June Supreme War Council Meeting

At the June SWC meeting, tensions between the Allies were raised, once again, when the issue of manpower was discussed. Foch raised concerns

---

[10] For more on amalgamation in early 1918, see Bruce, *Fraternity*, 144; Greenhalgh, *Foch*, 323–328; Kaspi, *Le Temps Des Américains*, 169–180.

[11] On the strength of the French army, see Doughty, *Pyrrhic Victory*, 368.

[12] For more on these negotiations, see Hanks, *Culture versus Diplomacy*, 209.

[13] Bruce, *Fraternity*, 15; Kaspi, *Le Temps Des Américains*, 243.

[14] On the issue of the relationship between the size of one's army and position at the peace table, see David French, *Lloyd George Coalition*, 9–10; Woodward, *Trial*.

about the British government's inability to find additional manpower to maintain the strength of their army. In response, the British and French members shifted the focus to American manpower by arguing that without these men to reinforce their lines, they might lose the war. The SWC meeting provided a forum to address these concerns and to once again pressure Pershing to amalgamate his troops with their armies.[15] Finally, Foch presented the less contentious issue of expanding the American army to 100 divisions by July 1919 as a solution to obtaining numerical superiority over the enemy.[16]

Foch was concerned about the contribution that British manpower could make to the Allied cause for the remainder of the war. He was distinctly unimpressed with the British ability to raise forces in 1918. A day earlier he had highlighted numerous ways the French had found men, while writing that, despite the SWC having raised in January the 'insufficiency of manpower obtained by British recruiting in order to keep up the British armies in France', little had been done by the British to remedy the situation.[17] Foch was most concerned that the size of the British army was decreasing faster than the AEF was increasing. In order to encourage both of his coalition partners to increase their manpower contribution, Foch drew upon information about the relative strength of the armies, estimating that, in France, the Allies had 150 divisions to the Germans' 204 divisions.[18]

Manpower was a sensitive issue for the British government as it struggled to balance the manpower requirements of the army with those of industry.[19] Less than a month earlier the British had faced the 'Maurice Debate' where Lloyd George had been accused of withholding manpower from his generals. The British representatives at the SWC were not going to allow the French to simply blame British recruiting practices for Allied manpower shortages. Lord Milner shifted the debate's focus by questioning Foch's figures stating 'that the Allies have 150 divisions ... [yet] yesterday this figure was presented as 160 and that

---

[15] For more detail on the debates in early 1918 over amalgamation of American troops, see Bruce, *Fraternity*, ch. 5; Doughty, *Pyrrhic Victory*, 419–424; Trask, *Supreme War Council*, 70–95; David R. Woodward, *The American Army and the First World War* (Cambridge, 2014), 89.

[16] 'Notes du Secrétaire' 1 June 1918, SHD-DAT, Fonds Clemenceau, 6N 61.

[17] Foch, 'Allied Armies in Defensive Battle', 1 June 1918, in *USAWW*, 2: 436.

[18] In reality, on 21 March 1918, the Germans had 191 divisions in the west (with a further 47 in the east). Fong, *The Movement of German Divisions*, 228.

[19] For more on the tension created between the British and the French over the issue of manpower, see Elizabeth Greenhalgh, 'David Lloyd George, Georges Clemenceau, and the 1918 Manpower Crisis', *The Historical Journal*, 50/2 (2007): 397–421.

he had heard it variously estimated'.[20] Milner was irritated that the British had not been asked to prepare figures for the discussion. And while Foch tried to ignore Milner's comments on the discrepancy in figures, the British Minister of War continued to press him, reminding Foch that the figures he had previously been given were '101 French divisions, 2 Italian and 4 American, making 107; 11 Belgian, making 118, and 51 English, making 169'.[21]

Lloyd George, too, was confused about Foch's estimates, enquiring as to why the French assumed the Germans could maintain 204 divisions in France 'when we, who have more reserves and men than they, must reduce our number of divisions'.[22] The British Prime Minister would not allow the issue to be avoided, raising the issue for a second time. He highlighted that the Allies had greater reserves than the Germans yet Foch assumed they could maintain 54 divisions more than the Allies. He asked 'if we would not be killing Germans in the meantime', which would reduce their divisions.[23] Foch defended his figures retorting that, 'this was because they managed better; that the Germans maintained 204 divisions with a population of 68 million; that the British with 46 million cannot maintain 53 divisions ...' hinting at his scepticism over British attempts to raise manpower.[24] Rather than reduce the figures for the German army, Foch eventually agreed to amend and increase the figure of 150 Allied divisions. Intelligence consistently estimated the enemy order of battle at 207 divisions.[25] Although he had been berated by the British representatives, these discussions allowed him to highlight an essential point – the Allies required a greater manpower contribution from the British. He reminded them that, 'if the number of British divisions is not maintained, we will fail'.[26]

In an attempt to increase the number of divisions they might field in 1918, the British raised the issue of amalgamating American manpower into their army. While Milner reassured Foch that the British could in fact maintain their divisions, Henry Wilson admitted that, to keep 47 British divisions intact, he required that Pershing allow 10 American divisions to contribute to British forces until August, at which point British recruits

---

[20] 'Conference on Transportation of American Troops', 2 June 1918 in *USAWW*, 2: 444; 'Notes prises par le Secrétaire au cours d'une conversation', 2 June 1918, SHD-DAT, Fonds Clemenceau, 6N 61.
[21] Conference on Transportation of American Troops', 2 June 1918.   [22] Ibid.
[23] Ibid.   [24] Ibid.
[25] 'Compte Rendu du Renseignements', Deuxième Bureau, 2 June 1918, SHD-DAT, Conseil Supérieur de la Guerre, 4N 27, No. 1445.
[26] 'Conference on Transportation of American Troops', 2 June 1918.

would be ready.[27] Throughout this meeting Pershing expressed his
concern about the ability to form his own Army. His partners wanted
him to ship infantry and machine gunners but, he argued, if he did not
also ship service-of-supply (SOS) troops then the American army would
never become an independent force. Foch's response was to continue to
highlight the dangerous situation the Allies were in due to their numerical
disadvantage. He explained that American infantry and machine gunners
were needed 'to avoid the immediate danger of an allied defeat in the
current period of time, given that the reserves at our disposal have to be
exhausted before those of the enemy'.[28] Foch expanded upon his thinking
during a special conference which dealt with expediting the transportation
of American troops to Europe. Not only did he press for more American
manpower to meet the immediate needs of the Allies, but he also recommended the Americans raise an army of 100 divisions to meet the future
needs of the coalition.

By the end of the meeting, tensions remained high. Milner submitted a
formal protest over the inaccuracy of the figures presented by Foch. The
Allies, however, were at least able to agree that the Americans should
send 170,000 infantry and machine gunners in the month of June and a
further 140,000 in July. Lloyd George said the British could provide the
additional shipping for troops and supplies, which reinforced an informal
policy of exchanging American manpower for British shipping. Of
course, as Milner highlighted, being part of a coalition meant compromis-
ing. Pershing said he could allow troops to remain with the British until
July or August; however, these dates were merely estimates from a
commander anxious to form his own Army, which in turn were interpreted by a partner equally concerned about bolstering its own army.
These competing desires led to misunderstandings between the British
and Americans throughout 1918 (as explored in this chapter and the
proceeding one).

The official minutes and resolutions of the SWC meeting give a
different perspective to the June gathering. They do not convey a sense
of disagreement between SWC members, but rather unanimity. This is
not surprising as the majority of the information in these minutes was

[27] Ibid; On 23 August, Haig hoped to keep 42 active divisions, 10 of which were dominion
divisions (excluding the 3 British divisions in Italy) on the Western Front in France after
1 November 1918. They aimed to maintain these divisions from 1st January 1919–1st
April 1919. B. B. Cubitt to Haig, 23 August 1918, CAB 25/66.

[28] 'Procès-verbal of the Second Session of the Sixth Meeting of the Supreme War Council',
2 June 1918, CAB 25/122. The record does not include detailed information about
discussions. Foch presented the figures and the SWC approved them. A telegram was
then sent to President Wilson.

presented as a telegram, which quoted Foch at length, but was signed by the French, British, and Italian Prime Ministers and sent to President Wilson on 6 June.[29] The content had to be a compromise and was reflected in Foch's assessment of the German divisions, which he reduced to 200 German divisions in France to the Allies' 162. These figures were presented to the US president to gain greater manpower resources from the Americans. The telegram highlighted that in order to obtain numerical superiority, which 'the Commander-in-Chief of the Allied Armies judges indispensable for the final victory', the Americans would have to comprise a total force of 100 divisions in France, as determined by the Generalissimo.[30] This idea entailed a massive expansion of the United States' programme given that the original one foresaw 30 American divisions (1.4 million troops) in France by 31 December 1918 that would be largely be preserved until 1919.[31] It was the first time such a figure had been recommended. As Pershing later recollected, the Allied generals 'grew more and more fearful lest the enemy might still have untold reserves ready to swell his forces ... so serious was the Allied situation regarded that it was no longer a demand for twenty-four divisions but for one hundred'.[32] In fact, the following day he described how the onslaught of the German forces had caused the atmosphere of the SWC to be one of depression.[33] In order to achieve the figure of 100 divisions, Foch requested that the Americans raise a minimum of 300,000 men per month. This would give the men three months of training in the United States before they departed for Europe. President Wilson replied positively to the Prime Minister's telegram, stating that he thought they might even be able to exceed estimates for manpower in 1919.[34]

[29] For a copy of this cable, see Général Mordacq, *Le Ministère Clemenceau: Journal D'un Témoin* (2 vols., Paris, 1930), 2: 57–59. Ambassador Jusserand (Foch) to Wilson, 5 June 1918, in *USAWW*, 2: 443–444. 'Second Session of the Sixth meeting of the Supreme War Council', 2 June 1918, CAB 25/122.

[30] Ambassador Jusserand to Wilson, 5 June 1918.

[31] Thirty divisions represented 1,372,399 troops. March, 'Annual Report of General Peyton C. March, Chief of Staff, United States Army, 1919', RG/165/84–8/158/1190; Woodward, *The American Army in the First World War*, 102.

[32] J. J. Pershing, *My Experiences in the World War* (London, 1931), 446.

[33] Pershing to the Adjutant General, 3 June 1918, in *USAWW*, 2: 449.

[34] Frazier to the Secretary of State, 3 July 1918, *FRUS*, Lansing Papers, 2: 271. As stated in this source, no reply can be found in either the Wilson Papers or the Department of State Papers. Lloyd George recorded in his memoirs that, 'Conceivably the 100-division figure was put forward in the hope that by asking for 100 American divisions we might get at least 50'; Lloyd George, *Memoir*, 2: 1829. Wilson's reply was mentioned by Tardieu. See Tardieu to the SWC, 'Procès-verbal of the First Meeting of the Seventh Session of the Supreme War Council', 2 July 1918, CAB 25/123; 'Unofficial Minutes', Bliss to Baker, 9 July 1918, Bliss/250.

The American government had refused to send a political representative to the June SWC despite Allied pressure to do so. Had they done so, the Allies surely would have pressured him to postpone the formation of an American Army; as it was, the American government did not want to interfere with General Pershing. It was aware of the developing relationship between Britain and the United States over the exchange of shipping tonnage for American troops training in British lines (which allowed the British to bolster their lines) – a relationship they preferred to maintain as they were in desperate need of this tonnage. Upon learning of Pershing's reluctance to attach his troops to Allied fronts, the American Secretary of War, Newton D. Baker, became concerned that Pershing was not following agreements with the British. In an attempt to prevent tension within the coalition, the American Chief of Staff, Peyton March, wrote to Pershing on 14 June warning, 'British here have been imperatively insisting on using those divisions as long as possible and question of supplies for the very large increase of troops now being floated is inevitably dependent upon the length of time the British retain, subsist and equip the troops allowed to them temporarily'.[35] The next day Henry Wilson wrote to Pershing on the same issue, reminding him that there was an agreement between Lloyd George and President Wilson. The CIGS was frustrated that Pershing would not send other divisions to train in the British zone and wrote that the American commander was being 'a little rough, to say the least'.[36] He also informed Pershing that Lloyd George was 'much distressed' over Pershing's decision.

On the issue of the amalgamation of American troops, however, President Wilson distanced himself. While the British and French governments attempted to outmanoeuvre Pershing by entwining President Wilson in the matter, the American president made it clear that he did not want to become involved.[37] President Wilson saw it strictly as a military and not political affair and thus left the issue to be decided by the military representatives in Europe. He responded to pressure by announcing, in June, that he would only consider schemes using American manpower if they came from the PMRs, as Versailles presented the needs of the coalition as opposed to those of the individual nations.[38]

As criticisms of Pershing by the Europeans continued, Colonel House became sympathetic to these complaints. As a result he recommended to

---

[35] March to Pershing, 14 June 1918, in *USAWW*, 2: 464.

[36] Henry Wilson to John Pershing, 15 June 1918, in *USAWW*, 2: 466.

[37] Lord Reading to Colonel House, 'middle of may' is all Seymour says. Reading also appealed directly to Wilson saying it was the suggestions of Lloyd George, 22 May 1918, in Seymour, *The Intimate Papers of Colonel House* (London, 1926), 3: 459.

[38] March to Bliss, 24 June 1918, in Trask, *Supreme War Council*, 95.

his government that Pershing's authority be modified by appointing a political leader in Europe that would restrict Pershing's role to solely a military one. Historian David Trask explains that, despite his earlier reservations that the Americans remain politically detached from their partners, 'House continued to think of inter-Allied cooperation primarily in terms of joint military effort in order to defeat Germany as quickly as possible'.[39] In this context, Pershing was becoming a hindrance to coalition relations.[40]

House was not the only American questioning Pershing's decisions. The War Department was also irritated to learn that Pershing was overextending his power in Europe and so decided that his role needed to be redefined. As March explained to the commander:

In the absence of a personal civilian representative of the President on the Supreme War Council, many matters which are political in character, although military in their inception, and which require the adoption of a policy by the United States have been handled by you ... the President handles himself so much of the diplomatic correspondence that heretofore he has been unwilling to definitely assign a civilian representative on the Supreme War Council.[41]

The lack of a diplomatic representative allowed Pershing to overstep his responsibilities. March framed the necessity of making changes to Pershing's responsibilities in the context of meeting the expanded military programme, describing how work in America was being doubled and tripled because the Allies took one military man's opinion in Europe to be policy when it was not. March said that the intricacies of enlarging a military programme (beyond simply getting the men from the draft) required someone who could respond within a day or two. Given the scope of issues – managing the army, dealing with finance and supply, and responding to questions of national policy – March recommended some new appointments be made. Despite Pershing's complaints that March overestimated his diplomatic responsibilities, the War Department decided to officially appoint another individual to this role. While a number of suggestions were made, Tasker Bliss was given the responsibility of 'diplomatic intermediary' in addition to his role as American PMR. Pershing was agreeable to this arrangement, as Bliss was not a threat to him, being a soldier and not a political type. In addition, Bliss worked well with the temperamental commander, believing it was part of

[39] Ibid., 93.
[40] For more on how Pershing was likely to have been replaced had the war continued into 1919, see Mark Grotelueschen, *The AEF Way of War: The American Army in Combat in World War One* (Cambridge, 2007).
[41] March to Pershing, 5 July 1918, March/22.

his duty to support Pershing even when he did not agree. The result was that Pershing spoke highly of Bliss. The downside of this relationship, however, was that Bliss became caught between supporting the ideas promoted by the AEF Commander and the War Department, both of which had quite different visions for the American army. Not surprisingly, this divergence often made it difficult for him to present consistent information to America's partners, which subsequently led to suspicion and tension between the coalition members.

The War Department reined in Pershing's authority in two other important ways. The first was that Edward R. Stettinius, who was Second Assistant Secretary of War, was sent to Europe to organise munitions with France, Britain, and Italy.[42] The second, was that the authority of the US Commanding General of the service-of-supply was expanded. This left Pershing, as commander of the AEF, to concentrate on leading, training, and employing American troops, while Foch was responsible for creating and executing the strategic plan of the combined armies. Baker attempted to placate Pershing by saying that these changes 'clear the way for your natural position as the leader of our combatant forces in France' meanwhile he reminded Pershing of the role that the PMRs held in Europe:

The President is adopting as a definite rule of action an insistence upon Inter-Allied military questions being referred to the Permanent Military Representatives. Our difficulty here has been that the British representative would present something for consideration without the knowledge of the French, or the French without the knowledge of the British, and when we took the matter up for decision we would sometimes find that the other nation felt aggrieved at not being consulted. As each of the Allied Nations is represented at Versailles, the President is now uniformly saying with regard to all Inter-Allied military questions, that their presentation to him should come through the Permanent Military Representatives who, in a way, are a kind of staff for General Foch and undoubtedly maintain such close relations with him as to make any proposition which they consider one upon which his views are ascertained.[43]

Baker framed this reorganisation as an attempt to reduce some of Pershing's burdens outside his role as military commander, but Pershing continued to insist that these other responsibilities did not consume much of his time.[44] Pershing, who met with Stettinius on 23 July, positively recorded 'He [Stettinius] seems imbued with the desire to

[42] Baker to T. W. Gregory (Attorney General), 14 June 1918, Baker/5/4.
[43] Baker to Pershing, 6 July 1918, Pershing/20.
[44] Pershing to Baker, 28 July 1918, Pershing/20.

cooperate with me and states that if I find he is not useful, I have only to say so and he will gladly go home', further praising that '[h]e has the right idea in deciding that the researches and reports of the various members of his party shall be made in conjunction with the American Expeditionary Forces'. However this assessment of Stettinius did not prevent the commander from communicating his own beliefs about the American army to the Allies, which undermined the roles of both Stettinius and Bliss.[45]

In July, the British Section at Versailles also challenged Pershing's notion of forming an independent army, with the idea of, instead, forming international divisions. These divisions would comprise 12 US infantry battalions and one US machine gun battalion. It was a way the Entente could continue to integrate American units into their own lines, and in reality, they would be American divisions commanded and supported by the British or French, although the British did not make this obvious.[46] Predicting American resistance to this plan, the British Section argued that as opposed to putting American citizens under British and French command, instead they were lending French and British artillery and auxiliary services to the Americans that would 'enable the latter's Infantry to inflict a decisive defeat on the enemy at as early a date as possible'.[47] As quickly as possible after their formation, these American troops would be placed under the AEF commander. Over time the British and French support troops would also be withdrawn leaving fully American divisions. Integrating forces in this way would quickly give the Allies the advantage over the Germans.

To make their case, the British Section estimated that the international divisions would affect numerical superiority by giving the Allies 2 million rifles; a superiority of 575,000 rifles by 1 July 1919 on the Western Front in France. While at the April SWC meeting the Allies extended the term 'Western Front' to include the Italian theatre, when it came to discussing the specific details of a policy for 1919 and a decisive offensive against the Germans that would win the war, the PMRs sometimes differentiated between 'the Western Front in France' and 'the Western Front in Italy'.[48] Focussed on the main body of the German army, estimates created for the numerical strength of the Allies and enemy on the

---

[45] Pershing diary, 23 July 1918, Pershing/2.
[46] Sackville-West, 'Strength of the Opposing Forces on the Western Front in 1919', 30 May 1918, CAB 25/122/SWC256. They used 'infantry' and 'rifles' interchangeably. They did not include machine gunners.
[47] 'M' Branch, 'Strength of the Opposing Forces on the Western Front in 1919', 1 July 1918, CAB 25/122/SWC250/1.
[48] 'Report of T. H. Bliss on the Supreme War Council', February 1920, Bliss/253/p. 72.

'Western Front' referred to the Franco-Belgian theatre (as is reflected by the exclusion of the forces on the Italian Front from the studies). They envisaged that, 'Our numerical superiority would give us the initiative and we could assume the offensive instead of being continually attacked and seeing the German Army steadily advancing towards the vital nerve centres of our military existence'.[49] To the British Section, 'This question of the formation of Anglo-American or Franco-American Divisions is therefore considered of the utmost importance and unless it is adopted a military decision against Germany will probably not be attainable before war-weariness and political events bring the war to an unsatisfactory conclusion'.[50] In presenting these international divisions as a solution to German numerical supremacy on the Franco-Belgian Front, they detailed Allied manpower assessments.

The British Section had made projections about Allied manpower and concluded that by 1 July 1919 British forces would comprise of 400,000 rifles (44 divisions), with 10 of these divisions being Colonial. Of these 44 division, 38 would be first-line divisions and 6 would be second-line.[51] They estimated that the French would have 461,000 rifles (65 divisions), which did not include two Czecho-Slovak divisions that the French hoped to create. The Belgian army would consist of 42,000 rifles (five divisions) and the Portuguese 20,000 rifles (two divisions), giving the Allies a total force of 1,388,000 rifles. In comparison they estimated that the Germans could draw infantry manpower from the following sources: 165,000 men in depots; 450,000 from the conscription class of 1920; 50,000 from revisions made to previous conscription classes; 86,000 (12 divisions) from the eastern theatre; 260,000 (20,000 per month) from POWs released from Allied custody; 325,000 from conquered territories; and 675,000 from returned wounded and sick soldiers. Altogether these sources represented 2,012,000 men. Including current forces and wastage, the total infantry strength of the German army on the Franco-Belgian Front at the end of June 1919 was estimated at 1,425,000 (178 divisions).[52] They predicted that these figures would continue to decrease until the class of 1921 became available in the autumn.[53] The estimate of 1,425,000 German rifles to the Allies' 1,388,000 rifles resulted in the Allies being inferior by 37,000 rifles and alarmingly meant that the Germans would maintain their numerical superiority over the Allies into July 1919 unless the Allies changed their approach to manpower. The British Section expressed deep concern over these figures, as

[49] Ibid.   [50] Ibid.   [51] Ibid.
[52] 'Class' meant that in the year mentioned, the men were 20 years old.
[53] 'M' Branch, 'Strength of Opposing Forces'.

they believed the Germans would be able to resume an offensive on the Franco-Belgian Front by March 1919, when they would have 220 divisions, and continue it until the autumn. This action would result in the war continuing into 1920 when one of Britain's partners might withdraw from the conflict due to war weariness. They argued that Germany would be able to increase its strength as it had access to materials in Russia.

A second advantage of adopting international divisions, argued the British Section, was that it would free up shipping, as the Americans would only have to transport infantry and machine gunners and not the auxiliary services. In their examination, if Pershing's programme were followed, the Allies would be unable to take the initiative in the spring of 1919. Meanwhile, in 1919 the British could maintain (supply with material) 60 divisions, even though they only had 40 divisions available due to manpower shortages, and the French could maintain (supply with material and auxiliary services) 103, even though they would only have 60 themselves. Rather than ship complete divisions, the Americans could instead ship the men to fill these divisions. They would have to send 130,000 infantry plus 10,000 machine gunners (to make up one machine gun battalion per division) per month from August 1918 to February 1919. This proposal did not mean that Pershing's cherished Army would never be formed. From December onwards the Americans could also ship one complete division per month to assist in its forming. In this way less shipping would be required by the Americans as these Anglo-American and Franco-American divisions would already have the necessary equipment and support troops in Europe. In addition, the divisions created would be first-line divisions as opposed to a mixture of first-line and second-line ones, and the British and French armies would be able to supply the Americans with experienced auxiliary services. While discussions about these international divisions re-emerged within British forums later in the year, they were never seriously considered by the Americans, as Pershing was adamant about forming his own Army and largely had the support of his government. The idea of international divisions does serve to illustrate how the Allies' concerns over numerical supremacy encouraged them to think of creative ways to gain manpower, as well it illustrates that the only consideration Pershing would take seriously for an increase over Allied rifle strength was the expansion of the American army.

Meanwhile, Foch, with the support of Clemenceau and the assistance of Tardieu (who had recently been appointed Commissioner for Franco-American War Cooperation), expanded the study on the requirements for the decisive campaign in 1919. Between the June and July SWC meetings the French government investigated the supply of machine guns, guns, aircraft, and other weaponry.[54] On 14 June Foch sent a note to Clemenceau about the serious material obstacles that faced the American army. It included a transport programme for the American troops in the second half of 1918.[55] He reinforced that 100 divisions were needed for 'a decisive victory in 1919' and to have 'undoubted numerical superiority' over the Germans, arguing that they would have between 220 and 240 divisions.[56] On 20 July Foch asked Clemenceau to call up the class of 1920 so that they could be trained for use in 1919. He explained, 'The year 1919 will be the decisive year of the war. From the spring, America will have delivered its greatest effort. If we want to shorten the struggle, we must, from that moment, give it all possible intensity and, consequently, have in our armies all the resources available'.[57] Foch envisaged 80 all American divisions in France by April 1919 and 100 by July 1919. His plan focussed on the rate of arrival of these troops, their training, the tonnage required to transport them, and how to supply them once they were in France. In particular he was concerned that they have enough horses to organise American units upon arrival in France and sufficient armaments for the troops. Central to his plan was the ability to ship these troops. Foch recognised that the programme required the British to continue to supply the Americans with shipping tonnage. Through the French Ambassador it was explained to Secretary Baker that:

His [Foch's] preliminary examination of the conditions has led him to the conviction that the help in tonnage presently supplied by England will be indispensable in its entirety or nearly so, up to January 1st 1919: for besides the transport of divisions proper, tonnage will be necessary for supplementary troops to fill the gaps, supplies of all sorts, horses etc., in proportion to the number of divisions.[58]

Foch wanted the Americans to coordinate with the French in asking the British government to supply this tonnage. Clemenceau also pressed for the issue to be discussed. He wanted the question of 'Can approximately sufficient troop and cargo shipping be made available to carry out above programme, month by month' settled before the next SWC meeting. The French Prime Minister also attempted to obtain this information through Bliss. If the French and Americans were prepared, then they could force the issue on their British partners.

---

[54] Bliss to Baker, 26 June 1918, Bliss/250; Tardieu confirmed it with his statement to the first meeting of the seventh session of the SWC, 2 July 1918, Bliss/250; CAB 25/122/SWC259.
[55] Foch, *Memoir*, 395.
[56] Foch, *Memoirs*, 396. He did not explain from where he obtained these figures.
[57] Foch to Clemenceau, 20 July 1918, *AFGG* 7/1, annex 178.
[58] Jusserand to Baker, 20 June 1918, Baker/6/4.

At the same time as Foch was drawing up the details for an expanded American programme, Pershing was writing to Baker about beginning the steps necessary to execute it. He asked that Baker increase the draft from 1.5 million to 2 million by the end of December 1918.[59] He made other suggestions on how they might improve the American war effort for the future, such as putting women in factories, billeting men in France, and getting equipment and armaments from the French and the British (all of which were already being done). Pershing was enthusiastic writing, 'I stand ready now, without waiting for detailed study, to say that we can do it'.[60] Pershing also described to March that he thought the war had to be ended as soon as possible as 'our allies are becoming so war-weary that I do not believe that they will hold out beyond another year'.[61] Although he said they should ship at least 250,000 troops a month to April at least, and likely beyond, he said that 400,000 troops a month was more desirable. The AEF commander estimated that if he had 2 million men in France by December than these men could receive four months training by April: 'With this number of men, I believe we can end the war next year ...'[62] While Pershing foresaw problems with transportation and supply he had faith that the Entente would assist them in meeting their needs. For instance he predicted that with France having an excellent crop that year, this would go a long way towards feeding American troops, and thus reduce shipments of food from the United States. In the case of transport, he argued that horses could be procured from France or Spain. On the issue of ports and rail-lines, Pershing had little concern that they could handle the extra men. He was also confident that the Allies would provide the artillery and equipment required by the expanded army. As he summarised:

I am very decidedly of the opinion that the above program should be carried out. It is important from every standpoint that it should be carried out. There is doubt in my mind as to whether our people at home will keep up their enthusiasm in the war if it is of long duration. The national desire is to push the war and the people will be, in every sense of the word, behind you in carrying out this plan. We cannot afford to allow the war to drag along and allow our people to become tired of it through losses or through failure to successfully conduct a vigorous and offensive campaign. Every argument that I can think of favors this view.[63]

---

[59] Pershing to Baker, 18 June 1918, Pershing/20.
[60] Pershing to Baker, 18 June 1918, Pershing/20. He referenced a plan that he outlined for the next ten months, but it is not included in these papers.
[61] Pershing to March, 19 June 1918, March/22; Pershing/123. Pershing to Baker, *USAWW*, 2: 476.
[62] Ibid.   [63] Ibid.

Pershing had no shortage of confidence in the ability of the coalition to support an enlarged AEF. After the war he attributed his confidence to the fact that 'In the course of our discussion, M. Clemenceau gave assurance that every possible effort to meet our deficiencies, including those in munitions and aviation, would be made by the French Government'.[64] Of course, given that the French had successfully assisted in training and equipping most of the American army throughout the war, his confident manner in mid-1918 was based on his fruitful experiences with the French.[65]

Pershing initially foresaw the American programme being increased to 66 divisions by 1 May 1919 (meaning a shipping rate of 250,000 men, or three corps, per month); however, after a discussion with Foch he agreed to increase this programme to 100 divisions. It was the situation in Russia and the idea that the Germans would move troops from this theatre to the Western Front that motivated Pershing to advocate this increased programme. After this meeting, which was held on 23 June between Clemenceau, General Foch, General Mordacq (Clemenceau's military aide), and General Pershing, the American commander's confidence further increased.[66] The main issue discussed was the rate of shipment required for the American programme, which they incorporated into a telegram that was co-authored by Foch and Pershing and sent to President Wilson. Their projections for what was required to win the war in 1919 were based on the assumption that in that year Germany would have 240 divisions; therefore, in order to obtain the numerical superiority required to defeat them, the coalition required 100 American divisions by July 1919.[67] The commanders drove home the necessity that President Wilson call up 300,000 men per month. They noted their concern over manpower shortages in the British and French armies, as well as 'new indications of probably substantial increase of German forces from eastern front ...'[68] In addition, after examining the example of the French army they established that 20 percent of forces would need to be replaced per annum, increasing the number of troops required per month.[69] Clemenceau instructed Jusserand to emphasise that manpower

---

[64] Pershing, *My Experiences*, 460.
[65] For training and equipping of the AEF, see Bruce, *Fraternity*, ch. 5.
[66] Mordacq, *Le Ministère Clemenceau*, 2: 91.
[67] Tardieu to Commissaire Français, 24 June 1918, Bliss/319. Telegram to Wilson is attached to this letter. In Foch's memoir he also gives the projection for German strength in 1919 as 240 divisions. Foch, *Memoir*, 395.
[68] Pershing to Chief of Staff and Secretary of War, 25 June 1919, in *USAWW*, 2: 482–483. Copy of this cable in Pershing, *My Experiences*, 461. More information on the figures can be found in Pershing to March, 25 June 1918, March/22; Pershing/123.
[69] Clemenceau to President Wilson, 23 June 1918, Bliss/319.

determined what shipping requirements should be, and that recruits could be readied before shipping tonnage was secured.[70] Tardieu later explained that the logic behind this request was that in the past unexpected tonnage had been found which allowed the transport of large numbers of troops. Foch further pressed the gravity of the situation by sending Wilson a separate note about the Germans reinforcing their lines in France with troops from Siberia.[71] President Wilson's response to the Foch–Pershing telegram was positive, and he agreed to keep up enlistment figures.[72]

Bliss gained information about the meeting on 23 June through Sackville-West, as the two men had been discussing the issue of supplying cargo tonnage for maintaining even 1 million men in France. It was rumoured that Pershing and Foch had agreed upon an even larger force than 100 divisions. At the current rate of shipping the Americans could have 48 complete divisions as well as some corps, army troops, and rear-area service troops by the end of 1918. Baker had estimated shipping figures for maintaining an army of 1 million men in France to be 2.5 million dead-weight tonnes per month. Bliss reasoned:

If your estimate is literally for a million men (including combatants and service of the rear men) then by the month of January, next, there will have to be a large increase to your 2,500,000 dead-weight tons for the maintenance of the army of 1,500,000 men that we would have in France. You will, therefore, see what a tremendous amount of tonnage would be required for the maintenance of an army of 100 combatant divisions, plus their service of the rear men. Sackville-West and myself came to the conclusion that such a force can only be contemplated for a campaign of 1920 and God knows that we hope the war will not last that long.[73]

The PMRs had reason for concern. They had already concluded that the war was unlikely to continue into 1920 due to the weakening morale of the Allies. Bliss estimated the 100 division programme alone meant 2.7 million rifles and 675,000 service men, meaning a total of 3,375,000 men. It would take extensive additional logistical support to field a force of this size, especially given that the 100 division programme was seen as being overly ambitious by some (explored further in Chapter 6).

---

[70] Ibid.   [71] Pershing diary entry, 23 June 1918, Pershing/2.
[72] 'Procès-verbal of the First Meeting of the Seventh Session of the Supreme War Council', CAB 25/123; 'Unofficial Minutes', Bliss to Baker, 9 July 1918, Bliss/250.
[73] Bliss to Baker, 26 June 1918, Bliss/250.

July Supreme War Council Meeting

The 100 division programme was discussed for a second time at the seventh meeting of the SWC held from 2 to 4 July. Tardieu presented the shipping schedule for the transporting of 100 American divisions, which he and Foch had compiled. Tardieu reported to the SWC meeting that, 'the French Government had been examining the questions connected with the supply of machine guns, guns, aircraft, etc. to the American troops as they arrive in France. As a result of these studies, it could be said that the French Government were in a position to supply all that was required, with the exception of horses'.[74] In fact, the French were already providing the Americans with almost all of their artillery, machine guns, and ammunition (and would continue to do so for the remainder of the war).[75] Despite this statement that they could supply *all* that the Americans required, this did not actually mean everything, as they still expected the Americans to ship over rolling stock and other munitions (he did not clarify what was covered by 'other munitions') to France. Tardieu explained that the largest challenge facing the Allies was the ability to find the shipping for these other supplies. His estimates on shipping were even greater than Baker's had been for supplying the expanded American programme in 1918: tonnage requirements of 2.5 million in July; 3 million in August; and 3.3 million in September. Beyond September he stated that 'the amount would go on increasing at a proportional rate since the quantity of supplies required to revictual would naturally increase with the size of the forces'.[76]

It was with Tardieu's discussion of shipping that Lloyd George 'boiled over' as Henry Wilson later described it. From Tardieu's speech, the extent to which Foch and Pershing had been working with the French and American governments to prepare a schedule for 1919, without including a British representative, was clearly revealed. Lloyd George wanted to know where they had obtained the figures for their study, as shipping was usually worked out by the British in the United States. The Prime Minister was irritated by the fact that the British, who supplied 150,000 tonnes of the 250,000 tonnes per month used to bring American troops to Europe, had not been consulted and bluntly felt that the issue had been sprung on them. Tardieu attempted to placate the British Prime Minster, explaining that it was a preliminary study to determine what was required for the future. He argued, 'It had always been intended that the United Kingdom should be consulted as soon as the

---

[74] 'Procès-verbal of the First Meeting of the Seventh Session of the Supreme War Council'.
[75] Bruce, *Fraternity*, 101.   [76] Ibid.

studies had been *completed* [emphasis added]'.[77] His wording did nothing to subdue the British representatives. Henry Wilson candidly summarised the entire session, 'This (7th) meeting of the Supreme War Council was the angriest we have had, but I was very anxious that we should give the French clearly to understand that they were not going to take us over, body and bones, and take charge of every theatre. We have done this plainly – if a little, and unnecessarily, roughly'.[78] Lloyd George asserted that tonnage would be determined between the British and the Americans. The British CIGS described it as 'a complete "deflate" for the French'.[79] Despite the suspicions of the British, it was not uncommon for Foch and Pershing to discuss the schedule for troop shipment ahead of conferences. Foch wrote that that when a schedule was not agreed upon ahead of time, much time was spent on this issue to the detriment of other Allied concerns.[80] And while they had not included Haig, they also had not included his counterpart in the French army, Pétain, either. Where the French representatives had been at fault was in presenting the figures to the SWC as a *fait accompli*, instead of allowing the British to properly prepare for the meeting.

The PMRs' Strategy Making

In addition to being given responsibility for organising shipping data, Bliss also considered strategy for the 1919 campaign as part of his role as PMR. At the July SWC meeting, planning for 1919 was officially added to the PMRs' responsibilities as well. While the generals made their own investigations for the campaign of 1919 (which focussed on operations), the PMRs were instructed 'to study the military situation in its broadest strategic aspect, taking into consideration all such factors as political developments, the naval and shipping situation, the utilisation of new instruments of warfare, or all new tactical methods, etc, and to consider them over the whole field of actual or potential warfare'.[81] As an Allied body, they were expected to create plans from an international perspective, and, unlike the Commanders-in-Chief, they had the luxury of time in which to do their planning, as they did not have to concern themselves with immediate operations.

---

[77] Ibid.   [78] Henry Wilson diary, 4 July 1918, in Callwell, *Henry Wilson*, 2: 114.
[79] Ibid., 112–113. Bliss also recorded that the French study of tonnage 'seemed to greatly irritate' the British Prime Minister, Bliss to Baker, 3 July 1918, Bliss/250.
[80] 'Notes on a Conversation with General Foch at Chaumont', 17 June 1918 in *USAWW*, 2: 468.
[81] 'Resolution No. 7, Seventh Session', 4 July 1918, CAB 25/122.

Lloyd George, in an attempt to rein in the power held by Foch, suggested that the PMRs be able to consult the commanders independently of the Generalissimo while creating their study of the campaign for the autumn of 1918 and 1919. There is no record of this item being discussed in the procès-verbal of the July SWC meeting nor did Bliss mention it in his summary of this gathering.[82] The explanation is that the British later amended the SWC resolutions to include this issue in an attempt to restrict Foch's powers.[83] The resolutions, drafted in English by Maurice Hankey, were then passed around after a long day at the conference. Neither of the two French representatives read English, and yet they hastily went ahead and accepted the minutes. Nineteen hours later, upon looking over the document, Weygand noticed the extra inclusion. When Foch learned of it he threatened to resign. In Weygand's memoirs, he describes how Clemenceau returned to Versailles late the same evening to discuss Foch's position with the British Prime Minister who 'went into a real state of rage'.[84] The resolution was amended, stating that the PMRs would plan for future operations in consultation with Foch, but the plans they submitted would be separate from Foch's own. The dispute between the French and British over the wording continued for an additional number of weeks resulting in the heightened suspicion of both governments towards one another.[85]

From July to 10 September the PMRs drafted and exchanged plans on the future campaign until they reached an agreement in the form of Joint Note 37. As part of their examination of the global nature of the war, their study highlighted the predominance of the Franco-Belgian theatre and characterised the German army as the main enemy (the additional theatres have been explored in previous chapters). These two conclusions were agreed upon from the onset of the PMRs' studies of future warfare. Unlike their studies of the other theatres of war, strategy for the Franco-Belgian Front required very little discussion between the PMRs and when they did do so, it was usually done in terms of determining when would be the best time to take up the offensive. In turn, this timing relied on when the Allies would have enough of a numerical superiority to defeat the Germans. Aware of the fragile state of morale on the British home-front and in the French and Italian armies, the PMRs argued that superiority had to be established for the year 1919.

---

[82] There is no record of this discussion in the procès-verbal. It should have been discussed between 'The Yugo-Slav question' and 'the press question'. Bliss did not mention it in his summary of the meeting either, CAB 25/123; Bliss to Baker, 9 July 1918, Bliss/250.

[83] For additional information, see Greenhalgh, *Foch*, 383.

[84] Weygand, *Mémoires; Idéal Vécu* (3 vols., Paris, 1950), 1: 551.

[85] Shumate, *Allied Supreme War Council*, 862–869.

Throughout 1918 the PMRs created a series of studies that compared Allied and enemy numerical supremacy. Both the British and French Sections had access to intelligence. The British Section gained intelligence from the War Office, GHQ, and its own information-gathering in the field. The British Section saw at least some of GHQ's intelligence summaries, as they received papers that were exchanged between the War Office (D.M.O., P. de B. Radcliffe) and the British liaison at Foch's GQG (Brigadier-General C. J. C Grant). This information included précis of action on the battlefield as well as some intelligence summaries.[86] The French PMR received intelligence from Deuxième Bureau, which included estimates of the enemies' order of battle. They also received analysis reports from Troisième Bureau (operations).[87] The PMRs shared and discussed this information (meanwhile the Allies shared intelligence information through the Inter-Allied Commission which functioned outside the SWC).[88] Given Versailles' proximity to the French Front, its officers visited the battlefield to collect data which informed their reports. Working with additional information from both the War Office and GHQ, from March to December 1918, an officer from 'E' Branch, Hereward Wake, created a series of reports showing the strength and movement of the enemy across all theatres.[89] Wake used information which identified German units to extrapolate figures for the Germany army's strength in all theatres. For example, he concluded that, given all German divisions on the Franco-Belgian had been identified, 34 remained on the Russian Front.[90]

Even with this information, however, the PMRs continued to overestimate the capabilities of the Germans. Their reports were heavily biased by their analysis of past experiences (the German spring offensives), as opposed to intelligence. The intelligence reports they did receive tended to underestimate news they received about the German army's struggles. The time period in which the PMRs created their reports is also significant: beginning their work in early July and finishing in September, it was during these two months the military commanders *slowly* began to realise that the Germans were 'beaten, but not broken' as Douglas Haig told

---

[86] See entire folder, WO 158/85. British GHQ's intelligence created two reports, the *Daily Intelligence Summary* and the *Daily Summary of Information*. Finnegan, 'Military Intelligence', 37.

[87] See 4N 27 for information passed to the French Section.

[88] Michael Occleshaw, *Armour against Fate: British Military Intelligence in the Frist World War* (London, 1989), 177.

[89] March-December 1918, Bliss/320. There is a gap in the reports from September to November.

[90] Wake, 'Summary for the week', 20 July 1918, Bliss/320.

Foch on 25 October.[91] This pessimistic outlook towards the defeat of the German army remained prevalent up to, and even past, the signing of the armistice.[92]

The American Section was the first to produce a draft for Joint Note 37. While examining all of the theatres of war, it made clear that the main theatre was the Franco-Belgian Front. It pointedly explained that a numerical superiority of 30 divisions had not resulted in a 'decisive offensive' for the Germans in the spring of 1918, nor for the Allies in 1916 and 1917. Therefore they recommended that the Allies wait until they had a numerical superiority of 50 divisions before launching a 'continued offensive'. The situation in Russia made it difficult for the PMRs to predict when this superiority would occur, leading them to review various scenarios. In the first, the Americans assumed that the Germans would not receive troops from the Russian Front. In this case the Allied forces would increase steadily from 1 November (exact figures could not be stated as available tonnage was not known), and by the spring or summer of 1919 the Allies could begin their drive against the Germans in France and Belgium. In a second scenario, in which the Germans were able to transfer 32 divisions from Russia to France, the Allies would have to delay their decisive assault to the mid-summer or autumn of 1919.[93] The American recommendation was that local object-ives remain limited and that the Allies focus on counter-attacks for the remainder of 1918, which would allow them to save their strength for an offensive in 1919.[94]

The officers in the British Section had difficulty in understanding the American figures. By their calculations the Germans would be able to maintain their strength throughout the winter, as in September 1918 the 1920 Class would be available to reinforce the German army. They thought the Americans were being too optimistic in suggesting the Allies would obtain numerical superiority over the Germans in 1918. With a shipping rate of three divisions per month and no German troops being transferred from Russia to the Franco-Belgian Front, the Allies would

---

[91] Haig to Foch, 25 October 1918, WO 158/85.

[92] For British attempts to assess German manpower and how these estimates influenced strategy between 1915–1917, see Louis Halewood, '"A Matter of Opinion": British Attempts to Assess the Attrition of German Manpower, 1915–1917', *Intelligence and National Security*, 32/3 (2017).

[93] Between 13 July to 31 August the British Section calculated that the Germans had a minimum of 35 infantry and 6 cavalry divisions on the Russian Front while the Austro-Hungarians had 15 ½ infantry, plus 4 ½ cavalry divisions. Wake, 'Summary for the week', Bliss/320.

[94] American Section, 'Allied Operations in the Autumn and Winter of 1918 and Summer of 1919', 15 July 1918, CAB 25/84.

still only have a superiority of 70,000 rifles by 1 April 1919 (1,729,000 Allied rifles to 1,660,000 enemy rifles). According to estimates received by the British PMR from the War Office, on 1 July 1918, the enemy had a superiority of 220,000 rifles.[95]

British pessimism was also illustrated in 'M' Branch's separate study on 'The Strength of Nations in Morale and Their Power of Endurance'. It expressed concern that, with the exception of the United States, war weariness was spreading in the belligerent nations, as exemplified through lowered morale in the armies and by internal unrest on the home-fronts. They thought the Latin 'races' were particularly susceptible to collapse. Furthermore, they also doubted even the ability of the American spirit to remain high for a prolonged period of time. Recognising that these were citizen armies that were not disengaged from home-front morale, they argued that the war had to be concluded in 1919 rather than 1920.[96] 'A' Branch was also pessimistic about the sprawling time-line for the Allies to win the war. In particular, they recorded that, due to manpower shortages, the war could not be won in 1919, but would continue until 1920.[97]

The branches of the British Section also completed their studies on 'What Constitutes Winning the War?' at the same time as they were considering plans for 1919. 'M' Branch defined complete victory as the ability to dictate their terms to the Central Powers. They wrote that complete victory could no longer be obtained, as the Allies military effort was likely to become exhausted before the enemy was defeated. Within this context, winning the war now meant 'a conclusion reached where the Central Powers, after strong military or economic pressure, offer to negotiate on grounds which are acceptable to the Allied Powers'.[98] As the Central Powers now had access to Russian resources, they no longer thought the blockade alone could achieve this result. Still, they hypothe-sised that a combination of military effort and blockade could win the war, advocating the use of 'auxiliary' means that would destroy civilian targets through large air raids. Another way to win the war would be if the Central Powers, like Russia, collapsed internally.[99]

---

[95] 'M' Branch, 23 July 1918, CAB 25/84, minute sheet, 2.
[96] 'M' Branch, 'The Strength of Nations in Morale and Their Power to Endure', 25 July 1918, CAB 25/84. For more on the issue of the relationship between sustaining efforts on the battlefield and sustaining home-front morale (in Britain), see Brock Millman, *Managing Domestic Dissent in First World War Britain, 1914–1918* (London, 2000).
[97] 'A' Branch, 'How Are We to Win the War in 1919?' 21 July 1918, CAB 25/84/SWC280.
[98] 'M' Branch, 'What Constitutes Winning the War', 25 July 1918, CAB 25/84.   [99] Ibid.

Before the British Section completed its report, the Allies had successfully defended against the last of the German spring offensives and had
undertaken their own successful attack at Soissons. While in reality the
collapse of German resistance had begun, the commanders had not yet
accepted this fact. Given that the PMRs were one step removed from the
battlefield, it took them even longer to learn about and digest events.
Between 20 July and 31 July, the attitude of the British Section changed.
The draft joint note approved and sent to the other PMRs by Sackville-
West on 31 July did not incorporate the former level of pessimism.
Instead, the British Section recommended that the Allies execute the
policy accepted in Joint Note 12 – that now was the time to move from
active defence to the offensive. American troops had bolstered the position of the Allies both materially and morally: 'In France also a decision
favourable to the Allies would finally be decisive for it would involve the
defeat of Germany and without German aid the remainder of the Central
Powers would fall to pieces'.[100] They did not give a date when 'a final
decision would be made', but they did estimate it would occur around
mid-summer 1919.[101] By applying pressure on all fronts they believed
they could overcome the advantages that interior lines gave to the Central
Powers. They reinforced that the 'final decision' had to be won on the
Franco-Belgian Front and that this decision could only be obtained once
they had a 'sufficient superiority' over the Central Powers. They even
went as far as to give specific objectives in the Franco-Belgian theatre:
'The Allies must . . . free themselves from all anxiety as to the position of:
1. The Channel Ports 2. The Bruay Mines 3. The communications
through Amiens and across the Somme to the West of that place. 4.
Paris'.[102] These operational objectives were the same ones that Foch had
given to the Commanders-in-Chief at Bombon on 24 July and the same
objectives that Henry Wilson presented to the War Cabinet on 25 July.

Henry Wilson's Plan, 1919

On 25 July, the British CIGS presented a memorandum to the War
Cabinet, in which outlined his ideas on British policy for 1918–1919.
His study began by describing how, as the Germans were understrength,
all the German army could do in 1918 was make one more attack on a
large scale.[103] However, this attack could allow the Germans to take
Paris, separate the British and the French forces, or divide the French

---

[100] British Section, 'Proposed Joint Note', 31 July 1918, CAB 25/84; Bliss/324.
[101] Ibid.   [102] Ibid.
[103] Henry Wilson, 'British Policy 1918–1919', 25 July 1918, CAB 27/8/273; CAB 25/85.

army in two. He argued that the Allied response had to be to ensure the safety of the existing front line in France, recommending they do so by pushing the Germans away from 'vital strategical objectives, such as the Channel Ports, the Bruay coal mines, the Amiens centre of communication and Paris' through a series of small operations in 1918. With the Western Front secured, the Allies could focus on building up resources and manpower 'for the culminating military effort at the decisive moment'.[104] Like the PMRs, Wilson assessed when the best time for the decisive assault would be – 1919 or 1920. While Wilson was pessimistic about the Allies' ability to win the war in 1919, he did argue that 'the culminating period for our supreme military effort' should be made no later than 1 July 1919 as that timing was more advantageous to the Allies than waiting until 1920.[105] His concern was the Allies could not maintain their war effort into 1920:

The war weariness in Great Britain, the exhaustion of France and Italy, and the impatience of America, who will by that time have been at war for over 2 years, will oblige us to strike in 1919 or to stop the war. Indeed there will be difficulty in tiding over the period from the political point of view even up to the middle of 1919. The moment the anxieties of the present situation are allayed we shall be faced in this country with grave industrial unrest, and a strong recrudescence of pacifist feeling. It must be realised that all enthusiasm for the war is dead. The genuine longing for peace that undoubtedly exists among even the patriotic majority of all classes, especially the women, would probably find more active expression than it does already but for their reluctance to be associated with the unpatriotic minority of avowed defeatists and the exasperation caused by their blatant propaganda. High wages and separation allowances no doubt act as an anodyne but affect only a portion of the population.[106]

In addition, if the Allies allowed the war to continue into 1919, the Germans would have time to solidify their position in Russia and in Asia. Access to resources would allow them to counterbalance the effort the Americans were making for the Allied cause. It would also give Germany a better position with which to negotiate a peace settlement. For these reasons the CIGS pressed for a decisive campaign in 1919.

The primary factor on which the success of the Allies relied was manpower, which in turn was heavily dependent on the ability of the Allies to raise, train, equip, transport, command, and maintain in the field a large American army. The PMRs estimated that the American army would steadily increase in relation to the declining armies of the European allies. Drawing upon the British Section's estimates on manpower for both the Allies (although his estimates for American manpower

[104] Ibid.   [105] Ibid.   [106] Ibid.

were reduced by two divisions from that of the PMRs' study) and the Central Powers up to 1 July 1919, Wilson argued that the Allied forces would have a superiority of 400,000 rifles by this date (if the Americans fielded 65 combat divisions and had an additional 13 depot divisions). This superiority in strength would not be enough to defeat the Germans. Although the American War Department had warned they could not guarantee the 100 division programme, Wilson advocated that the United States send these divisions by the summer of 1919. He estimated that the expanded programme would give the Allies a superiority of 580,000 rifles. If the Allies could increase their manpower and support it through mechanical means, it would 'give us a fair chance of achieving substantial military success, while if the more favourable contingencies should arise our success should be decisive'.[107]

Henry Wilson also had to address the manpower crisis his country faced. He estimated that Britain would keep 59 divisions in the field during the current crisis but that afterwards they were going to scale down to 43.[108] To compensate for their lack of manpower, Wilson planned to expand the mechanisation of the British army by increasing the number of machine guns, aeroplanes, and tanks and to improve the training of troops. He went as far as to suggest a large-scale attack of 10,500 tanks on a 50 mile front.[109] He also wanted to recall troops from other theatres, especially Salonika – replacing the four British divisions with Indian ones.[110] If the Allies were to win the war they required more of everything to do so.

Wilson's ideas, however, were quite radical compared to those of the British Commander-in-Chief, who was flabbergasted by the CIGS' proposal. Haig wrote directly on the memo next to the Wilson's manpower and machine estimates: 'I do not agree with these figures' and on the first page of Wilson's memo, he scrawled, 'Whoever drafted this stuff will never win any campaign!'[111] While Haig had a positive view of tanks, he did not believe that entire campaigns could be planned around them.[112] The PMRs, too, took a more traditional approach, advocating the increased production of mechanical means as Foch dictated.[113] Whereas Wilson foresaw tanks replacing infantry, and hence greatly reducing

---

[107] Ibid.
[108] See Millman, *Pessimism and British War Policy*, for more on Henry Wilson's perspective, as his work is heavily based on Wilson's thinking.
[109] Henry Wilson, 'British Policy 1918–1919'.   [110] Ibid.
[111] Douglas Haig's notes on Henry Wilson's 'British Policy 1918–1919', n.d., WO 256/33.
[112] Harris, *Men, Ideas and Tanks*, 164.
[113] For other ideas on mechanical warfare at the time, see Harris, *Men, Ideas and Tanks*.

casualties, Foch envisaged them acting usefully, but more modestly, as a support weapon for more traditional infantry-artillery attacks.

On the same day Wilson presented his memo to the War Cabinet, the War Department informed the Entente that it had decided on the 80 division programme, giving the PMRs more accurate figures on which to build their report. The PMRs agreed that to win the war they required a supremacy of 1 million rifles over the Germans on the Franco-Belgian Front. They used the idea that one side had always had a superiority of 250,000 in this theatre – the Allies through to 1917 and the Germans at the beginning of 1918 – without breaking the other side. As Bliss explained to Baker, German success in the spring of 1918 was due to the fact that the Germans had half the distance to travel to reach the Allies' vital points and that, if they had had double their superiority (500,000), then they would have reached them. Following this logic, in order to reach the German army's 'vital points', defined as 'points which will cause the whole German line to crumble', the PMRs believed they needed twice what the German figure for success would have been – that is a 1 million superiority in rifle strength and a 'more or less approximate superiority in machine guns, artillery, airplanes, tanks, etc'. – given the extra distance to reach these areas.[114]

Also to be considered was the rifle strength of the Allies by 1 July 1919, for which both the British and American PMRs created studies. The Americans estimated that British rifle strength would shrink to 420,000, French to 656,000, and the Belgians to 42,000.[115] Where the British study deviated was on the French figure, which it reduced to 461,000. In addition, the British Section placed American rifle strength at 780,000, whereas Bliss argued that the 80 division programme would give the Americans a rifle strength of 1,184,000, plus a further ten divisions (169,000 rifles) that would have been in France for less than two months. The PMRs also did not agree over the forces that the Germans would have on the Franco-Belgian Front in 1919, as a number of variables altered their estimates: the number of troops the Germans could bring from the East; the number of Russian troops they might enlist; and the success of the Allied intervention in Siberia to hold forces there. Given these factors, the PMRs recognised the hypothetical nature of their estimates. While the British Section had already estimated that the Germans had 32 divisions (277,000 rifles) that could be used in such a way, it now estimated the Germans had an additional 400,000 recruits

[114] Bliss to Baker, 9 August 1918, Bliss/250; American Section, 'Estimate of Comparative Rifle Strength, Western Front', 4 August, Bliss/324.
[115] American Section, 'Estimate of Comparative Rifle Strength'.

from the Russian border states, which could be in France by 1 March 1919. In contrast, Bliss did not include this figure in his estimates, nor did he include any troops that the Germans had supporting the Austro-Hungarians against Italy, which could potentially be moved to France.[116] The American PMR estimated that the 80 division programme would give them a superiority in combatant strength (of divisional infantry, including machine gun components) of between 647,200 to 924,400 rifles (or 70 to 110 divisions), depending on whether the Germans moved an entire 32 divisions to the Franco-Belgian Front or not. With these divisions they estimated the Germans would have 1.65 million rifles and without them 1.38 million rifles.[117] These figures also considered that only 70 of the US divisions would be trained to fight by 1 July 1919. Not ignoring Pershing's desire for a 100 division programme and desperate to gain numerical superiority over the enemy in 1919, Bliss estimated that if the Americans could meet this expanded programme, it would give the Allies a rifle superiority of 1.13 million without the German use of Russian divisions and 850,000 with these extra enemy divisions.[118] It was the 100 division programme that could give the Allies the 1 million rifle superiority they believed was needed to win a decisive victory.

The British War Office initially used the figures presented by the British Section until the Adjutant General's Branch and the General Staff completed a joint study in August that was based on more recent evidence, including an update of the enemy and Allied armies in light of the heavy fighting they had incurred to July 1918.[119] Unlike the PMR, the War Office argued that evidence they had received illustrated the Germans had sustained heavy casualties and thus, 'All units appear to be under establishment and it is a fair estimate to reduce correspondingly their man-power resources by anything from 100,000 to 150,000 men below the infantry establishment of 750 men per battalion, to which they were recently reduced'.[120] In calculating the German army's strength, they estimated that the Germans could move ten divisions from Russia; however, they did not include any Austro-Hungarian forces that could be moved to the French Front, nor did they consider it likely that they Germans would recruit men in occupied Russian territories in substantial

---

[116] Bliss to Baker, 9 August 1918, Bliss/250.
[117] The precise estimates by the American Section were 1,654,800 rifles and 1,377,600 rifles.
[118] The precise estimate was 1,127,000 rifles. Bliss to Baker, 9 August 1918, Bliss/250.
[119] War Office, 'Allied and Enemy Strengths', 13 August 1918, WO 158/107; CAB 25/85; The papers of Alfred Milner, Viscount Milner, Bodleian Libraries, University of Oxford, 361 (hereon MS. Alfred Milner).
[120] Ibid.

numbers. In comparison to the PMR estimates, the War Office reduced the German army's strength from 1.23 million to 992,000 rifles.

Heavy fighting in 1918 had also taken its toll on Allied strengths, as the War Office study reflected. Highlighting that the French army strength was down due to severe fighting in July, they argued that the British army would have to sustain heavy causalities up to 1 July 1919, adjusting the PMRs' estimates for 1 July 1919 from 400,000 British rifles to 311,000 and 461,000 French rifles to 402,000. As the Belgians had undertaken less fighting than expected, they increased their rifle strength from 42,000 Belgian rifles to 43,000. The War Office also increased American rifle strength from 780,000 to 840,000 as training time for American soldiers had been decreased, thus allowing them to field men at a faster rate. The estimate of 20,000 Portuguese rifles remained the same (though Haig thought it 'useless to include these fellows!').[121] Unlike the PMRs, the War Office also argued that the British could add to their estimates of British manpower by using 'B' divisions – giving the British an additional five divisions.[122] They also considered that if Ireland were conscripted (with recruitment beginning in October 1918) the British army would gain an additional 10 divisions, bringing the maximum strength of the British army to 430,000 rifles by 1 July 1919. The War Office concluded that with these extra British divisions, the Allies would have a rifle superiority of 743,000 and 624,000 without them

The reduction of British manpower also affected relations between Lloyd George and Clemenceau, as the French remained suspicious that the British were withholding manpower, a suspicion that was enhanced after the French conducted its own study on the availability of men in Britain (compiled into the Roure report). As Lloyd George explained to Clemenceau, after the French Prime Minister accused him of withholding 2 million men from service in the British army, Britain's manpower had to be used to supply coal, shipping, munitions, and other resources to the Allies and for this reason more men could not be combed out of industry.[123] As Elizabeth Greenhalgh has described, the inequality of service between the British and French resulted in the latter conscripting more men despite their smaller population.[124] Lloyd George's

---

[121] Haig's on Henry Wilson's 'British Policy 1918–1919', n.d. WO 256/33.

[122] Henry Wilson described 'B' men as 'nearly "A" men'. Wilson quoted in Keith Grieves, *The Politics of Manpower, 1914–18* (Manchester, 1988), 196. Ranking divisions was done based on men's fitness levels. Greenhalgh, *Franco-British Co-operation over Munitions Production*, 409.

[123] Lloyd George to Clemenceau, 30 August 1918, LG/F/50/3/17.

[124] Greenhalgh, 'Franco-British Co-operation over Munitions Production', 401. She also addresses the issue of higher recruitment rates in the *French Army*, 408–409.

explanation did little to quiet Clemenceau, who insisted that British could increase their manpower contribution in the coming year. He explained that further sacrifice had to be made to achieve victory: 'the goal which seems to me to be necessary to our efforts if we do not wish to expose ourselves to an extension of the war, is to approach the campaign of 1919 with all our units at maximum strength, so that the High Command has in its hands all the necessary assets, to take the decision straight away. I do not seek to look further than that'.[125] Throughout 1918 the two Prime Ministers continued to disagree on Britain's manpower contribution, heightening tension between the Allies. Pershing too, was concerned about the explosive situation created between his partners over the issue of British manpower.[126]

On 6 August the French Section submitted its plan for the autumn of 1918 and the year of 1919. Like their counterparts, they recommended that the Allies move to the offensive, as suggested in Joint Note 12. The Western Front in France should be secured from attack, and the Allies should prepare the way for the offensive in 1919 so that, 'it can be executed in the best conditions and with the most powerful means".[127] Like Henry Wilson, Foch, and the British Section, the French PMR suggested that offensive action should focus on reducing the German salient in the direction of Amiens, that it should free the mining region of Béthune, and improve the Allied position on the Côtes de Meuse. The latter operation would take place with the idea that a subsequent operation would occur towards Briey and recover useful railway lines and waterways. However, the French Section advocated these offensive actions only if they did not wear out the Allied forces for an offensive in 1919 (similar to Pétain's concerns). The Allies should take the offensive early in the spring of 1919, otherwise the Germans would do so. This action would prevent Foch from having to commit the troops in unfavourable ways: 'These operations must be based on the front from the North Sea to Switzerland and be conducted with the maximum of resources. A decision can only be obtained through a series of successes won over the German armies and pursued relentlessly so as to achieve the disorganisation of these armies and the final destruction of their resistance force'.[128] In terms of material means, they

---

[125] Clemenceau to Lloyd George, n.d., LG/F/50/3/18.
[126] Pershing to President Wilson, 9 July 1918, Wilson/97.
[127] French Section, 'Projet de Plan d'Operations pour les Armées Alliés pendant l'automne 1918 et l'Ete 1919', 6 August 1918, Bliss/324; CAB 25/84.
[128] Ibid.

recommended the increased employment of tanks, aviation, and armaments as Foch requested.

The PMRs Meet with Foch, 26 August 1918

The French draft clearly illustrated that the PMRs had to base their studies on Foch's view, as did the first draft produced by the Americans.[129] Sackville-West explained to Belin that in order to obtain data about the Allied armies it was necessary to go through Foch rather than approach the Allied Commanders-in-Chief directly.[130] Bliss's communications to March highlighted the extent to which the PMRs were guided by the Generalissimo. The PMRs had met throughout July to informally discuss their draft joint notes, which the PMRs, with the exception of the Italians, then sent to Foch for his review. Prior to this meeting Bliss told March that ultimately the PMRs would have to agree with Foch: 'what is to be done or attempted on the other theatres must be made to fit in with what General Foch thinks should be aimed at on the Western Front'.[131] The one exception was if Foch recommended sending forces to a theatre outside the Franco-Belgian one. Bliss and the War Department agreed that the French Front was the decisive theatre and all American manpower would be put into action there.[132] This was an important point to clarify with the coalition partners. As he prepared for his meeting with Foch and the other PMRs, Bliss was aware that while the PMRs were in agreement over the main points the Allies placed more emphasis on fields outside the Franco-Belgian theatre.[133] President Wilson thought these sort of expeditions were futile.[134]

The meeting between the PMRs and Foch revealed that they were all in general agreement on plans for the autumn of 1918 and the year 1919. Afterwards Bliss described the meeting to Baker:

The main point was that every effort must be made by the Allies to thoroughly and crushingly beat the Germans *on the western front in France next year* ...

Marshal Foch then made a statement that was somewhat disquieting to me. In the main it was

That British and French divisions must be maintained at, at least, their present strength through next year, *at all costs*.

---

[129] American Section, 'Allied Plans of Campaign for the Autumn 1918 and for the Year 1919', 1 August 1918, CAB 25/84.
[130] The British PMR to the French Section, 29 July 1918, Bliss/246.
[131] Bliss to March, 5 August 1918, Bliss/250.
[132] March to Bliss, 26 August 1918, Bliss/251.
[133] Bliss to Baker, 9 August 1918, Bliss/250.
[134] March to Pershing, 12 August 1918, Pershing/123.

That 100 American divisions must be in France by July 1, 1919.

That tonnage must be provided at any sacrifice to enable the U. S. to do this.

He constantly reiterated that it was man-power that he wanted; as much artillery, tanks and aviation as he could get, but that it was 'man-power' and again 'man-power' that he wanted.

In answer to my question he told me that he should make this declaration at the next session of the Supreme War Council. If he does this, the Allies will have the issue clean-cut for their decision. Can they do it? Will they do it?

Marshal Foch holds these views in full light of the success he is now meeting in his present offensive against the Germans ... General Pershing told me on Sunday that he was sure that the Marshal would make these demands. As he and the Marshal worked out the 100-division program together they may still be in accord as to its necessity. This I do not now know.[135]

Bliss found Foch's statement 'disquieting' because Baker and Wilson had a different opinion on manpower and the campaign of 1918 than did Pershing and Foch. Furthermore, studies by the American Section had highlighted the necessity for the 100 division programme. Despite that the War Department had approved the 80 division programme, Bliss made estimates for both the 80 and 100 division programmes. In this way he was able to support the War Department and both Foch and Pershing.

Sackville-West was surprised that Foch did not give the PMRs more information about his plans, but rather focussed on manpower, the need for 100 division programme by the Americans, and for the British to maintain their current number of divisions.[136] After this meeting, the British drafts adopted a positive tone, advocating that the Allied attitude should be offensive. Once again they argued that to achieve decisive results, the Allies required 50 percent to 60 percent superiority over the Germans, estimating that the Allies would have a numerical superiority of 800,000 or 1 million men (a superiority of 55%) by 1 July 1919. However, despite these numbers they still considered the Germans to be a formidable enemy, which in turn meant they had to be cautious as:

It will not be possible to defer our offensive operations until July 1st – operations will have to begin in the Spring or the enemy might regain the initiative, but the gradually increasing pressure of numerical superiority will become decisive in July, 1919, and the increasing rate of production of aeroplanes, tanks and other mechanical contrivances is expected to give to the Allies a superiority of strength as regards material at least as pronounced as that which can be anticipated in personnel.[137]

---

[135] Bliss to Baker, 27 August 1918, Bliss/250. Bliss also wrote about the meeting to March on 3 September. Bliss to March, 3 September 1918, Bliss/250.
[136] Sackville-West to Hankey, 27 August 1918, LG/F/23/3/10.
[137] British Section, 'Proposed Joint Note', 30 August 1918, CAB 25/84.

The general tactics that should be used against the Germans were to attack on a wide front to exhaust the enemy and achieve a breakthrough. The British Section also described the French Front as 'the decisive front ... operations on all other fronts must be made to play a subsidiary role, and must be considered in relation to their probable effect on the situation in France'.[138] For the rest of 1918 the goals should be to prevent the enemy from recovering and 'to carry out such offensive operations as are required for the preparation of the Campaign of 1919'.[139] The PMRs expected the commanders-in-chief to inform them of their plans, but beyond this they wanted to draw attention to the importance of the 'Bruay Coalfield to be worked to its utmost capacity in order to save the shipping now employed in bringing coal from England to France'.[140]

Overall, the PMRs' drafts were in general agreement with one another on the main points. Prior to discussing Joint Note 37 for a final time, the Italians submitted their own draft. They illustrated concern that the Germans might rest over the winter and shorten their line which would allow them to hold on the Western Front. Concerned the Allies would not have a large superiority in the spring of 1919, they warned that a battle of attrition might set in. For these reasons they suggested an attack occur in Italy instead (as explored in Chapter 4), with the Allies supplying the necessary resources to make it a success. Overall, the Italian note only affected strategy in France to the extent that the Allies did not withdraw their remaining forces in Italy for use on the French Front.

The final Joint Note 37 approved by the PMRs firmly placed Foch at the centre of Allied military decisions. While the British Section had advocated increased use of mechanical means throughout their draft notes (although never to the same extent as the CIGS), in this final copy the PMRs highlighted Foch's role in determining objectives and material for the future conflict, which included his making decisions on *materiale* (munitions, tanks, aviation). Bliss also supported the Generalissimo by reinforcing that American manpower should be determined by Foch, which was reflected in the final note agreed upon. The Allies had:

to spare no effort to accumulate in the shortest possible time the greatest possible numerical superiority. For this purpose it is very important that American troops should continue to be sent to France, to the exclusion of other theatres of operations, and to be placed at the disposal of the Marshal Commanding-in-

---

[138] Ibid.   [139] Ibid.   [140] Ibid.

Chief the Allied Armies in France [sic], until such time as the Supreme War Council may decide otherwise and with this object in view the necessary tonnage should be made available.[141]

The final joint note emphasised the predominance of the French Front and Bliss had insured that it was clear American manpower be sent and used here.

The secondary theatres were given an assisting role to that of the Franco-Belgian Front, subordinate to and harmonised with it (as explored in Chapters 2–4):

Operations in the other theatres of war must be made to play their part in the decision sought for on the Western front by contributing to the moral and material exhaustion of the enemy. But such operations must not be allowed to absorb resources which are required by the Armies of the Entente on the decisive front. The defeat of the Central Powers in any of the subsidiary theatres of war could only be a step on the road to the defeat of Germany: it could not bring about the final decision.[142]

The PMRs concluded their note by reiterating that by bringing all of these military means to bear on the enemy, they would achieve 'peace through victory'.[143] During the months of July and August, when the PMRs did their main planning, they never internalised the intelligence they received about the German army. Aware that German 'wastage' was high after the spring offensive, they still calculated that the strength of the German army in July was 205 divisions, a figure which had only fallen to 198 by the end of August.[144] This pessimism was not just experienced by the PMRs though, as French intelligence set the figure at 207 in July, down to 184 by November.[145] The British PMR did, however, report that discipline in the German army was waning and that divisions continued to be disbanded to bring others up to strength.

The War Department Investigates the Expanded Military Programme

After receiving information on the June SWC meeting, the War Department began to seriously consider the requirements for expanding the American war programme. By 2 July March responded to Pershing's letter from 19 June (actually he had sent three other letters but Pershing

---

[141] 'Joint Note No. 37', 13 September 1918, CAB 25/122/SWC320; Bliss/324/SWC316/1.
[142] Ibid.   [143] Ibid.
[144] Bliss/320 contains a series of reports on enemy strengths created by British 'E' Branch.
[145] Greenhalgh, *Foch*, 485.

had not received them) about expanding the programme to 100 divisions. March explained:

Things are going along here now at a very high speed. We got the twelve billion dollar appropriation bill through both Houses with practically no difficulty at all. We found in the hearings that both the Senate and House Military Committees were backing our tremendously expensive program without concerning themselves much about minor details. In fact, the attitude of the Committees on that point was highly patriotic.[146]

In his letter, Pershing had illustrated his concern with cantonments for men of the expanded military programme. These issues did not concern March; however, he explained that, 'the difficulties of the War Department really arise from demands outside of this country'.[147] This included demands from the British and French Embassies in Washington (represented by Lord Reading and Jusserand respectively) and various nationalities requesting recognition, money, and troops. March wrote:

My own opinion ... is that the only possible military solution of the situation is to raise the American Expeditionary Forces in France to such numerical strength as will permit it to drive through the German lines, and the ultimate result of such a drive, as I see it, will put the attacking forces in a position to dictate terms of peace that will prove the salvation of the small units all over the world who are claiming our protection.[148]

March's solution to these problems was a large American force that would win a military victory and allow the Allies to dictate the peace terms.[149]

As part of the investigation into the expanded military programme Baker considered the material necessities for a large American force. While Pershing wanted to push forward with 100 divisions Baker reminded him: 'great as our capacity is in industry, it takes time to build new factories, get the necessary machine tools, and bring together the raw materials for any large increase in our industrial output ... These involve, of course, questions of clothing, small arms, ammunition, transportation, and training'.[150] As Baker and March continued their investigation on the feasibility of the 100 division programme they highlighted

---

[146] March to Pershing, 2 July 1918 and Pershing/123; March/22.   [147] Ibid.
[148] Ibid.
[149] Baker replied to this specific letter [18/19 June] on 6 July, but he had also already received the cable from Foch about the enlarged division. Pershing had also amended the figures in cable 342-S after he met with Foch on 23 June, RG/120/267/3176/1305.
[150] Baker to Pershing, 6 July 1918, Pershing/20. Baker said that the Operations Committee of the General Staff would investigate these issues. Once these studies were drafted, the War Department would then have to consult the War Industries Board to see if the manufacturing facilities could be provided.

their concerns with shortages in port facilities, wool (for uniforms), and artillery, as well as the complications that shipping more horses would cause. As Baker explained to Bliss on 8 July:

March and I are studying together the 100-division program, but are finding it full of burrs. The latest one presented to me is that all the ports in France, and all the berthing space there, if devoted to the exclusive use of America, would not, on present calculations, be adequate for the 100-division program. Other shortages which are causing us anxiety are wool and artillery. And if it turns out that we are going to have to resume the shipment of horses in any large numbers, the ocean tonnage problem gets a new complication. As you know, our intention has for some time been to develop 100 divisions by 1920, but to push that consummation ahead a whole year is not easy, to say the least, even if it should turn out to be possible with the maximum aid from the British and French. I note in one of your cablegrams the suggestion that General Foch and General Pershing have even a larger program than those under consideration for America. I am not willing to believe that anything is impossible, no matter what it is, but at present it looks as though I would need Aladdin's lamp for the 100-division program, and just what additional magic the larger program [the 110-division] will require, I do not know.[151]

Despite these initial concerns, Baker's confidence in the ability to meet an enlarged programme grew. He and March pinpointed the changes required to make the 80 division programme a reality. The French and British would have to be consulted over their ability to meet the American deficits in heavy artillery and transportation (troops and cargo) until the American artillery and shipping programmes were expanded (as will be explored in the next chapter on resources). Manpower requirements also had to be met. To meet Pershing's earlier shipping request of 250,000 men, Baker suggested that the United States maintain a constant 1 million men in training at home. These soldiers would receive four months of training before being sent to Europe.[152] The draft age would have to be changed in order to obtain men in these numbers. From Congress, the War Department would also have to procure billions of dollars in additional funding for the enlarged programme.

Baker supported the idea of an enlarged programme, especially given that it was framed in the context of ending the war as soon as possible. In a letter to Pershing on 6 July he reminded the Commander-in-Chief of his earlier proposal for a 60 division programme, but wrote that, 'when the 100-division program came to me it occurred to me that we ought to study the situation with the view of determining the maximum amount we can do. I have the feeling that this war has gone on long enough and if

---

[151] Baker to Bliss, 8 July 1918, Bliss/250.
[152] Baker to Pershing, 6 July 1918, Pershing/20.

any exertion on our part or any sacrifice can speed its successful termination even by a single day, we should make it'.[153] In response, the War Department began to investigate the possibility of fielding 60, 80, and 100 divisions by 1 July 1919. The War Industries Board assisted the War Department in these studies. Baker asked Pershing to refrain from making any statements to the Entente until these were completed. He did not want his coalition partners to think they had agreed to a programme if they could not execute it. Bliss reassured the Secretary of War that he had made it clear that the Allies should not rely on the 100 division programme until the American government gave full instructions to do so.[154] Another reason for proposing a larger programme was that it motivated the American government to achieve more. As Baker explained, 'One of the happy effects of the recent accelerated shipment of troops has been that we have out-stripped our promises and, if I judge correctly the effect of this in Europe, it has been most agreeable and heartening'.[155] In this way, planning for the future could improve the present situation.

By 20 July Baker had completed his studies on the expanded programme, which included information for 60, 80, and 100 division programmes. The studies were so straightforward that he told the President it would take no more than ten minutes to go through them.[156] Three days later the Americans approved the 80 division programme (having 80 divisions in France and 18 at home meaning 3.36 million men in France and a total of 4.85 million overall) to be completed by 30 June 1919 provided the above conditions could be met.[157] The War Department believed the legislation for men and money would easily pass, that the British promise that troop ships already in use by the Americans would continue to be available, which seemed to the War Department to 'practically take care of that deficiency', and that the French would continue to supply guns, carriages and ammunition 'at least as rapidly as they have been furnishing them up to the present time'.[158] Despite a lack of precision in their figures, they remained confident that the programme

---

[153] Ibid. Baker expressed a similar opinion in a letter to Walter H. Page (American Embassy, London), 28 June 1918, Baker/13(a)/12.

[154] Bliss to Baker, 3 July 1918, Bliss/250.

[155] Baker to Pershing, 6 July 1918, Pershing/20.

[156] Baker to Wilson, 20 July 1918, Baker/8/8; Wilson/97.

[157] War Department to American Section, 23 July 1918, Bliss/329.

[158] War Department [March] to American Section, 17 August 1918, Bliss/329, cablegram no. 80; 'Annual Report of General Peyton C. March, Chief of Staff, United States Army, 1919', RG/165/84–8/158/1190/p. 4. For 1918/19 fiscal plan see RG/120/267/3176/1312. For rates of equipment furnished to the AEF by the French and British see Bruce, *Fraternity*, 105.

could be completed. Baker's general attitude was that they should push to obtain greater goals, but that they should not overestimate the abilities of the American war machine.

The Commanders on the Enlarged Programme

As the Allies began to successfully counter-attack in France in early July, Foch addressed the question of 'what is needed to bring victory to the cause of the Allies?' In a study which he discussed with the Allied Commanders-in-Chief, he answered that, 'It demands an incontestable numerical superiority, as number of divisions greater than that of the enemy. The number of our divisions is inferior. It is necessary then to increase the number of our divisions as soon as possible and as rapidly as possible'.[159] Foch highlighted the need for the Allies to maintain all present French and British divisions. In order to do so, American troops would need to support the weakened divisions for 'As long as the battle lasts or threatens to reopen …'[160] Although Foch had agreed to the formation of the United States First Army three days earlier, he still encouraged Pershing to delay its actual establishment until 1 October 1918. For 1919 Foch envisaged that the French, British, and American armies would launch an offensive on the front of Arras-Argonne Forest.[161]

Pershing was to study this plan before the commanders met to discuss it. He disagreed with Foch's objectives, which were to release the railways, whereas Pershing wanted to attack into Lorraine.[162] He did not think Foch's objectives would bring victory in 1919, writing that 'This final victory can only be had by reaching the vitals of Germany and by destroying her armed forces'.[163] Pershing assessed that these 'vitals' were in Lorraine and that they should move directly into that region. Pershing also disagreed with Foch's assessment of German numerical supremacy. He wrote:

There is even now great doubt as to any considerable numerical superiority on the part of the Germans. The unquestioned superiority of the enemy at present is believed to be due to his possession of the initiative and its accompanying benefit to morale rather than to any more numerical superiority. The effort of the United States should give both the advantage of superior numbers and of the initiative before spring.[164]

---

[159] 'Conversation between the Commander-in-Chief and General Foch Relative to an American Sector', 13 July 1918, RG/120/268/3143/986.
[160] Ibid.   [161] Ibid.   [162] Ibid.   [163] Ibid.   [164] Ibid.

The morale of the British and French troops, he said, would be improved once the Allies took the initiative. Hence, he did not see the need to integrate American troops into their divisions: 'In any event it seems unwise to associate our troops with troops who could only be drawn into an attack by our immediate presence'.[165] Pershing reminded Foch that he was not obliged to go along with the Allied Generalissimo's plan and that he could demand a sector for the Americans 'so that we may develop on our own lines in our own way'.[166] Pershing knew the Allies were relying on American manpower and used it as leverage to form an independent American Army as early as possible. Pershing thought the war could be won in 1919 if the Allies not only attacked in Northern France, as Foch desired, but also in Lorraine where the Americans believed they could make a major contribution. He would not delay the formation of the American army, which came into effect 10 August 1918, ending his amalgamation controversy with Foch.

The Commanders Meet at Bombon

Operational discussions for 1919 culminated on 24 July 1918 when the commanders met at the Château Bombon to discuss the shape of future warfare. Foch expanded upon the points he had raised at his earlier meeting with Pershing. Pleased with the ability of the French army to stop the fifth German offensive (the prelude to the Soissons counter-attack), he instructed that the time was ripe for the Allies to move onto the offensive. He estimated that the Allies had greater reserves than the Germans and described the poor state of the two German Armies: 'an army of occupation sacrificed, without effectives, kept for a long period on the front; and manoeuvring behind this fragile façade, a shock army, the object of the German High Command's care, but already strongly depleted'.[167] Foch was also positive about the superiority of Allied aviation, tanks, and artillery. While the Germans were struggling to keep up their unit strength with effectives, the United States was sending over a minimum of 250,000 troops per month. The Generalissimo planned to launch a series of offensives to take strategic railway points. Yet despite his positive attitude, Foch planned for the war to continue into 1919.

Foch's operational plan was to focus on 'releasing the railroads indispensable to later operations of the Allied Armies': Paris-Avricourt (Marne region) in the operations that were presently underway; Paris-Amiens

---

[165] Ibid.   [166] Ibid.
[167] 'Mémoire lu à la Réunion des Commandants en Chef des Armées Alliées', 24 July 1918, RG/120/267/3111/2667.

through a combined British-French offensive; and Paris- Avricourt (Commeroy region) by the Americans.[168] After these operations Foch wanted to concentrate in the north on pushing the enemy back from Dunkerque and Calais, as well to release the mining regions. He envisaged two attacks either in conjunction or separately. Foch was uncertain 'How far the different operations planned above will carry us in space and time ...' but he did believe it was essential also to begin plans for an offensive at the end of the summer. He was aware that the Germans were likely to withdraw to shorter lines. In reality, while they may have retreated beyond the Hindenburg line, these defences were designed to meet the Allied armies of 1916 not those whose tactics and firepower had developed in 1918.[169]

Weygand later recollected that the room was filled with silence after Foch presented, what Wegyand called, his modest plan. The commanders expressed concerns about the state of fatigue of both the British and French armies as well as the inexperience of the American one.[170] Foch instructed the commanders to report back to him within two to three weeks' time on what men and material they thought could be made available from 1 January to 1 April 1919. He gave them a list of questions to answer which he hoped would assist in standardising the army systems.[171] Foch also pressed the Commanders-in-Chief to instruct their governments on the essential war material for them to focus production on.[172] Pétain was the only commander to send a written response back to Foch, but Haig and Pershing had verbally agreed with him.[173] In Pétain's response he agreed with Foch on the general operations but expressed concerns about having the resources to commit French troops to the operations that would free the northern mines and ports.[174] Pershing, was thrilled about this meeting, claiming it as the moment 'the American Army has been recognized as a participant, as such, alongside the allies'.[175] Weygand, however, wanted concrete information from the Americans, pressing Pershing to learn what the Americans would

---

[168] 'Mémoire lu à la Réunion', 24 July 1918.
[169] Prior and Wilson, *Command on the Western Front*, 349–350.
[170] Weygand, *Mémoires*, 1: 585.
[171] 'Forces que chacune des armées alliées peut metre en ligne le 1er janvier et le 1er avril 1919', 24 July 1918, RG/120/267/3111/2667.
[172] 'Notes on a conversation between General Foch, General Pétain, Sir Douglas Haig and General Pershing on July 24, 1918 at Cheateau Bombon', RG/120/268/3143/986; *AFGG* 7/1, annex 277.
[173] Foch to Pershing, 24 July 1918, RG/120/267/3111/2667; Foch, Memoirs, 430–1; Weygand, *Mémoires*, 1: 585.
[174] Pétain to Foch, 26 July 1918, *AFGG* 7/1, annex 325.
[175] Pershing to Baker, 28 July 1918, Pershing/20.

produce in terms of guns and ammunition. Foch was still concerned about shortages of horses, and he wanted more motorised vehicles. He also highlighted the importance of tanks. And while Foch was critical of Lloyd George giving tanks an exaggerated importance, the Americans recorded that at this meeting Foch 'expressed the opinion that under present conditions the possibilities of an offensive depended on the number of tanks that are available'.[176] Pershing recollected that the Allied Generalissimo knew that they would be short on tanks in 1919, and that while Foch recognised their importance, he never mentioned them in the numbers that others did.[177] In September, as Foch was successfully pushing back the Germans and experiencing high rates of loss to his infantry, he became concerned that the Allies might be overproducing tanks and aircraft, which required large numbers of men that could instead be used as infantry.[178]

Final Attempts by Commanders to Obtain 100 American Divisions

Despite Allied successes on the Marne in July and at Amiens in August, Foch continued to press for the 100 division programme (ignoring the War Department estimates on the 80 division programme) while encouraging Pershing to do the same.[179] In early August, Lloyd George had informed Clemenceau that the British would have to reduce their tonnage being used for the transport of troops and that they would no longer be able to supply the Americans with cargo tonnage (explored further in Chapter 6). Anxious to receive more American manpower, Foch turned his attention to obtaining resources from Washington. His own studies concluded that it would be difficult for the Allies to transport and supply 100 American divisions for 1 July 1919; however, he believed that it would be less difficult for the Americans to do so. The motivational point was that the war could be won in 1919 if the Americans made the effort:

---

[176] 'Notes on a conversation between General Foch, General Pétain, Sir Douglas Haig and General Pershing on July 24, 1918 at Château Bombon', RG/120/268/3143/986.

[177] Pershing, *My Experiences*, 506.

[178] Reading notes on an interview with Foch, 3 September 1918, The National Archives, Foreign Office Papers, [hereon FO] FO/800/224/170.

[179] In September Foch focussed on transportation and railway arrangements to June 1919. He explained how the French needed the assistance of the Americans. The programme he described had been agreed upon by the French War Committee in consultation with the American Director General of Transportation. Foch to Pershing, 17 September 1918, Pershing/75.

In the present state of things, taking into consideration the value of which the American Army gives proof each day, it is rational and wise to foresee the end of the war in 1919, if the American government and the American people do everything in their power to increase as rapidly as possible the strength of this army and make it 100 divisions strong by July, 1919.[180]

Pershing was reluctant to send this telegram as he 'was afraid that [it] might have a tendency to irritate the President rather than to urge him to action'.[181] In his memoir, Pershing recalled that Foch was 'thoroughly committed to the larger programme. He said that in his opinion the Allies should make an effort to win the war in 1919, that the British were tired, that the French were worn out, and that we must hasten the arrival of American divisions'.[182] Pershing recommended that they discuss the issues of shipping with Secretary Baker when he arrived in Europe. By the end of August Foch was operationally interested in keeping the Germans disorganised by attacking.[183]

Despite Foch's central role in advocating an expanded programme, Bliss believed he did not go far enough in publicising his ideas. He believed that much of the confusion over prioritising needs could be reduced if Foch stated what was required for a final campaign in 1919 – that way a supreme effort could be made.[184] Throughout his correspondence with March and Baker, Bliss reiterated that the dominant idea should be to win the war. Foch's opinions as to when to end the war and the forces required to do so were key to achieving this goal. Bliss explained to Baker that the people of Europe might force their governments to accept peace if Germany granted terms, and therefore 'they would be very much helped in withstanding German allurements by the knowledge that a definitely and openly expressed hope was being held out to them, that if they endure these sacrifices a few months longer and even increase them if necessary, the war will end the way they want it and they can demand their own terms'.[185] Three days later Pershing and Bliss met to discuss the expanded military programme. From Pershing's

---

[180] Foch to Pershing, 14 August 1918, ibid.
[181] Pershing diary entry, 15 August 1918, Pershing/2. Pershing also answered Foch verbally via Colonel Mott.
[182] Pershing, *My Experiences*, 558–559.
[183] 'Notes on Conversation between General Pershing and Marshal Foch on August 30 1918 at Ligny-en-Barrois'. This conversation and the one on 2 September 1918 at Bombon both focussed on future operations and how Foch might use American manpower, meanwhile Pershing insisted the Americans get their own sector. 'Notes on Conference between Pershing, Marshal Foch, and General Pétain at Bombon', 2 September 1918. RG/120/268/3143/986.
[184] Bliss to Baker, 9 and 22 August 1918, Bliss/250.
[185] Bliss to Baker, 22 August 1918, *PWW*, 51: 36.

perspective he was delighted that he and the American PMR agreed on, 'establishing closer relations ... about the 100 division program which we have each independently been urging on Washington'.[186] Bliss, aware the approved programme comprised 80 divisions, urged Washington to pressure Foch to openly state what the programme should be, as then this confusion would be ended. Taking these concerns seriously, Baker in turn wrote to President Wilson suggesting the President write to the three other government heads and ask them to confront Foch about the military programme for 1919: 'General Bliss feels that we would all then be able to work toward a definite program and count just the sacrifices each country would have to make to carry it out'.[187] Instead the issue was left for Baker to solve on his trip to Europe in autumn 1918.

The final major discussions that both Pershing and Foch had about planning for 1919, in fact, occurred when Secretary Baker visited Europe in September 1918. Holding separate discussions with the two commanders, the central issue was the American programme. Despite the War Department's decision of 18 July to complete an 80 division programme, throughout July and August Pershing and Foch continued to discuss the campaign in 1919 in light of an expanded American programme of 100 divisions. Baker was surprised to learn that Pershing had ignored the War Department's instructions. Whereas the War Department's estimate pointed to an 'aggregate total force A. E. F. by June 30, 1919, 3,760,000, including wastage replacements of 400,000' in Europe, 'Authorities here contemplate a total force by the same date of 4,700,000 ... That is, the A. E. F. included sixteen depot divisions as a complement of the eighty'.[188] Baker asked March to officially remind GHQ of the 80 division programme and the figures it encompassed. March explained to Pershing that that the commander's expanded programme meant 1.13 million troops more than the War Department estimates.[189] Pershing, however, would not accept this smaller programme.[190] On 29 September GHQ wrote to the War Department to explain their shipping programme and to justify their larger figures. They argued that their programme was in fact based on 80 divisions by 1 July 1919 but that the difference was that the War Department calculated an American Division at 40,000 men whereas GHQ calculated it at 52,000

[186] Pershing diary entry, 25 August 1918, Pershing/2.
[187] Baker to Wilson, 22 August 1918, Baker/8/6.
[188] March to Baker, 23 September 1918, quoted in Palmer, *Baker Papers*, 2: 346.
[189] March to Pershing, 25 September 1918, RG/200/19/4/2; RG/120/267/3176/1309.
[190] For information on how Pershing tried to gain control of supply in October, see Beaver, *Baker*, 186.

(including corps and army troops). In addition 800,000 SOS troops and 600,000 replacements, or a total of 4.76 million.[191] Pershing attempted to place pressure on the War Department to alter these figures by informing them that Foch and America's partners understood the 80 division programme in the same way as GHQ and that any confusion was caused by the War Department's incomprehension of the basis of American divisions.[192] However, Baker's meeting with Foch on 27 September dispelled this disagreement. Baker learned that the Generalissimo's needs for winning the war in 1919 were less than those for which Foch had been earlier advocating. As Greenhalgh has explained, although Foch recorded in the GQGA diary that 100 divisions were still required to win the war, in reality he told Baker it could be won with 40 divisions. Foch likely contradicted himself as he had a habit of asking for more than he required.[193] In addition, the military situation had drastically improved for the Allies, as the Bulgarians had sued for an armistice, Allenby was advancing in Palestine, and the Germans had begun to put out peace feelers, of which Foch was aware.[194]

Greenhalgh's revelation about Foch's manpower requirements bring into question the estimates made throughout 1918 by the Allies. Did they intentionally exaggerate what they needed to achieve victory? In examining their pessimistic attitudes throughout the year, the answer, at least partially, can be found in the Allies' reaction to the German spring offensives. The Allies' near-failure in March 1918 resulted in their overestimating German capabilities throughout 1918. In turn they overestimated what they needed to defeat the Germans. By the signing of the armistice the German and Austrians had approximately 3.53 million troops on the Western Front to the Allies 6.43 million soldiers.[195] The Germans had serious manpower deficiencies: the 1919 Class had already been incorporated into the army and both regiments and divisions were being dismantled to provide drafts to bring the others up to strength. While the class of 1920 had been trained, but not used in the frontline, they would provide at most an additional 300,000 recruits.[196]

---

[191] Avery Andrews (G1) to Chief of Staff, 1 October 1918, RG/120/267/3176/1309.

[192] Pershing to March, 2 October 1918, RG/120/267/3176/1309.

[193] Greenhalgh, *Foch*, 448. Also see as Baker recollected in an interview to Palmer that Foch told him the 40 division figure. Palmer, *Newton D. Baker*, i: 346.

[194] On Foch, see Greenhalgh, *Foch*, 448.

[195] Alexander Watson, *Enduring the Great War: Combat, Morale and Collapse in the German and British Armies, 1914–1918* (Cambridge, 2008), 188–189.

[196] Herwig, *Germany and Austria-Hungary*, 441–442.

Intelligence historian James Beach has described the complicated picture presented by GHQ intelligence about the German army. Beach explains, 'Since early October German reserves had been assessed as being fewer than twenty divisions across the whole Western Front [France/Belgium], of which only about five were considered "fresh". Documents and prisoners also continued to suggest a collapse in German morale, showing indiscipline and even mutinies in the rear areas'.[197] By the end of September the Allies were aware the Germans had serious supply issues, including an inadequate number of supply dumps for the number of German troops on the Franco-Belgian Front and a shortage of petrol and horses for the moving of goods.[198] However, this was only part of GHQ's analysis, as Beach explains:

more significantly, intelligence indicated that the Germans were conserving the 1920 Class as a reservoir of fresh manpower. Indeed, one incident was reported whereby men of the 1920 Class who had reached a frontline unit were ordered back to their depot to comply with this policy. Therefore, in his statement to the War Cabinet, Haig highlighted the likelihood that, if operations continued over the winter, the Germans would be given 'several months for recuperation and absorption of the 1920 Class'.[199]

Although by the second half of 1918 GHQ Intelligence functioned well, they failed to recognise the weakness of the German army, as there was a tendency to ignore both the political situation inside Germany and to dismiss information from interviews with German POWs, not the least on the deteriorating situation within Germany itself. The result was that the British were not as in tune with the strength and capabilities of the German army as they could have been.[200] In this context, the PMRs were not alone in overestimating German capabilities.

The Allies also had difficulty in accepting that the German units were considerably below strength and that morale in many was rapidly ebbing. In the Allied nations it was customary to reduce establishments, in order to keep the existing units close to full strength. In contrast, the Germans retained divisions that were severely understrength.[201] Thus, when the Allies identified a particular German division they were facing, they assumed it was close to its established strength or at least could (and would) be made up to that fighting strength in the near future. In cases where they did acknowledge that these divisions were understrength,

---

[197] Jim Beach, *Haig's Intelligence* (Cambridge, 2013), 317.   [198] Ibid., 315.
[199] Ibid., 317.   [200] Ibid., 319.
[201] Greenhalgh notes that, while the German establishment strength of a division in October 1918 was 11,643, one division was found to have as few as 720 men. Greenhalgh, *Foch*, 486.

they were reluctant to extrapolate this as typical over the entire German army. So while the Allies were competent in identifying the German order of battle, which was one of the primary goals of intelligence, this did not reveal the actual strength of the German army.[202] Overall, the Allies did not want to underestimate the German strength for a second time – a prudent course but one which increasingly overestimated German fighting capabilities and correspondingly Allied requirements to overcome them. Even as the Allies pushed the Germans beyond the Hindenburg line, they did not fully comprehend that the enemy was collapsing. The Allied military leadership believed that the Germans could still hold on to their frontier. Thus, while the forces required by the Allies were overestimated, their concerns over the capabilities of the German army were founded on past experiences and pessimistic readings of intelligence. The Allies may not have known the exact forces the Germans had sent to the French Front for the German spring offensives (they moved 48 divisions from 1 November 1917 to 21 March 1918); however, they knew the Germans had successfully mustered the manpower to break through Allied lines.[203] It is not surprising that the PMRs, fearful that the Germans would use their superior interior lines of communication to move further forces from the east, also allowed for a wide margin of error when calculating the numerical supremacy they required to defeat their main enemy.

The Franco-Belgian Front was at the centre of Allied planning for a campaign in 1919. It was a widely held belief that the war would continue into 1919 and that victory had to be achieved in this theatre against the main body of the German army. Even the PMRs, who had a unique global viewpoint, were convinced that the war would be won in the Franco-Belgian theatre with the secondary theatres playing an important role in holding down enemy forces. It was through an overwhelming numerical superiority that this goal would be achieved. As the Americans remained opposed to the idea of substantial amalgamation of troops, coming to form their own Army in August, the expansion of the American army became the main solution to obtaining numerical supremacy over the Germans in 1919. As the commanders, the War Office, and the individual PMRs all estimated Allied and enemy strength on the Franco-Belgian Front for 1 July 1919, a number of variables, in particular the ability of the Allies to raise manpower and the extent to which the Germans would transfer manpower from the East to the West, led to

---

[202] For more on identifying German order of battle, see Finnegan, 'Military Intelligence'.
[203] Fong, 'The Movement of German Divisions', 229.

variation in their predictions. However all groups were aware that they needed as much manpower as they could field, and as such the military leaders of the Allied nations continued to press for the American government to fulfil the 100 division programme. As American manpower hinged on shipping and supply, it is to the coordination of resources that the next chapter turns.

6   Building a Bridge to France: The Role of Resources in Creating an Allied Strategy for 1919

> Let me put it this way – in our general war program, the whole question comes down to a question of manpower. We are not engaged in a war which means simply taking care of the soldiers that we ourselves raise and send to the front. Right at this moment, I have on my desk demands that have to meet the situation in Baku City with the English, with the whole Mesopotamia campaign, with the campaign that is started in Siberia, with the campaign in Archangel, with the campaign along the whole western front. In other words, this country's resources have got to be used for the whole world.[1]

The American War Department's assessment of what was required to fulfil the 80 division programme involved a complex system of procuring funds for the enlarged programme, drafting and clothing the troops, transporting them to Europe, disembarking and moving them from the ports, training them, and finally supplying them in the field. Exploring the many facets of the reality of the expanded American programme is outside the scope of this work. Instead, this chapter uses the Allied Maritime Transport Council as its central focus to explore two main issues facing the Allies: transporting and supplying the American troops. When the War Department approved the 80 division programme in July, both issues were at the forefront of their concerns. Although by the summer of 1918 the convoy system had neutralised the submarine menace and shipbuilding finally equalled shipping losses, the expanded military programme significantly altered the shipping situation for the second half of 1918 and the year 1919.[2] By this time, the European Allies had expected that the Americans would be contributing shipping to the overall war effort; instead, implementing the 80 division programme meant that the Americans would require further assistance from their

---

[1] Baruch to the National Federation of Building Industries, 22 August 1918, Baruch/499.

[2] Fayle described how submarine losses were lower in June and July 1918 then they had been since the Germans began their policy of unrestricted submarine warfare. He also explained how the ship building programme had begun to replace ships at the rate of wastage. C. Ernest Fayle, *Seaborne Trade* (3 vols., London, 1920–1924), 3, 367–369.

coalition partners and would continue to draw upon already stretched Allied shipping resources. Originally receiving assistance with troop transport from the British in the latter half of 1918, the American government further increased its demands by asking for substantial assistance with cargo tonnage as well. Furthermore, American demands did not confine themselves to shipping tonnage. The 80 division programme placed stress on already limited munitions resources too, as the Americans pressed both the British and the French for assurance that they could assist with the supply of artillery and shells until their own programme came through in 1919.

At the centre of these discussions were the various bodies of the Supreme War Council. The Americans insisted that discussions take place via this forum, giving the SWC – most notably the AMTC and the Inter-Allied Munitions Council – a prominent role. When the American Secretary of War, Newton D. Baker, travelled to Europe in the autumn of 1918 it was through the AMTC that he discussed shipping with the Entente partners. This chapter will explore the AMTC as a case study in determining shipping for the expanded American programme and examine the role of the IAMC in determining and meeting the artillery needs of the Allies. It will be built around a close examination of the discussions held and documents created by the Allies in their decision-making process at the time. Although the Allied process may often appear confused and conflicting, it reveals that disorganisation within the American military structure caused difficulties at the international level.

US officials, military and civilian, failed to provide their European Allies with official projections for their 1919 resource programmes, which resulted in a series of fluctuating estimates being used as a guideline for 1919. The French, who were supplying a significant portion of the AEF in return for raw materials, needed to know what resources the Americans required for the 1919 programme and what raw materials were available for France's own munitions program. Furthermore, they were concerned with the slow mobilisation and disjointed system of the American war machine.[3] The British became suspicious of their American partners as well. Conscious of the growing economic might of the Americans, which included the necessary expansion of its merchant marine, as well as Britain's financial indebtedness to them (which reached $5 billion by the end of the war) the British wanted to ensure that the American merchant marine was

---

[3] Kaspi, *Le Temps Des Américains*, 203.

being used to its full extent to execute the American military programme and not for trade.[4]

Adding further complication to the scenario was the unofficial policy
of exchanging manpower for shipping between the British and the
Americans, as the 1919 programme was intertwined with negotiations
for the use of American troops alongside the British Expeditionary Force
(as introduced in the previous chapter). Washington's request for additional shipping provided the British with another opportunity to gain
manpower from their partner. With the forming of the First American
Army in August 1918, the British could no longer demand amalgamation. However, they could request that when the Americans took up
their sector of the front line, this would reduce the length of the line held
by the British. As the British attempted to continue this exchange,
tensions that were difficult to overcome arose between the Allies. However, as this chapter will show, the Allies did not allow these tensions to
unhinge the coalition, and as such they were still able to coordinate
resources in order to defeat their enemy.

Finally, this chapter will serve to illustrate how the Allied political and
military leadership used resources to underpin the operational notion of
victory held by the commanders. It was not simply a matter of Foch and
Pershing receiving whatever manpower they requested; the American
War Department made the decision on the final troop numbers. From
there the resources to transport and supply these troops had to be
procured. Only then could the Allies bring to bear the necessary strength
to defeat the Germans in France.

The PMRs and Shipping

At the July SWC meeting Bliss once again had his duties in Europe
expanded – but this time by the SWC rather than by his own government. Before the July SWC had closed, Lloyd George, irritated with the
French for initiating discussions of shipping for the expanded military
programme, insisted that this question be considered by an Allied body
prior to an agreement being reached. The SWC members resolved that
Bliss should investigate whether the United States could provide the
tonnage to move and maintain 100 American divisions in the field by
31 July 1919. Reasserting the dominant position of the British on shipping matters, Lloyd George suggested (and it was agreed) that, if the
Americans were unable to supply all of the tonnage, then they should ask

---

[4] Burk, *Sinews of War*, 223. Burk writes that tension caused by lengthy discussions over
finances illustrated America's dominant position over the British, 162, 208–216.

the British to make up the shortage. In the meantime, the British would continue to supply the same quantity of tonnage for troop transport in August as they had in July (equivalent to shipping approximately 180,000 men).[5] Noteworthy is that, outside of the SWC meeting, Milner had already informed Pershing that Britain would provide transport for 250,000 men per month for the next year.[6] Between July and late September, when Baker finally decided to travel to Europe, Bliss was one of the few American representatives with whom the Entente communicated for information on future campaign plans. The SWC agreed to withhold discussions on shipping until these studies were completed. Because of the dramatic unfolding of the war from the summer of 1918 onward and the slow progress of these studies, the political side of the SWC was never again used as a forum to discuss shipping. Thus to learn of the role of shipping on campaign planning it is to the sub-committees and delegates of the SWC that one must turn.

While Bliss was given a central role in shipping matters he was only able to present the information that the War Department and American shipping authorities made available to him. The War Industries Board (WIB), whose main role was 'to obtain the materials required for carrying out the military program of the United States and the Allies, with as little dislocation of industry as possible', had difficulty determining what these materials should be. The problem lay with the War Department, which frustratingly kept changing the figures on which the American military programme was based.[7] Exasperated, the WIB members complained repeatedly that they were 'acting without facts'. As historian Daniel Beaver has correctly argued, the Americans were a difficult partner to work with because they could not supply essential information to their Allies as they frequently did not have it for themselves.[8] Originally the Americans had told the British they would build 6 million tonnes of shipping per year, but due to disorganisation they had failed to produce these results.[9]

While waiting for shipping information from the American government, Bliss and his staff studied the transport situation, including troop, cargo, and animal (mules and horses) transport in their estimates. They

[5] 'Unofficial Minutes of SWC Meeting of 1st Session of the 7th Meeting', Bliss to Baker, 2 July 1918, Bliss/250; 'Procès-verbal of SWC meeting of 1st session of the 7th meeting', 2 July 1918, CAB 25/122/SWC259.
[6] 'Sufficient Tonnage Available', Pershing to Chief of Staff and Secretary of War, USAWW, 2: 484; Pershing to Secretary of War and Chief of Staff, 27 June 1918, RG/120/267/376/1312; Pershing to Reading 26 June 1918, USAWW, 2: 485.
[7] Baruch to President Wilson, 29 November 1918, RG/61/12/73/827.
[8] Beaver, Newton D. Baker, 173.   [9] Burk, Sinews of War, 162.

intended that this study should give the European Allies an approximate idea of what would be required by the Americans, as opposed to finalised figures. Originally based on the 100 division programme advocated by Foch and Pershing at their meeting on 23 June, estimates for troop transport were updated on 2 August to reflect the War Department's revised 80 division programme.[10] However, despite the fact that the War Department had reduced the number of animals per infantry division from 6,522 in January to 4,712, with additional reductions in August to 3,772, Bliss continued to draw his requirements for animals from figures provided by Tardieu, which had been created in consultation with Foch and Pershing.[11] These men accounted for approximately 8,100 animals per division with an additional 1,170 replacement animals per month.[12] In addition, Bliss differed in his calculations because he expected these animals to be shipped from America, whereas Tardieu assumed some could be found within Europe.

Horses were an essential component of transportation. Trucks had problems using roads, mechanics were rare, and many people did not know how to drive, whereas many people knew how to handle horses. Trucks were mechanically unreliable, and there was no chance to standardise fleets of them as there were too many different small manufacturers of trucks in Britain and the United States. By the end of the war the majority of short-range transport (from railway sidings to the front) was still done by horses. So while Bliss's figures were over-exaggerated, he was responding to the requests of the commanders-in-chief who were greatly concerned they would meet serious transportation issues in the near future if horses were not procured.

Bliss's figures relied on six other assumptions: first, that an average of four gross tonnes per man would be required for the transportation of personnel; second, that maintenance supplies would average 30 lbs. per day for each man; third, that an average of 12.6 dead weight tonnes (DWT) would be needed to transport draft animals; fourth, that deadweight space for cargo could be used at a rate of 15 percent on troop transports and 45 percent on animal ones; fifth, that for ships carrying troops, cargo, or animals the loading efficiency was 64 percent of the deadweight space; and sixth, that the average turn-round time for ships was 37½ days for troop transports, 75 days for cargo transports, and

---

[10] 'Approximate estimate of tonnage for plan of June 23, 1918,' n.d., Bliss/329; 'Revised estimate of Tonnage, based on program of 80 Divisions in France by June 30, 1919,' 2 August 1918, Bliss/319.

[11] On reduction of horses per infantry division, Stevenson, *With Our Backs*, 242.

[12] For Tardieu's figures, see 'Effectifs – Chevaux', 27 June 1918, Bliss/319.

Table 6.1 *Estimates for the American cargo and animal transport tonnage deficit, 1918–1919*[13]

	Divs. in France at end of month	Total tonnage of cargo and animal transport required by 80 divs.	Total tonnage of US cargo and animal transport now in transatlantic operation	Cumulative estimate of US ship construction at rate of 3 million DWT in 1918 and 10 million DWT in 1919	Apparent deficit
1918	–	–	1,066,000	–	–
July	28	1,708,520	–	–	–
Aug.	32 1/2	2,477,255	–	333,333	1,047,920
Sept.	37 1/4	3,029,275	–	666,666	1,296,690
Oct.	42	3,408,970	–	1,000,000	1,342,970
Nov.	46 3/4	3,763,035	–	1,333,333	1,363,702
Dec.	51 1/2	4,117,120	–	1,666,666	1,384,454
1919	–	–	–	–	–
Jan.	56 1/4	4,471,200	–	2,000,000	1,405,200
Feb.	61	4,825,350	–	2,833,333	1,259,350
Mar.	65 3/4	5,179,440	–	3,666,666	1,113,440
Apr.	70 1/2	5,543,515	–	4,500,000	977,515
May	75 1/4	5,887,595	–	5,333,333	821,595
June	80	6,241,670	–	6,166,666	675,650
Aug.	–	–	–	7,000,000	–
Total	–	–	–	–	12,688,486

70 days for animal transports.[14] Combining this information with construction figures provided by Edward Hurley, Chairman of the United States Shipping Board (USSB), Bliss compared American requirements with tonnage available in order to estimate the deficit from August 1918 to June 1919. He was then able to share this information with the other PMRs, who could then use it as an *estimate* for what the American programme required from the European Allies (see Table 6.1).

[13] This table was made by combining a series of figures drawn up by the American Section in 'Approximate Estimate of Tonnage', and 'Revised estimate of Tonnage', Bliss/319. It is unclear as to whether these figures just include those to transport horses and cargo or whether it also includes further cargo tonnage to keep them in the field (oats and food).

[14] 'Approximate Estimate of Tonnage', and 'Revised estimate of Tonnage', Bliss/319. DWT was the maximum weight of cargo, passengers, and fuel that a vessel could carry. Gross tonnage was the total measured cubic contents in tonnes (2240 lbs to a tonne) of a vessel, using the arbitrary figure of 100 cubic feet being equal to one tonne. D.W.T was 35 percent less than a gross tonne. See 'United States Food Administration: Inter-office Memorandum', 31 August 1918, RG/165/94–8/190/1440; Fayle, *Seaborne Trade*, i: 6–7n4.

Table 6.2 *War Department estimates for the American tonnage deficit, 1918–1919*

Month	Deficit in DWT
August 1918	1,217,755
September 1918	1,185,384
October 1918	1,117,734
November 1918	859,949
December 1918	731,274
January 1919	497,016
February 1919	209,641
Total	4,818,753

Source: March to Bliss, 23 July 1918.[15]

Meanwhile, as Bliss was tabulating his own data, the War Department was doing the same. After an intensive study of resources, it completed its own programme on 23 July. The 80 division programme was decided on the basis of the information supplied by Charles Piez, Vice President of the Emergency Fleet Corporation (EFC) (a branch of the USSB). While Piez's report was not found in the shipping or War Department records, the War Department's estimations for cargo requirements are known.[16] Their figures varied greatly from those provided by the American PMR. The War Department assumed that the British would continue to provide troop transport at the current rates (shipping approximately 180,000 men per month) and that the British and French would continue to supply field guns and heavy ammunition to the Americans. However, they still estimated a serious cargo tonnage deficit (see Table 6.2).

[15] March to American Section, 23 July 1918, Bliss/329/no. 74. March did not give a detailed explanation of how these figures were calculated, nor did he provide one in his final report, 'Annual Report of General Peyton C. March, Chief of Staff, United States Army, 1919', RG/165/84–8/158/1190.

[16] The War Department based its military programme on a report received from Charles Piez, the vice president of the EFC. I was unable to find a copy of this report despite looking through the EFC files (RG 32) including Subject Classified General Files; Entry 8, Box 56 (which was to include, but did not, records of Charles Piez, who created the report for the Emergency Fleet), Box 73 (War Department), and Box 80 (Military Program); Entry 37, Division of Planning and Statistics, Statistical Reports, April 1918-Nov 1919 (records themselves state that they were 'weeded out with little regard for their historical value, with the result that much of what remains is fragmentary, although still useful'); and Entry 14, Records of Lester Sisler, 1917–1919 (Secretary of the USSB and the Emergency Fleet Corporation).

After February 1919 the War Department estimated that their shipping programme would be able to maintain cargo tonnage for their 80 divisions without assistance from the European Allies, provided the submarine threat remained neutralised, in comparison to Bliss's study, which relied on the Allies into June 1919. While the War Department foresaw a total deficit of 4.8 million d.w.t from August to the end of February, the American Section of the SWC had calculated that for the same period the shortage would be a total of 9.1 million DWT. The main discrepancy between this figures was a result of Bliss's inclusion of transport for animals which added an average of 550,000 DWT per month to the tonnage deficit.[17]

On 23 July the War Department sent these figures to Bliss so that he could transmit them to the European Allies; however, Bliss did not receive this telegram.[18] In fact, it took nearly a month before the War Department realised the instructions in this telegram had not reached the American PMR, at which point needs had to be reassessed.[19] Although the former had calculated the assistance necessary for the 80 division programme, the War Department was relying on Bliss to inform them on whether or not the Entente would support the Americans in their programme. Unaware, Baker continued to communicate his concerns about the 80 division programme to Bliss without resending the War Department's actual programme with its accompanying figures. In the days following, Baker explained to Bliss that the two concerns he had about fulfilling the expanded military programme had to do with cargo shipping (to supply the troops) and port facilities (for unloading supplies).[20] Baker requested that Bliss request from the British PMR the amount of cargo tonnage the British could provide to the Americans. From the French PMR, Baker wanted information on the capacity of French ports.[21] Baker informed Bliss that under the supervision of the USSB and Mr Schwab, its president, American ship building was moving steadily and would likely exceed tonnage estimates, as the tendency in the United States was to make conservative estimates. In contrast, Baker was reserved about French estimates on port facilities, explaining to Bliss,

[17] 'Table III: Animals in Plan for 80 Divisions', 2 August 1918, Bliss/319.
[18] March to American Section, 23 July 1918.
[19] On 17 August the War Department wrote to the American Section to inquiry why they had not responded to their cable on the 23 July [cable #74] regarding the 80 division programme, and why they were asking questions already answered in said cablegram. The War Department had to send its findings a second time. March to Bliss, 17 August 1918, Bliss/329/no. 80.
[20] Palmer, *Bliss*, 326.   [21] Palmer, *Newton D. Baker*, 272.

'The port situation, I confess, seems more or less insoluble from this end, and yet every estimate we get from France is hopeful, if not optimistic'.[22]

It was through the foreign press that Bliss learned of the USSB's new shipbuilding projections. With this information Bliss extrapolated that the Americans might still be able to meet the 100 division programme, as opposed to the 80 division one. As described in the previous chapter, the military leadership wanted to gain as great a numerical superiority over the enemy as could be achieved by 1 July 1919. Writing to Baker regarding these new figures, he explained:

should it do so you may be able to carry out the 100-division program, if we do not bring the war to a conclusion with a lesser force. On previous estimates of available tonnage I have feared that even the 80 division program is more than we can accomplish. But when we consider that the American division is double the strength of the German division, any approximation to the 80-division program will give us a magnificent force.[23]

An opinion held by few individuals at the time, Bliss considered it possible to end the war in 1918; however, this did not prevent him from advocating a large American programme.

Bliss continued his campaign for the enlarged programme by creating a draft joint note entitled 'Shipments of American Troops', which he submitted to the other PMRs. It supported Foch and Pershing's request for an enlarged programme by arguing 'that a force of not less than 80 American divisions in France by June 30, 1919, is a necessary condition to the successful completion of the war within a reasonable length of time; and ... this effort should be continued, if necessary to include 100 divisions as soon as practicable after June 30, 1919'.[24] He also went so far as to recommend to his partners that the American army take priority in shipping over the Allies' own import programmes. Bliss pressed, 'That all the Allied governments, including the United States of America, make every effort to furnish the shipping and artillery material necessary for this purpose, giving preference to the requirements of the American military effort over other demands for shipping'.[25] However the other members refused to agree to this draft note. Instead, they requested detailed information from Bliss about the American military programme. On 26 August, the Italian PMR once again asked Bliss for America's shipping requirements.[26] Two

[22] Baker to Bliss, 28 July 1918, Bliss/250/no. 5.
[23] Bliss to Baker, 31 July 1918, Bliss/250.
[24] American Section, 'Draft of Proposed Joint Note: Shipments of American Troops', 23 August 1918, Bliss/324.
[25] Ibid.   [26] Di Robilant to Bliss, 26 August 1918, Bliss/324.

Table 6.3 *Unofficial cargo deficit created by the 80 division programme*

Month	Deficit in DWT('000)
August 1918	650
September 1918	667
October 1918	729
November 1918	718
December 1918	767
January 1919	543
February 1919	881
March 1919	915
April 1919	1,000
May 1919	1,022
June 1919	913
Total	8,805

Source: 'Memo by the Ministry of Shipping', 17 August 1918, LG/F/35/2/78.

days later Bliss finally received the War Department's programme figures. He relayed this information as the actual requirements of the American army as opposed to simply estimates.[27]

The problem with the War Department figures, as described by the British Shipping Controller, Joseph Maclay, who had received this information from the British PMR, was that they were meaningless without further explanation. Maclay was unclear if the figures meant that the additional DWT could be given in August and then slowly be reduced over the following months, or if they required additional tonnage each month. Maclay wrote that these figures, 'are unsupported by facts or material of any sorts. There is nothing to show on what basis of supply the tonnage requirement is based, nor how far it has been brought into relation with new tonnage suitable for the service or how far it includes tonnage obtained by a drastic comb-out of other shipping interests'.[28] Maclay was suggesting that the Americans might have been withholding shipping for the military programme for use in transporting goods for profit. The only explanation he could offer for the imprecise nature of the latest American figures was that they were outdated. He had also received shipping figures presented by the American member of the AMTC (see Table 6.3). Although these figures were an unofficial statement of the

[27] American PMR to French PMR 'Transport of American Troops after the Month of August, 1918', 28 August 1918, Bliss/324.
[28] Maclay to Lloyd George, 23 August 1918, LG/F/35/2/78.

United States cargo deficit created by the 80 division programme, Maclay believed they were closer to the reality of American needs than the muddled War Department estimates.

In fact the estimates provided by the American member of the AMTC were closer to the ones drawn up by Bliss than by the War Department. Like Bliss, they estimated that the United States would run a shipping deficit into June 1919, and the 8.8 million d.w.t deficit was much closer to the 9.1 million DWT estimated by Bliss than the 4.8 million d.w.t figure provided by the War Department.[29] While Maclay believed the higher figures were closer to the reality of the American situation, he still thought the deficit could be reduced. Now that the United States was asking for assistance from the Allies, Maclay noted that they could press Washington, via the SWC, for a full explanation of their shipping programme. This action would allow the British to ensure that the Americans were making sacrifices equal to that of their partners – notably that they had reduced their shipping trade as much as possible to accommodate the American military programme. It was through the AMTC that Maclay wanted American assistance explained and justified so that the British could assess if they should provide shipping to the Americans. He was, however, positive 'that if great pressure comes, we can do something to meet it'.[30] From these discussions it was clear that the information being presented by the Americans was confusing. Not only did they fail to provide a detailed programme but, worse still, they had three different groups providing various British officials with remarkably different figures. Not only did it make it difficult for the Allies to assist them, but it also raised suspicions towards the American import trade.

The Lloyd George Telegram to Clemenceau

A telegram sent on 2 August from Lloyd George to Clemenceau had the ability to de-rail the 80 division programme. The British Prime Minister explained that it was no longer possible for the British to supply the Americans with cargo tonnage and that, in addition, they would have to reduce the tonnage they were providing for troop transportation. Lloyd George was adamant that 'it must not be forgotten that the greater part of the American troops were brought to France by British shipping and that because of the sacrifices made to furnish this shipping our people have the right to expect that more than 5 divisions of the 28 American Divisions now in France should be put in training behind

---

[29] The precise estimates were 8,805,000 DWT, 9,100,286 DWT, and 4,818,753 DWT.
[30] Maclay to Lloyd George, 23 August 1918, LG/F/35/2/78.

our lines'.[31] Pershing, who had obtained a copy of this telegram and sent it to the War Department, understood it to be a reaction of the British to the formation of an independent American army, which was true. This formation had come at the time when Haig was preparing to use American troops, which the British had shipped and trained. Instead, Pershing asked that they be released so he could form his independent army. Understandably, Haig was furious.[32]

The AEF commander was alarmed that Lloyd George was going to use the next SWC as a forum to discuss various ways in which American troops could be used with the British army – including an American army dependent on the British for supplies and the creation of 'international' divisions (an idea already floated by the British PMR and described in the previous chapter). Pershing was convinced that one of these scenarios would be pressed upon the Americans in exchange for shipping, and noted that the Prime Minister's attitude was at variance with his earlier support of the enlarged programme. Ever wary of British intentions, he also believed this to be an attempt by the British and Italians to hinder 'too friendly' relations between the Americans and the French.[33] Fortunately for Pershing the August and September meetings of the SWC were postponed, and when it did meet in October it was to discuss armistice terms. A meeting with the British Ambassador to the United States, Rufus Isaacs, 1st Marguees of Reading, over the issue of shipping did little to quiet Pershing's suspicions. As Pershing put it to Baker, 'the increase of British tonnage for our use seemed to hinge on the allotment of a greater proportion of our troops for service with their armies'.[34]

Lloyd George had in fact been authorised by the War Cabinet (in consultation with Maclay and Milner) to use shipping as leverage to encourage the French and Americans to take up more of the front line.[35] This telegram was part of a British campaign to gain manpower from the Americans.[36] Additionally, it fuelled animosity between the British and French over manpower, as Lloyd George attempted to force Foch to send American troops to the British for training. From the British perspective, they were frustrated that they had been providing their partners with such extensive shipping resources, and receiving little in return. By the end of the war the British had shipped approximately half of the

[31] Pershing to Baker, 15 August 1918, Pershing/20.   [32] Bruce, *Fraternity*, 254.
[33] Pershing to Baker, 15 August 1918.
[34] 10 September 1918, in Pershing, *My Experiences*, 579.
[35] F. P. Robinson to J. T. Davies, 9 August 1918, LG/F/35/2/75.
[36] Greenhalgh, *Victory*, 270.

American troops in France, and yet most trained in the French sector.[37] In addition, once the independent AEF was given a sector, it was near the French zone of operations, as opposed to the British. As Hankey, who had drafted the telegram for Lloyd George, explained, it reflected the Prime Minister's jealousy of both the French and American heads of state. He recorded in his diary, 'He [Lloyd George] fears that between Wilson & Clemenceau; between American success & French prestige; he and Great Britain will at the peace conference cut a poor figure'.[38] Lloyd George went as far as to instruct Hankey to 'rig' Maclay in any negotiations with the Americans over shipping.[39]

A memo on the 'Tonnage Assistance Rendered by Great Britain to the Allies' drawn up by Maclay and forwarded to Lloyd George assisted the Prime Minster in building his case. In July the British had shipped 185,000 out of the 300,000 American soldiers who had crossed the Atlantic.[40] This equated to a sacrifice of 250,000 tonnes of imports a month for the British.[41] The Ministry of Shipping employed (had on the register) a total of 15 million gross tonnes of shipping (4,050 merchant vessels) in August, plus an additional 900,000 tonnes which were found on Naval, Military, Allied, and Colonial Services making return journeys with imports from America. What made the contribution to American troop transport so significant was that it had to be allotted from within the 6½ million tonnes of commercial tonnage from which all imports for Britain came. This included the tonnage to transport food, munitions and raw materials (essential for Britain's war manufacturing). Thus shipping American troops at this rate reduced what the British had available by 250,000 tonnes.[42] On assessing the British war effort Maclay calculated that the French employed over 1 million gross tonnes of British shipping (45 percent of French imports and 50 percent of the coal used in France were transported in British ships). As well, Maclay estimated that more than 500,000 gross tonnes of British shipping were being used to supply the Italians (45 percent of Italy's total imports and

---

[37] Bruce, *Fraternity*, 166.   [38] Hankey diary, 1 August 1918, HNKY/1/5.
[39] Hankey diary, 25 July 1918, HNKY/1/5.
[40] Ministry of Shipping, 'Tonnage Assistance Rendered by Great Britain to the Allies', 8 August 1918, LG/F/35/2/75.
[41] For the American figures see Ibid.; for the total gross tonnage of the Ministry of Shipping, see Ministry of Shipping, 'Notes on Tonnage Position, August, 1918', 20 August 1918, LG/F/35/2/77.
[42] Ministry of Shipping, 'Notes on Tonnage Position, August, 1918'. The remainder of the 15 million gross tonnes was employed in the navy (2 million), military (1.85 million), and Allies (2 million). Naval ships included ships such as armed merchant cruisers, mine sweepers, and carriers, hospital ships, colliers, and oilers. Army ships included those for 'trooping' and moving stores, coal, nitrates. These are monthly figures.

75 percent of its coal were transported in British ships). Of the 1½ million tonnes of neutral shipping obtained by the Allies, most of it was employed by Britain's partners. In the context of this hefty shipping contribution it is not surprising that the British expected increased support in return.

Despite growing animosity towards the Americans, in reality the British were facing serious difficulties of their own – in particular shortages of coal for industry, as Lloyd George explained to Clemenceau in this telegram. Coal and manpower were related in that the British had had to comb out coal miners for army service in order to meet manpower shortages earlier in the year, with the obvious consequence that less coal was mined. On 12 August, Maclay and Winston Churchill, Minister of Munitions, urged the Prime Minister to address the coal shortage.[43] Despite the pressing concerns expressed by Lloyd George, Peyton March, the American Assistant Secretary of War, insisted that his government should continue to push ahead with the enlarged American programme. He did, however, recognise that it would take longer than the War Department had anticipated without the assistance of the British. Nonetheless, 'when the American shipping begins to come through', March assured Pershing, 'we will surprise the world'.[44]

The British were reluctant to provide shipping to the Americans, whose own merchant marine was expanding at a colossal rate (even though merchant ship construction was relatively poor compared to initial estimates of their shipbuilding capabilities).[45] In the last six months of the war they produced nearly 3 million tonnes of merchant ships (comparable to the total world output of any pre-war year).[46] President Wilson was also conscious that the American shipbuilding programme was affecting Anglo-American relations. In response Woodrow Wilson thought the American government should be cautious when making statements about the country's postwar economic plans, telling the chairman of the USSB not to make any public statements about American shipping after the war as 'the English, as I need not tell you, are making a great many determined efforts to see to it that only that they are not put at an economic disadvantage after the war, but that they secure now by as tight arrangements as possible every economic

---

[43] Maclay to Lloyd George, 12 August 1918, LG/F/35/2/76. For memos by Churchill, see 'The Munitions Position as Affected by the Prospective Shortage of Coal', 18 June 1918, CHAR/15/37 [995] and 'Coal and Iron Ore', 14 July 1918, CHAR/15/34.
[44] March to Pershing, 12 August 1918, Pershing/123.
[45] Trask, *Captains and Cabinets*, 207.
[46] Jeffrey Safford, *Wilsonian Maritime Diplomacy, 1913–1921* (New Brunswick, 1978), 153.

advantage that is within their reach'.[47] As he reminded Hurley, 'the impression made by past utterances has been that we, like the English, are planning to dominate everything and to oust everybody we can oust'.[48] He felt that the British had misunderstood American intentions, and that the only solution was to keep quiet, 'My object [being] to give them not even the slightest color of provocation or excuse for what they are doing'.[49] It was a difficult position for the Allies, as the British wanted American manpower and materials in Europe, but the expansion of America's merchant marine inevitably meant that the expansion of American trade after the war, so challenging Britain's economic position. In fact, it was Hurley's intention to do so.[50]

The Lloyd George-Clemenceau telegram also affected how Bliss approached his role as a liaison between the European Allies and his own government on the shipping programme. First, it affected his attitude towards the British. Bliss, like Pershing, responding with irritation to the telegram, interpreting it as an attempt by the British to obtain manpower in exchange for shipping. He told Baker:

The British seem to take it very much to heart that we are not going to feed our man-power into their organizations in order to enable them to maintain their previous number of divisions; also that we have not committed ourselves as a matter of policy to maintaining American divisions on the British Front. It is hard to believe that England, who is so vitally interested in the issue of the war, would allow this to stand in the way of her furnishing tonnage assistance provided she could possibly furnish it.[51]

Bliss went so far as to suggest the Americans force the Allies to provide the cargo tonnage and troop transport for the American programme. His anxiety to increase American manpower in Europe was heightened by his belief that the Allies might negotiate with the Germans before they could be defeated, as he believed the 'common people' might pressure them to do so. While militarily he thought the Allies had the ability to win the war in 1918, he also recognised home-front morale as a key component in achieving victory.[52]

The Lloyd George-Clemenceau telegram also resulted in Bliss relaxing his efforts to exchange information among coalition partners. It led him to believe the British had decided upon the shipping, and thus he did not need to provide them with additional information on American capabilities. Furthermore, he thought that the British and American experts, who were working together in London on shipping, had taken

[47] W. Wilson to Hurley, 29 August 1918, Wilson/99.   [48] Ibid.   [49] Ibid.
[50] Safford, *Wilsonian Maritime Diplomacy*, 154.
[51] Bliss to Baker, 22 August, 1918, Bliss/250/no. 17.   [52] Ibid.

the lead. With little information being sent to him from his government, Bliss did not push the matter. Meanwhile, Baker, upon learning of the telegram considered going to Europe to deal with tonnage, but decided he should remain in Washington to focus on getting the necessary legislation passed for the expanded military programme. It was Baker's belief that Bliss remained at the centre of shipping negotiations.[53] Once again, disorganisation and misunderstanding meant the Americans were not working to their full potential with their partners.

The AMTC Investigates Shipping

By August another Allied body, the AMTC, had become prominent in discussions for the expanded American programme. As Elizabeth Greenhalgh has explained, 'The greatest story at the heart of the SWC lay in the AMTC's ability to apportion neutral shipping and to provide coal'.[54] Indeed, she evaluates the AMTC as one of the greatest success stories of the SWC and illustrates how the Allies reorganised the transportation of coal to France and Italy in order to release shipping for use elsewhere. Building upon the groundwork she has laid, this section considers the AMTC's role in coordinating available shipping for the achievement of the 80 division programme. The AMTC was one of the many councils created when the Americans sent a mission under House to coordinate the American war effort with its coalition partners in November 1917. The idea for such a body stemmed from the Allies' frustration with their ineffective allocation of tonnage and poor communication networks.

When working on the AMTC's initial conception only Britain and the United States were represented despite that Clémentel (the French Minister of Commerce) had been advocating shipping control throughout 1917. It was not until they had laid the groundwork for this body that they invited the French and the Italians to join them at this forum. The representatives for the AMTC were: M. Loucheur (Minister of Munitions) and Clémentel for France; Lord Robert Cecil (the Under-Secretary of State for Foreign Affairs) and Sir Joseph Maclay (the Shipping Controller) for Britain; Sgr. Crespi (Minister of Supplies) for Italy; and R. B. Stevens (Vice-Chairman of the USSB) for America.[55] The AMTC was closely linked to the shipping controllers in each nation. While the AMTC

---

[53] Baker, 6 August 1918, in Palmer, *Newton D. Baker*, 2: 261.

[54] Greenhalgh, *Victory*, 274. For more on the AMTC and the movement of coal, see Fayle, *Seaborne Trade*, 3: 301–305, 372.

[55] Morrow to Stettinius, 5 May 1918, Albert and Shirley Small Special Collections Library, University of Virginia, Stettinius Papers (hereon Stettinius) Stettinius/87. In Salter's account, the Italians had two ministers, not one, the second being the Minister of

itself met monthly, it had a permanent staff that sat in London called the Allied Maritime Transport Executive (AMTE) whose members liaised between their governments on all shipping questions. As J. A. Salter, the British AMTC representative, described:

It was found possible to secure the necessary co-ordination and decisions partly through the liaison work of the members of the Executive, and party through telephonic and telegraphic arrangements, supplemented in certain cases by special visits ... By these and similar methods the necessary consultation and agreement were in practice secured without a formal meeting of the Council.[56]

Although the AMTC did not have executive power, the connection of its members to the shipping controllers at home, and the continuous work of the AMTC, resulted in the AMTC being at the centre of Allied discussions for shipping. While it was suggested by Lord Robert Cecil, the British representative at the initial AMTC meeting, that this body pool tonnage and establish an international body to control it, other representatives from both Britain and the United States adamantly disagreed.[57] Lord Curzon, Sir Joseph Maclay, and Mr Colby argued that such an international body would cause friction between the Allies, as neither the British nor the Americans would want their shipping decisions made by others, nor could they allow another body to make decisions which had the ability to so greatly affect civilian and military requirements. Instead it was recommended that the AMTC be a consultative body rather than an executive one.[58] Its objectives were first 'to make the most economical use of tonnage under the control of all the Allies', second 'to allot that tonnage as between the different needs of the Allies in such a way as to add most to the general war effort', and third 'to adjust the programmes of requirements of the different Allies in such a way as to bring them within the scope of the possible carrying power of the tonnage available'.[59] To achieve these results the AMTC encouraged *each* nation to tabulate its requirements for tonnage needed, tonnage available, and tonnage likely to be available in the future – a *massive* undertaking that was still underway when the armistice was signed.[60] For

Transport. Sir Arthur Salter, *Allied Shipping Control: An Experiment in International Administration* (Oxford, 1921), 189.

[56] Salter, *Allied Shipping Control*, 189.

[57] Clémentel had made a similar suggestion about the pooling of tonnage in August 1917. See Kaspi, *Le Temps Des Américains*, 152.

[58] 'Draft Report of a Committee appointed by the Anglo-American Conference on November 20th, 1917', Baker/15/13/p. 24.

[59] Ibid., 29.

[60] Raymond Stevens and George Rublee (American shipping Mission, London) to Baker, 26 September 1918, Baker/15/13.

neutral and interned tonnage, the vision was to share these ships based on who had the greatest need and allot them accordingly, as opposed to tonnage being kept by the country which had seized it. The AMTC eventually came to control 500,000 tonnes of neutral shipping, and while remaining shipping stayed under national control, the AMTC recommended how this tonnage should be used.[61]

The AMTC recommended that each country should attempt to furnish greater tonnage by combing it out from other areas 'such as that in South America ...', a clause clearly aimed at the American merchant fleet.[62] The European Allies demanded that the Americans increase their cargo tonnage by taking 'every possible step to bring into war service neutral and internal vessels now idle or out of war service'.[63] The AMTC also recommended that the Americans seek assistance from the Japanese. Finally, it wanted the United States to reduce imports (for the needs of civilian consumption) to free up tonnage that could be used for the military programme. While the AMTC did not allocate troops for the military programme specifically, it did make recommendations and predicted the effect the expanded military programme would have on the European Allies' supply needs for their armies, raw materials for both industry and their militaries, and food supplies for civilians.[64]

The French members of the AMTC, Clémentel and Loucheur, envisaged that this council would bring more American troops to fight in France by using Allied tonnage more efficiently.[65] The British and French governments suspected the Americans had not reduced their civilian imports as greatly as was possible. In August 1918, the British and French arranged to discuss American tonnage through the AMTC.[66] Tardieu, who was at the centre of Franco-American economic coordination, had been unsuccessful in gaining information on how the US was employing tonnage.[67] He had asked his deputy, Edward de Billy, who was at the head of the French High Commission in Washington to investigate this question. While Tardieu understood he would have to alter and even sacrifice French supply for the American programme, he required clear information on American requirements and capabilities. It was through the AMTC that the Entente could pressure the Americans to utilise more of their own tonnage for the military programme.

---

[61] Greenhalgh, *Victory*, 275.   [62] 'Draft Report of a Committee', Baker/15/13/p. 30.
[63] Ibid., 32.   [64] Salter, *Allied Shipping*, 193.   [65] Ibid., 129.
[66] Tardieu to de Billy, 26 August 1918, SHD-DAT, Collection Tardieu, 13N 17.
[67] Tardieu to de Billy, 15 August 1918 and de Billy to Tardieu, 20 August 1918, 13N 17.

Programme Committees

Simultaneously, a number of 'Programme Committees' were created to work alongside the AMTC.[68] These were referred to as 'investigating and planning' committees and were intended to cover the entire area of Allied imports.[69] The French initiated the idea of these committees, while the British had to be persuaded to agree to their adoption. Again the Americans preferred their representatives only observe these meetings rather than act as full participants. When appointing his subordinates to these committees, Stevens, head American representative on the AMTC, highlighted the need to select individuals who could act outside their national interests and coordinate Allied needs. He deemed this characteristic to be of higher value than technical understanding. Stevens explained to Washington the advantages these committees offered to the Americans:

By reason of its [America's] rapidly increasing construction of ships it will soon command an important and constantly growing share of the tonnage in the service of war needs. Therefore it has an obvious special interest in making sure that the credit and tonnage furnished by it are not wastefully or improvidently used. The purpose in creating the program committees is to secure this end.[70]

Despite Stevens' encouragement for the Americans to become full partners, President Wilson preferred to remain detached.[71] This significantly reduced the ability of the Americans to illustrate to their partners that they were making equal concessions. Furthermore, it disappointed the French and Italians who urged the Americans to join so that they would not be overshadowed by the British.[72]

Like the AMTC, the programme committees did not have executive authority. Each committee member was responsible for gathering the necessary information to detail the minimum requirements for their nation. Using this information the coalition could then come to an agreement with the other representatives for a joint Allied programme of purchases and imports.[73] One American member described these committees as, 'investigating and planning committees, to ascertain the

---

[68] For a diagram of how these committees worked, see Greenhalgh, *Victory*, 278; Hankey, *Diplomacy by Conference*, 10; Salter, *Allied Shipping*, endpaper.

[69] George Rublee to President Wilson, 20 June 1918, Baker/15/13.

[70] Stevens to Hurley, Gay, McAdoo, McCormick and Hoover, 15 May 1918, Baker/15/13.

[71] They did not become a full member until after Baker's trip to Europe in the autumn. Sir Arthur Salter, 'Allied Maritime Transport Council, 1918', http://archive.org/stream/cu31924027892607, 7.

[72] Stevens to Hurley, Gay, McAdoo, McCormick and Hoover, 15 May 1918.

[73] More on programme committees, Stevens to the Department of State, 12 June 1918, Baker/15/13.

facts by which the governments may be guided. There has been no thought of giving to these committees any power to control policies, or, indeed, any executive power whatever'.[74] They were naturally at the centre of discussions for future planning, being connected to both the coalition partners and the relevant departments within their national governments.[75] For example, the British government required the British department responsible for each commodity to select the representative for the programme committees and to assist them.[76] Programme committees included ones on jute, timber, and coal. Munitions and food were further organised into the Inter-Allied Munitions Council and the Inter-Allied Food Council (see Figure 1.1 Diagram of the Supreme War Council Organisation, November 1917). The heads of the Food Controllers of Italy, France, Britain and the United States met in London approximately every three months to 'agree upon a programme and methods of food imports embracing the needs of the Allied countries, and will determine questions of common interest and policy'.[77] These committees were also assisted by the War Purchases and Finance Council, which functioned on the same level as the AMTC. Established in August 1917 it oversaw purchasing in America.[78] These various committees allowed the four nations to discuss and agree upon import requirements for each commodity. The AMTC then considered all commodities as part of a wider Allied programme.

Prior to the first AMTC meeting in March, the goal of which was for each country through 'an interchange or views and mutual criticism to get a workable knowledge of the minimum requirements of each of the four countries', the American delegates met informally with various shipping authorities in France and Britain.[79] Dwight Morrow, who acted as an advisory delegate to Mr Stevens, described to Stettinius the situation in Europe in May:

If you were here now I think you would be surprised by the effect of the great German offensive upon the spirit of the English and French people. They realize that they are fighting for their lives. I adhere to the view that I have held from the

[74] George Rublee to President Wilson, 20 June 1918, Baker/15/13.
[75] The Quarter-master general was responsible for stores, jute, flax, hemp, hides and leathers, and mules and horses; the Ministry of Food for items such as meat and fats, sugar, oil seeds, and cereals; the Board of Trade for paper, cotton, timber, and tobacco; the War Office for wool; the Ministry of Munitions for munitions, metal, ores, nitrates, etc.; and the Ministry of Shipping for coke and coal. Salter, *Allied Shipping*, 194.
[76] Ibid., 181.
[77] AMTC 'Report of Action, July 16th to August 15th, 1918', 16 August 1918, Baker/15/13.
[78] See Greenhalgh, *Victory*, 181.
[79] Dwight Morrow (AEF) to Stettinius, 21 May 1918, Stettinius/87.

beginning, that Germany will look her most terrible when she is weakest. In making our own preparations, we should plan for a long War. In strengthening our hearts, however, we should never forget that 'if hopes were dupes, fears may be liars'.[80]

Morrow recognised the important role that the American army played in the notion of achieving victory. Within this image he assessed the relevance of shipping infantry as 'the biggest thing that America has done since we entered the war ... It may mean the difference between Germany winning or losing the world war'.[81] While Morrow worked on shipping through the AMTC, he also considered the needs of Pershing by consulting with Colonel Logan, who was the Head of the First Section of the General Staff and in charge of tonnage for the AEF.[82] Morrow was in a pivotal position between the AMTC, the American government, and GHQ. His opinion was that Pershing should use American troops with the Entente armies and wait to form an independent American army until the winter of 1918–1919. Morrow's approach illustrates how the members of the AMTC took a broad view on civilian and army shipping requirements.

No meetings were held by the AMTC between 25 April and 29 August; however, discussions and decisions about tonnage allocation continued through the AMTE. By July the biggest issue facing the AMTC was the increased American military programme.[83] In terms of troop transport, the AMTC estimated that while the existing arrangements would suffice to bring the men, 'the real problem is one of the carriage of supplies and horses'.[84] As they waited for shipping figures from the Americans, the British Section of the AMTC made loose estimates for the Allied shipping programme. They concluded that in order to maintain in Europe the men from the 80 division programme, 7–8 million DWT from the summer of 1919 onward would be required. Added to this figure was another 1–1½ million d.w.t for the transport of horses. The requirements for the 1919 programme represented a significant increase from 1918, as in the month of July 1918 the American army required only 2 million DWT.[85] Despite this challenge and the uncertainties expressed by the AMTC at the time, after the war Salter recalled that, given the rate of American shipbuilding and due to the fact that ship losses at sea had been significantly reduced, by July 'the corner was turned' on the issue of shipping.[86]

---

[80] Ibid.   [81] Ibid.   [82] Ibid.   [83] Salter, *Allied Shipping*, 195.
[84] Note on general shipping position quoted in Ibid.   [85] Ibid.   [86] Ibid., 196.

The Third Session of the AMTC

In August, the AMTC was embroiled with discussions on how to make up shortages in cargo tonnage for the American programme, and thus was placed at the centre of the creation of an Allied strategy for 1919. Throughout late July and August the AMTE had worked with the Inter-Allied Food Council in estimating requirements for the cereal year 1918–1919.[87] This programme encompassed all foods for all European Allies.[88] Initially the Food Council estimates were greater for the upcoming year by 4½ million tonnes than they had been for the cereal year 1917–1918. Upon reading these figures the AMTC insisted that the maximum programme presented by the AMTE be no greater than the previous year's programme. As the AMTE explained:

the Transport Council [AMTC] will not feel justified in asking the military and munitions authorities to reduce their demands upon tonnage (with a consequent reduction of the numbers of American soldiers available for next year's campaign) in order that such tonnage may be allocated to food as to enable and encourage consumption upon a more generous scale than during the past year.[89]

When thinking about future shipping, the AMTC figures for American cargo tonnage were based on 300,000 American troops being shipped per month.[90] Despite the Lloyd George-Clemenceau telegram, the AMTC still believed that the British would continue to supply troop transport at 'the present rate' (shipping approximately 180,000 men) to the end of December 1918. The AMTC received information about the American requirements from Bliss via the SWC.[91]

In response to these suggestions the Food Council divided its recommendations into two categories: 'priority tonnage' and 'balance of programme'. These figures were then discussed by the AMTC at its third meeting held during 29 and 30 August when it tentatively agreed that the food programme should consist of only 'priority tonnage', which was represented by a figure of 18½ million shipping tonnes, excluding military oats.[92] As the AMTC did not have all available information (it was still waiting for precise shipping information from the Americans as well

---

[87] The cereal year began in September. Margaret Barnett, *British Food Policy During the First World War* (New York, 2014), 50.

[88] For the specific details of the cereal year, broken down by source, see AMTC 'Allocation of Tonnage in the Cereal Year 1918–19', 27 September 1918, Baker/15/13.

[89] Letter from Transport Council to Food Council, 5 August 1918, reprinted in Salter, *Allied Shipping*, 306–307.

[90] AMTC 'Minutes of Third Session at Lancaster House, London, August 29–30, 1918', 30 September 1918, Baker/15/13/p. 20.

[91] Ibid., p. 21   [92] Ibid.; Salter, *Allied Shipping*, 198, 304–310.

as details of the IAMC's programme for the following year), a final decision was delayed until they met for a fourth time in late September.[93] Meanwhile the AMTC still hoped to persuade the Japanese to provide ships. The Japanese government had not responded to the Allied request for them to join the AMTC by the time the armistice was signed.[94]

Failure of the Americans to Send Programme Information

The AMTC did not examine the details of any military supply programme. Rather, it considered the demands that the military programmes would have on tonnage. By late August the AMTC was still waiting to receive shipping information from the Americans. On 27 August the American Ambassador described to President Wilson the complications created by the failure of the United States to present its programme for imports of food to the other Allies, pointedly adding that 'A direct message sent to some person here to the effect that the sacrifice of the Allies for the common cause is recognised by the United States which intends to cut its own trade to the bone would have a decided effect in obtaining, with regard to the Army program, prompt action'.[95] While the European Allies pressed the Americans to reduce its own imports, the American Food Controller, Herbert Hoover, responded that the Americans had organised so as not to use transatlantic tonnage for food imports with the exception of using 'some minor liner space and two tankers for oil', concluding that 'our food import program cannot interest allies [sic] and should be sufficient evidence of our stripping to the bone'.[96] Hoover's opinion was that it was dangerous to cut into priority food tonnage.

It was Baker, not Hoover, who had the authority to make final decisions about these programmes.[97] Although he did not send a complete programme to the British he did inform Colville Barclay, who was acting for Lord Reading, of the cargo tonnage situation for the American programme. In his letter he reminded the British that the Americans had already reduced cargo tonnage required for the 80 division programme by dropping the normal tonnage requirement for each man from 50 pounds per day for maintenance, replacement and reserve down to the absolute minimum of 30 pounds (with an added 250,000 tonnes per month of construction material). He argued that the American ship

[93] Salter, *Allied Shipping*, 304–310.   [94] Ibid., 202.

[95] American Ambassador at London (Walter Hines Page) to Woodrow Wilson, 27 August 1918, Wilson/99.

[96] Hoover to US Embassy in London, 7 September 1918, Wilson/99.   [97] Ibid.

building programme would significantly reduce the tonnage deficit in the immediate future, reminding Barclay that while in August 1918 the shortage was 1.2 million DWT, by February 1919 it was predicted to be down to 209,621 DWT.[98] Given these figures the Americans believed that by early 1919 they would be able to release much of the shipping loaned to them by their partners. Baker urged that the demands of the current crisis in cargo tonnage for the American programme be met, warning that General Pershing was already facing serious drains on his reserve supplies, 'which in a very short time will become so serious as to compel the Department to materially reduce troop shipments, if not stop them entirely'.[99] In reality Pershing was also sufficiently concerned about cargo tonnage, supplies, and shortages to advise his government to exchange food cargo for military cargo.[100] A day earlier March had informed Pershing that the War Department would not be able to meet his requests for horses and mules due to shipping shortages. The issue hinged on the British ability to supply the cargo tonnage.[101] Aware of this situation, Baker pressed the British Ambassador: 'I therefore, cannot urge too strongly the necessity for prompt action on the part of your government in supplying at the earliest practicable date sufficient additional cargo tonnage to meet the program agreed upon'.[102] This information was also communicated to both the AMTE and AMTC who incorporated it into their calculations for the cereal year 1918–1919.[103]

The Inter-Allied Munitions Council

The AMTC relied on the IAMC to supply it with munitions tonnage requirements for the cereal year 1918–1919. First conceived in 1917 and agreed upon by the Allies in October 1917, the IAMC was not formed until pressure created by the German spring offensives forced the coalition members to reconsider their munitions supplies.[104] The council comprised: the French Minster of Munitions, Louis Loucheur, assisted by M. Dumesnil (Under-Secretary of State for Military Aeronautics), General Mauclere, and Colonel Mercier; the British Minister of Munitions, Winston Churchill, assisted by Sir Charles Ellis, Mr W. T.

---

[98] Exact figure was 1,217,755 DWT, by February 1919.
[99] Baker to Mr Colville Barclay (the Charge d'Affaires, Ad Interim, British Embassy), 27 August 1918, Baker/5/4.
[100] Pershing to Baker, see letters from 15, 16, and 17 August 1918, Pershing/20.
[101] Palmer, *Newton D. Baker*, 2: 339.   [102] Baker to Colville Barclay, 27 August 1918.
[103] AMTC, 'Allied Program Committee', n.d. but it does state that it is a report prepared for the upcoming AMTC meeting on 30 September 1918, Baker/15/13.
[104] Greenhalgh, *Victory*, 272.

Layton, and Major-General Sir W. T. Furze; the Italian Under-Secretary of State for Munitions of War, H. E. Signor Nava, assisted by H. E. Signor Chiesa, Signor Quartieri, Lieut-General Marquis Claverino, and Dr A. Pirelli; and the American Assistant Secretary for War, Edward Stettinius, assisted by General Wheeler (Ordnance Department) and Mr L. L. Summers (WIB). A member of the War Department could also be asked to attend the meetings in order to speak for the General Staff. In addition the IAMC had a standing committee in Paris. It also worked closely with the Inter-Allied Statistical Bureau. Information relating to munitions was exchanged between the IAMC and the Inter-Allied Council on War Purchases and Finance, as well as with the Inter-Allied Shipping Council.

The IAMC was to meet every month to six weeks in Paris. Like the political body of the SWC it held preliminary meetings before the 'real' meetings.[105] It was to act as the 'clearinghouse' for all the other munitions bodies. Thus its members were 'to study, criticise, and make proposals in connection with munitions programmes' which included the military equipment of each army as well as the 'allocation and transport of raw materials for munitions to the various Allied countries'.[106] Munitions materials were defined as 'all products having steel or other metals as a base, and to all chemical products . . .'[107] It was also to receive all of the programmes from the sub-committees so as to deal with any conflicts. While it did not have executive authority, its role was to recommend programmes in consultation with both the Inter-Allied Council of Purchase and Finance and the AMTC, with whom it shared the same status. In case of disagreement this council would appeal to the political side of the SWC, Foch, or the governments involved. At its second meeting Churchill asserted that the IAMC should be established under the SWC, but that 'action . . . will proceed without the need of formal or special sanction in matters of routine'.[108] The relationship between the PMRs and this committee was such that the PMRs could attend the munitions meetings. All reports created by the IAMC were sent to the PMRs.[109]

The AMTC required munitions figures from the IAMC to accurately calculate shipping for the cereal year 1918–1919. Disorganisation within

[105] Stettinius to Thomas Nelson Perkins, 10 August 1918, Stettinius/87.
[106] 'Memorandum on the Organisation of the Inter-Allied Munitions Council', 4 June 1918, CHAR/15/34.
[107] Ministry of Munitions, *History of the Ministry of Munitions* (12 vols., London, 1918–23), 2, part viii, 44.
[108] Ibid., 45.   [109] Ibid., 46.

the American system meant that Stettinius did not receive complete information in order to make decisions causing him to lament:

We will never be able to derive full advantage from these situations until I am placed in a similar position:- that is to say, I must know the weak and high spots in the production programs of ordnance, and must also keep measurably in close touch with aircraft, so that what we want that our allies can supply and knowing what we can produce that they want, may be able to make trades and then make up shortages in certain lines of material.[110]

Although Stettinius found the first meeting of the IAMC to be 'wearisome' and 'rather ponderous', he came to realise its usefulness, particularly in the opportunity it presented to trade with the other members. For example, the British exchanged tanks for motors with the French.[111] Unfortunately, the American representative could not participate at these meetings to the same extent as his European partners as he did not have sufficient information about American production.

One of the main issues brought to the forefront of Allied munitions planning at the IAMC's second meeting held during 14 and 15 August 1918 was the programme for supplying the AEF in France for 1919. The Entente members were still unclear about the figures for the expanded military programme. At an informal meeting, Stettinius told his colleagues that the American government was aiming to field 80 divisions by the end of June 1919 and that the Americans would be unable to fully supply their own army with artillery and ammunition for the 1919 campaign. As part of planning for the future campaign, the IAMC members agreed to tabulate munitions statistics for the coalition.[112] A mere five days later, under pressure from Loucheur, Stettinius had obtained predictions for the American artillery programme. In gathering information as to what artillery Britain and France could supply the American army from the present time through to June 1919, Stettinius had turned to both W. T. Layton, the statistical adviser to the Ministry of Munitions in Britain, and Loucheur.[113] Then, with his own staff of approximately eight experts and alongside General Wheeler (Chief Ordnance Officer in France) and his staff at the Ordnance Department, Stettinius estimated a 'complete' statement of American needs (see Table 6.4).

---

[110] Stettinius to Perkins, 4 October 1918, Stettinius/87.   [111] Ibid.

[112] For how these values were calculated, see Greenhalgh, 'Errors and Omissions', 36.

[113] Stettinius to Layton requesting artillery information, 16 August 1918, Stettinius/85; Layton to Stettinius, 20 August 1918, Stettinius/87; Loucheur's response is explained to Baker by Stettinius, 26 August 1918, Stettinius/85; Stettinius to Bliss, 23 August 1918, Bliss/251.

Table 6.4 *American equipment requirements*

Type	Total requirements to 30 June 1919	From France	Equipment supplied to date	From Britain	Remainder to be supplied by US
Field guns	6,610	5,070	1,000	1,500	40
6-inch howitzer	3,000	2,190	400	710	100
6-inch gun	1,500	450[a]	150	180[b]	300
Heavy howitzer	763	0	–	450	313

[a] Plus an additional 200 modified range guns on howitzer carriages and additional 105-mm guns from Italy.
[b] Plus 220 60-pounders
Source: 'Note on the Equipment of the American Army in 1919', 2 September 1918.[114]

As shown in Table 6.4, the British and French were to supply the majority of artillery for the American programme. While tabulation of American artillery requirements represented a substantial effort by Stettinius, it still had to be approved by the War Department (and considered by the WIB). Stettinius had written to Baker in late August to ask him for definite instructions as to artillery and artillery ammunition requirements.[115] One possible explanation why the Entente representatives continued to wait for figures is that they did not recognise Stettinius' predictions as the official American programme since it had not been approved by his government. As a result they continued to pressure Stettinius for further information on the American programme.

Raw Materials

Another of the European Allies' concerns was getting enough raw and semi-manufactured materials to Europe, especially iron, iron ore, and steel. Many of the munitions, including motor transport, aeroplanes, and tanks, could be produced in European factories if the materials were available.[116] Raw materials were being requested by all of the European

[114] Table drawn from CHAR 'Note on the Equipment of the American Army in 1919', 2 September 1918, CHAR/15/34 and Layton to Stettinius, 20 August 1918, Stettinius/ 85. Slight revision were made to the American programme in early October, See 'Review of U. S. Artillery Program 66 Combat Divisions & 14 Depot Divisions', 4 October 1918, RG/120/267/3138/918. For information on how these results were compiled see Bliss to Baker, 22 August 1918, Bliss/250.
[115] Stettinius to Baker 26 and 27 August, Stettinius/85.
[116] IAMC, 'Note on the Second Meeting of the Council, 14th and 15th August 1918', 8 October 1918, Stettinius/85.

Allies. Italy wanted more steel and iron in order to increase its munitions production output. While the council recognised that Italy had comparative munitions stocks to France, these munitions would only suffice if Italy remained on the defensive (see Chapter 4 for Italy's operational plans in 1918). The French had also increased their demands for these two resources by 70 percent from the previous year. The German occupation of northern and eastern France for most of the war deprived France of 14 percent of all of its pre-war industrial production, including 63 percent of its steel and 81 percent of its iron.[117] As the French had supplied the Americans with ammunition in the past, and seemed likely to have to do so in 1919, the IAMC recommended that 'it [was] essential now for France to open out rapidly on ammunition production, the more so since the American supply of munitions is not yet forthcoming'.[118] France also increased its demands for railway material as Foch wanted a sizeable stock available in case large advances were made, especially as the enemy destroyed the railways as they retreated.

In trying to meet the American programme, the French were also running into serious problems with congested port facilities which also had repercussions for cargo tonnage. France's internal rail system was straining to transport the ever-expanding American army. The French required additional railways, as the ones they had were not sufficient to promptly clear the loading docks. As the French increased materials to expand their railway infrastructure (and to supply the Americans), this material congested its ports. Subsequently the turnaround of ships was delayed, causing a reduction in the amount of cargo tonnage a vessel could transport in a given period of time. As illustrated, the Allies were already concerned about the predicted cargo deficit for the 80 division programme. Any inefficiencies in utilising cargo tonnage were taken seriously, thus the British Admiralty, who had loaned cargo tonnage to the French, took action when they learned that not all of these vessels were being used to their full potential. In an attempt to accelerate the turnaround of ships in port, the British placed restrictions on the type of goods that could be transported in vessels they loaned to the French. The problem became that requirements imposed by the British did not always coincide with the materials the French had available to ship. Tonnage was sometimes wasted, as the vessels were not filled to capacity.[119] To the dismay of the French, the Admiralty took further action by removing

[117] Jean-Bapiste Duroselle, *La Grande Guerre des Français, 1914–1918* (Paris, 1994), 171.
[118] Stettinius/85; Steel Committee to IAMC, 26 September 1918, Stettinius/85.
[119] de Billy to Tardieu, 29 August 1918, SHD-DAT, Tardieu 13N 17.

three vessels previously used by the French and loaning them to the Americans.[120] It was in assessing the wider supply and shipping needs of the Allies that the AMTC and programme committees could improve efficiency by coordinating its members' needs.

The British Minister of Munitions' plans for the British army also hinged on the receipt of substantial raw materials from America. As early as March 1918 Churchill had a vision for the British army that compensated for the lack of British manpower through an increase in mechanical means of warfare: 'We should create, in order to attack the enemy in 1919', he observed, 'an army essentially different in its composition and methods of warfare from any that have yet been employed on either side'.[121] Mechanical means offered the opportunity to multiply manpower; however, the resources to create such an army competed with the needs of the expanded American programme.[122] Once again shipping tonnage, steel, and coal were limiting factors.

While offering to supply the Americans with heavy artillery and ammunition, Churchill was also willing to reduce the production of ammunition in Britain in order to continue the production of machine-guns, gas, aeroplanes, and tanks.[123] Churchill's production plans would equip the British army with the means to advance on the enemy. He had to balance each weapon's production costs with the results it could produce. In this way he found aeroplanes to be less useful for the campaign of 1919. As he wrote, 'There is no doubt that the demands of the Air Force on men and material are thought to be much in excess of the fighting results produced. There is no doubt that if Haig had to choose between 50,000 men for the Infantry and 50,000 men for the Air Force, he would choose 50,000 men for the Infantry'.[124] Churchill, however, was more supportive of tanks. He argued that they had proven to be of use in giving the Allies tactical superiority. 'It is the power of being able to advance a reasonable distance day after day remorselessly rather than making a very big advance in a single day', he asserted, 'that we should seek to develop. This power can only be imparted by Tanks and cross-country vehicles on the largest scale'.[125] The CIGS also supported the idea that tanks would assist the Allies in winning the war, writing to Churchill in early August to advocate their use: 'What I feel is that though our numerical

---

[120] 'Aide Américaine en tonnage' de Billy to Tardieu, 1 September 1918, Tardieu 13N 17.
[121] Churchill, 5 March 1918, quoted in Ministry of Munitions, *History*, 2, part i, 89.
[122] For more information on Churchill's ideas about mechanical warfare, see Harris, *Men, Ideas and Tanks*, ch. 5; Robin Prior, *Churchill's World Crisis as History* (London; Canberra, 1983), 80–82, 244–248.
[123] Ministry of Munitions, *History*, 2, part i, 96–97.
[124] Churchill to Lloyd George, 9 September 1918, CHAR/15/1.   [125] Ibid.

superiority next year will not be very great, yet we can add materially to that by our lead in mechanical means. If it is decided that we go for the Boche let us knock him out properly and in no half-hearted manner'.[126]

To meet his overall munitions programme Churchill proposed reducing the steel industries' consumption of coal by increasing imports of steel from America. For every one tonne of steel he received from the United States he could save four tonnes of British coal.[127] Churchill also had ideas about the Americans providing shell steel as well. He recommended that the shortage of artillery ammunition for the American army be relieved by the Americans receiving the shell production from American and Canadian factories that was previously allocated to the British. These shells would be filled in Britain. To meet this scenario the Americans would have to increase their shipment of shell steel, propellants and nitrates (to produce explosives). As Churchill explained, 'this material would be in substitution for material that would otherwise be required by the American factories to produce the French-type ammunition, there would be no net increase in the demand for tonnage'.[128] In essence Churchill was proposing that the British receive an increase in imports from the United States in exchange for ammunition, as opposed to the Americans supplying the French with raw materials in exchange for French ammunition. The production situation was further complicated by the fact that the Americans required both British and French ammunition to fire from the artillery pieces with which both the British and French had supplied them. Despite these ideas, Churchill's planning efforts were stymied, as he was reliant on the American Shipping Controller to inform him how much steel the United States would provide.[129]

In reality, although Churchill required steel from his North American partners, he did not have enough tonnage to bring it to Europe. The Steel Department ideally wanted 12 million ingot tonnes for the 1919 year but the Munitions Department was estimating that they would only receive 10 million tonnes in *total* for munitions.[130] Nor was the Ministry of Munitions going to receive as much coal as it required. Coal deficiencies for 1919 were estimated at 35 million tonnes out of a total of 250 million tonnes required. Despite the stupendous resources required by these mechanical means, overall Churchill was positive about the munitions

[126] Henry Wilson to Churchill, 8 August 1918, CHAR/15–1.

[127] The low quality of iron ore that the munitions industry had available meant that large quantities of coal were required to smelt the steel.

[128] 'Note on the Equipment of the American Army in 1919', 2 September 1918, CHAR/15/34.

[129] Churchill to Lloyd George, 9 September 1918.

[130] Ministry of Munitions, *History*, 2, part i, 96.

programme for 1919, telling Lloyd George 'that there will be enough to meet all reasonable needs'.[131] This optimism was partly a result of Allied coordination and the fact that discussions over munitions programmes had begun much earlier in 1918 than they had in 1917.

Within the United States, the WIB was facing difficult decisions about the allocation of steel. For example, in the case of steel plates, the EFC was demanding greater numbers of them to relieve its 1 million tonne shipping deficit created by the expanded military programme. Meanwhile Pershing had insisted he receive railway cars to clear the congestion in French ports. There was too little steel plate for both demands to be met and in this case the EFC's request was declined.[132] On 5 September Bernard Baruch, Director of the WIB, wrote to Mr Cromwell, Assistant Secretary of War, to inform the War Department, 'that there is such an acute shortage of steel today that not only is it impossible to meet the civilian requirements, but worse than that the military program cannot be met in full'.[133]

By September's end Churchill was still waiting to receive an official munitions report from the Americans which would inform him what they required from the British (he had only received a draft report). This information was essential for him to complete his own report on the British situation in 1919. From his talks with Stettinius, Churchill added to his earlier suspicions that the British would need to supply the Americans with ammunition, as opposed to the Americans supplying their Allies; however, he wanted confirmation from his American partner. If Churchill's suspicions were true, he would have to rework British munitions plans as he was not prepared to present the Cabinet with a plan based largely on speculation. Meanwhile he informed the Cabinet that, if the Americans were to meet the 80 division programme, the British and French would have to assist them. The outlook Churchill presented was positive as he focussed on the European Allies' ability to supply the Americans and illustrated his confidence in the ability of British factories to produce munitions if the Americans were to ship them raw materials. He asserted that he was, 'pursuing the policy of doing everything possible to equip the United States armies, and offering every assistance in my power'.[134]

During the meeting of the Artillery Committee of the IAMC, the WIB's representative informed the other members that steel requests in

---

[131] Churchill to Lloyd George, 9 September 1918.
[132] War Industries Board Meeting, 1 August 1918, Baruch/454/718.
[133] Baruch to Crowell, 5 September 1918, Baruch/454/760.
[134] Churchill 'Supplies to the United States Armies', 25 September 1918, FO 800/224/178.

America from the Allies were in excess of what was available. Stettinius argued that, if they provided the Europeans with steel from that allocated to their own industries, it would hinder the ability of the Americans to produce ammunition for their partners.[135] But, as Elizabeth Greenhalgh has noted, Pershing had informed the War Department in late 1917 that tonnage could be saved if the Americans shipped raw materials to Europe instead of transporting finished guns and shells which took up 1:7.5 ratio in cargo space. Raw explosives and powders were the exception, however, as they took up space nineteen-fold to their finished product.[136] It was finally agreed at this meeting, as recommended by Churchill, that the Americans would prioritise shell steel to the Allies, who would in turn supply the Americans with artillery ammunition. Afterwards, however, Stettinius amended the resolutions, giving them an extremely ambiguous wording. He wrote that the European shell steel demands (of which 110,000 tonnes per month were for France, 60,000 tonnes per month for Britain and 11,000 tonnes per month for Italy), 'should be given priority over the American shell manufacturing program to as great an extent as possible without interfering with the continued manufacture of shells in American plants'.[137] This was a complete reversal of the Allied agreement. Furthermore, the Americans wanted the AMTC to find the tonnage to ship to Europe any extra shell steel the United States could provide. Yet despite these changes a preliminary Anglo-American agreement was signed.[138]

The Third Meeting of the IAMC and Preparation for the Fourth AMTC Meeting

IAMC met for its third meeting on 28 September to finalise its programme for the upcoming year. It was essential that this information be sent immediately to the AMTC. Secretary Baker had arrived in Europe and expected to finalise shipping arrangements for the American programme at the next AMTC meeting. The first obstacle presented was that Stettinius was still unable to provide his partners with an official artillery programme for the United States in 1919. Without this information the IAMC was incapable of determining the extent to which the Americans required assistance from the British, French, and Italians. The European Allies had to move forward with their own programme

[135] Stettinius to March, 30 September 1918, Stettinius/85.
[136] Greenhalgh, 'Errors and Omissions', 28.
[137] Stettinius to March, 30 September 1918.
[138] Stettinius to Churchill, 19 October 1918, MUN/4/296.

plans for the upcoming year, despite the fact that American requirements would have an effect on their nations' production programmes. The result was that the coalition partners made loose agreements over munitions. The British and Italians agreed to continue to supply munitions to the Americans as promised, while the French decided to estimate the assistance the Americans would require and adjust their munitions programme once they received the American programme information. Stettinius responded positively to the arrangements with the British, as he found the information they provided to him to be consistent. With the French, however, he had doubts, describing how, to his great frustration, they frequently altered their plans. What Stettinius failed to appreciate was the French would adhere to the arrangement between their two nations, that if the Americans provided the French with raw materials then they would supply the Americans with munitions of equal value. But to accurately assess French production, they first needed to know what raw materials the Americans had available.[139]

Stettinius continued to feel that French demands of the American war industry were substantial (despite all the French were doing for the Americans). The French also potentially required labour from the United States.[140] Of course these raw materials and men took up shipping and would need to be accounted for in shipping estimates. Further, the requests were independent from the orders placed by the Ordnance Department, despite the fact that the WIB insisted that all requests for materials purchased in America had to go through the War Purchase and Finance Council.[141] As the example of steel demonstrated, the Americans did not have unlimited resources to provide to their partners. The French kept constant pressure on the Americans by frequently updating their programmes and asking the Americans to provide their programme details. While Stettinius was at times frustrated with his French colleagues for bombarding him for information, America's coalition partners required solid data about America's military programme and production in order to plan for the upcoming year.

Beyond the omission from the Americans, the IAMC was unable to provide information about railway, motor transport, tank, and aircraft requirements, and thus these were also excluded from the statement it sent to the AMTC. This failure was partially the result of poor organisation. While committees for tanks, aircraft, and transport already existed

---

[139] On production arrangements, see Bruce, *Fraternity*, 106.
[140] Greenhalgh, 'Errors and Omissions', 28.
[141] 'Meeting of the War Industries Board held Thursday, October 24, 1918, at 10:30 A.M., Room 909, C. N. D. Building', Baruch/454/799.

under the PMRs, the members of the IAMC chose not to use them. Instead they wanted to establish their own programme committees which would be directly subordinate to the IAMC rather than the PMRs.[142] It was recognised that creating sub-committees was a slow process. As such, the IAMC could have increased its success if it had have used the committees available to it, rather than forming new ones that were not established in time to make a contribution to planning for 1919.

As a result of this disorganisation, the IAMC was only able to provide the AMTC with a summary of the total munitions requirements of Britain, France, and Italy for the year 1 September 1918 through 31 August 1919.[143] In turn, the AMTC and War Purchases and Finance Council did not have figures to work with. Without the details of the programme, and what they were going to ship, it was impossible for the AMTC to accurately tabulate requirements for shipping.

Prior to the fourth meeting of the AMTC, the AMTE finalised its report on the cereal year 1918–1919. Munitions were only part of the programme. It had finally received an estimate of the total carrying capacity for the import requirements of Britain, France, and Italy as calculated by the statistical departments. The total seaborne imports were estimated to be 72.5 million tonnes for that year, a figure divided between coal (25.2 million tonnes), raw materials (8.4 million tonnes), munitions (17.8 million tonnes), and food (27 million tonnes). The programme committees submitted their requirements for tonnage which the AMTC then compared to the tonnage available. In this way the AMTE was able to scrutinise the tonnage figures. It was from the latter two areas – munitions and food – that the AMTE thought tonnage could be reallocated to the American programme. Once again the AMTC criticised the figures for food imports, recommending a reduction of the food programme by 5 million tonnes, dropping it to a total of 22 million tonnes.

In their section on munitions shipping requirements, officials were concerned that shipping available for munitions, at 17.8 million tonnes, would leave a deficit of 4.2 million tonnes. To alleviate some of this burden, the AMTE reasoned that the demand for munitions (and raw materials used to make them) were highest in the autumn and winter as the belligerents prepared for their spring campaigns, and that food stocks were highest after the autumn harvest. At the time, all signs indicated that 1918 would yield a large harvest. Given this relationship, the AMTC

---

[142] IAMC, 'Note on the Second Meeting of the Council', 8 October 1918, Stettinius/82.
[143] For a detailed breakdown of Allied tonnage demands, see IAMC, 'Tonnage Demands for the Cereal Year' n.d., Stettinius/85.

determined that food imports could be safely substituted for munitions during the upcoming autumn and winter.[144] Beyond this suggestion, the AMTE could make no further recommendations without having a complete programme from the IAMC.

Preparations for the AMTC meeting brought to the forefront the problems caused by the Americans' failure to supply their partners with information. In their 'Short Report with Special Reference to Supply Programme for American Troops' prepared prior to the AMTC meeting, once again the Entente pressed the Americans for more information, emphasising that, given the brief summary provided by the IAMC, they did not understand the extent to which these estimates provided for artillery and ammunition shells for the Americans. They also questioned whether the shipping requirements for the American programme would be in addition to the figures presented. Having received Baker's monthly estimates on cargo tonnage, the AMTC converted them so they could be expressed in terms of European imports, the result being an additional deficit of 2 million tonnes. Aware that the coalition was meeting in Paris to discuss artillery and ammunition supplies for the Americans, the AMTC still did not know the extent to which the final figures would affect this 2 million tonne estimate.[145]

Meanwhile, the AMTE was concerned that the extra shipping for the American programme had still not been secured. As it recorded, 'the Council should not recommend at this moment any reduction in the embarkation of American soldiers in spite of the grave conditions of the import programmes as indicated above, but should be prepared to recommend such a reduction, if necessary, in the embarkations of next year in order to meet any crisis that may arise in the imports of food or other supplies at the time'.[146] Following this idea, the AMTE took the initiative to secure shipping for the American army's supplies by approaching the British government. For September and October, the British agreed to provide 200,000 tonnes of cargo shipping. The AMTE also hoped to acquire an additional 300,000 tonnes of shipping before the year's end by further reducing European imports.[147] This extra shipping would go some way towards reducing the cargo shortages presented by the War Department (see Table 6.2).

---

[144] Salter, Allied Shipping Control, 208.

[145] AMTC, 'Short Report with Special Reference to Supply Programme for American Troops' n.d. (but it does state that it is a report prepared for the upcoming AMTC meeting on 30 September 1918), Baker/15/13.

[146] AMTC, 'Cereal Year, 1918–1919', 27 September 1918, Baker/15/13; Stettinius/85.

[147] Salter, Allied Shipping Control, 206.

Baker Travels to Europe

It was between the two AMTC meetings that Baker travelled to Europe to work out the enlarged military programme for 1919 with his coalition partners. Beyond sorting out the size of the American force, the other two issues to be discussed were shipping and munitions. Baker was optimistic about his trip, telling President Wilson that 'the tremendous effort which America is making, and the vast force which we will have in 1919 will win the war, if our allies want it won, and are willing to make any correspondingly devoted effort'.[148] President Wilson wanted Baker to work towards a complete programme of cooperation with the Entente and thus instructed him to discuss and formulate all elements involved in the military programme for 1919.

The first issue that Baker had to settle, in order to reach a shipping agreement with his European partners, was the discrepancy that existed between the War Department's programme and that of Pershing. As was stated in the previous chapter, when Baker arrived in Europe he realised that Pershing was still presenting the Allies with figures for the 100 division programme. Beyond illustrating the confusion between the War Department and Pershing, these differences in programmes had a real effect on Allied coordination. The 'Military Program' approved by Baker included drafting and shipping rates for American manpower (see Table 6.5).

The figures in Table 6.5 illustrate the heavy fighting the Americans expected to undertake in 1919, as reflected in the shipment of replacement troops. By shipping an additional 2.76 million troops, the American army would reach its 80 division target by 30 June 1919 (3.76 million men, including wastage replacements of 400,000).[149] However, the figures provided by Pershing had led 'authorities here [to] contemplate a total force by the same date of 4,700,000 million or 940,000 more than our figures. The authorities here interpret Eighty Division program as meaning eighty combatant divisions, with sixteen depot divisions, which in effect gives a total force approximately equal to ninety-six divisions'.[150] Baker was appalled to learn that Pershing conceived of transporting 300,000 troops per month from August to December 1918 and 350,000 per month from January to June 1919.[151] As Table 6.5

---

[148] Baker to President Wilson, 17 August 1918, Baker/7/6.
[149] Baker to March, 23 September 1918, RG/200/19/4/2; RG/120/267/3176/1312.
[150] March explained to Pershing that the commanders expanded programme meant 1,130,00 troops more than the War Department's estimates, March to Pershing, 26 September 1918, RG/120/267/3176/1312.
[151] Fox Conner to Chief of Staff, 29 September 1918, ibid.

Table 6.5 *American manpower requirements for 'Military Program',*
1918–1919

Date	Men to be drafted (,000)	Rein- forcement troops (,000)	Replace- ment troops (,000)	Total troops shipped (,000)	Total in AEF rifles (,000)/ divisions	Remaining in US rifles (,000) / divisions	Total US Forces rifles (,000) / divisions
1918							
30 June	–	–	–	–	1,000/24	1,450/18	2,500/42
31 July	345	200	50	250	1,235/-	1,545/-	-/-
31 Aug	250	200	50	250	1,470/-	1,545/-	-/-
30 Sept	200	200	50	250	1,705/-	1,495/-	-/-
31 Oct	155	200	50	250	1,945/-	1,400/-	-/-
30 Nov	150	185	45	225	2,160/-	1,325/-	-/-
31 Dec	150	175	25	200	2,350/52	1,275/18	3,675/70
1919							
31 Jan	100	160	15	175	2,515/-	1,200/-	–
28 Feb	200	160	15	175	2,675/-	1,225/-	–
31 Mar	300	200	35	255	2,885/-	1,290/-	–
30 Apr	300	175	75	250	3,060/-	1,340/-	–
31 May	300	150	100	250	3,210/-	1,390/-	–
30 June	300	150	100	250	3,360/80	1,440/18	4,850/98
Total	2,750	2,155	605	2,760	–	–	–

Source: War Department to Chief of Supply Bureaus, 25 July 1918.[152]

illustrates, in fact the War Department had planned to send between
175,000 and 250,000 men depending on the month.[153] Given the shortage of cargo tonnage to supply the enlarged AEF, additional shipping

[152] War Department memorandum to Chief of Supply Bureaus, etc., 25 July 1918, RG/
120/267/3176/1312.

[153] The greatest number of troops sent in one month has been recorded differently by
various individuals. Vice Admiral Gleaver (commander of convoy operations in the
Atlantic, 1917–1919) recorded that it was 311,359 in July 1918. In contrast, March
wrote that 306,000 men were embarked in July 1918, 'Annual Report of General
Peyton C. March, Chief of Staff, United States Army, 1919', RG/165/84–8/158/1190/
p. 9. Salter recorded that in July a total of 305,000 men were shipped (Salter, *Allied
Shipping Control*, 268). March and Salter's figures are consistent with David Stevenson,
who cites 'Draft Report on Shipping Control, 1914–1918', 27 April 1921, TNA
(Ministry of Transport) MT/25/86. Stevenson puts August as the month which saw
the highest number of American troops shipped at 314,700. Stevenson, *With Our Backs*,
345; Albert Gleaves, 'A History of the Transport Service', (updated 3 February 2014)
https://archive.org/stream/historyoftranspo00gle#page/92/mode/2up, 90.

would be used for that purpose, not bringing the additional troops Pershing desired.

The problem was that Pershing's figures, which were much too large, had confused the British shipping authorities. The result was that 'estimates of requirements and tonnage made here are in excess of our estimates due to the inclusion of the 16 Depot Divisions . . .'[154] Not only were these figures central to the provision of adequate troop transport, but they were also the figures on which cargo tonnage was based. The inefficiencies caused because the War Department and Pershing were not working on the same programme were twofold. At the national level, it meant that the War Department was not preparing the men and resources that Pershing required in Europe. The War Department ensured that certain types of troops (service-of-supply, auxiliary, infantry, machine gunners) and resources were ready to be shipped to Pershing. However, Pershing complained that he was not receiving the soldiers he had requested. At the international level, the Americans complicated Allied relationships by not communicating what their shipping needs were.

Pershing's composition of troops to be shipped also conflicted with attempts by Baker and the SWC to coordinate resources across the coalition. Pershing wanted first to send a large proportion of services-of-supply troops before sending more divisions, so that by September there would be 40 complete American divisions in Europe. For the months of October and December he requested that no divisions be shipped and that instead the available tonnage be used to make up shortages of howitzer material, animals, replacements, services-of-supply troops, and other equipment. As of January 1919 troop transport should begin by sending six divisions per month, plus replacements. GHQ envisaged decreasing the number of services-of-supply troops being sent to June 1919. As artillery material became available Pershing would then request Corps and Army artillery units. In November four divisions would be sent while the remaining 36 would be shipped from January to June 1919, bringing the GHQ troop transport programme to 80 divisions. Impatient with the execution of his plans, Pershing highlighted how the shipping of combat troops earlier in the year to meet the needs of the European Allies and the War Department's own plans had resulted in serious problems for the AEF:

---

[154] Baker to March, 23 September 1918.

Due to the necessity of bringing over only Infantry and Machine Gun units to meet the critical situation that existed in April and succeeding months, the needs of the S. O. S. and of auxiliary units were not met. The shortage thus caused has grown in the past three months due to failure to follow our calls given in our priority cablegrams. Today we are about 129,000 Army Troops; 93,000 Corps troops; 83,000 S. O. S. troops and 65,000 replacements. The formation of Corps and Armies is meeting with delays because the necessary auxiliary troops are not here. Divisions have come with shortages in personnel aggregating 45,000 men to date. We have not the troops necessary to replace even our ordinary causalities.[155]

Pershing was fixated on the United States building the infrastructure required by the American army, which included building and improving railroads, ports, harbours, training facilities, and hospitals, whereas the War Department was focussed on working with the Entente to create or borrow these facilities.

The War Department urged a regular flow of divisions, and responded to this telegram by reminding Pershing that 'the number of men in the United States military program by July 1st, 1919 has been clearly stated to our Allies as well as to you?? [sic]' Furthermore, 'The demands for tonnage made upon Great Britain were not based upon divisions or other units but upon the number of men which we propose to transport and the necessary cargo tonnage to supply that given number of men'.[156] The War Department did agree to meet the deficiencies in services-of-supply troops and said that each month four divisions would be shipped, as they assisted in filling the ships to capacity. March also reprimanded Pershing for establishing his own totals for division strength, pointedly reminding him that: 'The strength of divisions is fixed by approval of the War Department and is clearly known here ... You will plan your operations upon the basis of the maximum strength in France stated in the forgoing? [sic] and set forth in detail by months in the approved program already forwarded to you by courier'.[157]

By early October the influenza epidemic had begun to disrupt the military programme, distracting from the conflict between the War Department and Pershing. Instead of trying to convince Pershing on the form the American army should take, March explained that, due to influenza, 'It is ... impossible to tell exactly which organizations called for will sail by 31st October'.[158] But it was hopeless getting Pershing to

---

[155] Pershing to March, 30 September 1918, RG/120/267/3176/1312.
[156] March to Pershing, n.d., From the dates referenced in the letter it was sent between 1 to 11 October 1918, RG/120/267/3176/1312.
[157] RG/120/267/3176/1312.
[158] March to Pershing, 10 October 1918, RG/120/267/3176/1312.

adjust his figures, no matter what the circumstances. On 5 November G-3 (Operations) was still railing against the War Department figures, and when it presented its shipping programme for January to June 1919 it still included an additional 1 million men.[159]

Beyond attempting to resolve the discrepancies with Pershing's programme, while in Europe Baker worked through the AMTC to obtain shipping for the American programme. Upon his arrival in London, Baker found that shipping arrangements for the programme were already underway. Lord Reading had been given the responsibility for working out the cargo tonnage situation.[160] The American PMR, having previously met with Reading, was given the impression that shipping would materialise if Allied shipping authorities met in London to discuss their priorities.[161] On 17 August the British Ministry of Shipping had made a similar recommendation – asking the Americans to advise the AMTC about the troubles they were having in meeting their own shipping needs. One month later to the day British and French representatives met once again to discuss shipping. While the American representative, General Hines, asked the British for 400,000 d.w.t, the British said that no more than 250,000 DWT could be allocated.[162]

Meanwhile Baker had to wait to meet with Reading as the British Ambassador had fallen ill. After delaying discussions for a number of days, Reading promised Baker 200,000 DWT for export use (this was the same tonnage that the AMTE had worked to secure). Reading also informed Baker that the British were willing to divert tonnage to the American programme as long as the Americans assisted the Allies with their essential needs later in the year when the Americans could contribute their newly completed merchant ships. Baker's understanding of the agreement was that the British had conceded that these ships would still be controlled by the Americans rather than the AMTC, and that, while the former would listen to the advice presented by this group, they would reserve the right to decide when their partners' needs were greater than their own. For their part, the British urged the Americans to participate

[159] G3, 'Priority of Troop Shipment', 5 November 1918, RG/120/267/3176/1312.
[160] Reading's correspondence in FO/800/225 (papers to and from William Wiseman) does not mention his discussions with the Americans over shipping.
[161] Bliss to March, 3 September 1918, Bliss/250; Baker to Pershing, 23 September 1918, RG 200/19/ 4/2.
[162] War Department (Transportation Service), 'Summary of Efforts Made to Obtain Shipping from Every Source (French Excepted) Followed by Synopsis of Correspondence', n.d., RG/165/84–8/190/1140/p. 6.

more fully in the meetings of the AMTC by displaying their detailed programme of needs.[163]

A day after the armistice with Bulgaria was signed, on 30 September, Baker was invited to Lloyd George's house in Suffolk. The Prime Minister was too ill to travel to London, but wanted to discuss shipping with Baker before the AMTC meeting, which was postponed until that Tuesday. Present at dinner were Lord Reading, Lord Milner, Sir Joseph Maclay, 'and an officer of the British General Staff, (not Sir Henry Wilson, but I have forgotten his name)'.[164] The conversation throughout dinner was cordial; however, upon the completion of the meal Lloyd George made a long statement about the shipping situation. While the assembled officials were all in agreement that an arrangement could be made, they disagreed over how American manpower should be used once the soldiers arrived in Europe.

Lloyd George detailed his dissatisfaction with the extent to which American troops had been used with the British army and believed that these troops had been brought over in British ships to assist not only the French, but also the British. He made it clear that, in his opinion, this was part of an agreement between the British and the Americans. Only two divisions had been brigaded in British lines – the rest had been allocated to the French. Furthermore, Lloyd George was concerned that given British manpower shortages, unless the Americans took up more of the British line, there would not be enough men to allow rest for the weariest troops over the winter months.[165]

The previous day Lloyd George had reminded Maclay, when instructing him on the upcoming AMTC meetings:

I therefore want once more to press upon you the decision which I communicated to you some weeks ago that we must not commit ourselves to any further shipping contribution to America until we have cleared up the position in reference to the use which is to be made of American troops in France ... I feel myself compelled as a trustee of the interests of the British soldier to insist upon this policy being carried out quite relentlessly in your dealings with the French and the Americans. It cannot be treated as if it were merely a question of how many ships you can spare. If we are forced to take more men out of ship yards and coal mines to keep up a long line, you certainly cannot give ships, and therefore these questions hang together, and I shall be obliged if you will bear that in mind in mind in your discussions tomorrow.[166]

---

[163] Baker to Wilson, September 23, 1918, in Link, *PWW*, 51: 94–95.
[164] Baker to Pershing, 2 October 1918, Pershing/20.
[165] Lloyd George to Maclay, 29 September 1918, LG/F/35/2/82.   [166] Ibid.

Maclay had disregarded the Cabinet's instructions to use shipping as leverage with the Americans, which irritated the British Prime Minister and forced him to take up the issue directly with Baker.[167] Lloyd George described to the American Secretary of War a number of situations when American troops had been prepared to go into battle with the British only to be withdrawn by Pershing. According to Baker, Lloyd George believed 'that the effect of the whole business was that for all their [British] pains and sacrifices for training our troops there and equipping them they had gotten no good out of them whatever and that the American troops had not been of any service to the British'.[168] Lloyd George urged Baker to allow American troops to assist their British partners.

Baker responded by explaining the American position to the unhappy prime minister, pointing out that it was his understanding that the American government increased the amount of manpower sent to Europe in response to the lack of reserves in the French and British armies. The agreement forged by Baker and Reading made it clear that these American troops would form an American Army as of 1 August 1918. Further, while American units might train with the British and French, Pershing had the authority to call them back at any time. Baker stressed that at no time did the Americans intend to feed their soldiers into the British or French Armies, and expressed confusion at the mis-understanding – reminding Lloyd George that the American position had been clearly communicated, orally and in writing, by both himself and President Wilson. Later writing to Pershing, Baker warned:

It left on my mind a very strong feeling that Lloyd George frankly wants Americans to remain with the British both as a stimulus and for the fraternization which he describes and that he is very suspicious that the French are desiring to monopolize the Americans and so come out of the war as our principal friend without their having been any real opportunity for co-operation and understanding between the British and Americans.

I, of course, gave him no assurances whatever, and when he asked me what expectations I thought he ought to have about the use of American troops I replied shortly that I thought he ought to expect the American Army as such to exist in the same sense as the British Army . . .[169]

Both Lloyd George and Baker held their positions without compromis-ing. This discussion illustrates the fundamental confusion between the British and Americans over expectations for American manpower: the Americans believed they were making a contribution by forming their independent Army and holding their own part of the front, while the

---

[167] Lloyd George to Milner, 29 September, 1918, LG/F/38/4/20.
[168] Baker to Pershing, 2 October 1918, Pershing/20.   [169] Ibid.

British expected them to support the Entente armies directly in exchange for shipping and supplies. Furthermore, it also illustrates Baker's support of Pershing's decision to form an independent AEF and his refusal to succumb to the European Allies' pressure for assistance.

Final AMTC Session

Despite these quarrels over the creation of an American Army, the fourth AMTC meeting, held from 30 September to 2 October 1918, went smoothly. The IAMC, AMTC, and Inter-Allied Food Council all attended this meeting to discuss the allocation of shipping tonnage. The two main issues to be resolved were the American deficit in cargo tonnage and the schedule for European cereal imports. By combining the discussion of these two issues, the coalition exercised its strengths and was able to reduce tonnage imports in order to ship more military cargo from the United States. Discussions began after Baker made it clear that the 80 division programme was the approved American plan deemed necessary by the War Department to win the war. The members then turned their attention to finding ways to reduce imports to Europe. They reasoned that, even if food imports were reduced to 22 million tonnes from the original 27 million requested by the Food Council, munitions shipments would not match full requirements. Between Britain, France, and Italy munitions requirements amounted to 22.8 million shipping tonnes; however, the AMTC announced that this amount of shipping could simply not be provided.[170] Churchill's response was to recommend that rather than attempt to force the munitions programme through, the IAMC should instead reduce its shipping requirements down to 19 million tonnes (11 million for Britain, 6.125 million for France and 1.75 million for Italy). In addition, the AMTC members agreed with a recommendation from the AMTE that munitions should be prioritised above food for the first months of the cereal year. Munitions would come first but then food stocks would be replenished in spring 1919. While this scenario was agreed by the AMTC, in reality the members recognised that tonnage needs would have to be constantly reassessed and structured around what was available to be shipped. For this reason they created a Tonnage Committee in London that was to

---

[170] The precise estimate was 22,785,000 shipping tonnes. 'Minutes of 4th Session of the AMTC', Stettinius to Baker, 24 October 1918, Stettinius/85/no. 24; Baker 15/13; AMTC, 'Draft Minutes of the Fourth Session Held at Lancaster House, London, S.W.1, September 30th, October 1st and 2nd, 1918', Baker/15/13. Changes to these minutes are found in Stevens (American Shipping Mission) to Baker, 28 November 1918, Baker/15/13.

work alongside the AMTC.[171] Although the Allies may have been able to reduce their food imports in autumn 1918, the American schedule still did not fit this programme. The Americans had the foodstuffs available to send immediately, not the extra raw materials, so that the recommendations agreed to on paper did not fit the reality of the situation.[172] Still, as Margaret Barnett has noted, the British government was willing to risk its food stocks to end the war as soon as possible.[173] This agreement was less of a gamble than appears at first glance as earlier in the year the Americans had sent 300,000 tonnes of its grain reserves to France and Italy which had been prioritised for shipping above munitions. Thus by June 1918 both Reading and Hoover were confident that the Allies had enough food for the next 12 months.[174]

The fourth meeting of the AMTC also reinforced Baker and Reading's discussions of a few days earlier. It was now formally agreed that the British would provide 200,000 tonnes for cargo shipping in October, with an allocation of 300,000 tonnes in both November and December. The British also stated that any space found through the release of double bottom ships would be allocated to the Americans for supply. In return, Baker was willing to assist the European Allies with shipping from April 1919 onwards. He also decided to coordinate the American programme with those of the European Allies and follow the guidance of the AMTC by disclosing the American shipping and import programmes.[175] The War Cabinet approved the resolutions of this meeting.[176] March later recorded that this agreement would nullify the cargo deficit predicted for the expanded American programme.[177] Tardieu's impression of this agreement was that Baker had excluded the French from his initial talks with the British about shipping. This situation fuelled French jealousy and concern that the Americans and British were growing closer due to their shared language and culture, which was difficult for the French to compete with.[178] Tardieu, however, was not alarmed or surprised with the resolutions of this meeting, as they did not deviate from earlier discussions held by the AMTC.[179] In this way, the AMTC acted as a channel for communication.

---

[171] Ministry of Munitions, *History*, 2, part viii, 47.
[172] Stettinius to Baker, 2 October 1918, Stettinius/85.   [173] Barnett, *British Food*, 192.
[174] Ibid., 187.   [175] Beaver, *Newton D. Baker*, 175.
[176] War Cabinet 487, 'Extract from Minutes of Meeting Held on 11th October 1918 at 11.30 am.', MT/25/76.
[177] 'Annual Report of General Peyton C. March, Chief of Staff, United States Army, 1919', RG/165/84–8/158/1190/pp. 11–12.
[178] Kaspi, 189.
[179] Tardieu to Reading, 9 September 1918; Tardieu to de Billy, 4 October 1918, SHD-DAT, Collection Tardieu, 13 N 17.

To reinforce the War Department's programme, Baker informed Pershing of the agreements made by the AMTC, writing, 'In effect this amounts to a present approval of our programme with the reservation that in view of the constantly changing situation we are all free to meet any new crisis should it arise, by fresh consultations and determinations'.[180] It was clear that shipping and munitions would be based on the 80 division programme. Baker also used his trip to Europe to better coordinate information between the AMTC and the American SOS, strongly encouraging Pershing to accept liaison between these two bodies.[181]

Immediately before Baker left Europe he sent General Hines to see General McAndrew for a final word on shipping. Overall, Baker was positive about his visit: 'I think we will all go home to the United States with fresh enthusiasm for our end of the work and I hope you will soon feel in Europe the effect of our work in the States'.[182] He listed the four major issues for the Americans still to resolve as: the shipping of both animal and motor transport; supply; manpower; and problems of promotion and tactical schools. When Baker wrote to Wilson on 6 October to update him on the state of relations in Europe his tone was also positive: 'Army has renewed attack and is progressing. Tonnage situation favorably cleared up'.[183] Bliss, on the other hand, was less optimistic. Finding his partners to be difficult now that the Germans had approached Wilson for an armistice, he told March that the Americans were being used by the Allies, explaining how on the issue of munitions, for example, the Allies had already begun to claw back what they had promised. On the previous day Bliss had met with Stettinius, and the American munitions expert informed him that after having reached 'a fairly satisfactory conclusion', he soon found that he was 'running up against a decided indisposition on the part of the British and French to give us the help which they promised'.[184] Bliss was not surprised. As he relayed to March, 'from various little indications that have come to my notice, it seems to me somewhat evident that the European Allies will attempt to minimize the American effort as much as possible. They think they have got the Germans on the run and that they now do not need as much help as a little while ago they were crying for'.[185]

This assessment was somewhat unfair. The British and French representatives were still working hard to prepare the Americans for the 1919 campaign. Following on from the AMTC meetings, Churchill pressed

---

[180] Baker to Pershing, 2 October 1918.   [181] Ibid.   [182] Ibid.
[183] Baker to Wilson, 6 October 1918, quoted in Beaver, *Newton D. Baker*, 177.
[184] Bliss to March, 14 October 1918, Bliss/250/no. 29; Wilson/101.   [185] Ibid.

Loucheur to clearly outline the shipping and purchasing programmes to the AMTC's programme committees and to War Purchase and Finance Committee.[186] Stettinius was schedule to return to Washington to ensure the American war machine was in line with its European partners. Both Loucheur and Churchill wanted to ensure the programme committees provided Stettinius with accurate estimates prior to his departure.[187] The British and French Minister of Munitions expressed some concern about getting the committees organised in a short span of time; however, they do not illustrate a reluctance to assist the Americans.[188]

By 26 October, Baker, like Stettinius and Bliss, had changed his opinion, becoming frustrated with his British partners. He wrote to Lord Reading asking for an update on why British shipping promised to the Americans had not been sent. As agreed at the AMTC meeting the British were to loan the Americans 200,000 tonnes of cargo in October and 300,000 tonnes in both November and December. In reality they provided 204,000 tonnes in October, while the scheduled loan for the other two months was never forthcoming due to the armistice.[189] In fact, the Americans shipped most of their own cargo during the war; less than 5 percent was transported by the European Allies.[190] Meanwhile, Mr Stevens urged the War Department to resurvey the American ships being used in non-essential trade so that they could be redirected to meeting the 80 division programme. As late as 30 October 1918, the Americans were still pushing their partners for assistance in realising the 80 division programme, insisting that Pershing's demands for railroad equipment, animals, motor transport, and other supplies be met.[191] When the British responded to American requests, they cited that the reason they were not providing the shipping promised was because they had learned, through the WIB, that the Americans continued to use 2 million tonnes of shipping that was in excess of their minimum needs for their own import trade.[192] The British were rightly angered. This was a vast amount of shipping given that 200,000 gross weight tonnes could

---

[186] Churchill to Loucheur, 10 October 1918, SHD-DAT, Conseil interallié de l'armement et des munitions, 10N 142.

[187] P. Hanson to R. Bazin (on behalf of Loucheur to Churchill), 24 October 1918, SHD-DAT, Conseil interallié de l'armement et des munitions, 10N 142.

[188] Loucheur to Stettinius, 25 and 28 October 1918, 10N 142.

[189] Salter, 'Report Executive, October 16th to November 15th, 1918', Baker/15/13/ no. 195.

[190] Correlli Barnett, Strategy and Society (Manchester, 1975), 45.

[191] War Department (Transportation Service), 'Summary of Efforts Made to Obtain Shipping from Every Source (French Excepted) Followed by Synopsis of Correspondence', n.d. RG/165/84–8/190/1440.

[192] Beaver, Newton D. Baker, 177.

ship four complete American divisions. In the shadow of armistice negotiations it provided Britain with a reasonable excuse not to turn over this tonnage, and it bolstered Britain's fears that America's primary interest was increasing her maritime commerce.

While historian Edward Parsons has shown the extent to which the expansion of the American merchant marine challenged the supremacy of Britain's merchant fleet, he argues that jealousy caused the British to withhold shipping in October 1918.[193] The British did use shipping as leverage in an attempt to improve the state of their own army. The inability of the Americans to supply their partners with their shipping programme and assets certainly frustrated the British. However, as David Stevenson argues, post-war competition was not the only factor that contributed to reduced shipping rates in the autumn months; the influenza epidemic also had a negative impact.[194] An examination of troop transportation figures supports Stevenson's argument, as it illustrates that the British continued to ship large numbers of American troops to Europe until the influenza epidemic affected the number of troops which could be sent. The transport records illustrate that, although only 94,214 Americans were conveyed to Europe in British ships in October as compared to 134,576 the previous month and 137,745 in August, the Americans themselves only transported 72,092 in October, a substantial decline from the 107,025 they had shipped the previous month.[195] Furthermore an examination of correspondence between the War Department and Pershing in the month of October also illustrates the stunting effects influenza had on realising the 80 division programme. By 23 October, March was writing to Pershing to inform him that almost all camps in the United States had been quarantined and, therefore they had had to cancel or suspend almost all of the draft call-ups. While they continued to send troops in October, March reported that 'Only a few thousand of replacements needed for ... November are in service [and] nearly all organizations on schedule are under strength'. Moreover, 'In order to keep transports filled we have to ship any kind of troops that are available without regard to any priority?' Not all was hopeless, however, as March concluded, 'Influenza situation has improved in the Army and

---

[193] Edward B. Parsons, 'Why the British Reduced the Flow of American Troops to Europe in August–October 1918', *Canadian Journal of History*, 12/2 (1977).

[194] David Stevenson, *With Our Backs*, 347–348.

[195] These are the figures in Gleaver, *A History of Transport Service*, 90. The figures used in the table drawn by David Stevenson (from 'Draft Report on Shipping Control, 1914–1918', 27 April 1921, MT/25/86) indicate a similar trend. Stevenson, *With Our Backs*, 347.

in civilian population in Eastern United States, so we hope for early improvements in above conditions'.[196]

Back in Washington there were serious concerns that the 80 division programme was too ambitious. Adjusting building programmes and industry within the United States took time. It was not until 26 September that the weekly reports of the WIB began to reflect the War Department's new programme even though the War Department had approved it on 18 July.[197] At the War Priorities Board meeting, the efficient Major-General George W. Goethals, the Director of the Purchase, Storage, and Traffic Division of the General Staff within the Quartermaster Corps in Washington (and who after the war oversaw the building of the Panama Canal), stated his concern that the United States did not have sufficient shipping to transport troops, equipment, and munitions, nor could they be adequately supplied with food. Although they had munitions, equipment, and supplies ready for transport, there was no shipping available to move these goods. The only source available to provide it was the Emergency Fleet Corporation, which was having difficulty building ships due to:

the lack of application of the employees in the shipyards in the performance of the tasks assigned them, notwithstanding their every demand for increase in wages and otherwise has been met, coupled with inefficiency in the management of some of the shipyards, rather than a shortage of the number of men employed in such shipyards or a shortage of materials, equipment or supplies needed in the construction of ships ...[198]

The members of the EFC were concerned by the War Department's plan to continue to transport large numbers of troops without the cargo ships to supply them. In response they prioritised the building of cargo ships above all other ship building. Still, EFC officials realised the gravity of the situation and pressed the War Department to reconsider the rate of troop transportation given that they could not meet the minimum requirements to supply American troops. On 29 October Baruch, recording in his diary a conversation he had had with General Goethals, noted that 'I spoke to him of shipping and told him it was bad, and that

[196] March to Pershing, 23 October 1918, RG/120/267/3176/1312.
[197] War Department, 'Weekly Survey by the Central Bureau of Planning and Statistics: Week ending September 15, 1918', Baruch/515. These 'Weekly Reports' illustrated how far the Americans lagged in production of aircraft, munitions, etc. By 19 September the requirements data sent by the War Department to the Planning and Statistics branch of the WIB still did not reflect all of the necessary changes to meet the 80 division program.
[198] Navy Department to Baker, 30 October 1918, RG/61/13/86.

we could not possibly get through with our programme'.[199] Goethals assessed that the Americans could only fulfil 75 percent of the programme. Hurley agreed, stating that his ship yards were only 50 percent efficient due to labour problems and inefficient organisation. The following day Baruch raised the issue with Baker, but the Secretary of War adamantly disagreed with Goethals, retorting that the latter did not have all the necessary facts to make such a sweeping statement. Baruch's concern led him to appeal to Baker's superior, but Baruch was rebuffed by the President, being told to work out his concerns with Baker.[200] Unfortunately for Baruch, Baker maintained his 'can-do' attitude for the remainder of the war despite the concerns raised by the heads of the WIB and the EFC and the Quartermaster – all of which were central to the realisation of shipping and supplying the 80 division programme. Fortunately for the War Department, the difficulties they would have faced in 1919 were never realised.

The disorganisation of the American army and subsequent inability to produce detailed shipping and munitions programmes, the jealousy experienced by the British over the Franco-American relationship, and the suspicion and animosity invoked by discussions over the use of American manpower were all real difficulties faced by the Allies in 1918. Although the American shipbuilding programme was immense, the United States never had enough ships in its service to transport and supply the AEF. Despite these obstacles, the coalition partners were able to reach agreements through the organs of the SWC, most notably the AMTC and IAMC. Using these two groups as a platform, Baker and Stettinius succeeded in making arrangements with their partners for troop and cargo tonnage as well as a munitions agreement which saw the British and French providing the Americans with much of the heavy artillery and ammunition that they required. The AMTC allowed the Allies to consider these issues from an Allied, as opposed to a national, perspective, and provided a forum for discussion and criticism. Through joint estimations for the upcoming year the Allies were able to make loose plans to assist one another. Together the coalition partners were able to meet the difficulties posed by the American deficit in shipping tonnage and the Allied deficit for the cereal year. They were also able to optimise the carrying capacity of their ships by examining the shipping process as a whole, as space on ships could be utilised that would otherwise have gone to waste. For instance, heavier cargo was combined with lighter cargo so

[199] Baruch diary, 29 October 1918, Baruch/499/p. 20.   [200] Ibid.

that ships were transporting goods at their maximum capacity. In this way fully 50,000 tonnes of shipping a month was saved.[201]

While these agreements were not all-encompassing and they did not always fit with the reality of the situation on the ground, they did express a concrete desire and effort by the coalition to realise the 80 division programme. The bodies of the SWC continued to grow and develop as the Allies required, and certainly in the cases discussed functioned effectively. Baker had promised to supply his Allies with detailed programme information; however, meetings, such as the one due to be held by the AMTC for 21 October, never took place.[202] Plans for 1919 never reached maturity, since by the time Baker reached Washington on 14 October Germany had approached President Wilson for armistice terms and attention was turned to negotiating a settlement.[203] The disintegration of Allied resource agreements in late October was not a reflection of poor Allied relations, but of the competing interests of the Allies. As long as the coalition members shared the common goal of defeating the Germans on the Western Front, they worked together. Thus, as the Allies slowly realised the war would be won with fewer resources than they had planned for in the 1919 campaign, the Europeans naturally began to withhold resources from the United States.

[201] Fayle, 3: 395; Salter, *Allied Shipping*, 213–215.
[202] Salter, 'Report Executive, October 16th to November 15th, 1918'. Salter explained how 'Insufficient time had elapsed before the conclusion of hostilities to get this programme (the Inter-Allied Munitions program for October 1918 to September 1919) into full working order, but the Executive had been able to arrange for all the tonnage asked for by the Tonnage Committee of the Munitions Council'. Baker/15/13/no. 195.
[203] Baker to Bliss, 14 October 1918 and Bliss to Baker, 27 October 1918, Bliss/250.

Conclusions

> One should not confuse the terms of an armistice with the conditions of peace. The armistice has the objective of assuring the victorious armies such a situation that their superiority is clearly established.[1]

Unbeknownst to the Allied coalition, on 3 October 1918, when the Germans approached President Wilson for a peace based on his Fourteen Points, victory was near. While the American President and German government continued to exchange a series of notes during the month of October to determine the basis for an armistice, the coalition members in Europe met to discuss its terms. They considered a series of drafts before settling on a final version. This section first examines the terms created by the PMRs and their naval counterparts from the Allied Naval Council, a sub-committee of the SWC which liaised with the PMRs on naval matters.[2] These terms will then be compared to the ones accepted by the SWC to show how closely the PMRs' terms paralleled broader thinking being done by the Allied political and military leadership. Contributing to the literature that explores how the Allied political and military leadership doubted German intentions and feared that the enemy would use the winter to regroup and mount a formidable defence, this study argues that, just as had been the case when preparing plans to fight into 1919, during the drawing-up of armistice terms the idea of a German menace remained in the forefront of Allied decision-making.[3] While this section is concerned with the Allied notion of victory, as opposed to national war aims, it does not discount their importance.[4]

---

[1] Georges Clemenceau as quoted in 'Supreme War Council: Procès-verbaux of the Four Meetings of the Eighth Session of the Supreme War Council, held at Versailles, October 31–November 4, 1918', 31 October 1918, CAB/25/123/I.C.85/p. 5.

[2] For more on the ANC's work, see Trask, *Captains and Cabinets*.

[3] Greenhalgh, *Foch*, ch. 17; Bullitt Lowry, *Armistice 1918* (Kent, OH, 1996).

[4] See Lowry for a detailed study of how the Allies achieved their major (national) war aims through the armistice. For British aims, see French, *Lloyd George Coalition*, 162–186; for French aims, see Stevenson, *French War Aims Against Germany*, 115–132; and for American ones, see Trask, *Supreme War Council*, 151–175.

It evaluates the extent to which the terms prepared and accepted by the Allies fulfilled their earlier notions of victory – namely the military defeat of the Germans on the Franco-Belgian Front – arguing that the Allies wanted to achieve through the terms of the armistice what they had not yet achieved on the battlefield.

Having avoided discussions of a political nature throughout 1918, the PMRs first explored armistice terms together when the Committee of Prime Ministers (of Britain, France, and Italy) asked them to meet with the ANC for a series of joint meetings. They were presented with eight conditions that the Committee of Prime Ministers stated should guide their discussions. Bliss, who was in bed with influenza, learned that the joint meeting was to take place the following morning, on 8 October. Feeling the meeting had been 'sprung' on him, and despite staying up for much of the night considering the terms of the armistice, he was too ill and underprepared to attend.[5] Instead he sent his chief of staff, the secretary of the American Section, and a naval representative in his place, instructing all of them to take no action. The result was that the Americans did not contribute to the draft created by the PMRs. This was not unwelcome to the European Allies, who were concerned that President Wilson would overshadow them in determining the armistice and the subsequent peace terms. In fact, they had already deliberately excluded the Americans from armistice discussions by meeting as the Committee of Prime Ministers as opposed to the SWC, thus preventing the American representatives from sitting in on their sessions while President Wilson carried out his exchanges with the German government.

On reading the terms suggested by the Committee of Prime Ministers, Bliss became concerned that they were not strict enough. He cabled Washington for instructions, explaining that these terms did little to guarantee that Germany would return its possessions in Russia and Romania, instead only asking for the evacuation of territory in the West, territory that the Germans knew they would lose come spring 1919. Bliss was more amenable to the terms drafted by the PMRs and ANC, as their implementation would result in the immediate disarmament of Germany.[6]

An armistice is an agreement between belligerents to cease fighting for a period of time; however, the PMRs wanted to ensure that the terms of the armistice meant that the Germans would be unable to renew

---

[5] Bliss to Baker, 9 October 1918, Bliss/250; Wilson/100.
[6] Copy of the PMRs terms, 8 October 1918, Bliss to Baker, Bliss/252. Also see this file for the exact terms presented to the PMRs by the Committee of Prime Ministers which will not be repeated here.

hostilities. Their terms were based on the idea that the Germans could not be trusted and thus they insisted that:

the Allied Governments cannot lose sight of the fact that the Government of Germany is in a position peculiar among the nations of Europe in that its word cannot be believed, and that it denies any obligation of honor. It is necessary, therefore, to demand from Germany material guarantees on a scale which will serve the purpose aimed at by a signed agreement in cases amongst ordinary civilized nations.[7]

Consequently, to ensure that they would not be deceived by their adversary, the PMRs demanded the immediate reoccupation by Allied troops of territory evacuated by the enemy; the German surrender of all arms, munitions, and supplies between the front and the west bank of the Rhine (as most of the German army was situated in this territory, the reality of this clause was near total disarmament); and finally the return of Allied prisoners of war (while enemy prisoners could be used 'for the reparation of the wilful damage done in the occupied area by the enemy, and for the restoration of the areas').[8] In Alsace-Lorraine they demanded the surrender of the fortresses of Neu Breisach, Strasburg, Thionville, and Metz as well as the fortifications and city of Lille. If they could gain these objectives from the Germans then any resumption of hostilities would ensure the Allies had the military advantage in France.

Their naval terms were far-reaching, too. In addition to the cessation of submarine warfare, the PMRs and ANC called for withdrawal of all enemy surface ships and submarines to bases which would be determined by the Allies; surrender of 60 submarines at specified Allied ports; movement of enemy air forces to bases specified by the Allies; identification of enemy minefields and the right to sweep these; removal of enemy forces from both the Belgian and Italian coasts, as well as the surrender of enemy stores and equipment along these coasts; evacuation of the Austro-Hungarian navy from all ports outside its own territory; and evacuation of the Black Sea ports and the transfer of all warships and material found there. Heligoland (used as a German submarine base) would also be surrendered. The Allied economic blockade was to continue. Furthermore, the Allies demanded that no more damage should be done to any areas by the enemy army and navy before evacuating.[9] The PMRs and ANC jointly recommended that the Germans be given four weeks to withdraw from the territories – not the two to three months the latter had estimated would be required for an orderly withdrawal – knowing that

[7] Ibid., 2.   [8] Ibid.   [9] Ibid.

they would be forced to abandon war materials and that generally the army would fall into disorganisation.[10]

The terms put forward by the PMRs and ANC were asking for a surrender as opposed to merely a ceasefire. As Bliss articulated:

it is intended to make inevitable the reply which Germany must make. Of course, it may be that she feels beaten to such a degree that she will accept such conditions as a precedent to an armistice, but I doubt it. But of course it is not an armistice in the ordinary sense of the word. It looks to me as though it were intended to say, 'We will not treat with you on the terms of President Wilson's fourteen propositions or on any other terms. Surrender, and we will then do as we please'. It looks to me as though it were intended to say to the United States that these are the conditions which the United States must inform Germany are the necessary precedent to considering any proposition for an armistice.[11]

Bliss's comment illustrates how the German request for an armistice (ceasefire) evolved into a surrender. Throughout his negotiations with the Germans, President Wilson came to a similar conclusion. While he eventually got the Germans and Allies to agree to terms based on his Fourteen Points, he warned the Germans that they would have no say in the terms of the armistice, which would be prepared by the military leaders.[12] In effect, he was asking for a German surrender. Passing all communications to the European Allies, President Wilson sent Colonel House to Europe to represent him at the SWC where armistice discussions would be finalised.

Although the PMRs' document was accepted by the Committee of Prime Ministers and supported by Henry Wilson, it went no further and was not approved by the individual governments. Instead the SWC considered draft armistice terms put forward by Foch. His terms focussed on the Western Front as opposed to the more global terms drawn up by the PMRs. In her study of the Generalissimo, Elizabeth Greenhalgh argues that Foch was confident that, if the Germans refused to sign the armistice, the Allies could force them to do so through continued military pressure and, while he did not ask for complete disarmament of the Germans, his terms ensured that they would have had great difficulty in resuming hostilities.[13] It was on 31 October, once House had reached Europe, that the SWC met to discuss, accept, and strengthen Foch's terms. In a number of ways, the final conditions agreed on were stricter and did more to ensure the military defeat of Germany than had the terms drawn by the PMRs. Both groups called for cessation of all hostilities and the evacuation of all territory the Germans

[10] Lowry, *Armistice*, 19.   [11] Bliss to Baker, 9 October 1918.   [12] Dallas, *1918*, 84.
[13] Greenhalgh, *Foch*, 475.

occupied. While the SWC did not ask for surrender of material between the present front and the west bank of the Rhine, they did require the Germans to evacuate these territories within 15 days of signing the armistice, which would inevitably mean the abandonment of their war materials. The Allies also required the surrender of substantial war materials (which the PMRs had not asked for) including 5,000 guns, 25,000 machine-guns, 3,000 trench mortars, and 1,700 fighting and bombing planes.

The final terms called for the evacuation of all of Alsace-Lorraine with its subsequent occupation by the Allies and Americans, as opposed to the PMRs' request for taking only the major fortifications in this area. The final note ensured that if the war were to continue it would be fought on German territory, as they demanded the evacuation of the west bank of the Rhine and the seizing of the principal Rhine crossings as well as bridgeheads on the east-side of the river. It also gave France two of its major war aims – the return of Alsace-Lorraine and the establishment of the Rhine as a strategic frontier.

The logistical problems that the Allies had been facing in 1918 on the Franco-Belgian Front were also considered and represented in the armistice terms, in that the Allies demanded that German civilian and military personnel continue their employment in communications sectors including on railways, bridges, and waterways. Additionally they called for the enemy to surrender 5,000 locomotives, 150,000 wagons, and 5,000 lorries to the coalition. The railways of Alsace-Lorraine were also secured. These demands ensured that the coalition armies would have the logistical and communications networks to move into German territory if the war were to be resumed.

In the East, not only did they crush German imperial ambitions but they also laid to rest their fears of the Germans gaining access to material resources. They did so by demanding the dissolution of the treaties of Bucharest and Brest-Litovsk as well as requiring the Germans to stop the supply of any materials they had been receiving from Romania and Russia. Further, the Allies were to be given access to the eastern frontier via Danzig or the Vistula.

The naval terms of the final armistice were also stricter than those suggested by the PMRs and ANC. They included clauses for the surrender of all German submarines, and the internment of 6 battle cruisers, 10 battleships, 8 light cruisers, and 50 modern destroyers in neutral or Allied ports. As well, the Germans were to evacuate the Belgian coast and turn over war materials such as merchant vessels and naval aircraft. They were to evacuate the Black Sea ports and surrender all Russian warships they had seized, allaying fears that the Germans might use these ships in the Mediterranean.[14] Finally, the Allies were to have freedom of access to and from the Baltic. The entire German merchant marine was also dismantled as the armistice terms made all ships liable to seizure by the Allies. Meanwhile the coalition partners would add to their own growing merchant marine as the Germans were to return all of the merchant ships they had interned.[15] In essence, the terms of the armistice crippled the German navy and merchant marine, ensuring that if the war continued the Allies would have unrestricted movement at sea to transport the men and material deemed necessary to defeat the Germans. If the Germans were using the armistice to regroup, as some individuals believed, the terms of the armistice ensured that the Germans would remain militarily defeated. The naval terms also met the British war aim that the German fleet be dismantled.

Yet the armistice did not resolve concerns about the German menace. At a meeting held on 2–3 December between the political and military leadership of the coalition, there was some concern about what would happen if the Germans did not sign the peace treaty. No one mentioned continuing the war into Germany; instead, it was agreed that they would take another reprisal measure such as seizing an additional bridgehead. The Allies did, however, ensure they had the capabilities to defeat the Germans if Berlin were to resume hostilities. As Foch explained during a discussion of the possibility of 'Army of Occupation in Germany':

To occupy the left bank of the Rhine and the Rhinelands, a total of 41 Allied Divisions was to be employed. Of these, 17 were French, 11 British, 9 American, and 4 Belgian. This force was adequate, should the enemy show any intention of renewing hostilities, to defend the Rhine and to cross it if necessary. These dispositions were to last until the signature of the Peace Treaty. The force could, no doubt, be reduced, but there were many unknown data both respecting the length of occupation that might be required and the extent of territory it might be advisable to occupy.[16]

Even as the Allies demobilised their forces and learned of the internal collapse of Germany, they prudently continued to make military plans to continue the war against Germany.[17] While the Allied political leadership discussed the peace treaty, Foch and the Admiralty explored plans to invade Germany in case it became necessary to do so in 1919. The idea of the German menace persisted in the minds of the Allies. In the end,

---

[14] See Trask, *Captains and Cabinets*, 251.

[15] 'The Armistice Agreement with Germany' in Barclay, *Armistice 1918*, 132–145.

[16] 'Imperial War Cabinet with Representatives of French and Italian Governments', 3 December 1918, CHAR/27/53/I.W.C.41.

[17] 'Study of Possible Advance of American Troops into Germany',10 February 1919, RG 120/268/3157/1128.

the Allies did not have to march to Berlin. Although the war did not end how (or when) they had planned, the armistice ensured that the military defeat of Germany would be maintained, even if the Allies had a difficult time accepting this to be true.

With the armistice the Allies were also on track to achieving many of their national aims. For the French: Alsace-Lorraine was to be returned; the Rhine was to be evacuated and could act as a strategic frontier; and the German military had been crippled. For the British: the threat of Germany hegemony had been broken and its fleet dismantled.[18] Signing the armistice also ensured that the Americans did not overshadow their 'Associates' in 1919 and allowed the Allies to focus on how they might combat the spread of Bolshevism in wake of the Russian Revolution. Through his initial negotiations with Germany, President Wilson had convinced the Germans and Allies to draw up a peace based on his Fourteen Points – so achieving his main war aim. It was at the peace table that each ally would have to ensure their aims were fulfilled.[19]

Evaluating the SWC

In its attempt to coordinate a coalition war and create an Allied strategy, the SWC was challenged by a number of factors. The first factor was inexperience. The coalition partners had no experience of conducting a multi-national war of this scale. By 1917 they understood that an institution for coordination was necessary if they were to achieve victory, but they did not have a blueprint for this organisation nor instructions on how it should function. The SWC had to be shaped and had to evolve at the same time as the war was being conducted. Furthermore, this factor of inexperience was complicated by a second factor – that of varying views on what the SWC should achieve. Lloyd George envisaged a body that would allow him to rein in the military leadership, whereas the French and Americans thought it should bring about unified command. Having barely survived the Battle of Caporetto, the Italians were looking for additional support from their partners. As these goals were achieved, the PMRs and SWC evolved to undertake more specific issues, most notably, creating a policy for the autumn of 1918 and year 1919 and negotiating the increase in American manpower.

The issue of varying perspectives on the role of the SWC was further complicated by the fact that Painlevé, not Clemenceau, had been the

---

[18] Lowry, *Armistice*, 163.
[19] See Margaret Macmillan, *Paris 1919: Six Months That Changed the World* (New York, 2003); Michael S. Neiberg, *The Treaty of Versailles: A Concise History* (New York, 2017).

prime minister when the British and French leadership created the SWC. Clemenceau was less receptive to this body, as he saw it as a stepping stone to unified command. When it initially failed to achieve this goal, he ignored it as much as possible. Despite this aversion to the SWC, and in particular Clemenceau's attempt to ignore it on issues relating to the Balkans, the fact that the Americans chose to employ the SWC as a major forum for communication meant that he was forced to do so too. Clemenceau also used it to gain information on British action in the Middle East.

In the American case, its political and military leadership lacked experience in conducting a large scale war as well as a coalition one. The result was that as they were negotiating with their European partners, they were also testing the mechanisms of their own war machine. American inexperience, the rapid rate at which they wanted to expand their programme, and the dysfunctional command structure led the War Department and Pershing to provide vastly different figures on the American programme to their partners. This in turn complicated shipping requirements. It was difficult for the coalition to support the American programme if the Americans themselves did not know what they required. These shipping and supply problems would have been difficult to overcome in 1919.[20]

President Wilson's attitude toward the SWC added a level of complexity to this forum while also giving it greater authority by his willingness to use it as a main source of communication with his European colleagues. The American government, which did not want its freedom of action limited by its partners, maintained its title as an 'associate' power, yet the SWC acted as an instrument by which the Americans functioned more like an 'ally' in their coordination of strategy and resources. In fact, in the SWC documents the term Allies incorporated the United States. At the same time, the American president's determination to remain politically detached allowed him to choose the issues in which America would became involved and that stance in turn dictated the actions of the coalition members on certain issues. The SWC members were forced to summarise their concerns and present them to Wilson. In response, the European partners tested Wilson's resolve on remaining politically detached, which in turn intensified friction between the coalition members. On one hand, Wilson ensured that the SWC recommendations remained of a military nature; on the other, he did make it difficult

---

[20] Woodward, *The American Army and the First World War*, 196.

for the Allies to reach wide-ranging strategic decisions because he was trying to maximise his freedom of action in the postwar world.

President Wilson did allow his military services to negotiate and act with their counterparts abroad. When the Americans sent additional representatives to Europe to negotiate agreements, they did so largely through the sub-committees of the SWC. During Baker's trip to Europe in the autumn 1918 to work out the details of the expanded American programme, for instance, it was through the AMTC and the IAMC that he chose to work. The American army, and the American boards which mobilised resources for it, chose to deal with their British and French counterparts essentially through the SWC. In turn, the Allies realised that the SWC was not just the best but actually the only place where they could negotiate with the Americans on the single most important issue: the deployment of American forces for 1919.

Wilson's stance also made Bliss's role as PMR an essential line of communication between Washington and the Europe. Bliss was not only the American PMR but also the main American representative in France. He successfully liaised between the European Allies, the American War Department, and Army Chief of Staff at a time when the AEF commander and American War Department were following different programmes, and when two of his close colleagues, Peyton March, the Chief of Staff, and John Pershing, the commander of the American Expeditionary Forces, despised one another. He had a knack for handling difficult personalities and while all three men were four-star generals, Bliss's ego did not prevent him from making sound decisions. His role was central, as his assessments of both the situation in Europe and America's partners were communicated to the President via Secretary Baker. In this way, what was discussed at the SWC affected relations between the Americans and their European partners. American unwillingness to have a political representative on the SWC served both to give Bliss's role greater importance and also to cause greater confusion, as his partners naturally attempted to glean the political opinions of the American government from him. And while he found this position frustrating at times, he was able to balance the demands of his government and his European colleagues. Bliss could not resolve all of the problems created by the dysfunctional command structure of the American army, but he did mitigate them. So while the Americans enabled the SWC, they also created significant friction through their inexperience and political aloofness.

The SWC met the challenges of inexperience and difference of visions with shifts in responsibility and decision-making. When Foch became generalissimo the role of the PMRs changed. Their main responsibility became to consider policy for autumn 1918 and 1919 alongside Foch.

Despite what has been written about the PMRs being used by the British to undermine Foch, this study has shown how the decisions made by the PMRs reinforced Foch's role as generalissimo, especially when dealing with the transfer of troops between Italy and France and when editing Joint Note 37 'Military Policy for the Autumn 1918 and Year 1919'. Even the content of this note reasserted Foch's authority. The American government instructed Bliss to support the Generalissimo and, since Bliss believed in the importance of having unified command, the American government's support of Foch was ensured. By working with Foch and incorporating his ideas into their strategic plan for 1919, the PMRs further gave authority to their work. However, while it may have been logical for the PMRs to act as an Allied general staff to Foch, and while it was suggested by President Wilson that they do so, the PMRs were never appointed to this role as Foch did not trust them.[21]

The PMR's support of Foch brought the Allies closer to unity through the SWC. The intended result was that the committee structure built under the SWC would coordinate resources in line with the Allied strategy that the PMRs were creating in consultation with Foch. In this way the political side of the SWC, the PMRs, the Allied Generalissimo, commanders-in-chief, and general staffs would all be working in unison toward a shared vision of victory in 1919. Problems and grievances would be aired on the floor of the SWC for all of the Allies to discuss. The SWC was to consider issues that were bilateral as well. That is why the transporting of American troops, for example, was discussed through the AMTC and not just between the United States and Great Britain. The mechanisms for this level of coordination were coming into place by the end of 1918. Transiting to this level of coordination was difficult and only worked when national interests were best served by a coalition. Otherwise, national interests took precedence. Increasingly, it was to be a coalition war effort – but a voluntary one.

The fourth factor that challenged the SWC was its lack of executive authority. Allied coordination worked best on the Western Front, where the British, French, Americans, and Italians all had substantial bargaining chips, and therefore they had to negotiate. Furthermore, on the Franco-Belgian Front they had a shared understanding of the German menace. In the Balkans and in Palestine and Mesopotamia negotiations

---

[21] Greenhalgh, *Victory*, 222. Greenhalgh does not examines the relationship between Foch and the PMRs after July, when the PMRs were drawing their plans. In not doing so, the work done by the PMRs, which underpinned Foch's position as generalissimo, is missed (although she does consider the PMRs' armistice terms). Her assessment of the PMRs is from Foch's perspective, thus she does not consider the important role that Bliss had in representing his government in Europe.

were more difficult, first, as there was a hegemonic power in these theatres that could undertake unilateral action if it deemed it necessary, and second, because they did not agree on the enemies' intentions. Defeating the Ottoman Empire or the Bulgarians was not a distinct strategy on its own, but as this work has shown, these theatres were part of a global strategy to defeat the Germans. Those advocating offensives in the secondary theatres made one of two arguments: by detaching one of Germany's partners, the Germans would be more easily defeated in 1919; or that by attacking in these theatres it would draw or hold forces away from the Western Front. Agreeing on which theatre should take precedence was difficult due to competing national interests.

This fourth factor connects directly to the fifth challenge, which was that the PMRs' recommendations were only one source of advice that the political leadership could draw on when negotiating or justifying their actions. The PMRs competed with the various general staffs and theatre level commanders. On the British side of the war, this situation was complicated by Lloyd George's attempt to gain greater control over strategy from the military leadership. This allowed him to use the SWC and advice of the PMRs when it suited him or draw on the advice of the commanders in the field or CIGS when it did not. With a variety of military advice available from multiple nations, it was unclear as to who determined strategy in the secondary theatres. Was it up to the hegemonic power to decide strategy? Or was action in each of the theatres now a coalition decision given the effects they had on one another? The ambiguity of the situation allowed the national powers to continue to jockey for position in these theatres. The clear focus on the Western Front left limited resources to be used in the peripheral theatres, placing the British and French at odds over whether the Balkans or the Middle East held greater importance. Both parties attempted to limit information going to their partners. Furthermore, when one party was seen as undertaking unilateral action it was used as justification for behaving in a similar manner. These elements created a volatile situation between the British and French.

In investigating and recommending an Allied policy in the secondary theatres, what the PMRs discovered was that their national interests varied tremendously. Discussions over the role that each theatre played in a global strategy also illustrated how the SWC acted as a forum through which compromise could be reached. In Palestine and Mesopotamia, Lloyd George advocated action against the Ottomans in early 1918 and was supported by the PMRs; in contrast, Clemenceau and the Americans preferred to focus on the French Front. The Allies came to a compromise which saw the British pursue action in the Middle East as long as it did not distract from efforts being made on the Franco-Belgian Front. Similarly, in Macedonia, the French wanted to initiate offensive action whereas the British, Americans, and Italians preferred a defensive stance. French pressure for an offensive resulted in the continued discussion about what form action should take in this theatre, until finally the Allies agreed to an offensive to begin in the autumn of 1918.

Despite these various challenges, the SWC was able to improve communication, coordinate essential resources for the 1919 campaign, and support a junior partner. However, it also had limitations, particularly in its reaction to unfolding events, and in its assessment of the enemy.

Communication

The SWC provided an avenue for the coalition to discuss and be informed of the actions of its members. Discussions and disagreements over the role that secondary theatres should play in winning a global war had the potential to alienate the coalition partners. However, as this study has shown, differences in opinion were accepted (and sometimes ignored – as was certainly the case in Macedonia) because the coalition partners knew the key to defeating Germany was coordination and compromise, which was in everyone's interest by 1918 and certainly for 1919. The PMRs proved able to create a cohesive strategy for 1919, and to inform the making of strategy in 1918, without discussing or agreeing on political war aims. With the creation of an Allied body was also the creation of an expectation that any member could raise an issue and discussion would occur. Despite attempts to limit information, none of the coalition members could ever rid themselves of this expectation and pressure. The result was that this channel of communication gave the PMRs and SWC members a solid understanding of their partners' positions in these theatres. While the secondary theatres were not coordinated to the level of the Western Front, the SWC still provided each member with information from which they could then base their own actions.

Throughout all of these discussions, the Franco-Belgian Front was recognised by all to be the main theatre of war. When a large-scale offensive in any of the secondary theatres became unrealistic in 1918, due to the threats developing on the French Front, the PMRs still deemed these theatres essential because of their ability to draw off and fix the resources of the Central Powers. Discussions about the role of these secondary theatres always made clear that the main effort of the coalition would be on the Western Front against the Germans. The PMRs, along with Foch, the commanders-in-chief, and the various

SWC sub-committees consistently underpinned the notion of a war-winning strategy which focussed on the build-up of 80 American divisions in the Franco-Belgian theatre by July 1919, even if the specific actions in Macedonia, Palestine, and Mesopotamia could not be agreed on.

Resource Coordination

By the spring of 1918 a number of sub-committees had been established under the SWC to coordinate Allied resources – the AMTC, AMTE, and IAMC. To function, these groups required information from their national counterparts. Creating programme schedules within these bureaucracies was complicated by the fact that the American War Department and American army required time to adjust their organisations to the realities of fighting a large scale war with partners. The result was the inability of the Americans to produce a military plan which described the needs of their military in terms of shipping and supply. Despite these omissions and the confusion caused by the American War Department and AEF Commander presenting different programmes for the American army, the Allied coalition was still able to make estimates and reach agreements. The European Allies planned to reduce cereal imports in early 1919 in order to assist with the supply of the expanded American army; the Americans prioritised the shipment of shell steel to the Allies in exchange for ammunition; and the British agreed to continue to provide the requisite troop transport to the Americans. The problems that the American army would have faced in 1919 with regard to shipping and supply had to do with a shortage of material in America and the overestimation of their own abilities rather than with the inability of the coalition to negotiate with one another. In this way the SWC served as an essential forum for the coordination of Allied resources.

Overall, the SWC represented a remarkable effort by the Allies to set-up an extensive committee structure on an unprecedented scale, doing so in less than a year. Unlike in the Second World War, where the nations could draw on the experience of the First World War and the interwar period's creation of the League of Nations, the Allies were forging new ground in establishing the mechanisms for coalition warfare. At the same time as they faced the challenges of mobilising and running a national war effort, they had to navigate how to coordinate at the international level. In addition, this had to be done between countries that were relatively equal partners (with the exception of Italy), with the result that one party could not dominate the others, as was more and more the case in the Second World War. At times, the agreements made through the SWC were bilateral; however, in these cases the SWC served to make the other partners privy to these actions. Increasingly throughout 1918 major decisions were made collectively with the SWC providing the necessary forums.

Support to a Junior Partner

In Italy, discussions focussed on improving the transportation lines between France and Italy, as the SWC recognised the interdependent nature of these two theatres, which jointly became known as the Western Front. The Italians persuasively argued that they were still vulnerable to attack, and the SWC members feared that if they did not support them, then the Italian theatre was likely to collapse. In turn this would potentially open a road for the Central Powers to attack southern France, and, at the least, to free up Austro-Hungarian and German combat troops for use elsewhere. The Italians, even as junior members, were able to push their case through the SWC, and even if the support forthcoming was not as extensive as the Italians had wanted, the SWC was correctly able to assess what this partner needed, thus sustaining the Italian Front throughout 1918.

Limitations of the SWC

Planning versus Unfolding Events on the Ground

The PMRs were unique in their global perspective and the fact that they had the luxury of considering a long-term coalition policy without having to make immediate decisions. They sat together in constant session, considering the war from the Allied perspective. In some ways this meant that their planning was detached from the reality of the situation on the ground, especially as events unfolded so rapidly in autumn 1918. It also meant that sometimes their plans were aborted before they could be executed by the coalition governments, as was the case with Joint Note 12 ('Campaign in 1918') when the Germans launched their offensive in spring 1918. In this way, the SWC's lack of executive authority could be evaluated as a benefit. The commanders were able to respond quickly to the enemy precisely as they did not have to wait for a slow decision by a committee. Ultimately, the Allies were willing to sacrifice the future for the present.

As we have seen, the SWC and its committees looked toward the future and made recommendations for the procurement of resources. This had an impact on the present, in so far as the commanders were able to use these resources to exploit their enemies' weaknesses. The original American military programme was for 40 divisions to be fielded by 1919. This programme was altered and intensified in response to the German spring offensive; however, the increased programme of 80 divisions, and the attempt to create a shipping and munitions programme to match, was a reflection of the Allies commitment to win the war in 1919. It was also a response to their overestimation of the German menace.

For the British and the French, a victory in 1918 was also more appealing than one in 1919 for political reasons. The substantial superiority the Americans would have in manpower over their partners would see them do much of the fighting in 1919. Thus, the war was likely to be interpreted as an American victory. Ending the war while the British and French still had sizeable militaries, and thus influence, would prevent President Wilson from dictating the peace terms.

Intelligence Failures

The SWC unsuccessfully evaluated the Germany army's size and abilities. One of the problems was that the SWC did not have an Allied intelligence body to rationalise these estimates and ensure that they were consistent between nations. While the PMRs did share some intelligence information, it was incomplete. The Italian failure at Caporetto, followed shortly by the devastating German spring offensives, ensured that the Allies would never again underestimate their adversary. While the Allies were aware of some of the weaknesses of the Bulgarian, Turkish, and Austro-Hungarian forces, they viewed the Germans as an unrelenting menace which, through the advantage of interior lines of communication, could easily shift forces to launch an offensive in any one of the theatres of war. This fear of German capabilities even caused them to doubt intelligence that contradicted their deeply rooted perception of the enemy's military potential. The inevitable result was that the Allies overestimated the manpower and material resources required to defeat the Central Powers. Insecure about the vulnerability of home-front morale in France, Italy, and Britain and unable to trust the information they had about deepening war-weariness on the German home-front, this perception of the daunting German menace was carried through to the drafting of the armistice. It had real consequences for the terms presented to the Germans. Although this mentality may seem illogical in retrospect, the Allies knew it was better to overestimate their opponent so as never to be caught unprepared by the Germans again.

SWC Legacy

The SWC left a legacy for the Second World War. In the run-up to the outbreak of the Second World War, the complex structure of the SWC was drawn on, in varying degrees, by British and French officials who were attempting to establish an allied body for coordinating strategy and military action.[22] As in the First World War, the Second World War SWC was complicated by tensions in civil-military relations, institutional limitations (lack of executive authority), and personality clashes. Yet the SWC was able to create an important communication network, as well as an Anglo-French Co-ordinating Committee to handle shared economic challenges.[23] The pressure of an intensifying war and an inability to make rapid decisions meant that Churchill replaced this model with an Anglo-American one.

The Second World War SWC was obsolescent, whereas the First World War SWC survived because it was able to evolve and expand to meet Allied needs. It provided the best and only mechanism for coordinating Allied strategy and resources. The fact that it was comprised of four members who all contributed essential components to the coalition meant that the Allies were forced to use this forum. While the Germans exhausted themselves in 1918, rapidly declining in strength after their spring offensives, the Allies were not only able to bring over American troops in staggering numbers, but were also able to resolve logistical problems that continued to stymie the German's military effort. In fighting a multi-theatre war, the coalition partners had to make decisions about the allocation of their limited resources. Through the SWC and its sub-committees they did so in a relatively harmonious way. Crucially agreeing that Germany was the main enemy, the Allies coordinated how to defeat Germany, making decisions on when to fight (1919), where (Western Front, with the other theatres drawing off enemy forces), and by what means (shipping and equipping 80 American divisions to do the majority of the fighting). Furthermore, in 1918 the SWC successfully addressed the concerns of its partners, which ultimately contributed to keeping its junior partner (the Italians) in the war.

Expanding beyond studies on 'how the war was won' this study has examined the mentalities of those creating an Allied strategy for the

---

[22] William J. Philpott, 'The Benefit of Experience? The Supreme War Council and the Higher Management of Coalition War, 1939–40', in Martin Alexander and William J. Philpott, eds., *Anglo-French Defence Relations between the Wars* (Basingstoke; New York: Palgrave Macmillan, 2002), 210–211.

[23] Ibid., 219.

autumn of 1918 and the year 1919. Although much had been achieved by November 1918, many of the results of this successful and coordinated planning had not yet been seen – and thanks to the 'premature' ending of hostilities – would not be seen. This has led historians to underestimate the role of the SWC in coordinating an Allied policy. In the end it was unnecessary to bring all 80 American divisions to Europe, along with all the necessary war materials, to defeat the Germans. The coalition was able to draw up terms which ensured the military defeat of Germany, terms which the Germans signed. As the Allies turned their attention to creating peace, their considerable plans and efforts were put aside, having been ambushed by victory.

Bibliography

Manuscript and Archival Sources

Britain

Bodleian Libraries, University of Oxford
The papers of Alfred Milner, Viscount Milner
The uncatalogued papers of James Rennell Rodd, first Baron Rennell
Churchill College, Cambridge
Amery Papers
Churchill Papers
Hankey Papers
Rawlinson Papers
House of Lords Record Office, London
Lloyd George Papers
Imperial War Museum, London
Wilson Papers
The National Archives, Kew
ADM 137/836 (Reports of the Allied Naval Council, 1918)
CAB 25 (Supreme War Council)
CAB 27 (War Cabinet Committees)
CAB 45 (Hankey Papers)
FO 800 (Lord Reading Correspondence and Papers)
MT 25 (Ministry of Shipping)
MUN 4 (Ministry of Munitions)
WO 32 (War Office: War of 1914–1918)
WO 106 (Directorate of Military Operations and Intelligence)
WO 158 (GHQ Correspondence and Papers)
WO 256 (Earl Haig Papers)

France

Service Historique de la Défense – Département de l'Armée de Terre, Château de Vincennes
4N (Conseil Supérieur de la Guerre, Section française)
6N (Fonds Clemenceau)

10N (Conseil interallié de l'armement et des munitions)
13N (Collection Tardieu)

United States

The Albert and Shirley Small Special Collections Library, Virginia
Edward Stettinius Papers
Library of Congress, Washington, DC
John Pershing Papers
Newton D. Baker Papers
Peyton March Papers
Robert Lansing Papers
Tasker Bliss Papers
Woodrow Wilson Papers
National Archives, Washington, DC
RG 32 (Records of the United States Shipping Board)
RG 61 (War Industries Board)
RG 107 (Records of the Secretary of War)
RG 120 (G3 and Supreme War Council)
RG 165 (War Department, General and Special Staffs)
RG 200 (Experience of the American Expeditionary Force)
Seeley G. Mudd Manuscript Library, Princeton
Bernard Baruch Papers
US Army Military History Institute, Carlisle, PA
Tasker H. Bliss Collection
William Starey Browning Papers

Printed Primary Sources

[Les] Armées françaises dans la Grande Guerre, 103 vols. (Paris: Imprimerie Nationale, 1922–1938).

Barnes, J. and D. Nicholson (eds.), *Leo Amery Diaries* (London: Hutchinson, 1979–1980).

Department of State, *Papers Relating to the Foreign Relations of the United States, The Lansing Papers, 1914–1920*, 2 vols. (Washington, DC: Government Printing Office, 1940).

Dutton, David (ed.), *Paris: 1918: The War Diary of the British Ambassador, the 17th Earl of Derby* (Liverpool: Liverpool University Press, 2001).

Hancock, W. K. (ed.), *The Smuts Papers* (London: Athlone Press, 1956).

Historical Section, Department of the Army, *United States Army in the World Wars*, 17 vols. (Washington, DC: US Government Printing Office, 1948).

Link, A. S. (ed.), *The Papers of Woodrow Wilson*, 69 vols. (Princeton: Princeton University Press, 1966–1994).

Seymour, Charles, *The Intimate Papers of Colonel House*, 4 vols. (London: Ernest Benn, Ltd., 1926–1928).

War Office, *Statistics of the Military Effort of the British Empire during the Great War, 1914–1920* (London: H. M. Stationery Off., 1922).

Secondary Works

Aldrich, Robert, *Greater France: A History of French Overseas Expansion* (Basingstoke: Macmillan, 1996).

Allain, J.-C., 'Le France Et Les Armistices De 1918 En Orient', in Helenē Michaēlidou (ed.), *La France Et La Grece Dans La Grande Guerre: Actes du Colloque Tenu en Novembre 1989 à Thessalonique* (Thessalonique: Université de Thessalonique, 2012), 25–44.

Andrew, Christopher M. and A. S. Kanya-Forstner, *France Overseas: The Great War and the Climax of French Imperial Expansion* (London: Thames and Hudson, 1981).

Anonymous, *The Supreme War Council* (Boston: World Peace Foundation, 1918).

Barclay, Brig, *Armistice 1918* (London: Dent, 1968).

Barnett, Correlli, *Strategy and Society (The Spenser Wilkinson Memorial Lecture, 1974)* (Manchester: Manchester University Press, 1975).

Barnett, Margaret, *British Food Policy during the First World War* (New York: Routledge, 2014).

Beach, Jim, *Haig's Intelligence* (Cambridge: Cambridge University Press, 2013).

Beaver, Daniel R., *Newton D. Baker and the American War Effort, 1917–1919* (Lincoln, NE: University of Nebraska Press, 1966).

Bidwell, S. and D. Graham, *Fire-Power: British Army Weapons and Theories of War 1904–1945* (London: Allen & Unwin, 1982).

Bliss, Tasker H., 'The Evolution of the Unified Command', *Foreign Affairs* 1 (1922), 1–30.

Bruce, Anthony, *The Last Crusade: The Palestine Campaign in the First World War* (London: John Murray, 2003).

Bruce, Robert B., *A Fraternity of Arms: America and France in the Great War* (Lawrence, KS: University Press of Kansas, 2003).

Burk, Kathleen, *Britain, America and the Sinews of War, 1914–1918* (Boston: G. Allen & Unwin, 1985).

Callwell, Charles Edward, *Field-Marshal Sir Henry Wilson: His Life and Diaries*, 2 vols. (London: Cassell, 1927).

Cappellano, Filippo, 'Les Relations Entre Les Armées Italienne et Française Pendant La Grande Guerre', *Revue historique des armées* 250 (2008), 53–65.

Cassar, George, *The Forgotten Front: The British Campaign in Italy, 1917–18* (London and Rio Grance: Hambledon Press, 1998).

Cornwall, Mark, *The Undermining of Austria-Hungary: The Battle for Hearts and Minds (Basingstoke, Palgrave Macmillan, 2000)*.

Delmas, Jean, 'Les Opérations Militaires sur Le Front de Macédoine Octobre 1915 – Septembre 1918', in Helenē Michaēlidou (ed.), *La France et la Grece dans la Grande Guerre: Actes du Colloque Tenu en Novembre 1989 à Thessalonique* (Thessalonique: Université de Thessalonique, 2012), 3–12.

Doughty, Robert A., *Pyrrhic Victory: French Strategy and Operations in the Great War* (Cambridge, MA: Harvard University Press, 2005).

Duroselle, Jean-Bapiste, *La Grande Guerre des Français, 1914–1918* (Paris: Perrin, 1994).

Dutton, David, 'The Balkan Campaign and French War Aims in the Great War', *The English Historical Review* 94/370 (1979), 97–113.

The Politics of Diplomacy: Britain and France in the Balkans in the First World War (London; New York: Tauris, 1998).

Ellis, John and Mike Cox, *The World War I Databook: The Essential Facts and Figures for All the Combatants* (London: Aurum Press Ltd, 2001).

Fayle, C. Ernest, *Seaborne Trade*, 3 vols. (London: John Murray, 1920–1924).

Finnegan, Terrence, 'Military Intelligence at the Front, 1914–18', *Studies in Intelligence* 53/4 (2009), 25–40.

Foch, Marshal Ferdinand, *The Memoirs of Marshal Foch*, trans. T. B. Mott (London: Heinemann, 1931).

Fong, Giordan, 'The Movement of German Divisions to the Western Front, Winter 1917–1918', *War in History* 7/2 (2000), 225–235.

French, David, *The Strategy of the Lloyd George Coalition, 1916–1918* (Oxford: Clarendon Press, 1995).

Fuller, J. F. C., *Tanks in the Great War, 1914–1918* (London: J. Murray, 1920).

Gale, Tim, *French Tanks of the Great War: Development, Tactics and Operations* (Barnsley: Pen & Sword Military, 2016).

Gleaves, Albert, *A History of the Transport Service* [online text] (New York: George H. Doran Company, 1921). https://archive.org/stream/historyoftran spo00gle#page/92/mode/2up.

Gooch, John, *The Italian Army and the First World War* (New York: Cambridge University Press, 2014).

Greenhalgh, Elizabeth, 'Technology Development in Coalition: The Case of the First World War Tank', *The International History Review* 22/4 (2000), 806–836.

Victory through Coalition: Britain and France during the First World War (Cambridge: Cambridge University Press, 2005).

'David Lloyd George, Georges Clemenceau, and the 1918 Manpower Crisis', *The Historical Journal* 50/2 (2007), 397–421.

'Errors and Omissions in Franco-British Co-Operation over Munitions Production, 1914–1918', *War in History* 14/2 (2007), 179–218.

Foch in Command: The Forging of a First World War General (Cambridge: Cambridge University Press, 2011).

Greenhut, Jeffrey, 'The Imperial Reserve: The Indian Corps on the Western Front, 1914–15', *The Journal of Imperial and Commonwealth History* 12/1 (1983), 54–73.

Grieves, Keith, *The Politics of Manpower, 1914–1918* (Manchester: Manchester University Press, 1988).

Grotelueschen, Mark, *The AEF Way of War: The American Army in Combat in World War One* (Cambridge: Cambridge University Press, 2007).

Halewood, Louis, '"A Matter of Opinion": British Attempts to Assess the Attrition of German Manpower, 1915–1917', *Intelligence and National Security* 32/3 (2017), 333–350.

Hall, Richard, *Balkan Breakthrough: The Battle of Dobro Pole 1918* (Bloomington, IN: Indiana University Press, 2010).

Halpern, Paul, *The Naval War in the Mediterranean, 1914–1918* (London; Annapolis, MD: Allen & Unwin/Naval Institute Press, 1987).

A Naval History of World War I (London: UCL Press, 1994).

'The War at Sea', in John Horne (ed.), *A Companion to World War I* (Chichester: Wiley-Blackwell, 2010), 141–155.

Hamard, Bruno, 'Quand la victoire s'est gagnée dans les Balkans: l'assuat de l'armée d'Orient de septembre à novembre 1918', *Guerres mondiales et conflits contemporains* 46/184 (1996), 29–42.

Hankey, Maurice, *Diplomacy by Conference: Studies in Public Affairs, 1920–1946* (London: Ernest Benn Ltd., 1946).

The Supreme Command, 1914 to 1918, 2 vols. (London: George Allen and Unwin Ltd., 1961).

Hanks, Robert, K., 'Georges Clemencuea and the English', *The Historical Journal* 45/1 (2002), 53–77.

Harris, J. P., *Men, Ideas and Tanks: British Military Thought and Armoured Forces, 1903–1939*. (Manchester: Manchester University Press, 1995).

Amiens to the Armistice: The B.E.F. in the Hundred Days' Campaign, 8 August–11 November 1918 (London: Brassey's, 1998).

Henniker, Colonel A. M., *Transportation of the Western Front 1914–1918* (London: H. M. Stationary Office, 1937).

Herwig, Holger, *The First World War: Germany and Austria-Hungary, 1914–1918* (London: Arnold, 1997).

Hughes, Matthew, *Allenby and British Strategy in the Middle East 1917–1919* (London: Frank Cass, 1999).

Kaspi, André, *Le Temps des Américains* (Paris: Publications de la Sorbonne, 1976).

Keene, Jennifer, *The United States and the First World War* (Harlow: Longman, 2000).

Kitchen, James, *The British Imperial Army in the Middle East: Morale and Military Identity in the Sinai and Palestine Campaigns, 1916–18* (London: Bloomsbury, 2014).

Larcher, M., *La Guerre Turque dans la Guerre Mondiale* (Paris: Chiron, 1926).

Liddell Hart, Captain B. H., *History of the First World War* (London: Pan, 2014).

Lloyd, Nick, *Hundred Days: The End of the Great War* (London: Penguin, 2014).

Lowry, Bullitt, *Armistice 1918* (Kent, OH: Kent State University Press, 1996).

Macleod, Roy and Jeffrey Johnson (eds.), *Comparative Perspectives on the Chemical Industry at War, 1914–1924* (Dordrecht: Springer, 2006).

Macmillan, Margaret, *Paris 1919: Six Months That Changed the World* (New York: Random House, 2003).

Martin, Gregory, 'The Influence of Racial Attitudes on British Policy towards India during the First World War', *The Journal of Imperial and Commonwealth History* 14/2 (1986), 91–113.

Melton, Carol, *Between War and Peace: Woodrow Wilson and the American Expeditionary Force in Siberia, 1918–19* (Macon, GA: Mercer University Press, 2001).

Millman, Brock, *Managing Domestic Dissent in First World War Britain, 1914–1918* (London: Frank Cass, 2000).

Pessimism and British War Policy 1916–1918 (London: Frank Cass, 2001).

Ministry of Munitions, *History of the Ministry of Munitions*, 12 vols. (London, 1918–1923).

Mordacq, Général, *Le Ministère Clemenceau: Journal d'un Témoin*, 2 vols. (Paris: Plon, 1930).

Neiberg, Michael, S., *The Second Battle of the Marne* (Bloomington, IN; Indiana University Press, 2008).

The Treaty of Versailles: A Concise History (New York: Oxford University Press, 2017).

Occleshaw, Michael, *Armour against Fate: British Military Intelligence in the First World War* (London: Columbus Books, 1989).

Palazzo, Albert, 'Plan 1919 – The Other One', *The Journal of the Society for Army Historical Research* 77/309 (1999), 39–50.

Palmer, Frederick, *Newton D. Baker: America at War*, 2 vols. (New York: Dodd, Mead & Company, 1931).

Bliss, Peacemaker: The Life and Letters of General Tasker Howard Bliss (New York: Dodd, Mead & Company, 1934).

Parsons, Edward B., 'Why the British Reduced the Flow of American Troops to Europe in August–October 1918', *Canadian Journal of History* 12/2 (1977), 173–191.

Pershing, J. J., *My Experiences in the World War* (Hodder and Stoughton: London, 1931).

Philpott, William J., *Anglo-French Relations and Strategy on the Western Front, 1914–18* (London: Macmillan, 1996).

'Squaring the Circle: The Coordination of the Entente in the Winter of 1915–16', *English Historical Review*, 114 (1999), 875–898.

'The Benefit of Experience? The Supreme War Council and the Higher Management of Coalition War, 1939–40', in Martin Alexander and William J. Philpott (eds.), *Anglo-French Defence Relations between the Wars* (Basingstoke; New York: Palgrave Macmillan, 2002), 209–226.

Attrition: Fighting the First World War (London: Little, Brown and Company, 2014).

Prior, Robin, *Churchill's World Crisis as History* (London; Canberra: Croom Helm, 1983).

Prior, Robin and Trevor Wilson, *Command on the Western Front: The Military Career of Sir Henry Rawlinson 1914–1918* (Barnsley Pen & Sword Military Classics, 2004).

Rochat, Giorgio, 'The Italian Front, 1915–18', in John Horne (ed.), *A Companion to World War I* (Chichester: Wiley-Blackwell, 2010), 82–96.

Safford, Jeffrey, *Wilsonian Maritime Diplomacy, 1913–1921* (New Brunswick, NJ: Rutgers University Press, 1978).

Salter, Sir Arthur, *Allied Maritime Transport Council*, 1918 [online text], Cornell University Library. http://archive.org/stream/cu31924027892607.

Allied Shipping Control: An Experiment in International Administration (Oxford: Clarendon Press, 1921).

Schwarz, B., 'Divided Attention: Britain's Perception of a German Threat to Her Eastern Position in 1918', *Journal of Contemporary History*, 28/1 (1993), 103–122.

Sfika-Theodosiou, Angeliki, 'The Italian Presence on the Balkan Front', *Balkan Studies*, 36/1 (1995), 69–82.

Sheffield, Gary, *Forgotten Victory: The First World War Myths and Realities* (London: Review, 2002).

Sheffield, Gary and Peter Gray (eds.), *The British Army, the Hundred Days Campaign and the Birth of the Royal Air Force, 1918* (London: Bloomsbury, 2015).

Sheffy, Yigal, *British Military Intelligence in the Palestine Campaign, 1914–1918* (London: Frank Cass, 1998).

Smith, Leonard V., Stéphane Audoin-Rouzeau, and Annette Becker, *France and the Great War 1914–1918* (Cambridge: Cambridge University Press, 2003).

Stevenson, David, *With Our Backs to the Wall: Victory and Defeat in 1918* (London: Penguin, 2012).

Strachan, Hew, *The First World War: To Arms* (Oxford: Oxford University Press, 2001).

Terraine, John, *White Heat: The New Warfare, 1914–1918* (London: Leo Cooper, 1992).

To Win a War: 1918, the Year of Victory (London: Cassell, 2000).

Thompson, Mark, *The White War: Life and Death on the Italian Front, 1915–1919* (London: Faber, 2008).

Townshend, Charles, *When God Made Hell: The British Invasion of Mesopotamia and the Creation of Iraq, 1914–1921* (London: Faber, 2010).

Trask, David, *The United States in the Supreme War Council: American War Aims and Inter-Allied Strategy* (Middletown, CT: Wesleyan University Press, 1961).

Captains and Cabinets: Anglo-American Naval Relations, 1917–1918 (Columbia: University of Missouri Press, 1972).

The AEF and Coalition Warmaking, 1917–18 (Lawrence: University Press of Kansas, 1993).

Ulrichsen, Kristian, *The Logistics and Politics of the British Campaigns in the Middle East, 1914–22* (Basingstoke: Palgrave Macmillan, 2011).

Wallach, Jehuda L., *Uneasy Coalition: The Entente Experience in World War I* (Westport, CT: Greenwood Press, 1993).

Watson, Alexander, *Enduring the Great War: Combat, Morale and Collapse in the German and British Armies, 1914–1918* (Cambridge: Cambridge University Press, 2008).

Ring of Steel: Germany and Austria-Hungary at War, 1914–1918 (London: Allen Lane, 2014)

Weygand, *Mémoires; Idéal Vécu*, 3 vols. (Paris: Flammarion, 1950).

Woodward, David R., *Lloyd George and the Generals* (Newark, NJ: University of Delaware Press, 1983).

The Military Correspondence of Field-Marshal Sir William Robertson, Chief of the Imperial General Staff, December 1915–February 1918 (London: Associated University Presses, 1990).

Trial by Friendship: Anglo-American Relations, 1917–18 (Lexington: University Press of Kentucky, 1993).

Field Marshal Sir William Robertson: Chief of the Imperial General Staff in the Great War (London: Praeger, 1998).

Hell in the Holy Land: World War I in the Middle East (Lexington: The University Press of Kentucky, 2006).

The American Army and the First World War (Cambridge: Cambridge University Press, 2014).

Unpublished Theses

Hanks, Robert K., 'Culture versus Diplomacy: Georges Clemenceau and Anglo-American Relations during the First World War'. PhD diss., University of Toronto, 2002.

Shumate, Thomas Daniel, 'The Allied Supreme War Council 1917–1918'. PhD diss., University of Virginia, 1952.

Index